Performance Appraisals & Phrases

FOR

DUMMIES®

by Ken Lloyd, PhD

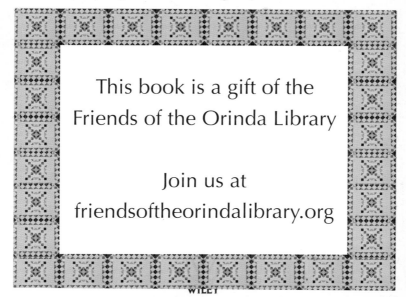

This book is a gift of the
Friends of the Orinda Library

Join us at
friendsoftheorindalibrary.org

WILEY

Wiley Publishing, Inc.

Performance Appraisals & Phrases For Dummies®

Published by
Wiley Publishing, Inc.
111 River St.
Hoboken, NJ 07030-5774
www.wiley.com

For general information on our other products and services, please contact our Customer Care Department within the U.S. at 877-762-2974, outside the U.S. at 317-572-3993, or fax 317-572-4002.

For technical support, please visit www.wiley.com/techsupport.

Wiley also publishes its books in a variety of electronic formats. Some content that appears in print may not be available in electronic books.

Library of Congress Control Number: 2009931757

ISBN: 978-0-470-49872-9

Manufactured in the United States of America

10 9 8 7 6 5 4

WILEY

About the Author

Ken Lloyd, PhD, is Vice President of Planning and Development for Strategic Partners, Inc., in Chatsworth, California. He is also a nationally recognized consultant, author, and columnist who specializes in organizational behavior, communication, and management coaching and development. As a consultant, Ken has worked in a wide range of industries including healthcare, apparel, financial services, electronics, and entertainment. His long-running workplace advice column appears in numerous newspapers and their Web sites, along with his Web site, www.jerksatwork.com.

He is the author of the widely-acclaimed *Jerks at Work: How to Deal With People Problems and Problem People* (Career Press, 1999; revised edition, 2006), which has been translated into numerous languages, including Chinese, Japanese, Polish, and Korean. He also authored *151 Quick Ideas to Recognize and Reward Employees* (Career Press, 2007) and *Be the Boss Your Employees Deserve* (Career Press, 2002), and he co-authored *Ultimate Selling Power: How to Create and Enjoy a Multimillion Dollar Sales Career* (Career Press/Penguin Books, 2002) and the best-selling book, *Unlimited Selling Power: How to Master Hypnotic Selling Skills* (Prentice Hall, 1990), now in its ninth printing. Ken is also the author of *The K.I.S.S. Guide to Selling* (DK Publishers, 2001), part of Dorling Kindersley's Keep It Simple Series. He also wrote the business film *Communication: The Name of the Game* (Roundtable Films and Video), award winner at the National Educational Film Festival and the American Film Festival.

Ken is a frequent television and talk-radio guest. He has appeared on ABC's *Good Morning America,* CNN, and NPR's *Morning Edition,* as well as KABC, KTLA, and the Fox Morning News "Ask the Expert" segments. He received his BA from UC Berkeley and his PhD in Organizational Behavior from UCLA. He taught for many years in the MBA Program at the UCLA Anderson School of Management, and he continues to lecture at various universities and speak before numerous organizations. Ken is a member of the American Psychological Association and the Society for Industrial and Organizational Psychology.

Ken lives in Encino, California with his wife, their three children, and their Golden Retriever.

Dedication

To Roberta, of course!

Acknowledgments

A book such as this requires a solid team to bring it to its full potential. At every phase of this project, I received extremely helpful feedback, guidance, and support from several terrific people. And ironically, it is their performance appraisals of my performance that have played a key role in strengthening this book.

In this regard, I would like to thank Charles P. Leo, Professor of Management at the Graziadio School of Business and Management at Pepperdine University. Dr. Leo conducted a patient and thorough technical review of the manuscript, and he provided numerous insightful comments and suggestions.

I also offer thanks to Donovan R. Greene, PhD, one of the foremost organizational psychologists and executive coaches. Dr. Greene has been a longtime source of expertise in a wide range of managerial areas. He not only conducts outstanding seminars on performance appraisal, but also serves as a great role model when actually conducting appraisals. I thank him for all the early lessons in this important area.

I also thank the entire team at Wiley Publishing. Mike Baker, Acquisitions Editor, provided outstanding direction for this project from day one. Another key player on the team has been the project's editor, Elizabeth Kuball. She is truly an editor's editor, with outstanding ability not only in terms of writing, but also in terms of project management.

I would like to give a posthumous thanks to the father of "back-timing," L. K. Lloyd, who also happened to be my father. A master in many fields, L. K.'s abilities to manage by wandering around and conduct performance appraisals that helped his employees learn, grow, and advance are truly legendary.

I also offer a very special thanks to my home team. First, I am very fortunate to have a fantastic research librarian, friend, and wife, Roberta. And I feel equally fortunate to have three wonderful children, Jessica, Stacey, and Joshua. If there were performance appraisals for a wife and children, they would all be rated as "exceptional" in every category.

Publisher's Acknowledgments

We're proud of this book; please send us your comments through our Dummies online registration form located at http://dummies.custhelp.com. For other comments, please contact our Customer Care Department within the U.S. at 877-762-2974, outside the U.S. at 317-572-3993, or fax 317-572-4002.

Some of the people who helped bring this book to market include the following:

Acquisitions, Editorial, and Media Development

Project Editor: Elizabeth Kuball

Acquisitions Editor: Mike Baker

Copy Editor: Elizabeth Kuball

Assistant Editor: Erin Calligan Mooney

Editorial Program Coordinator: Joe Niesen

Technical Editor: Charles P. Leo, PhD

Senior Editorial Manager: Jennifer Ehrlich

Editorial Supervisor and Reprint Editor: Carmen Krikorian

Editorial Assistants: Jennette ElNaggar, David Lutton

Cover Photos: © Workbook Stock

Cartoons: Rich Tennant (www.the5thwave.com)

Composition Services

Project Coordinator: Patrick Redmond

Layout and Graphics: Reuben W. Davis, Melissa K. Jester, Christine Williams

Proofreader: John Greenough

Indexer: Claudia Bourbeau

Publishing and Editorial for Consumer Dummies

    Diane Graves Steele, Vice President and Publisher, Consumer Dummies

    Kristin Ferguson-Wagstaffe, Product Development Director, Consumer Dummies

    Ensley Eikenburg, Associate Publisher, Travel

    Kelly Regan, Editorial Director, Travel

Publishing for Technology Dummies

    Andy Cummings, Vice President and Publisher, Dummies Technology/General User

Composition Services

    Debbie Stailey, Director of Composition Services

Contents at a Glance

Table of Contents

Part IV: The Part of Tens 315

Chapter 18: The Top Ten Words to Include in a Performance Appraisal 317

Chapter 19: The Top Ten Behaviors Meriting Special Recognition 323

Index... 331

Introduction

● ●

As the time to conduct performance appraisals approaches, many managers experience one or more of the following feelings: anxiety, nervousness, nausea, aggravation, frustration, confusion, fear, stress, or dread. Frankly, based on the way that many companies put together their performance appraisal programs, these reactions aren't surprising.

The good news is that today's performance appraisals are user-friendly, easily administered, and an essential component of effective management. Performance appraisal plays a central role in developing your employees and enhancing their performance and productivity. As such, the appraisal process plays a key role in adding value to your employees — and ultimately to your department and your company at large.

And as for those negative feelings aroused by performance appraisal, the antidote is in your hands!

About This Book

I wrote this book to identify every key piece of the performance appraisal process, and to provide up-to-date information and tools to help you effectively manage them. Every chapter stands on its own, and you can jump around this book as much as you like, without missing a beat.

If you're interested in (or concerned by) a particular aspect of performance appraisals, you can flip right to it and hit the page running. For example, if you're interested in how to conduct an appraisal session, there is a chapter just for you. And the same applies if you're interested in knowing more about the kinds of performance appraisals, how to gather the right performance data, how to avoid mistakes, how to follow up with employees, and how to do just about anything else when it comes to performance appraisals.

If you're interested in seeing the best phrases to use in the process, there are nine whole chapters of phrases — more than 3,200 phrases in all — waiting for you!

Conventions Used in This Book

I don't use many conventions in this book, but I do use a couple that you should be aware of:

- ✔ Anytime I refer to a Web address, I put the address in `monofont`, to make it easier for you to spot.

- ✔ I alternate the use of masculine and feminine pronouns for gender equality.

What You're Not to Read

Although I encourage you to read the whole book, you can still build your performance appraisal skills if you pass on anything marked with the Technical Stuff icon. (For more on icons, see the "Icons Used in This Book" section, later in this Introduction.)

This book has thousands of phrases that you can use when evaluating your employees, but you certainly don't need to read every single phrase. Think of these phrase chapters the way you would any other reference book — search for what you need when you need it and leave the rest for later.

Foolish Assumptions

As I wrote this book, I made a number of assumptions about you:

- ✔ **You're responsible for appraising employees.** I assume that you're in a supervisory or managerial position, and that one of your responsibilities is to appraise the performance of each of your employees.

- ✔ **You're nervous, anxious, or annoyed with performance appraisals.** And you're seeking new, user-friendly, and productive ways to carry out your responsibilities in this area.

✔ **You want to build your performance appraisal skills.** Whether you're new to management or you're an experienced veteran, I assume that you aren't satisfied with your current appraisal skills and you're looking for a way to improve them.

If at least *one* of these assumptions sounds like you, then this book has some sound advice for you.

How This Book Is Organized

I've divided this book into four parts. Although the order of the parts basically follows the same sequencing that you would follow in the actual performance appraisal process, you can easily target any section and find all you need to know without having to read anything that precedes or follows it.

Part I: When It's Time to Appraise Your Employees

This part provides you with the full range of foundational information on the performance appraisal process. I cover the widespread and major roles that performance appraisal plays, as well as the vast array of performance appraisal systems, techniques, and forms, and the effectiveness of each.

Part II: Working Your Way through the Process

In this part, you find the best ways to carry out each of the performance appraisal steps. I give you hands-on information on topics that cover the full range of planning and preparation, gathering and analyzing employee performance data, completing the evaluation forms, and avoiding the most common mistakes.

This part concludes by focusing on the best ways to work with your employees in establishing performance and developmental goals, and then following up with appropriate coaching, guidance, feedback, and support.

Part III: Phrases and Expressions That Work

Part III provides the best appraisal phrases to cover the full spectrum of employee performance. There are over 3,000 such phrases, and they're specifically designed to encourage employees to continue their successful performance, while simultaneously energizing them to make appropriate improvements in areas where problems are found.

Part IV: The Part of Tens

Every *For Dummies* book ends with the Part of Tens, and this book doesn't drop the ball on that tradition. Here, I offer ten powerful words to include in any performance appraisal, and ten employee behaviors that deserve special recognition in a performance appraisal. When you're short on time, this is the part for you!

Icons Used in This Book

Throughout this book, I use three different icons to highlight different points. Here's what they mean:

 I use the Remember icon to emphasize a point for you to keep in mind whenever you're conducting appraisals.

 The Tip icon highlights particularly effective ways for you to carry out various performance appraisal steps.

 The Technical Stuff icon flags information that focuses on, well, technical stuff — in other words, stuff that you can safely skip without missing the main point.

When you see the Warning icon, take heed: This icon marks common mistakes or problems that you can sidestep if you know where to look.

Where to Go from Here

If you're about to begin the performance appraisal process, your first stop should be the beginning of this book, namely Chapter 1. If you're ready to schedule a performance appraisal session, Chapter 6 has all the information you need to cover all the bases. To avoid making the most common mistakes in the process, it would be a real mistake to miss Chapter 7. And if you're seeking the best appraisal phrases for your employees' performance, you can easily find them right now in Chapters 9 through 17. You can use the table of contents and index to locate the information you need — including phrases to use in your written appraisals. Or just dive in anyplace that looks interesting to you!

Part I

When It's Time to Appraise Your Employees

The 5th Wave By Rich Tennant

When's the last time we conducted a serious employee performance review?

In this part . . .

*P*erformance appraisals play a remarkably wide range
of roles. Instead of being an isolated annual event,
appraisals are but one component in the overall process
of performance management. Within this framework, a
state-of-the-art performance appraisal system generates a
vast array of positive and productive outcomes.

The chapters in this part show you how appraisals motivate your employees, build their self-insights, and set the
groundwork for training and developmental programs, all
the while enhancing individual and departmental
performance.

You also find a snapshot of the wide range of appraisal
systems, techniques, processes, and forms, along with
insights into their strengths and weaknesses. Looked at in
a slightly different way, these chapters conduct a performance appraisal of the various performance appraisal
systems.

Chapter 1

Building Success with Performance Appraisals

* *

In This Chapter

▶ Facilitating the performance appraisal process from start to finish

▶ Generating great results with state-of-the-art performance appraisals

▶ Using performance appraisals to build your employees and their productivity

* *

*M*any managers see the performance appraisal process as an administrative rite that consumes a lot of time, while producing little more than frustration, confrontation, and piles of paperwork. This reaction is totally understandable if your company is relying on a performance appraisal system that has fallen woefully out of date.

However, as I explain in this book, the performance appraisal process *can* play a remarkably powerful role in building your employees, as well as their performance and productivity — when it's done right.

Part of the problem with the appraisal process is that managers often see it as an isolated annual set of steps that are separate from all other managerial responsibilities. In actuality, today's performance appraisals are integrated into your ongoing managerial functions, year-round.

As a manager, a key part of your role is to maintain strong contact with your employees and provide them with ongoing coaching, guidance, and feedback. These steps are called *performance management.* As part of the performance management process, there is a specific time — typically once a year — when managers gather all the performance data on their employees, analyze it, document it, and then provide employees with specific feedback. This piece of the performance management process is *performance appraisal*.

Laying the Foundation

In order to take full advantage of the wide range of measurable benefits associated with state-of-the-art performance appraisals, you need to start with a few foundational steps.

Recognizing the roles of performance appraisal

Managers who view performance appraisal as an isolated annual event tend to regard documentation as its sole and primary purpose. Although documentation has a place in the process, it sits beside numerous equally important functions:

- ✔ Motivating employees
- ✔ Educating employees
- ✔ Clarifying performance expectations
- ✔ Increasing self-awareness
- ✔ Building your managerial skills
- ✔ Communicating and reinforcing company values
- ✔ Establishing performance goals and developmental goals
- ✔ Establishing training and reviewing its effectiveness
- ✔ Setting the bases for promotions, transfers, and raises
- ✔ Preventing legal problems

I discuss all these functions in greater detail in Chapter 2.

Seeking additional sources of feedback

Most people think that the only source of feedback during the appraisal process is the manager herself. Although the manager's role in the process is central and essential, the quality and effectiveness of the entire process is significantly upgraded when two additional sources are included.

These two primary additional sources — self-evaluations and 360-degree feedback — provide insights that lead to the continuation of excellent performance and improvement of sub-par performance.

Turn to Chapter 3 for more on these types of feedback.

Strengthening your role

As your employees' manager, you play the central role in the performance appraisal process, because you're still the primary source of feedback.

In order to effectively carry out this responsibility, one of the most important foundational steps is to have a clear understanding of the different types of performance appraisal systems that are available, along with the pros and cons of each. This information helps you understand, enhance, and succeed with any system that you may be using.

Here are your options for performance appraisals (all of which I cover in greater detail in Chapter 3):

- Essays
- Graphic rating scales
- Checklists
- Forced choice methods
- Employee ranking
- Critical incidents
- Behavioral checklists
- Management by objectives

Successfully Navigating through the Appraisal Process

With the foundation in place, you can take some specific preparatory steps that help set the stage for highly effective and productive performance appraisals.

Generating the right mindset and the right plans

As I explain in Chapter 4, an essential step in the appraisal process is to establish a performance appraisal mindset in which you:

- ✔ Truly see yourself as the leader.
- ✔ Set positive expectations regarding the entire process.
- ✔ Take productive steps to identify and overcome any fear or reluctance you may be experiencing regarding the appraisal process.

By applying specific strategies to build your self-awareness and empathy, you'll greatly enhance your understanding of your employees as well as your skills to appraise them. When you combine these steps with some advance planning, anticipation of the kinds of questions you may encounter, and preparation of the kinds of answers that you can provide, you reduce your personal reluctance and increase your confidence.

Accumulating and examining performance data

In order for your feedback to have relevance and a lasting impact, you must base it on specific examples of employee performance. You can't glean this information from quick visits with your employees, nor is it accessible at the last minute.

As I explain in Chapter 5, accurate appraisals require a real understanding of your employees' performance throughout the evaluation period. The only way to effectively reach that high level of understanding is by sharpening your observational skills, continuously managing by wandering around, and using all your senses in the process.

In addition to carefully monitoring your employees' performance, you can enhance the quality, reliability, accuracy, and acceptance of your performance appraisals by familiarizing yourself upfront with other important pieces of data as well (such as job descriptions, last year's appraisal, performance objectives, notes you've been taking, employee files, and previous performance evaluations).

Marginal data gathering leads to useless feedback, which leads to employee resistance.

Preparing evaluations

After you've reviewed all the performance data from a variety of sources, the next step is to complete the evaluation form. These forms vary from one company to another, but some overarching principles will help you handle this step more easily and effectively. Some of these steps include evaluating your best employees first, entering your written comments before the numerical ratings, and considering how your employees will feel when they read your comments.

Your comments will generate resistance if they're invalid, unsubstantiated, or focused on personality instead of performance.

Conducting highly effective appraisal sessions

After you've completed evaluation forms with ratings that are based on direct observations of your employees' performance, behaviors, and results, you're ready for the face-to-face performance appraisal sessions.

Because you're providing your employees with feedback, coaching, and guidance throughout the evaluation period, your employees already have a clear understanding of how they've been performing on the job, so you've all but eliminated the likelihood of resistance or defensiveness during this meeting.

Some of the key steps that will help make these meetings even more successful include

- Understanding your objectives for the meeting itself
- Setting an agenda
- Practicing any comments that may be difficult to express
- Bringing your notes and relevant forms and files with you
- Entering with positive expectations
- Preventing interruptions
- Scheduling sufficient time for the appraisal
- Selecting a private venue for the appraisal

As you hold appraisal sessions, you also need to take some key steps when opening the discussions, giving your employees opportunities to talk, engaging in active listening, reviewing objectives and results, analyzing critical incidents, discussing strengths and areas needing improvement, going over the final rating, and properly concluding the sessions — all of which (and more) I cover in Chapter 6.

Avoiding mistakes

As you navigate through the performance appraisal process, be sure to note and avoid the common errors that can instantly undo all your efforts in this area. As I outline in Chapter 7, some of the strategies to identify and deal with these errors include

- Accurately assessing recent events
- Removing bias and stereotypes
- Ending the halo-and-horns effects
- Thinking twice about first impressions

> ✔ Understanding the contrast effect
>
> ✔ Controlling your emotions
>
> ✔ Avoiding the central tendency and skews
>
> ✔ Eliminating labeling, arguing, defensiveness, excessive talking, postponed sessions, and surprises

Taking follow-up actions

Although some managers believe that the appraisal process ends when the performance appraisal session ends, that ending is actually more of a beginning.

With the evaluations completed, you'll have plenty of data to use in developing real goals with your employees (namely, goals that are clear, specific, prioritized, challenging, measurable, and supported by action plans). In order to be truly effective, these goals should be in sync with company goals as well as your goals, and they should be designed to enhance your employees' performance, productivity, and development.

With these goals in place, your next step is to manage by wandering around and providing your employees with ongoing communication, coaching, guidance, and feedback. By doing so, you'll be able to keep your employees on track to meet their goals. You'll also be able to identify and correct any number of departmental issues before they become serious problems.

With the appraisal process functioning as but one component in the performance management process, a cycle is actually developed: First, you and your employees jointly establish and agree upon specific performance and developmental goals. Then you provide ongoing coaching and feedback throughout the evaluation period. When the time for performance appraisals arrives, both you and your employees know exactly how they've performed, so you have no difficulty creating the evaluation or conducting the face-to-face sessions. And after you've completed those sessions, the goal-setting process starts anew. Chapter 8 contains a detailed discussion of this cycle and the follow-up actions you need to take.

Using Effective Phrases and Expressions

Your written comments in the performance appraisal process offer an excellent opportunity to present compelling, long-lasting, and motivational feedback to your employees. In order to do so, the phrases you use must be specifically designed to energize your employees to continue and even surpass their excellent performance, while simultaneously helping them to understand and upgrade their questionable performance.

The best way to reach this objective is to identify the key areas of performance and then provide powerful phrases that target the full range of employee behaviors. With this in mind, Chapters 9 through 17 provide more than 3,200 such phrases.

With a state-of-the-art performance appraisal system in place, backed up by the best phrases to use in this process, you're in an excellent position to enhance the performance and productivity of your employees, your department, and your company.

Chapter 2

What Performance Appraisals Do for You and Your Team

In This Chapter

▶ Unlocking unexpected motivational powers

▶ Providing education through evaluation

▶ Fulfilling administrative needs

*P*icture yourself as an archer, your bowstring fully extended and ready to sail an arrow toward the target 50 yards down the range. You carefully aim and let the arrow fly. But this is a different kind of range — you can't see where your arrow actually lands. You have no way of knowing if you hit the target or the bail of hay behind it. As a result, you don't know what to improve, how to improve, if you're actually improving, or whether you need to improve at all. What you do know is that archery is no longer interesting, motivating, or fun.

Welcome to life without performance appraisals.

Everyone needs feedback. Without it, you have no way to learn, grow, and fully reach your potential.

The problem is, many managers see appraisals as annual rituals that drag them and their employees away from their work, seemingly satisfying no one but the human resources department. And this feeling is natural — after all, most businesses haven't taken the time to explain the purpose of appraisals or train their managers in how to conduct them.

Performance appraisals shouldn't be isolated events that stand starkly removed from the rest of your managerial responsibilities. As a manager, you're communicating with your employees on a regular and frequent basis. You're providing them with assignments, updates, information, and feedback on their work. You may even be writing up their performance on various projects during the course of a year.

By taking these steps, you're engaging in what's called *performance management*. And within the framework of performance management, there is one point each year when you provide your employees with formal and documented feedback regarding their performance. That piece of the process is called the *performance appraisal*.

If I told you I knew about an easy-to-use managerial strategy that improves employee motivation, focus, insights, and growth, you'd probably be intrigued — especially if that strategy were free. Good news: Performance appraisals have all these intriguing advantages, and many more!

In this chapter, I explore the rationale behind performance appraisals. I also give you steps you can take to easily, seamlessly, and effectively incorporate performance appraisals into your managerial style.

Harnessing the Motivational Power of Appraisals

Motivation is the process that energizes employees and propels them to pursue their goals. Well-designed and well-executed performance appraisals have a strong motivational impact. Appraisals have the power to motivate employees because they provide a number of interconnected benefits:

✔ **They demonstrate the need for improvement.** If employees don't have a clear understanding of how they've been performing, they can't be motivated to make any improvements. After all, if they haven't been told that there are issues regarding their expertise, their communication, or the quality or quantity of their work, and if they don't sense that any improvements are needed, then they certainly won't be motivated to work harder in these areas.

✔ **They meet higher-level psychological needs.** Researchers continue to find that recognition is one of the most powerful forms of motivation for large numbers of employees. Although you can find numerous possible sources of recognition on the job, performance appraisals are an opportunity for employees to receive formal, significant, and enduring recognition from their manager. This prospect is particularly energizing for that large percentage of employees who have strong needs in this area.

✔ **They build a sense of personal value.** When managers take the time and effort to carefully review, analyze, document, and discuss performance with employees, the underlying message to the employees is that they're important and valuable, and this alone is quite rewarding, whether the feedback is positive or not.

✔ **They enhance personal development.** Performance evaluations are motivational for employees who are looking to enhance their personal learning, growth, and development. Appraisals are a highly valuable source of information, insights, and tools necessary for such progress. Performance appraisals are similarly motivational for employees whose needs are centered on achievement, goal attainment, and sensing personal effectiveness, respect, and trust.

✔ **They turn employees around.** When employees are performing poorly, performance appraisals can provide the wakeup call that they need to get refocused and reenergized. Perhaps a struggling employee has been given a verbal warning, and maybe she was written up along the way. This type of negative documentation is often perceived as self-serving for the company, and it can easily generate resentment, anger, and defensiveness, none of which is much of a precursor to improved performance. With performance appraisal, however, the purpose of the session is not strictly disciplinary, so the employee is more likely to walk in with a more receptive and open mind. As a result, your comments regarding an employee's questionable performance have an excellent chance of being heard and generating action as a result.

✔ **They increase satisfaction.** When performance appraisals meet the employees' needs in such areas as gaining recognition, sensing achievement and competence, experiencing growth, and meeting objectives, they're also contributing to the employees' job satisfaction, and this is one of the most important elements at work today. When employees are satisfied, some of the most visible indicators are reduced turnover, absenteeism, and tardiness.

On the flipside, when employees are subjected to a shoddy or even nonexistent performance appraisal system, the opportunities to fulfill these higher-level employee needs are substantially reduced.

If you think about this in psychological terms, when the employees' needs are not being met on the job, employees are likely to try to meet them elsewhere. The result can be joining another company or simply spending less time on the job and more time on activities that *do* meet their needs — and those are the very pursuits that can cause them to miss work or be less than productive when they're at work.

Just as a solid performance appraisal system is motivational, the lack of such a system undercuts motivation and fosters a growing sense of dissatisfaction, frustration, and confusion. Employees who aren't given regular performance appraisals become hapless archers who don't know where their arrows have landed.

Educating while Evaluating

Performance appraisals are also important because of the numerous ways in which they contribute to employee education and development.

In order for anyone to learn, he needs to receive feedback on his performance. Performance appraisal is an outstanding educational tool because the entire process is based on providing feedback. Employees learn a great deal about themselves through performance appraisal, whether the appraisals take the form of self-evaluations or evaluations from their managers, peers, and others in the workplace. (For more information on the types of appraisals, turn to Chapter 3.)

Feedback: Would you like a little formality with that?

There are actually two types of feedback:

✔ **Informal feedback:** Informal feedback is brief and intermittent advice, typically provided spontaneously or in a casual discussion. When you provide your employees with informal feedback, it's often regarded as passing news that may or may not require much attention or action. Your employees may hear what you're saying, but you have no guarantee that they're actually listening or learning.

✔ **Formal feedback:** Formal feedback is a planned and structured discussion in which the objective is to give the employees clear and specific information regarding their performance. This automatically means that your employees' attention levels are more likely to be turned up and tuned in. Employees enter this session with the expectation that they're about to receive key information regarding their performance. This expectation sets the stage for them to listen more attentively to what you're saying.

In this section, I fill you in on the many ways in which performance appraisals can help your employees — and you! — learn and grow.

Setting expectations

When an employee starts a new job, she's typically provided with a job description that spells out her responsibilities and functions, which, ideally, helps her understand *what* she's supposed to do. But in order to perform at peak levels, employees also need to know *how* they're supposed to work. This type of information is not usually found in a job description, but it's critical when the time comes for the employee to be evaluated.

A performance evaluation plays a powerful educational role by providing employees with an essential counterbalance to their job description. By understanding the content of the job description as well as the content of the performance evaluation, an employee is armed with full knowledge of the meaning of excellent performance. This knowledge can actually help draw out such performance.

Building self-awareness

Performance evaluations have the unique power to help employees throughout the company build their self-awareness, whether they're being evaluated or doing the evaluating. The better that employees truly understand themselves, the better they'll be able to learn, grow, and perform on the job. If their self-insights are marginal, their work is likely to be marginal, too.

Generating insights for your employees

A well-crafted performance appraisal is one of the most powerful tools for increasing your employees' self-awareness. With greater understanding of their strengths and weaknesses on the job, it's far easier for them to be more focused, goal-oriented, and productive.

An effective way to teach your employees is to focus on them as individuals, instead of taking a one-size-fits-all approach to education. As an educational process, performance appraisal is 100 percent focused on your employees as unique individuals.

Although most of life's experiences offer a degree of learning, there is a random aspect to many such experiences. Incorrect, inappropriate, or meaningless lessons can be learned at any time, often leaving a person on the sidelines, in the wrong game, or generally out of it. But this doesn't happen with performance appraisals. When they're conducted properly, information is direct, factual, and specific, and it's tailored to just one person (namely, the employee you're evaluating).

The feedback that your employees receive during a performance appraisal has extra credibility for one main reason: You're providing it. Employees are more likely to believe and internalize your comments because you've observed and analyzed their performance, and because you're one of the most important people in their lives. If you're unsure about this, just ask them.

Points of reflection

When you look at yourself in the mirror at home, you're essentially getting a look at yourself from one perspective. Granted, it's an accurate view, but it isn't the *complete* view. If you have full-length folding mirrors that allow you to see yourself from many different angles, you're sure to get a more thorough look and a good deal more information, for better or for worse.

The same principle applies to performance appraisals. The feedback you provide to your employees essentially holds up one mirror that gives them a look at themselves, while feedback from others in the workplace holds up many mirrors from entirely different perspectives. With all this additional data, there are great opportunities for additional self-awareness and growth.

And if your company's appraisal system gives employees the option to complete self-evaluations, there are even more opportunities to build self-awareness. When employees take the self-evaluation option seriously, they tend to spend some quiet time truly thinking about their performance, productivity, skills, knowledge, and other key elements that are central to their jobs. The mere act of sitting down and looking honestly at their work not only helps them understand their performance on the job, but also helps them understand themselves.

At the same time, when employees take this option casually and automatically rate themselves as outstanding in every category, the opportunities for self-awareness will arrive when you sit down with them and paint a more accurate picture.

And if your company's appraisal process includes feedback from the employees' peers and subordinates, the opportunities for self-awareness and growth are multiplied.

Generating awareness for yourself

As a manager in the performance appraisal process, you have three key opportunities to build your *own* self-awareness. (You didn't think your employees were the only ones who had something to learn, did you?)

- ✔ The feedback that you receive from your own manager can be a major help in strengthening your self-awareness, just as your comments do for your employees.

- ✔ If you opt to complete a self-evaluation form, you, too, are afforded the opportunities for self-awareness that accompany this step in the process.

✔ If your company uses a 360-degree feedback program (see the nearby sidebar, "Points of reflection"), your peers, employees, and others in the workplace can enhance your self-awareness on a wide range of workplace behaviors, including planning, organizing, communicating, delegating, and leading.

With a greater understanding of how you're perceived in these areas (and in many others that are part of managerial performance), you, too, now have the advantage of looking at yourself in many mirrors. You can truly see yourself as others see you, and that is one of the premier building blocks for self-awareness.

Increasing your managerial effectiveness

While you're carrying the various responsibilities that are part of the performance appraisal process, you're also profiting from one of the less apparent roles that this process plays. By definition, in order to conduct effective evaluations, you need to have finely tuned observational skills. Without such skills, your reviews will be full of misstatements and mistakes, and the one-on-one sessions with your employees will miss the mark. When you have excellent observational skills, you're empowered with accurate firsthand data, one of the true keys to building successful evaluations.

Managers quickly learn that one of the best ways to gather accurate data about their employees is to engage in a highly regarded practice called *managing by wandering around.* This doesn't mean having constant face time with your employees every day, but it does mean that you get out of your office frequently and visit with your employees in their work areas.

When you take these steps, you end up creating a mental grid for yourself in which you can file the behaviors and actions that you observe. And the more frequently you use this framework with your employees, the more astute an observer you become.

As you spend time in a department gathering performance appraisal data, an important byproduct is that you're likely to gather firsthand information about new developments, problems, issues, and concerns. In many cases, these matters may not have been brought to your attention until they've morphed into full-blown crises.

Plus, face time with your team has a positive impact on their motivation and morale. When a manager spends time with her employees, the employees simply feel better. The unspoken message is that the employees are important and valuable, and that's a message you want to convey.

There is more to observation than meets the eye. If you really want an accurate picture of employee performance, think about observing with *all* your senses. The next time you wander through the work area, turn up your antennae and concentrate on what you're seeing, hearing, touching, and even smelling. In every respect, this is a sensible way to manage. (Turn to Chapter 5 for more on managing with all your senses.)

Transmitting company values

Performance appraisals educate the employees on the company's culture. For example, some companies place a premium on independence, creative thinking, and assertiveness, and language in their appraisals reinforces these types of behaviors.

Other employers may speak glowingly of their support for such behaviors, but they don't mention them in their performance appraisals. In fact, in such companies, these behaviors may be viewed as trouble-making, boat-rocking, or arguing. Their reviews may emphasize such qualities as "obedience," "respect," and "following company procedures."

Performance appraisals spell out valuable information regarding the behaviors that are valued and rewarded in the company. If employees want to succeed and thrive in a given company, paying attention to which company values are highlighted in their performance appraisals is essential.

Understanding and meeting goals

A performance appraisal is an excellent time to confirm that the employees understand your goals, as well as the goals for your department and the company at large.

Employees are often provided with this information when they join a company, but that can be the first and last time that they ever hear anything about it. Performance appraisals offer the perfect time to clarify and reinforce the company's objectives and align the employees' goals with your goals.

The better your employees understand the objectives, especially reasonably challenging objectives, the more motivated they'll be to meet them.

Defining a career path

When employees receive performance-based feedback through the appraisal process, it's as if they've plugged into a navigation system that pinpoints their exact location on their career path. But employees need to know more than where they are — they need to know if they're on the right road, and if that road is taking them where they want to go.

Through the appraisal process, you gain a better understanding of each employee. This insight is generated from the most valuable indicator of a person's strengths and weaknesses — namely, her behavior. People can talk about performance, standards, and goals, but their performance on the job speaks much louder.

With in-depth knowledge of each employee, a manager is in the perfect position to work with an employee to help set the most appropriate career path and objectives. Employees should be receiving some of this feedback on a regular and informal basis throughout the year, but performance appraisals guarantee that they receive a current road map at least once a year.

When performance appraisals are overlooked or given short shrift, employees will still be on a career path — but their navigation system will be turned off.

Identifying training needs and evaluating the results

Before you implement any educational program, whether conducted on the job or in sessions that are held off-the-job, the most critical step is to determine the areas in which your employees actually need to be trained. The data that you generate through performance appraisals provide a solid basis for determining training and educational needs, whether on an individual or departmental basis.

For example, maybe you find a significant number of evaluations that point to problems in teamwork and cooperation. This finding would highlight a need for training in these areas, such as a team-building program. On the other hand, if the performance review data indicate that there are no teamwork or cooperation problems, even the best team-building program in the world will be of only marginal value.

 In the world of training, excellent programs are described as having a high degree of *transference,* meaning that the information learned in these programs can be readily applied to the attendees' jobs. Training that is conducted without consideration for the employees' needs is destined to have minimal transference at best, and this means minimal interest, attention, and learning. For example, in order to perform more effectively on their jobs, apparel designers don't need training on tax laws.

When a training program is completed, one key step is to evaluate its effectiveness. And one of the best ways to do this is to compare performance evaluations prior to and after the training. If the evaluations included consistently low ratings and negative comments on teamwork and cooperation prior to the training, while the ratings and comments became more positive in later evaluations, then the training most likely worked. However, if later evaluations show that the ratings and comments remained poor or even dropped, then the issue needs to be revisited.

 When employees are provided with clear and specific examples of performance where they fell short, and they understand the consequences associated with continued poor performance, their interest in taking corrective steps is significantly enhanced. As a result, they enter an educational program as motivated learners, which is essential for learning to occur.

Aiding Administration

Performance appraisals play a key role in several administrative areas. As a result of the data generated through the appraisal process, you're better able to make good decisions about a wide range of matters that directly impact your employees, your department, and the company at large.

These decisions, many of which are life changing for the impacted employees and critical for the organization, are best based on facts, and one of the best sources of such facts is performance appraisals. With accurate hard data in hand, employment-related decisions are easier for managers to make — and they're easier for employees to understand and accept.

Setting the groundwork for promotions

One of the strongest motivators that many employees bring to the job is focused on being promoted.

As manager, you can look back on an employee's performance over a given period and have a general impression regarding his promotability. However, if you base a promotion decision on feelings rather than findings, you actually generate difficulties in three distinct arenas.

- **Problems for the promoted employee:** Without accurate performance data, you're likely to promote the wrong person. In such a case, the outcome is obvious. Namely, she's likely to fail. This creates an entirely new menu of problems that await you, such as extra time monitoring, coaching, counseling, disciplining, and perhaps terminating this individual. Plus, you've lost an employee who probably was performing satisfactorily in her original position and became just a marginal person in the newly filled position.

- **Problems for the employee who is not promoted:** By promoting the wrong person, you've most likely also upset at least one other person in the department — namely, the person who deserved to move up the ladder.

This person is likely to be upset and believe that promotions in the department are unfair and arbitrary. These types of feelings eat away at an employee's motivation, commitment, and performance — which means one of your best employees is now dissatisfied.

✔ **Problems for the rest of the team:** Employees get a strong sense of which co-workers are actually deserving of promotions. When they see a promotion decision that ignores a truly outstanding co-worker, they too develop doubts about the role of equity and merit in the department. Such doubts can chip away at their attitudes and job behaviors as well.

When the wrong person is promoted, dissatisfaction is promoted throughout the department.

Setting the groundwork for job transfers

A transfer can be a great way for an employee to advance his career and undergo a significant growth experience. Although the new position may be essentially at the same level as the employee's current position, a transfer allows him to have an expanded opportunity to learn, acquire new skills, work with different people, and possibly open a wider and more suitable career path.

If you have a job opening and an interested employee asks to be considered, whether through a job-posting system, internal advertisement, or simply word of mouth, you'll need some accurate performance data in order to make a good decision. Certainly some important information can be gleaned by an interview, but the decision needs to be based on more than a friendly conversation.

Assuming there is mutual interest, the next step is to speak with the applicant's manager. Just keep in mind that any number of factors can contaminate the data that the manager provides. For example, that manager may be upset that her employee wants to make a change, which could lead to some biased comments.

Here's where performance appraisals again enter the scene. When you're looking at an employee who wants to be transferred, one of the best steps is to review all the appraisal data on him. And if you have multiple applicants, this approach can help you put all of them on a level playing field, matching each against the other on comparable work-related skills and behaviors.

Establishing meaningful raises

The raises that you provide to your employees can lead to positive, neutral, and negative reactions, all heavily influenced by the performance appraisal process itself.

Garnering bravos for the raises you give

With solid performance appraisal data, you can look back at clear, specific, and consistent measures of performance for each employee on your team. Instead of trying to recall how an employee did or simply relying on gut feel, a state-of-the-art performance appraisal system allows you to accurately focus on such factors as quality, quantity, communication, cooperation, attendance, and much more. As a result, you're able to base your raise decisions on factors that are fair, consistent, and tailored to individual performance.

When raises are based on accurate, fair, and measurable behaviors and outcomes, all your employees are literally on the same page. With a clear link between performance and pay increases, the entire process becomes more transparent, equitable, and motivational.

One of the major sources of pay-related dissatisfaction is not the actual amount of an increase. Instead, the dissatisfaction emanates from what is called *pay equity*. For example, a person may be satisfied with a raise until she finds out that a co-worker with less skill, training, or productivity has received an equal or larger raise. When this happens, that satisfying raise instantly morphs into a source of dissatisfaction, frustration, and demotivation. You can prevent this from happening by making sure that the raises you grant are clearly related to your employees' performance.

Dodging rotten tomatoes after you hand out raises

If raises appear arbitrary or unfair, employees view them negatively. When employees believe they've met all the criteria for a specific raise, but they're granted a lower raise for no apparent reason, their reaction will be a combination of dissatisfaction, disappointment, distress, and resentment. And these feelings aren't likely to energize employees to put forth extra effort in the future.

In fact, when an employee believes that he is under-rewarded, he has a conscious or unconscious tendency to get even with the company. The attitude goes something like this: "If they're going to shortchange me, I'm going to shortchange them." And employees do this by cutting back in such areas as quality, quantity, commitment, and dedication.

On the other side of the coin, believe it or not, employees generally don't like being over-rewarded. When they receive a raise that greatly exceeds their expectations, their reaction is not necessarily positive. In these scenarios, many employees experience a combination of guilt, nervousness, and anxiety. They don't sense the feelings of competence and accomplishment that accompany a reasonable raise, and they wonder if there are strings attached to this unexpected windfall.

Putting your employees to sleep with your raises

Sometimes raises elicit a ho-hum response from employees, indicating that the pay increase neither dissatisfies nor energizes them.

This response is typically what you see when all employees receive essentially the same raise, year after year. In this scenario, the raises are simply expected, and the employees believe that they're automatically entitled to them. When raises have nothing to do with performance, they actually become background noise. Employees typically receive them with a shrug, and there is no measurable positive impact on motivation or performance.

The employer spends money and gets nothing in return. And by the way, the only time these raises impact employee behavior is when an employer eliminates them. So, although such raises have no motivational power, the raises will demotivate employees if they're reduced or removed.

Preventing legal problems

One of the less obvious but equally important roles of performance appraisals comes from the legal protection that they can provide.

Evaluations without raises

Some managers wonder if they should conduct performance evaluations when an employee isn't going to be given a raise. Maybe the employee doesn't deserve a raise, or maybe the company's financial situation has led to a freeze on all raises. Either way, evaluating performance is still very important.

If an employee's raise is being denied because of performance issues, the evaluation helps the employee understand not only the specific areas in which she has fallen short, but also the consequences of her actions or inaction. The process also gives an employee the key tools that she can use to do better in every respect in the future.

Employees should also be evaluated if financial developments have caused a company to freeze raises. Even if there is no raise, all the motivational and administrative benefits of the process still apply. Plus, when employers opt to eliminate performance evaluations during tough times, other problems develop down the road. For example, when raises are reintroduced, there can be confusion over how to reward employees when no evaluative data exists.

In today's workplace, you must fairly, fully, and formally document employee performance before you take any kind of action — positive or negative, promotion or termination. Such documentation is extremely helpful in preventing legal claims and in dealing with claims if they're made.

The documentation associated with performance appraisals can clearly demonstrate that decisions on such matters as work assignments, transfers, promotions, and raises were made on the basis of performance and merit.

At the same time, if an employee is struggling on the job and is ultimately terminated, the data and feedback in his performance review will provide strong documentation showing that the employee was well advised regarding performance issues, and was equally well informed regarding the consequences of continued questionable performance.

If an employee is terminated and she's surprised, don't be surprised if she considers legal options.

Chapter 3

The Types of Performance Appraisals

In This Chapter

▶ Building on self-evaluations

▶ Capitalizing on the input of others

▶ Strengthening your skills with a full range of appraisals

*P*erformance appraisals come in three main categories: feedback from the employee himself; feedback from the employee's co-workers and customers; and feedback from you, the manager. In order to generate the most thorough and accurate feedback for your employees, the best approach actually combines all three components.

The feedback that you provide is a critical part of the process, but it isn't necessarily the first step in the annual performance appraisal. You can build a better foundation for your feedback by first gathering performance data from two other workplace sources: the employee who is about to be evaluated, and the employee's associates.

In this chapter, I walk you through each of the three types of evaluations, showing you how they work together to give you the full picture of an employee's performance.

Feedback from the Employee: Self-Evaluations

One of the most powerful ways to open the evaluation process is to have your employees do a self-evaluation. There is nothing complicated about this step. All you need to do is give the employee a blank copy of the exact form that you're using and ask her to complete it for herself.

Encourage her to truly think about her performance during the year and to be totally honest and forthright. In addition, let her know that you'll be carefully looking over her self-evaluation and you'll be considering her ratings and comments when determining her performance appraisal.

Be sure to tell your employees that this isn't a bargaining game, where their 5 and your 3 for the same factor average out to a 4. They should be as honest as possible and not overrate themselves to try to balance out a low score they expect to receive from you.

Some companies exclude the self-evaluation step altogether, while others merely recommend it. If your company offers the option to include self-evaluations, seize the opportunity and ask all your employees to evaluate themselves. The advantages of self-evaluations cover a broad spectrum:

- ✔ **They demystify the process.** When employees sit down and complete the same evaluation form that you'll be using, any mystery in the process is immediately wiped out.

- ✔ **They help employees focus their behavior.** The better employees truly understand the criteria on which they're being judged, the better they're able to target their efforts on the job.

- ✔ **They send a motivational message.** Employees view the opportunity to evaluate themselves as an indicator of respect and trust and as a sign that their ideas and inputs are important and valued — all of which motivates them to work harder and care more.

- ✔ **They improve communications.** Your understanding of your employees' appraisals leads to a more open, focused, and effective discussion when you meet with them.

If you've given an employee a low rating on a factor that he sees as an area of significant accomplishment and success, the discussion can become tense, argumentative, and sidetracked. By reviewing an employee's self-evaluation in advance, you'll be able to either prepare for this difference of opinion or make an adjustment in this particular rating (for example, if you somehow overlooked some compelling aspects of the employee's performance).

Especially revealing are the areas in which you've rated your employees higher than they've rated themselves. Don't lower your rating just because you came in higher than your employees. Instead, discuss this point with them — it's a great opportunity to provide recognition and support.

The way in which employees approach self-evaluations is quite revealing. Whether they realize it or not, self-evaluations are actually work assignments. Employees who simply plug in all the same scores and make no effort to elaborate on their ratings are giving you additional insight into their work ethic, attitude, and motivation.

Feedback from Others: 360-Degree Feedback

You can learn a great deal about the performance, productivity, and overall effectiveness of your employees by gathering feedback from selected associates at work.

Known as *360-degree feedback,* this evaluative technique provides employees with performance-based feedback from a dozen or so anonymous raters in the workplace — including peers, subordinates, additional members of management, customers, and vendors — all of whom have had work-related dealings with the employees being evaluated.

These raters are asked to complete questionnaires that focus on the performance of individual employees. There is no single and widely accepted form or format for 360-degree feedback, and the approach varies in terms of areas probed, numbers of questions, and types of questions.

Some of the forms that the evaluating individuals complete are lengthy questionnaires with hundreds of questions, while other forms have fewer than 20 questions. Some forms are developed and implemented internally, while other forms are the work of outside experts.

The underlying premise of 360-degree feedback is that if one manager can gather meaningful data about an employee from the top-down angle, a significant amount of additional performance data can be gathered by looking at an individual from all the other angles and degrees.

A professionally operated 360-degree feedback program can be an excellent source of feedback for whoever is being evaluated. But what to do with this feedback is hotly debated among human resources experts. Some experts contend that 360-degree feedback should be part of an employee's formal appraisal, while others contend that such data should be limited to employee development.

The resolution to this conundrum is for you to carefully consider any 360-degree feedback that you obtain as part of the performance appraisal process and use it as a source of additional data but not as a *key* factor in determining ratings. Because you've been managing by wandering around and providing your employees with ongoing coaching, feedback, and guidance, you already have a clear idea of their performance. The data from 360-degree feedback can help support the ratings that you provide.

Besides, employees tend to be receptive to feedback from their peers and others at work when such information is used for training and development, but they tend to be less comfortable with the prospect of having peers and other individuals impacting their evaluations, raises, or promotions.

Feedback from You

Several performance appraisal systems exist, from classic to cutting-edge. Some of these systems work better than others, and there is some overlap among the various systems. The most successful systems are tailored to the companies in which they're used. No matter what performance appraisal approach your company uses, there is one element that can make any of them work better, and that element is *you*.

If you do all the following, you're likely to generate highly effective evaluations:

✔ Keep the evaluation process transparent.

✔ Jointly establish fair and challenging objectives.

✔ Maintain a high degree of contact and communication with your employees.

✔ Engage in regular coaching.

✔ Focus on behaviors and results.

✔ Use meaningful and appropriate phrases when providing feedback.

In this section, I cover the various types of appraisal systems your company may use.

Writing essays

If the word *essay* gives you the same queasy feeling that you had in high school English class, you're not alone. Essays were among the earliest performance evaluation techniques — and they're among the most trying as well.

As the name implies, this approach consists of little more than a manager's written overall opinion of each employee's performance. Under this system, when the end of the year rolls around, a manager is typically handed a form that reads something like, "Please evaluate your employee's performance during the year." The rest of the page is blank — and, interestingly enough, so is the manager's face. Armed with little more than a hint of guidance, the manager writes whatever comes to mind.

For managers who find writing to be a chore, and evaluations to be a bore, the write-up typically contains a few scribbled points that may or may not relate to the employees' performance. Such comments are generally off the cuff, off the top of their heads, and, as a result, off target. There is no reason to assume that such information will have even a hint of accuracy, relevance, or usefulness to employees.

The situation isn't much better for managers who are more verbose. They may fill up the page with words, but all of it may be irrelevant. The form doesn't provide a framework for them to follow, nor are they given any direction regarding rating criteria and focus. As a result, their essays tend to be filled with impressions, biases, distortions, and rambling comments that run far astray from the real meaning of performance appraisal.

Whether the essay-writer is terse or wordy, you can only imagine what a one-on-one session with the evaluated employee would be like. With the essay written by the minimalist, the evaluated employee will feel short-changed, ignored, and insulted. And in the session conducted by the purported wordsmith, the evaluated employee will be instantly defensive and ready to argue each point vociferously. Neither scenario sets the stage for an open discussion in which actual performance, behaviors, and outcomes are discussed and reviewed.

When an evaluation form provides no structure in terms of topics, techniques, and criteria, the raters can provide highly impressionistic feedback that can easily wander far from work itself. This type of form can lead to biased and discriminatory comments (whether intentional or not), which can lead to legal problems for the company.

There is still a place for essays in the evaluation process — but not lengthy diatribes, and not at center stage. Instead, today's essays should be short, focused, and performance-related, and they should be provided along with your rating or ranking of your employees. At the heart of these mini-essays are the specific, targeted, job-related phrases that are among the most powerful tools for performance appraisal and improvement — the kinds of phrases I provide in Part III of this book.

Using graphic rating scales

Graphic rating scales are among the most common tools in the performance appraisal process. They typically contain a list of the following, which employees demonstrate on the job:

> ✔ **Traits and characteristics:** Traits and characteristics are parts of an employee's personality. As such, they tend to be quite stable and unlikely to change over time, especially as the result of a performance appraisal.

Rating scales that focus on traits and characteristics tend to run into trouble. Traits and characteristics are difficult to identify, measure, and evaluate, and there isn't much an employee can do with feedback in this area. For example, when you give an employee a low rating in "self-esteem," she can't go back to her workstation and start working on that.

✔ **Competencies:** Competencies are the overarching, measurable, and observable attributes deemed necessary for successful performance on the job. Depending upon the position, they can include such topics as knowledge, supervisory skills, communication, and problem solving.

✔ **Actions and behaviors:** Actions and behaviors are the specific, observable, and measurable behaviors that employees have taken in the course of carrying out their job responsibilities. Feedback in this area is factual and performance-based. This type of feedback is easier for employees to understand, accept, and act upon.

✔ **Results:** Results are the benchmarks, outputs, and objectives that your employees achieve. Feedback in this area is clear, specific, measurable, accurate, and based upon the employees' meeting specific agreed-upon standards. Appraisals that focus on objectives are easier for you to structure, because the data speaks for itself. At the same time, appraisals in this area help employees focus their attention on the right targets, which can be motivational as well.

The forms usually include a numerical scale, often from 1 to 5, indicating whether the employee is outstanding, excellent, competent, marginal, or unsatisfactory in each described area.

Some of these forms also include a section where you can write comments and phrases to further describe the employee's performance. This is where you would include specific examples, supporting data, and meaningful phrases to support the ratings you provide (see Part III).

Graphic rating scales offer several advantages:

✔ The forms are easy to design for most organizations.

✔ The forms have a clear rating scale, with a description of the level of performance associated with each numerical ranking.

✔ The forms are easy to complete, and they don't take much time.

One main problem with graphic rating scales occurs when they focus on traits and characteristics rather than performance. Other problems are caused by errors that managers make when completing these forms (see Chapter 7).

Choosing checklists

Another basic evaluation method relies on checklists, the most common of which is a broad listing of work-related behaviors, characteristics, and outcomes. With this list in hand, you place a checkmark indicating "yes" or "no" next to any of the descriptors that apply to the employee who is being evaluated.

A variation on this method is the weighted checklist. This approach uses the same process, but the descriptors in the checklist are given different values based on their role and importance in the employee's position.

In either case, you total the scores and determine the employee's overall rating.

The checklists approach is a quick way to evaluate an employee. It can be used to evaluate employees in any position.

At the same time, the checklists approach has some noticeable deficiencies:

✔ **It's incomplete.** Some key outcomes and performance measures can be missing from the checklist, while other measures don't lend themselves to the simplicity of a "yes" or "no" response.

✔ **It's uncontrolled.** Without specific performance indicators, various biases can enter the equation.

> ✔ **It's muddled in the middle.** Managers can encounter additional difficulties when using this approach for employees who are neither stars nor strugglers — people who fall somewhere in between a definite "yes" or "no" response.

Forcing the choice

Some managers have the tendency to give many employees the same ratings, whether positive, neutral, or negative. Although this problem can be addressed by training, some employers opt for an appraisal method called *forced choice*.

Under the forced choice approach, managers use a list that contains several groupings of four statements. Each of the four statements describes a work-related behavior. Developed through careful prior analysis (typically conducted by outside specialists), two of these statements (the weighted ones) are most typical of the performance of excellent employees, and the other two statements are unrelated to the performance of excellent employees. However, they all look equally positive to the manager doing the evaluation.

For each grouping of four statements, you select any two statements that appear to best describe the employee you're evaluating. When you select either or both weighted statements, the employee's appraisal score is increased. When you select the non-weighted statements, there is no impact on the employee's score.

The good news is that there is greater objectivity when you don't really know how positively or negatively you're rating your employees. Without the influence or distraction of specific rating scales, you're more likely to focus on behaviors rather than scoring. Plus, this method eliminates the tendency to give all employees the same rating.

Still, there are some downsides to consider:

> ✔ The actual process of determining the groupings of statements calls for considerable technical expertise, which can be costly.

> ✔ This approach can leave out some of the specific behaviors associated with the quality and quantity of an employee's work or attainment of goals.

> ✔ The process can be annoying to complete, especially when managers feel forced to select an inaccurate option when none of the statements applies.

When the design of an evaluation form overlooks important behaviors and provides no leeway for a manager to tailor his responses, the most likely outcome is an evaluation session that is uncomfortable for the manager and his employees.

Ranking employees

Referred to as *multi-person comparison methods,* these appraisal strategies match each employee's performance with that of her peers and then generates a rank order from top to bottom.

In some cases, comparing employees can be based on any number of criteria conjured up by the managers themselves. In fact, it can be as basic as asking managers to rank their employees from the best to the worst. In other cases, the ranking process and strategy can be more focused, structured, and sophisticated.

Multi-person comparisons work best when you have large departments or groupings of employees in the same evaluation unit.

Forced distribution

The forced distribution approach is a lot like that high school or college class you had that was graded on a curve. In the workplace, the manager doing the evaluating is supposed to look at each employee's performance, compare it to the performance of the employee's peers, and then place each employee in an appropriate percentile grouping — slotting the top 5 percent to 10 percent in the "excellent" group, the bottom 5 percent to 10 percent in the "poor" group, 15 percent in the "fair" group, 15 percent in the "very good" group, and the balance in the "competent" group.

Some companies believe in the forced distribution approach so strongly that they terminate employees who land in the bottom group.

Here are the advantages of forced distribution:

- ✔ It eliminates the possibility of a manager giving all employees similar or equal ratings, whether unduly low or unduly high. By definition, the evaluations are going be spread out from highest to lowest, even if the range is quite narrow.

- ✔ The forced distribution scale forces managers to put some serious thought into their evaluations.

- ✔ This approach is more likely to highlight the real factors that are used to measure success in a company.

- ✔ Some employers contend that this approach leads to higher-caliber employees, especially if the bottom ranks are eliminated each year.

On the flip side, here are some of the drawbacks to the forced distribution approach:

- ✔ It can have a negative impact on teamwork because employees sense that they should set aside any notion of working as a cohesive entity, and instead focus their attention on outdoing, outperforming, and outshining their co-workers whenever possible.

- ✔ If the program is used for several years, the bottom 10 percent has been getting better and better, and the prospect of continuing to eliminate employees in this grouping can have a chilling effect across the company.

- ✔ This approach may not be successful in laying the appropriate groundwork for employee development and growth.

Pairing up

A second well-known multi-person comparison method is called *paired comparisons*. With this approach, the manager pairs an employee with another person in his department or work unit; then he looks at the pairing and chooses the better performer from the pair. He pairs the better employee with another employee in the department, and evaluates that pair to see who is the better performer. As employees continue to be matched up in pairs with each other, the manager continues to choose the better performing individual.

When all the possible pairings and selections have been made, it's time to total things up. Employees who are selected more frequently move toward the top of the list, while those who are selected less frequently drop toward the bottom. Ultimately, there is a rank ordering of employees from the highest to the lowest. Those at the top receive the top rewards, such as raises, while those at the lower end receive lower-level rewards, if any at all.

This approach prevents all employees from getting the same ranking, and it can be used in many departments across a company.

At the same time, this process can easily be subjective, and factors other than performance can leak into the mix. In fact, popularity can play a greater role than performance.

Finding critical incidents

Critical incidents are a special category of employee behaviors that focus on two distinct areas: particularly outstanding behaviors and particularly questionable behaviors. The critical incidents method of performance appraisal is based on managers spending time during the year observing and gathering behavioral data on their employees, while looking extra carefully for those critical incidents.

At the end of the year, the managers take out all their notes on these critical incidents and categorize them as either positive/satisfactory behaviors or negative/unsatisfactory behaviors. An employee's rating is then heavily influenced or even determined by which pile of data is taller — the satisfactory or the unsatisfactory.

Here are the advantages of the critical incidents approach to performance appraisal:

- ✔ **It's based on direct observations.** The greatest strength of this approach is that performance evaluations are based on actual performance that is observed firsthand by the employee's manager.

- ✔ **It's time-tested.** In this approach, managers gather data over a full year, so it's less likely to be influenced by a mad last-minute scurry for data or the undue impact that can be associated with an employee's most recent behaviors.

✔ **It provides more face time.** By definition, the critical incident approach encourages managers to spend time on the floors with their employees, which allows them to provide more coaching, guidance, and feedback, while also learning more about overall developments in the department

On the other hand, the critical incidents approach has some drawbacks:

✔ **It delays the giving of feedback.** In order for feedback to be truly effective (whether the feedback is positive or negative), it should be linked as closely as possible to the behavior in question. With critical incidents, a greater emphasis may be placed on gathering data and tallying it than actually using it to inform, educate, and motivate employees.

As the distance between behavior and feedback increases, the value of feedback decreases.

✔ **All satisfactory and unsatisfactory behaviors are not equal.** Throughout the year, a person may display many excellent behaviors but only one unsatisfactory behavior. In that case, her pile of satisfactory behaviors would be much greater than her pile of unsatisfactory behaviors. But weighing the number of satisfactory behaviors against the number of unsatisfactory ones can lead to an erroneous conclusion if the one unsatisfactory behavior cost the company its best client, or its computer system, or its line of credit.

In order to increase the accuracy and utility of the critical incident method, managers who use it should attach a numerical value to each positive and negative behavior.

✔ **Although managers should engage in managing by wandering around, the critical incident approach can cause managers to spend too much time on the floors.** If the manager is constantly wandering around with his employees, the employees can start to feel as though the team is being micromanaged.

Going paperless

Many companies rely on paperwork for completing, communicating, and documenting performance appraisals, but a burgeoning industry is offering a wide range of Web-based applications to cover virtually every aspect of the performance appraisal process. With these paperless solutions, it's easier for managers to:

✔ Oversee, coordinate, and expedite the appraisal process.

✔ Eliminate masses of paper and paperwork.

✔ Collect and analyze a wide range of performance data.

✔ Maintain high levels of employee involvement in every step of the performance appraisal process.

✔ Track the employees' progress toward their goals.

There are several outstanding providers of online performance appraisal tools and systems. The pricing of these online solutions varies by provider and by the programs and tools that you select. The best approach is to visit the Web sites, look over the range of offerings, and find out more about features, benefits, and costs of the solutions that appeal to you.

Some of the best providers are the following:

✔ **EchoSpan (`www.echospan.com`):** EchoSpan offers a full range of Web-based feedback and evaluation tools that you can easily customize and implement, including 360-degree feedback, goal-setting and management, dashboards that facilitate the process, tailored reports, and expert advice.

✔ **GroteApproach (`www.groteapproach.com`):** Grote-Approach offers online performance appraisal software with a library of competencies that you can tailor to your company, self-evaluations, a dashboard to track the process, 360-degree feedback, online approvals, and the full range of reporting.

✔ **Halogen Software (`www.halogensoftware.com`):** Halogen offers a full array of performance appraisal software that is Web-based and includes highly customizable forms, dashboard reporting, goal setting and management, competency libraries, and career planning.

✔ **SuccessFactors (`www.successfactors.com`):** Tailored more to businesses in the small to mid-size range, this Web-based performance management solution includes a broad range of tools such as online evaluations, 360-degree feedback, goal planning and setting, and reporting through a customizable dashboard.

Using rating scales tied to behavior

Instead of relying on behaviors that can be appraised in any position in a company, one well-known appraisal method takes the process into a different arena and bases evaluations on specific behaviors required for each individual position in an individual company. This approach is known as *behaviorally anchored rating scales* (BARS).

Development of BARS evaluations requires an in-depth understanding of each position's key tasks, along with an understanding of the full range of behaviors displayed by individuals in carrying out such tasks. You rate these behaviors for each employee; then you anchor each behavior to points on a rating scale, which indicates whether the behavior is exceptional, excellent, fully competent, or unsatisfactory. The result is a rating scale for each task.

For example, in a hypothetical position of human resources coordinator, one of the job holder's responsibilities is to complete status change notices, which update the personnel system regarding changes in employee pay, position, title, supervisor, and personal data. The BARS method for this specific task in this specific job could read as follows:

> 5 — Exceptional performance: Accurately completes and submits all status change notices within an hour of request.

> 4 — Excellent performance: Verifies all status change notice information with requesting manager before submitting.

> 3 — Fully competent performance: Completes status change notice forms by the end of the workday.

> 2 — Marginal performance: Argues when asked to complete a status change notice.

> 1 — Unsatisfactory performance: Says status change notice forms have been submitted when they haven't.

The BARS approach offers several key advantages:

- ✔ **It's behaviorally based.** The BARS system is totally focused on employee performance. Ideally, it removes all uncertainty regarding the meaning of each numerical rating.

- ✔ **It's easy to use.** The clear behavioral indicators make the process easier for the manager to carry out and the employee to accept.

- ✔ **It's equitable.** With its heavy emphasis on behavior, the evaluation process comes across as fair.

- ✔ **It's fully individualized.** From the standpoint of consistency within a company, BARS is designed and applied individually and uniquely for every position.

- ✔ **It's action-oriented.** With an understanding of the specific performance expectations and standards of excellence, employees can much more easily take steps to improve their performance, and they're more likely to do so as a result.

Like any method, BARS isn't perfect. Here are some of the drawbacks to the BARS approach:

- ✔ **The process of creating and implementing BARS is time-consuming, difficult, and expensive.** Each BARS form must be created from scratch for every position in the company.

- ✔ **Sometimes the listed behaviors still don't include certain actions required of the employee, so managers can have difficulty assigning a rating.**

- ✔ **It's high maintenance.** Jobs change over time, which means that BARS requires a high degree of monitoring and maintenance.

- ✔ **It's demanding of managers.** In order to successfully conduct BARS evaluations, managers need detailed information regarding the actions of their employees. Gathering such data can be quite time-consuming, and many managers end up letting this slide.

Managing by objectives

Another well-regarded and widely used approach to performance appraisal is called *management by objectives* (MBO). By definition, under this method, you evaluate your employees on the basis of results.

MBO is more than performance appraisal — it's a construct for managing the entire organization. Its breadth includes the organization's vision, values, strategies, goals, and performance measurement.

MBO begins with managers at the top of the company setting goals. Then managers and employees at each successively lower level develop their own goals. Employees' goals are designed to support the goals of their own managers. In this way, the entire organization is linked together in the pursuit of objectives.

The focus is on outcomes that are clear, specific, measurable, and supported by action plans, benchmark dates, and deadlines. All aspects of the goal-setting process also apply to the employees' personal and developmental goals, such as building their skills or knowledge base.

After employees meet with their managers to establish their goals and action plans, the employees return to work newly energized and focused on specific short-term and longer-term targets. Simultaneously, their managers monitor the employees' performance, provide coaching and support, remove barriers or help employees overcome them, and make adjustments and course corrections as necessary. The employees' performance and progress are clear, measured, documented, and transparent every step of the way.

Employees are highly motivated through MBO because they've been able to actively participate in the process of setting goals, instead of simply having the goals dumped on them. Their involvement in this type of decision making helps meet many of their higher-level needs for accomplishment, achievement, recognition, and self-worth.

When the time arrives for the annual appraisal, there is no mystery or surprise in the evaluation — a plus both for managers and the employees they're evaluating. With MBO, employees clearly know how they've been doing along the way because they've been given regular managerial feedback starting from the point when the objectives were originally set. Because employees know where they stand, they aren't likely to be resistant, argumentative, or defensive.

As part of the annual appraisal process, employees and their managers establish objectives for the coming year, and the cycle starts anew.

MBO brings a wide range of advantages to the appraisal process:

- ✔ **It helps build relationships between managers and employees.** MBO includes a great deal of contact and communication between managers and their employees, which builds camaraderie, communication, and trust — all key elements in strengthening teamwork.

- ✔ **It fosters a comfortable climate in the workplace.** MBO helps build an atmosphere of respect and trust within a given department and beyond.

- ✔ **Because managers work directly with employees to identify and solve problems, MBO improves the quality of decision making and problem solving.**

- ✔ **It's fair.** Employees are evaluated on the basis of their performance and attainment of goals, which is regarded as fair and energizing.

- ✔ **It's quick and easy.** Performance evaluation forms associated with MBO are a breeze to complete. Typically, they spell out each objective as established at the beginning of the cycle, and then provide a space for the manager to summarize the results.

Some MBO forms also include a scale that asks for a numerical assessment of the employees' success in meeting their goals. These scales guide the managers in the rating process by including specific descriptions of excellent, good, fair, and poor levels of goal attainment.

Part II
Working Your Way through the Process

The 5th Wave　　　　By Rich Tennant

"How'd my performance appraisal go? She said I was supercalifragilisticexpialidocious, and if you can tell me what that means I'll tell you how it went."

In this part . . .

*T*he chapters in this part provide you with hands-on tools to make performance appraisals smooth, functional, and highly effective. Starting with the steps you should take to prepare for evaluations, these chapters carry you through data gathering and analysis, planning and logistics, and ultimately conducting highly productive appraisal sessions.

Although tipping points and tripping points await unwary managers, these chapters show you how to easily prevent or manage all of them. They also tell you what to do after you've completed the evaluations. This part is where you find the great benefits that are associated with goal setting, managing by wandering around, and providing your employees with ongoing coaching.

With these strategies, you'll literally and figuratively be in a great position to build your employees' performance — and build your employees as well.

Chapter 4

Getting Started

● ●

In This Chapter

▶ Developing a mindset that strengthens the appraisals you provide

▶ Preparing yourself for any questions your employees might ask

▶ Organizing the appraisal process

● ●

*W*ith so many appraisal forms, techniques, and strategies at your command, you can easily become sidetracked and overlook the most important element in the entire performance evaluation process: *you!*

Researchers continue to find that, although it's obviously important for companies to select and implement performance appraisal systems that match their culture, style, and standards, the individual who conducts the evaluations is the key factor in determining the effectiveness of the system itself.

Think of your company's performance appraisal system as a car — in fact, think of it as a high-performance car. And think of yourself as the driver. If you're not driving the car or the appraisal process, neither will go very far.

Building Your Evaluation Mindset

Before you start looking at your employees, you need to look at yourself. In order to provide the most relevant, compelling, credible, and effective appraisals, you need a mindset that is fully supportive of the process. Managers who approach performance appraisal as a ritual, a chore, or an isolated event undercut their own effectiveness before they even start.

To have the right mindset, you need to:

- ✔ See yourself as a leader.
- ✔ Set positive expectations.
- ✔ Overcome your own fear, reluctance, and resistance.
- ✔ Gain self-awareness.
- ✔ Empathize with your employees.

With this foundation in place, you'll be in a much better position to understand and analyze your employees' performance and, ultimately, to help each individual achieve greater productivity, growth, and satisfaction.

Seeing yourself as a leader

One of the primary reasons that managers struggle with the performance evaluation process is that they haven't mentally crossed the bridge to management. Perhaps they were promoted over their workplace friends, maybe even long ago, but they still see themselves as part of the old group rather than as a member of management.

These managers are the ones who don't want to give their employees any negative feedback because they're afraid that their friendships will be disrupted. For these managers, being liked is more important than being a leader.

If you're concerned about upsetting your employees because you have to deliver negative performance-related feedback, you haven't fully crossed that bridge to management. And until you do so, the evaluation process is going to be uncomfortable for you and meaningless for your employees.

Managers who want to be effective leaders while simultaneously remaining buddies with their employees find that these two desires don't mix. By continuing to play the buddy card, they undermine their influence, power, and ability to guide the team to meet its goals. Plus, instead of coming across as likable, managers who act this way appear weak.

A manager needs to act like a manager, and that includes providing employees with honest, accurate, job-related feedback, especially during the performance appraisal process. Acting like a manager generates something more important than popularity: It generates respect — and managers who are respected tend to be well liked.

Unless you see yourself as a manager, your employees won't see you as one — and they won't accept or act on the information you give them during the performance appraisal.

Setting positive expectations

Your expectations are directly linked to your employees' performance and, hence, to the performance appraisal process itself. Why? Because your expectations have a measurable impact on how your employees ultimately perform on the job. Not only do you need to have accurate expectations, but the expectations you set for your employees need to be positive.

If you expect an employee to perform poorly, you telegraph that expectation in many subtle and not-so-subtle ways:

- **On the subtle side, your body language can clearly signal your negative expectations.** You may have the perpetual hint of a frown when communicating with the employee. Your brow may be furrowed, your arms may be crossed, and you may even shake your head in an almost imperceptible way.

- **On the not-so-subtle side, you may talk and behave in a way that clearly communicates your negative expectations.** You may speak curtly; frequently use the word *no* in your comments; give better assignments to other employees; and give minimal signs of thanks, appreciation, and recognition.

Your employees pick up *all* these cues — whether subtle or obvious. They internalize your cues and act accordingly, which leads to negative attitudes and diminished performance.

At the same time, when you expect your employees to do well, you deal with them in an enthusiastic, upbeat, and supportive style. You tend to smile and nod more, and your speech is likely to be more animated and filled with the word *yes,* as well as with encouraging phrases. The work you assign and the feedback you provide tell the employees that they're terrific, and they respond with terrific performance.

Think of expectations as self-fulfilling prophecies.

Your expectations have a major impact on your employees' performance and ultimately on the evaluations that you conduct.

As you prepare yourself to appraise your employees, think of your employees as individuals, and then consider the expectations that you've established for each one of them. You'll find that the employees for whom you have low expectations are, indeed, the weaker performers, while the better performers are the employees for whom you have high expectations.

The annual performance appraisal is a perfect time to take a careful look at your expectations for all your employees and then commit to building more positive expectations for each of them. Be sure to express positive expectations during the performance appraisal process.

Overcoming fear, reluctance, and resistance

When you're confronted with the prospect of several performance appraisals looming on the horizon, you may feel queasy. In fact, some of the more common reactions that managers have to performance appraisals are fear, reluctance, and resistance.

If you're experiencing any of these emotions, the best way to dig yourself *out* of them is to dig *into* them. After all, if you carry these feelings into the performance appraisal process, they'll carry you and the process far from where you want to go.

Eliminating fear

Fear is an emotion that is aroused by imminent danger — whether real or imagined. In the case of performance appraisals, fear belongs in the imagined file. Instead of sensing that there may be significant danger in the various stages of the appraisal process, managers have more mundane fears that can hold them back, such as:

✔ **A fear of looking foolish:** Managers who have this fear are primarily concerned that their ratings, comments, and face-to-face appraisal sessions will put them in situations that highlight their lack of knowledge, lack of accurate information, and even lack of managerial skills.

✔ **A fear of confrontation:** Some managers are also afraid that their one-on-one sessions with their employees will turn into arguments and disagreements. Instead of opening the door to these encounters, some managers simply opt to provide unwarranted positive reviews to avoid confrontation. Unfortunately, these reviews don't do anyone any good.

Providing undeserved positive reviews in order to avoid a confrontation doesn't qualify as a method of *overcoming* fear. Actually, it's a method of *surrendering* to fear.

Fortunately, there are two major steps that you can take to help yourself overcome your fears about conducting performance appraisals:

✔ **Spend more face time with your team.** Not only will this strategy help you gather the factual, specific, and job-related performance data you need to create and provide a valid evaluation, but it will demonstrate to your employees that you aren't pulling data out of thin air.

In every respect, your firsthand knowledge provides you with first-rate confidence.

✔ **Become an expert in your company's performance appraisal system.** If you're thumbing through the documents and rating forms the night before an evaluation, you're likely to miss key points, emphasize the wrong points, and move in a direction that has nothing to do with the evaluation or its objectives. Plus, your employees will react negatively to any or all of these indiscretions, bringing out the very behaviors that you fear.

A key source of fear is a perceived lack of power. When you have in-depth knowledge of your employees' performance and the appraisal system, your fears will be alleviated — because knowledge is power.

Just as your expectations about your employees' performance will strongly influence how they ultimately perform, the same applies to your expectations about how the performance appraisal process will go. If you enter the process expecting an embattled exchange, that's precisely what you're likely to get. On the other hand, if you approach the process with positive expectations, it's far more likely to go well.

Eliminating reluctance

Managers who are reluctant to provide performance reviews aren't necessarily *afraid* of conducting appraisals. They're just hesitant, tentative, and likely to defer the process until a later date — a much later date.

One of the primary sources of this reluctance stems directly from a manager's prior experiences with performance evaluations — both the kind they gave to other employees and the kind they received from their own managers:

- **Problems with reviews you gave:** If you've had difficulties providing performance appraisals in the past, you're likely to feel reluctant to give another appraisal now. Perhaps you gave reviews based on information that wasn't fully substantiated, or maybe you had to give an employee a negative review when he expected a great review. Either way, the outcome most likely was conflict. And now you're reluctant to enter the ring again. That reaction is a normal one — after all, you don't want to repeat a less-than-pleasant situation.

- **Problems with reviews you received:** You can also experience reluctance about conducting performance appraisals if you had a particularly dissatisfying experience when you were on the *receiving* end of an appraisal. Perhaps you had a manager who evaluated you unfairly or focused on traits and characteristics that had nothing to do with your performance. Because you don't want to put your employees through this type of ordeal, you're reluctant to appraise them at all.

By definition, *reluctance* is not an absolute refusal to conduct the process. Instead, it's a hesitancy to do so until you reach more of a comfort zone. You can take a couple of key steps that can help you get to that place of comfort:

✔ **Set goals for yourself.** When you carry out most of your other managerial functions, you establish specific objectives, strategies, and deadlines — do likewise for performance appraisals. Try to determine the measurable outcomes that you'd like to achieve from this process, and spell them out in specific terms. These objectives can focus on actual improvements in employee performance, upgrading of employee skills, and achieving greater results.

When you include specific objectives and an action plan as part of each appraisal, your reluctance will decrease. You're implementing the appraisal process similarly to your other managerial functions.

✔ **Practice.** A second important way to overcome reluctance is to build your appraisal skills. One way to do this is to conduct a mock evaluation session with one of your fellow managers or your company's human resources (HR) representative. The practice will increase your comfort level with the process, and the feedback provided in this mock session will help fine-tune your skills and confidence.

Eliminating resistance

When managers resist performance appraisals, they flat-out oppose it. Typically, resistance doesn't have anything to do with being afraid. Instead, managers who resist appraisals tend to believe that the process is an unnecessary intrusion on their time or that it doesn't provide them with useful results.

When some managers first look at performance appraisal materials, their brains go immediately into overload. The result is that they either close the file or set the pile aside. This step, also known as avoidance, does nothing to help them. In fact, although they may physically remove the performance appraisal materials, they still know that the appraisals must be completed. And whenever that thought resurfaces, the queasy feeling returns, along with another round of avoidance.

For some managers, conducting real performance appraisals is very different from what they've been doing in the past, which leads to additional resistance — they want to avoid change. (See the "Resistance to change" sidebar for more on this topic.)

Resistance to change

Some managers resist performance appraisals because appraisals call for a change in long-term and well-established daily behaviors. It doesn't take long for someone to say, "Well, it's human nature to resist change." But believe it or not, this may not be the case.

If you were told that you were going to experience a gigantic change in your life, a change so profound that it would definitely change your relationship with your employer, family, friends, and community at large, would you resist it? Well, it's human nature to resist change, so the answer must be "yes," right?

But what if this gigantic change is that you just won the state lottery and a cool $50 million? That's probably a major change for you, but would you resist it? If not, how can it be human nature to resist change?

The answer is clear: Change itself is not automatically resisted. But people do resist the unknown elements of change. When a change is being introduced, people instantly wonder how it'll impact them. And when the change is filled with unknowns, they resist it.

The best way to reduce resistance to change is to make the entire process more transparent. The more people know about the change, the more they're able to make an intelligent judgment about the best way to react to it. This applies to any change that people encounter in life, including the actions that they're expected to take in the course of a performance review. Taking the time to practice the evaluation process is a great way to reduce your resistance to it.

If you find that your approach to the performance appraisal process is best described as resistance, you can take two key steps to help remove this barrier:

✔ **Consider the advantages.** Instead of approaching the appraisal process as a time-consuming exercise with minimal usefulness, take a look at the potentially positive outcomes associated with it, especially in terms of advantages for you. For example, with a well-tuned appraisal process, your employees are likely to be more satisfied, energized, and productive, which means that your department will be more successful.

At the same time, if you resist the process, the likelihood of these outcomes will diminish, and you'll be forced to spend more time trying to focus and motivate your team. In fact, you're likely to spend more time on *those* efforts than you would have spent on the evaluation process.

✔ **Demystify the process.** Grab the appraisal materials by the horns and read them. One particularly effective strategy is to sit down with a couple of managers or even the HR representative and do a point-by-point run-through. As you'll no doubt find, the process is not as daunting as you thought. And as your familiarity and understanding increase, your resistance will decrease.

Gaining self-awareness

Effective performance appraisals require managers to have considerable insight into their employees, but this task is virtually impossible for managers who lack insight into themselves. When self-awareness is lacking, managers easily miss the main event when appraising their staff and focus on performance issues that are secondary, off the mark, or simply meaningless.

At the same time, self-awareness is a personality trait that employees and managers can't just snap into place overnight. Upgrading skills in this area takes time, focus, and practice. Still, if you want to carry out excellent performance appraisals, you need to address your self-awareness and, if necessary, do some building in this area.

One of the most valid and effective sources of information that can strengthen your self-awareness is the feedback that you've received over the years. Here's the catch: If you've been in denial mode and deflected all negative feedback, you've blocked out information that could help you see yourself more accurately, make some upgrades, and ultimately see others more accurately as well.

With that in mind, one of the best ways to build your self-awareness is to carefully consider the feedback that you receive from the credible sources in your life. This doesn't mean that you have to roll over every time someone says something about you that doesn't sit well, but it does mean that you should truly *listen* to what others are saying and then try to make an honest judgment.

Walking the walk

One of the key ways in which your self-awareness directly impacts your performance appraisals is the extent to which you literally and figuratively "walk the walk" that you expect of your employees. The more you understand yourself in this area, the more effective your evaluations will be.

For example, if you have a casual attitude toward safety and your employees are well aware of your lackadaisical comments and behaviors in this area you won't have much credibility and impact if you try to emphasize safety when evaluating your employees. This applies to *every* component of the performance evaluations that you provide.

As a manager, you need to continuously monitor the degree of consistency between your behaviors and the standards you're using to evaluate your employees' performance:

✔ **Your self-evaluation:** Regardless of whether your manager requires you to complete a self-evaluation, do one — even if it's just for yourself. This self-evaluation will give you a hands-on opportunity to see whether you're truly performing at least at the level that you expect of your own employees. Go through every component of the evaluation process and look honestly at your specific performance on each factor.

✔ **Your support for the process:** In order for your performance appraisals to have real significance, you need to not only get actively behind them but also let your employees know that you're doing so. If you make offhand negative comments about the appraisal process, or if your evaluations run late, your employees will respond in kind, not only verbally but behaviorally.

✔ **Your questions:** In order to continue to build your self-awareness, ask yourself the following key questions — and answer honestly. As you do so, the self-portrait you paint will help you see and evaluate the work of your employees more accurately.

  ✔ What are my greatest strengths and weaknesses?

  ✔ What am I most and least proud of at work?

  ✔ What is my greatest success? What is my greatest failure?

  ✔ How would my manager describe me? How would my co-workers describe me? How would my employees describe me? How would my friends describe me? How would my family describe me?

  ✔ What steps am I taking to continue my growth and development?

If the feedback you receive starts to fall into a pattern or common theme, you should definitely give it a second thought, or even a third. In particular, pay attention to feedback from:

- ✔ **Your manager:** Part of your manager's job is to observe and evaluate your performance, which requires her to learn a lot about you. Your manager probably gives you feedback throughout the year, as well as during your performance review. If you want to build your self-awareness, take this feedback to heart.

- ✔ **Your co-workers:** Your fellow employees spend a lot of time with you every day. Some of the feedback they provide may come out during informal conversations, but you may also have the benefit of their insights through a 360-degree feedback program as well (see Chapter 3 for more on 360-degree feedback). Either way, your co-workers have lots of data on your personality and performance. Their comments, insights, and suggestions are definitely worth considering.

- ✔ **Your friends:** By definition, true friends are open and honest with each other, which means that they can provide you with feedback that can enhance your self-awareness. When you're with your friends, you're free to be yourself — certainly more than you are in the workplace — which means that your friends see a much wider range of your behaviors. As a result, when friends give you feedback, it's worth hearing.

- ✔ **Your family:** Your family knows you in an entirely different context, but — like it or not — your family does know you. For some people, feedback from family members is wrapped in so much emotional baggage that it's difficult to accept. Nonetheless, if you truly want to build your self-awareness, try to set some of your own baggage aside and listen to what they have to say.

- ✔ **Professionals:** If you've taken any tests during the employment process — including tests in such areas as personality, math, reading, job knowledge and aptitudes, and even physical abilities — go back and look at that data. If you've ever met with a career counselor or mental health professional, take a second look at what he said to you as well. Because these are professional observations, they merit some extra observation from you.

✔ **Yourself:** The messages that you give yourself will provide you with some of your most compelling self-insights. Maybe you're too hard on yourself, or maybe you don't expect enough from yourself. Either way, listen to what you say to yourself during the course of the day. Each message gives you one more piece of useful data.

If you pause to look at your behaviors and listen to your own messages, you can gain significant insight into your confidence, self-image, ethics, attitude, self-control, communication skills, interpersonal skills, energy, and much more.

Empathizing with your employees

Empathy is the quality of sensing the feelings and thoughts of other people. As you may expect, empathy is a particularly valuable and desirable quality for any manager to have.

During the performance evaluation process, your ability to feel what your employees are feeling will help you craft written and verbal feedback that will be more meaningful and useful to them. When employees sense that you feel what they feel, their trust in you increases, as does their acceptance of your messages.

Managers who are low in empathy tend to resort to a one-size-fits-all style of appraisal, but they soon find that this approach doesn't fit at all.

Although you can't develop empathy overnight, you can take some steps right away to upgrade your skills in this important area:

✔ **Understand your own feelings.** The better you understand your own emotions and feelings, the better you'll be able to experience the emotions and feelings of others. You can build your abilities in this area by stepping back and taking a good hard look at yourself in situations in which your emotions are actively in play. Feedback from the significant others in your work life and personal life can also help you strengthen these abilities.

✔ **Widen your network.** The more people you know, and the more varied and diverse the situations in which you place yourself, the greater your opportunities will be to enhance your ability to empathize with others. As you experience the ways in which others display empathy, you can learn from their examples and try to emulate their behaviors.

✔ **Practice empathy.** In the various interactions that you have with others, whether in the workplace or in your personal life, try to direct your thinking onto what other people may be feeling, sensing, and seeing.

The more you can see and experience the world from the perspective of those around you, the more compelling and effective your evaluations will be.

Playing the "What If?" Game

By identifying the most difficult questions that your employees can ask during the appraisal process, and then coming up with answers to those questions, you increase the likelihood that your evaluation sessions will be successful.

Many of today's highly successful salespeople try to come up with the most difficult questions that a customer can ask and then develop solid answers to them. This is called the "What If?" game, and it applies to the performance appraisal process as well.

Being stunned by an employee's questions isn't pleasant; neither is stumbling around for answers. By reviewing some of the more frequent questions that employees ask during the face-to-face sessions, along with sample answers, you increase your likelihood of keeping your appraisal sessions on track and on target.

The following answers may not be perfect for your individual situation, but they can give you an idea of the direction to take:

Question: Why am I not getting a raise?

Answer: When you and I originally set goals for this year, we agreed that raises would depend on how successfully you met them.

Question: Why is my raise so small?

Answer: Your raise is in line with what we talked about when we set up the goals.

Question: What did you rate Joe?

Answer: Everyone's rating is confidential.

Question: I thought my performance was better than that. Why did you rate me so low?

Answer: I based the ratings on direct observations of your work that we talked about during the year. Let's talk about the specific ratings that you feel are too low.

Question: Why don't you like me?

Answer: Actually, I do like you. But your evaluation isn't based on that. It's based totally on your performance.

Question: Who told you I did that?

Answer: None of this is based on comments from any single person.

Question: Doesn't loyalty count for anything?

Answer: Loyalty counts a lot, and you received strong ratings in areas that dealt with commitment and dedication.

Question: What do I need to do to get higher ratings?

Answer: Great question. Let's talk about it.

As part of the performance evaluation process, meet with your fellow managers, discuss the most common and difficult kinds of questions they've faced during the evaluation sessions, and then work together to craft some excellent answers to each. This approach is the perfect way to play the "What If?" game.

Planning and Scheduling

As the time for the performance evaluation grows near, you need to move into an administrative role to handle the planning and scheduling of the process.

Set dates and times for all of the key benchmarks in the process. One of the best ways to do this is to use a process called *back-timing*. With this approach, you establish the specific date that you want to conduct the sit-down session with each individual employee and then work backward to set up the benchmark dates for all the activities that need to occur prior to the meeting.

Start the process by contacting each employee at least six weeks ahead of the proposed date. For example, if you want to have your review sessions with your employees in mid-December, contact each of your employees by November 1 to set up a mutually acceptable day and time for your one-on-one session.

When you and one of your employees have agreed on a date and time to meet, set up advance benchmark dates for that meeting to occur:

- ✔ **Six weeks before the meeting (as soon as you've set up a date and time for the meeting):** Meet with the employee, discuss the evaluation process, and give the employee the self-evaluation form. Advise the employee of the due date for this form (see "Four weeks before the meeting," later in this list). Reserve a conference room if you don't have a private office. If you're using 360-degree feedback (see Chapter 3), advise these individuals that you'll need their input on this employee within two weeks.

- ✔ **Five weeks before the meeting:** Assemble all your performance data, notes, and documentation for the employee.

- ✔ **Four weeks before the meeting:** The employee returns her self-evaluation form to you. If you use 360-degree feedback, those forms are returned to you at this point as well.

- ✔ **Two weeks before the meeting:** Complete the review of your documentation, self-evaluation form, and 360-degree feedback.

- ✔ **One week before the meeting:** Complete the first draft of the employee's evaluation. Review the recommended raise, if any.

✔ **Three days before the meeting:** Finalize the raise, if any.

✔ **Two days before the meeting:** Finish the final draft of the employee's evaluation. Plan the agenda for the meeting.

Be sure to put each of these benchmark dates on your calendar. By setting specific dates for every step of the process, you're able to give your employees the time and attention that they deserve for their performance appraisals.

Without planning ahead, you can easily let the time slide by. Then, all of a sudden, there are three days left and you haven't even gathered all the information and documentation, let alone reviewed it and completed the evaluation materials. You can save yourself a lot of stress, and ensure that your performance appraisals are a success, by getting ready ahead of time.

Chapter 5

Gathering and Analyzing the Data

*M*ost managers understand the necessity of basing performance evaluations on workplace behaviors, competencies, and results. But there is less of a consensus and understanding of how to gather and analyze this information. If you don't pay enough attention to this part of the process, you end up with flawed performance data — and equally flawed evaluations.

The information that you need in order to precisely and productively evaluate your employees' performance won't suddenly appear on your desk. Gathering what you need for this process is a year-round responsibility, and handling it effectively helps not only in the performance evaluation process but also in the daily process of managing your employees.

Numerous workplace sources and resources provide the kind of information that's essential for an accurate and meaningful performance appraisal. Of course, as important as these resources are, you're the most important resource of all.

You're at the center of the entire evaluation process for your employees. You're most familiar with them, you've spent the most time observing them, you have access to more data about them than anyone else in the company, and you're the one who will ultimately make sense of all the information and turn it into an accurate and relevant appraisal for each of your employees.

If you scrimp in the data-gathering phase, your evaluations will show it, and so will your employees' reactions.

In this chapter, I show you the state-of-the-art methods to gather, analyze, and utilize the most important performance data on each of your employees.

Managing with All Your Senses

One of the most important ways to gather the kind of information you need to appraise your employees' performance is to manage by wandering around and spending time side by side with your employees as they do their work.

By intermittently visiting your team, you gather some excellent firsthand performance data. Plus, you're carrying out several key functions in the realm of performance management (for example, providing coaching, guidance, support, and feedback right at the point when your employees need it most).

When you spend time working with your employees, you can easily get so caught up in their projects that you miss other subtle yet important developments that are occurring simultaneously. One key way to capture the less obvious, yet strikingly important, subtleties is to apply all of your senses to your managerial style. Together, your five senses — hearing, touch, taste, sight, and smell — play a key role in understanding the world around you, and that world includes the workplace. Even if one or more of your senses is impaired, your other senses still provide extremely valuable data.

Here's how you can expand each of your senses:

> ✔ **Hearing:** When you meet with your employees, don't just listen to what they're saying. Listen to the speed of their delivery; the length of their sentences; and their

vocabulary, pitch, tone, and volume. Try to listen for any other sounds in the department, from disgruntled whispers to possibly malfunctioning equipment.

✓ **Smell:** Most managers don't enter a meeting with their employees thinking about what they're going to smell, but that's exactly what you should do. By tuning into your sense of smell, you may discover alcohol, illegal substances, mold, fumes, and even extreme perfumes, all of which could be tip-offs in terms of employee performance.

✓ **Touch:** Carefully consider what your sense of touch is telling you when you meet with your employees. For example, when you pick up a piece of your employees' work, ask yourself if it's heavier or lighter than it should be. If your employee was supposed to provide you with a brief report but he delivers one that immediately feels as heavy as a phonebook, that may raise some questions about his performance, regardless of the contents.

✓ **Sight:** The next time you meet with your employees in their work areas, take a careful look around. Look at their desks, the photos on the walls, the piles on the credenzas, the in-baskets, the junk on the floors, or the half-open drawers. Most managers walk into an employee's office or workstation, have their meeting, and then leave. If you take the time to look around, you'll actually be able to see into your employee.

✓ **Taste:** When it comes to evaluating employees, *taste* is more figurative than the other senses. For example, when you meet with some employees, the discussion may leave a bad taste in your mouth and give you a gut feeling that something is amiss. On the one hand, you can easily ignore these feelings and refocus on the task. But, by doing so, you may be overlooking information that you should be taking into consideration. If you're getting a bad visceral reaction, acknowledge it and try to figure out what's behind it.

In each of these ways, the real message is to try to draw all your senses into your interactions with your employees. By combining this data with the broad array of performance data, you're more likely to generate deeper and more useful information and insights, followed by more accurate and effective performance evaluations.

Focusing On the Entire Year

In order for your performance appraisals to be effective, you need to maintain regular communication, contact, and coaching with your employees throughout the entire evaluation period (typically, one year). Your employees shouldn't have any doubt about how they're doing. If they run into performance glitches, issues, or problems, they should feel confident that you'll identify and address these situations quickly.

Think of it this way: You're conducting mini-appraisals and feedback sessions all year.

Still, many managers base their annual performance evaluations on selected chunks of time and individual incidents during the evaluation period, rather than on the entire period. When they do this, they end up short-circuiting the evaluation process — and their employees.

Managers offer many excuses for gathering limited data, but all are dubious at best:

- ✔ **There's not enough information.** This claim typically means that the managers haven't been wandering around or focusing on the myriad available sources of performance information. And now, with evaluations around the corner, they don't have any clear and specific examples of their employees' performance.

  With limited data, their evaluations suffer from a lack of thoroughness, specificity, and meaningful examples. Employees typically react to this type of feedback with denial, defensiveness, and disappointment.

- ✔ **There's not enough time.** This pronouncement comes from managers who may be aware of the various sources of performance data, but who lack a true sense of interest, involvement, and commitment to the evaluation process itself.

  These managers base their judgments on limited and arguably questionable performance data, and they tend to rely on general impressions. The employees' reactions to their appraisals will again be distress, but they'll also feel a sense of frustration and humiliation in seeing the minimal amount of time and interest that their managers put into their appraisals.

✔ **There's enough information already.** For these managers, the rationalization is that people don't change very much, so it makes just as much sense to do a cut-and-paste and provide the employees with essentially the same evaluation as last year.

This approach is thoroughly dissatisfying and upsetting to employees, especially those who sincerely tried to improve their performance, competencies, and results. More than likely, they won't make that "mistake" again.

✔ **The most recent behavior is most important.** Instead of taking the time to look at an entire year's worth of performance, these managers rely heavily on recent events, whether positive or negative. They then justify their stance by claiming that these events are more important than events from months long gone by.

If you want your employees to do next to nothing for the first few months and then come to life in the final quarter of the year, this plan is perfect. It punishes the employees who give their all throughout the year. It also punishes employees who had a great year, only to hit even a minor stumbling block toward the end of the year.

✔ **Only a few incidents really matter.** Managers who rely on this excuse believe that there's no need for a year's worth of data because it only takes a few critical incidents to really understand employee performance.

This belief is problematic for a couple reasons:

- The critical incident method (see Chapter 4) includes numerous incidents from throughout the year, not just a few.

- When a manager relies only on a few key incidents, there is no way to know how accurately these incidents reflect the employees' overall performance. With limited performance data, the evaluations can be unduly positive or negative, both of which will be unfair not only to the employees who are being evaluated but also to the rest of the department.

✔ **I already know these are strong employees.** These are the conflict-avoidance managers, the ones who view the appraisal process as a time to praise rather than appraise. Their evaluations are filled with happy talk and language designed to build bonds of friendship and goodwill with their employees. They enter the process with the preconceived notion that their employees are terrific, and that's how they appraise them, regardless of the facts.

Providing employees with recognition and building a strong working relationship with them is important, but that's not appraisal — that's another activity altogether: team building.

✔ **I already know these are weak employees.** These managers use the performance appraisal process as an opportunity to strike back or put down their employees, regardless of the employees' accomplishments or achievements during the year. The twisted idea behind this approach is that the employees need to be tougher, and those who can take this heat will stand out and stand up for themselves.

This macho approach generates little more than annoyance, frustration, and hostility from the employees. For those who have worked hard and met their goals, this type of feedback tells them that their efforts and accomplishments during the year were meaningless.

Regardless of explanations or rationalizations, appraisals that fail to look at the full range of employee performance and competencies throughout the entire year are destined to fail.

There are four additional advantages associated with performance evaluations that cover a full year:

✔ **They put the employees on a level playing field.** It isn't fair to have employees in one department evaluated on a few samples of performance during the past month, while other employees are being scrutinized for an entire year.

✔ **They're accurate.** When evaluations are based on performance data gathered over the evaluation period, the employees' ratings are not excessively downgraded because of a couple of mistakes they made. When evaluations cover only a few critical incidents or a few weeks, any number of invalid and unwarranted conclusions can be drawn.

✔ **They're motivational.** If employees see that all of their behaviors throughout the year will be considered as part of their performance evaluation, they're more likely to be motivated to maintain high standards and output throughout the year.

✔ **They lead to better documentation.** If a need arises to look back at an employee's performance, data that covers the entire evaluation period is very useful.

Accessing the Information

One of the main determinants of the effectiveness of your appraisals is the quantity and quality of performance-based information that you gather. This information provides the foundation and support for the evaluations you create as well as for the feedback that you provide. If the information is thin or flimsy, the same will be said of your appraisals.

In any company, numerous resources can provide you with important performance-based data. Your notes on your employees' performance are at the top of the list, but several resources beyond your notes provide additional insight into your employees' performance — and give your evaluations additional impact.

Getting back to basics

Before looking at your notes or at any other resource related to performance appraisals, there are three basic preparatory steps you need to take.

Checking out job descriptions

Take a look at your employees' job descriptions. You need to be sure that the criteria you're using to evaluate your employees' performance are actually part of their job today.

As the year goes by, any number of formal responsibilities can slip by the wayside, while other roles, expectations, and standards can slip in and take their place. Sometimes this happens so subtly that neither you nor the employees notice it, but by the end of the year, their jobs can only bear a slight resemblance to what they were when the year began.

When you find that a job has changed but the job description has not, you need to make a decision: Either update the job description or update the employees and let them know that they need to refocus their energies and efforts back onto the central responsibilities that were originally assigned to them.

Reviewing last year's appraisal

Assuming that your employees worked for you last year or worked for another manager in your company last year, another important early step is to take a look at last year's evaluation. Presumably, that evaluation contained areas in which the employees needed to demonstrate some improvement. Identify those areas, as well as possible sources of such deficiencies, and keep them in mind as you conduct this year's evaluation.

For example, if a particular performance issue is interfering with an employee's effectiveness, it would be very helpful to know whether this is a new development or whether it's a problem that was apparent last year. If this is a new development, you can address it in the performance evaluation and offer some strategies to correct it.

At the same time, if this problem was addressed in the employee's evaluation last year, then you're dealing with two issues:

- ✔ There is a performance problem with this employee that needs attention and a plan of correction.
- ✔ This employee failed to take adequate action regarding an issue that was identified in last year's evaluation.

Revisiting the objectives

The final step is to go back to last year's evaluation and look at the specific objectives that you established with your employees for the current evaluation period. At this point in the process, you aren't evaluating their performance. Instead, your goal is strictly to familiarize yourself with the objectives and the priorities that were attached to them.

Reviewing your notes

When you regularly spend time on the floors with your employees, you're in the perfect position to observe their work and provide them with the coaching, feedback, guidance, and support that they need to do their jobs well. Your face time with them also allows you to gather data regarding all aspects of their performance.

Your notes don't need to be a detailed treatise. They can be a list that includes the dates, a few words describing the incidents, and a few more words describing their impact. When the time for the annual evaluation arrives, these notes will provide you with accurate firsthand information regarding your employees' performance during the entire course of the evaluation period.

If you rely on your memory for all this information, you probably won't remember exactly what happened, when it happened, and who did what to whom, especially over the course of a year.

When you go back over the log that you've kept on your employees' performance over the year, you'll find several areas that are rich sources of data for their evaluations:

✔ **Getting the job done:** Upon initial review, your notes are going to provide you with the factual information you need in order to determine whether your employees actually carried out all their job responsibilities.

The idea at this point is not so much to evaluate data as it is to gather it. Depending upon the job position, this is where you generate specific and measurable performance-related totals (such as sales calls made, number of designs completed, number of programs accepted or rejected, amount of errors, number of returns, number of projects completed on time, training programs attended, and the like). You can feed this information back to your employees, and it establishes a credible framework for the evaluative feedback that you'll also be providing.

✔ **Meeting objectives:** Your notes will tell you whether your employees met the agreed-upon objectives. Because you've already reviewed the objectives, you're also able to make an accurate judgment regarding the value of meeting one objective versus the value of meeting another.

✔ **Performing up to par:** Your notes will also show you how your employees handled the full spectrum of incidents that they encountered, all the way from carrying out the most important functions of their position down to their handling of the most basic chores. You can find clear and specific examples of your employees' key behaviors, actions, and interactions, and importantly, the results that your employees achieved in these myriad situations. You'll have clear documentation on how the employees handled each incident, as well as how each situation ended up.

✔ **Applying competencies:** Your notes will provide you with valuable insight into the full range of your employees' competencies in such areas as communication, technical knowledge, dealings with others, managing time, and so on. Although observing your employees' skills in these areas is important, it's even more critical for you to see how effectively your employees are able to apply these skills to their work. Your on-site observations will also provide you with firsthand data on your employees' commitment to upgrading their competencies, as well as their ability to impart their knowledge to others.

Reviewing the files

As part of the process of accessing and gathering a full range of information about your employees' performance during the year, take a look at each employee's file. The file can contain important pieces of performance-related data that can enhance as well as round out the information you've already assembled.

If other managers have work-related contact and dealings with your employees, you can gather additional information for the evaluations by discussing your employees' performance with them. Don't forget to ask your own manager.

Considering complaints

During the course of the year, complaints about an employee can be documented. The complaints could have come from other managers or employees, or possibly from customers or vendors.

If the complaints were focused on incidents that occurred early in the year, you may not be aware of them at evaluation time, unless you specifically check the employee's file.

Regardless of whether these complaints impact the employee's ratings, you need to be aware of them, review them, and calibrate the role you believe they should play in the employee's appraisal.

Considering compliments

As you look through your employees' files, you may also find letters, e-mails, and other documentation praising your employees. Compliments can come from people at any level within the company, as well as from outsiders who have contact with your employees. Depending upon the sources and incidents behind this praise, you may also want to consider this data in preparing your evaluation.

Be sure to mention these compliments when you're conduct-ing evaluation sessions. They'll motivate your employees to keep up the good work!

Reviewing reprimands

Your review of the files may also turn up some reprimands. You may have entered these reprimands in your notes, but they may have slid under the radar, which is why checking the employee files is so important.

When you find reprimands, consider the number of incidents, their severity, and any actions taken as a result, whether by the employee or the company. If the problematic behaviors are continuing, make a note of that.

Homing in on honors and awards

Companies provide awards for all sorts of behaviors, such as for volunteering, coming up with suggestions for safety or sustainability, or referring friends to come to work for the company. In addition, you may find honors that have been bestowed on your employees from outside organizations. If your employees have received awards of any kind, consider them as you compile the evaluations.

In some cases, honors and awards can be just enough to tip a given employee's evaluation into a higher range.

Mulling over milestones

Documentation associated with employees' efforts to continue their education and self-development is often found in their files. Look for information regarding classes, seminars, continuing education credits, certifications, degrees, and designations that your employees have pursued and achieved during the year.

In many cases, these milestones are met off-site, and, as a result, they may not appear in your notes. These accomplishments clearly fall in the area of competencies, and they're worth considering as part of the appraisal process. After all, by enhancing their knowledge and skills, your employees bring additional value to their jobs and to the company at large.

Reviewing the evaluations

If your company's appraisal process includes self-evaluations, or if you've opted to include them in the process, this is the time to look them over. The same applies to 360-degree feedback (see Chapter 3), if your company uses it.

Evaluating self-evaluations

When reviewing your employees' self-evaluations, the first step is to take a look at how your employees approached this assignment. Employees who are careful, thorough, and detailed in their approach to work will demonstrate these characteristics in the way that they complete their self-evaluations. At the same time, employees who are lackadaisical or careless will reflect these attitudes in this assignment.

After you've looked over the appearance of the forms, it's time to look at the content. Look carefully at the employee's ratings and try to get an overall sense of how she sees her own performance. If the employee's ratings are in sync with the data that you've generated, you can make three strong suppositions:

✔ Your employee has a realistic view of how she's been performing.

✔ You've been providing the employee with effective feedback during the course of the year.

✔ The employee is being honest in completing her self-evaluation.

As a result of these suppositions, you shouldn't have any trouble discussing your ratings during the evaluation sessions.

If you find that an employee's self-ratings are totally different from what his performance data indicates, a couple things could be going on:

✔ Either your employee is living in dreamland, or you haven't been adequately monitoring his performance and providing feedback.

✔ If you have overwhelming performance data to substantiate your views of the employee's performance, and you've been actively managing by wandering around, then the employee is naïve, lying, manipulative, or uninvolved and uninterested in the evaluation process.

As a result of these two possibilities, you may face some difficulties when you and your employee sit down to discuss the performance appraisals. Make sure you're thoroughly prepared with clear, accurate, and specific performance data.

Evaluating 360-degree feedback

Companies use 360-degree feedback for different purposes. Some use it for employee appraisal, some use it for employee development, and some use it for both. (See Chapter 3 for more on 360-degree feedback.)

If your company includes 360-degree feedback in the appraisal process, this is the time to review the findings. This data — gathered from an array of anonymous individuals, such as co-workers, managers, peers, customers, and others — can provide a good deal of additional insight regarding your employees' performance competencies and effectiveness.

If you've been provided with an overview of the 360-degree feedback findings, you should find significant overlap between this feedback and the data you've generated on your own. If there are major differences, stay with *your* assessments, because your data focuses more directly on your employees' specific job responsibilities and goal attainment.

360-degree feedback can help you further understand your employees and assess their performance, but this information should not be a substitute for your own appraisals, nor should it trump your own judgment.

Regardless of its role in the appraisal process, if your company uses 360-degree feedback, it's most helpful to bring the feedback into play when you're establishing a development plan with your employees.

Completing the Evaluation Form

After you've reviewed all the performance data from the various sources and resources that you were able to access, the next step is to complete the evaluation form. These forms vary from one company to another, but there are some overarching principles that can help you handle this step more easily and effectively:

✔ **Start with your best employees.** As a result of your direct observations and analysis of the performance data, you're probably able to name the better employees in your department. These employees should be the first ones that you evaluate.

By starting your evaluations with these individuals, you can clearly define, for yourself, the actual meaning of excellent performance. With this standard in place, you'll be able to interpret and evaluate the performance of the rest of your team more easily.

✔ **Write first, rate later.** Because many companies have evaluation forms that combine written comments with numerical ratings for each component that's being

evaluated, it can be difficult to know which to do first —
ratings or written comments.

The best approach is to go to a given item, write out your
written comments, and then enter a numerical rating.

When you write the numerical rating first, you may find
yourself adjusting your writing in order to match those
numbers. For example, if you think an employee is
average and you immediately enter an average numerical
rating, your writing will tend to confirm this rating. At the
same time, when you do your writing first, you aren't
consciously or unconsciously influenced to color your
comments to fit your predetermined numerical rating.

Many performance appraisal forms that call for written
comments also provide information on the kinds of
factors to consider in your write-up. Be sure to look over
these tips very carefully before starting your written
comments.

✔ **Think while writing.** By writing out the assessments of
your employees' performance in a particular category,
you're forced to think specifically about their actions,
their objectives, their competencies, and the outcomes
of their efforts.

Whether you're writing a positive or negative comment,
be sure that it's laced with examples and supported by
times and dates as you deem necessary. As you create
and review your written comments, adding appropriate
descriptive phrases as needed, you'll be generating a
clearer picture of your employees' performance and the
rating that it merits.

✔ **Consider how it will be read.** Don't forget that whatever
you write in the appraisals is going to be read by your
employees. If your comments are vague, unsubstantiated,
or focus on personality over performance, you're setting
the stage for problematic sessions with your employees.

Selecting a rating

After you enter your comments for each factor that you're
appraising, you're ready to enter a numerical rating (assuming
your form calls for one). The key to success with this step is
to fully familiarize yourself with the rating scale.

With many numerical rating scales, there is a mini-description associated with each number. For example, the rating form may list several behaviors associated with communication, accompanied by a rating scale that reads:

5 — Exceptional: Consistently exceeds expectations.

4 — Excellent: Frequently exceeds expectations.

3 — Fully competent: Meets expectations.

2 — Marginal: Occasionally fails to meet expectations.

1 — Unsatisfactory: Consistently fails to meet expectations.

Without the mini-description following each rating, it would be easy for each manager to have a different opinion on what *outstanding* means. The descriptions result in far greater consistency in the process.

One of the major concerns in the performance appraisal process is called *inter-rater reliability*. Essentially, this is the extent to which the 5 that you rate an employee is equivalent to the 5 that other managers rate their employees. With increased clarity in the evaluation forms, such as including mini-descriptions for each rating, the chances of increased inter-rater reliability improve. This reliability can be improved even further through training, practice evaluations, and additional information in the evaluation forms themselves.

At the same time, it's at least as important for a manager to maintain a high degree of internal consistency when rating employees — in other words, all the employees who merit the same rating from you in a particular category should be essentially performing at the same level. Even if a 4 from you is closer to a 3 from most other managers, the internal consistency of your ratings will allow your scores to be better understood if one of your employees is being considered for a transfer, a promotion, or even a layoff.

Describing strengths and weaknesses

With all your numerical ratings and written comments in place, some forms will pose additional questions, the most common of which focus on the employees' strengths and areas for improvement.

Strengths

When writing about your employees' strengths, your comments will be most effective if they focus on specific behaviors and competencies. For example, although it's nice for employees to hear that they "do excellent work," the focus is totally unclear and the employees can't anchor your comment to any particular action. So, although your employees would like to receive positive feedback in the future for their excellent work, they don't know which behaviors to repeat.

Your comments will take on more meaning, have a greater motivational impact, and have a longer shelf life if you phrase them in behavioral terms. For example, instead of saying that your employees do excellent work, give them specific examples of such work, such as "Provides extremely high-quality work on time." With this type of comment, your employees clearly know the two components that generated this positive feedback — quality and timeliness.

Weaknesses

When writing about your employees' weaknesses, the same basic framework applies. You need to be specific and avoid phrases such as "attitude could use improvement." Your comments will be more effective and more motivational if you leave out the word *attitude* and focus specifically on behaviors that are indicative of a questionable attitude, such as complaining, arguing, or refusing to help others.

After the review, part of your job will be to work with the employees to help them become more effective in the areas currently needing improvement. The more specific you are in your description, the better able you'll be to focus your developmental efforts. And because your employees understand the specifics of the areas needing improvement, they're likely to be more receptive to your guidance.

Determining an Overall Rating

As you work your way through the performance appraisal form, you'll start to get a sense of the overall rating of each of your employees. In some evaluation forms, the final rating is based on little more than this overall perception. In this case, you're asked to give your own overall rating of the employee based on all the comments and rankings that you've entered into the form. The best guideline in this case is to make sure that the overall rating you provide is consistent with the individual ratings that you've provided in each category.

The only time to stray from this strategy is if your employee has done extremely well or poorly in parts of the job that are truly the most important elements of the job itself.

 If you have full latitude in determining the final rating, you can add weightings to various areas that you evaluated in order to make sure that performance in those areas has a greater impact on the employee's final rating.

At the other end of the continuum, some performance evaluation forms include mathematical calculations and weightings for each of the ratings that you enter. In some cases, these forms are designed to take the ratings that you provide for each component, calculate an average score, and convert that into the overall rating.

 When you've finished writing the appraisals and made your final evaluations, set them aside for a few days. This will give you some time to think about them and let any of your concerns incubate. When you revisit these evaluations, you'll do so with a fresh perspective. Give each evaluation a final look, make any needed adjustments, and then lock them in as final. You're guaranteed to be more certain about your ratings, and more comfortable with them, after this second visit.

Chapter 6

Running a Productive Appraisal Session

*B*y the time you've completed your employees' evaluations, the scheduled dates for your one-on-one sessions loom large on your calendar. Some managers feel uneasy at this point. But I have good news for you: If you've worked through Chapter 5, you've already taken three major steps to quell such feelings:

✔ **You've gathered and documented accurate and specific performance data for each of your employees.**

✔ **In order to gather such data, you spent a lot of time in direct contact with your employees, providing them with feedback, coaching, guidance, and support.** In doing so, you've provided them with a clear understanding of your thoughts regarding their performance, so you've eliminated the element of surprise from the forthcoming session. And this means that the likelihood of resistance, defensiveness, or disagreement is dramatically reduced.

✔ **You've written performance evaluations that are thorough, fair, and focused on specific and measurable behaviors, competencies, and results, rather than on personalities.**

In order to have highly productive appraisal sessions with your employees, all you need to do at this point is prepare and plan for each face-to-face discussion and then make sure that you stick to your plan and run each session in an organized, businesslike, and positive style.

Setting the Stage for the Appraisal

A few days before the sit-down sessions, you can take several key steps that will greatly increase their effectiveness and improve their chances of succeeding.

Identifying your objectives

Your employees won't remember everything you say during their appraisal sessions. Because of the amount of information and the nature of the feedback that you're providing, employees often get overloaded and zone out a bit.

Plus, if an appraisal contains some negative feedback, or it's a positive appraisal but still lower than what your employee expected or wanted, she's likely to focus on this discrepancy and fail to absorb all your other important comments and points.

 Regardless of the nature of the feedback that you'll be providing, take the time to note two or three major points that you definitely want your employees to hear and remember. For example, these points may focus on specific competencies that your employees need to upgrade, various behaviors that are interfering with individual or departmental performance, or opportunities for growth and development.

By identifying these major points before the sessions, and then emphasizing and reemphasizing them during the sessions, you'll greatly increase the likelihood that your employees will leave with a clear understanding of the most important components of your feedback.

Setting an agenda

You don't need an iron-clad agenda for appraisal meetings because the dynamics of these sessions can draw the discussions into unplanned topics — and that's not necessarily a bad thing. After all, such topics can include unanticipated suggestions, complaints, and concerns that can help identify existing problems or prevent new ones.

However, when the discussion strays from what you had intended, you need to be able to eventually guide the discussion back to the main points that you need to cover. An agenda can help you keep your discussions on target.

Your agenda should include

- ✔ The highlights of your opening remarks
- ✔ The step-by-step sequence of the performance-related feedback that you're planning to provide
- ✔ A list of the key points that you want your employees to remember
- ✔ The point in the session where you plan to discuss the employee's raise (or lack thereof)
- ✔ The key points you want to make when closing the session

In developing your agenda, jot down some estimates on the amount of time that you're planning on spending on each item. Granted, some areas may take longer than you plan, but having a sense of timing will help you keep each session focused on the higher-priority topics and issues.

Scripting your delicate comments

When you have to provide negative feedback to an employee, knowing exactly what to say can be difficult. If you fumble for words and then hedge around a problematic issue or behavior, your employee will sense your apprehension and confusion and either shrug off your comments or seize the opening and challenge you.

One of the best ways to prevent this problem is to look carefully at the areas in which you're going to give some negative feedback and then write down exactly what you want to say. You don't have to give a lengthy diatribe — a well-crafted sentence or two can say it all.

Don't rush this scripting process. You may need to spend quite a bit of time, writing several drafts, to come up with the right handful of words, but they'll be valuable to you during the session. After you've scripted your comments, be sure to practice them aloud several times until you can say them easily and naturally.

Bringing the data

Before the evaluation session, decide which pieces of documentation you're going to bring. You don't need every piece of data that you touched in determining the ratings, but you should have some data at your side:

- ✓ **Evaluation forms:** Be sure to bring two hard copies of the completed evaluations. If your employee completed a self-evaluation, bring two copies of that as well.

- ✓ **The employee's file:** You aren't likely to need to thumb through the employee's file during the evaluation session, but if you do need to access some primary support data, having the files nearby is helpful.

- ✓ **Your notes:** If your employee raises questions about specific times and dates regarding the issues that you're discussing, having your log or notes nearby is helpful.

Setting positive expectations

Your expectations play a key role in many aspects of effective management (see Chapter 4), and they come into play again at this point in the performance appraisal process.

One of the most effective ways to increase the likelihood of a positive, open, and highly productive two-way conversation during an appraisal session is for you to set positive expectations. Visualize how you want each session to go — you'll have an easier time achieving your goals if you've visualized them.

Handling the Logistics

Several premeeting administrative steps play an important supporting role in determining the success of your sessions with your employees.

Scheduling the time

As part of the back-timing process, you most likely scheduled the discussion sessions with your employees several weeks in advance. At that time, your calendars and theirs probably had a fair share of wide-open spaces, but that's likely not the case anymore — now your schedules are jam-packed, and you need to make sure you've allotted enough time for each meeting.

Clearing the deck

Always place scheduled appraisal sessions at the top of your priority list. Remove all other projects, meetings, and tasks from your calendar during the hours that are scheduled for these sessions.

If other assignments come your way, or if other people want to meet with you during these scheduled times, do everything you can to defer or delay them until you've completed the sessions.

Clearing the deck also means clearing your desk. Remove, file, or cover all documents on your desk while you're conducting these sessions. If these documents are visible during the evaluation session, they can distract you and your employees — plus, they may reveal confidential information.

Blocking extra time

In most cases, you should schedule appraisal sessions to last an hour. Just to be safe, though, don't schedule any other appointments that end right before the evaluation sessions or start right after them. Leave yourself at least a 30-minute cushion both before and after every evaluation.

Dashing into an evaluation session after the scheduled starting time sends a message of disinterest and carelessness to the employee, and it's sure to raise his anxiety, distress, and ire.

Recognizing the role of reminders

When the times and dates for the sessions are around the corner, send e-mail confirmations to your employees. Make sure the confirmation e-mails are clear and direct, not wishy-washy. Don't ask an employee whether the date and time still works for her — remind her of the date and time you agreed on.

Unless a real crisis, crunch, or emergency occurs, avoid rescheduling these meetings. Each time an appraisal meeting is deferred, its role, impact, and significance decrease in the employee's eyes.

Giving out the appraisals

One of the most important decisions to make prior to the evaluation sessions is when to give the completed evaluations to your employees. You can opt to give them their formal evaluation forms at one of three different points.

When the session starts

Some managers start evaluation sessions by handing the completed evaluation forms to their employees. On the one hand, this approach reduces any mystery and doubt over the points to be covered in the sessions. The employees have an immediate idea of the focus and even the tenor of the discussion.

On the other hand, when managers hand employees completed forms at the beginning of the sessions, the employees tend to rush through the forms and typically have trouble absorbing all the detail. Feedback of any kind arouses emotions, and these heightened emotions further interfere with the employees' abilities to concentrate on what they're reading. Plus, most employees aren't comfortable sitting and reading their evaluations while their managers are staring at them.

When the session ends

At the other end of the spectrum, some managers discuss the entire evaluation with their employees, and then give out the evaluation forms at the end. Although this approach eliminates the speed-reading and concentration issues associated with handing out the forms at the outset, it has its own problems: When managers go point-by-point through evaluations that the employees haven't seen yet, employees typically hear the first few words of their managers' comments regarding performance in a particular area and then start to wonder how they'll be appraised on the next item.

Before the session

Many managers find that the best time to give the completed forms to their employees is *before* the sit-down sessions. Some managers give out the forms an hour or two ahead, while others give them out a day or two in advance.

Either way, the idea is to give employees a chance to understand their evaluations and remove any initial knee-jerk reactions. This approach gives the employees time to think more about their performance, formulate productive questions, and consider their own ways to make improvements where needed.

When you give the evaluations to your employees ahead of the discussion sessions, your employees come to these sessions better prepared to have a productive two-way conversation.

Selecting the right venue

As the time for your sit-down sessions with your employees draws nearer, carefully consider where you're going to hold the meetings. You can do a great deal of preparatory work and create the most perfect evaluations in the world, but if you hold the sit-down sessions in inappropriate locations, their effectiveness instantly evaporates.

One of the best places for your sit-down evaluation sessions with your employees is your office, as long as you have a private office. Only hold evaluations in your office if it's not a cubicle or workstation but rather a traditional office with a door and four walls that extend from floor to ceiling.

Even if your employees have their own private offices, you should still conduct the evaluations in your own office. Your employees will sense that they have more power and control in their own offices, but this can make it easier for them to resist or reject your comments, input, and guidance.

If you don't have a private office, try to reserve a conference room or an available private office if your company has any. The goal is to find a site where you can meet privately, confidentially, and out of the earshot of anyone else.

If you don't have a private office but your manager has one, ask her whether you can use it for your evaluations. Many managers will go along with this request, especially those who take the process seriously and expect their employees to do likewise. Your manager may also have some suggestions for other options or meeting areas in the company.

Keeping it private

The concept of privacy is central to an effective performance evaluation session. Without privacy, both parties in the session feel awkward, distracted, and unable to be totally honest. And if these sessions lack honesty, there's no point in holding them.

In order for evaluations to be productive, you need to have privacy both during and after the appraisal session.

During the session

In order to have an open and honest exchange, you need to have absolute privacy during appraisal sessions. This means that there are no visitors, audiences, or eavesdroppers of any kind.

After the session

The information that you discuss in appraisal sessions is private and confidential. Don't discuss the contents of these meetings with others unless necessary in the context of doing business (such as in terms of promotions, transfers to other departments, or staffing cutbacks).

You're not the only one who needs to keep the contents of appraisal meetings private. Employees shouldn't discuss their ratings or your comments with others — either to brag or complain. In fact, if you find out that employees have freely discussed their performance evaluations with their co-workers, you may want to note this as a critical incident in their next performance evaluations.

Performance appraisals don't contain state secrets, but as you wrap up your review sessions, give your employees a friendly reminder that you won't be sharing what you've discussed and that you expect them to do the same.

Holding the Meeting

When the time for the evaluation sessions with your employees arrives, several strategies will help make these meetings more effective from start to finish. You've already put the foundation in place, and now you're ready to build some solid review sessions.

Opening the discussion

Your opening comments will set the tone, tenor, and atmosphere for the entire discussion. Maybe you scripted them earlier (see "Scripting your delicate comments," earlier in this chapter), or maybe you're winging it. Either way, your initial comments in each session should do the following:

1. **Greet the employee.**

   Start by making friendly and welcoming comments to break the ice. To help further relax your employee, you can even ask a question or two about some informal topics that interest both of you.

2. **Set the framework.**

   This is the "here's what we're going to do" section of your opening. The idea is to give your employee an understanding of the structure of the meeting, including an overview of the topics and timing.

3. **Ask for questions.**

   If an employee asks questions that deal with your opening remarks or with matters that should be addressed on the spot, this is the time to answer them. However, if the questions pertain to matters that you plan on discussing later in the review, advise the employee of this fact and make a note to yourself so you don't forget to cover these topics later.

Leading the discussion

There is no single path for you to follow in order to conduct highly successful evaluation sessions. At the same time, when you're leading these discussions, ten steps will help make the meetings more interactive and productive:

1. **Let your employee talk.**

   If your employee has completed a self-appraisal, your first step is to indicate that you'd like to hear his thoughts. Although you already have a copy of the appraisal and you've looked it over prior to this session, tell your employee that you'd like to know more, especially in terms of his performance and results that he believes are particularly important, as well as the way in which he arrived at his specific ratings.

   If you or your company doesn't use self-evaluations, you can still encourage the employee's input at this point in the session by asking a question such as "How have things on the job been going during the past year?"

   Giving your employees the chance to discuss their actions, achievements, and competencies is rewarding to them because it further emphasizes your respect and trust, while also reinforcing your partnership with them.

2. **Give an overview of the session.**

   After you've heard your employee's thoughts regarding her performance, your next step is to give her a brief overview of overall topics that you'll be covering in the session.

3. **Focus on objectives.**

   This part of the discussion focuses on the agreed-upon objectives and the extent to which your employee met them.

4. **Focus on performance results.**

   The emphasis in this section is on the various additional performance-related outcomes that were the result of your employee's actions and efforts, even if such outcomes were not directly attached to the overall objectives.

5. Focus on critical incidents.

Your comments in this area are focused on the way in which your employee handled particularly noteworthy situations, whether positively or negatively.

6. Focus on competencies.

This is where you discuss instances in which your employee applied his skills effectively to the job, shared his knowledge with others, or took specific steps to further build his competencies.

7. Focus on points of agreement.

Whether based on your employee's self-evaluations or on her opening comments regarding her performance, your focus at this point in the session is on the areas in which your employee agrees with your ratings.

These points are typically the more positive ratings in your evaluation. Many of your comments at this point are focused on encouraging your employees to continue to engage in the behaviors that generated these positive outcomes and ratings.

8. Focus on points of disagreement.

This is the time to discuss the areas in which you rated your employee lower than he rated himself, whether based on his self-evaluation or his opening comments. Your objective is to learn more about your employee's rationale for giving himself ratings that are higher than yours and for him to understand the rationale behind the ratings that you gave.

This is not a negotiation session, and you should not revise your ratings based on your employee's comments. Even after you provide an explanation of the rationale behind your ratings, your employee may still disagree. However, that isn't a major problem as long as he truly comprehends the reasons why his ratings were lower than what he expected or wanted.

9. Focus on the overall rating.

At this point in the process, you and your employee have discussed all the key performance-related issues and concerns, and it's now time to discuss the overall rating. Your comments should focus on the steps you took to determine this rating.

If part of this overall rating is based on additional weightings that you placed on any of the areas within the performance appraisal, make sure that your employee understands the rationale and methodology behind this adjustment.

10. Focus on raises.

There is a good deal of debate among managers as well as management theorists as to where to place raises in the performance appraisal session. Some managers don't even think that raises belong in the session at all. Here are your options:

- **Bringing up raises in the beginning:** This approach is premised on the belief that employees don't pay much attention during appraisal sessions with raises at the end because they're fixated on what their raises will be. Letting them know at the outset is supposed to put an end to their wondering and allow them to pay attention to the feedback you're providing. However, if they expected a better raise, they may end up being consumed with their disappointment and not hear what you're saying anyway.

- **Bringing up raises toward the end:** Here, the idea is to provide employees with a clearer understanding of the relationship between their performance and the raise they receive. After giving glowing reviews, you're ideally able to provide a direct reward for the employees' stellar behavior, demonstrating the clear link between better performance and better rewards. The same principle applies in reverse, when you're providing less of a reward (or no reward) for less-than-stellar performance. The primary concern with this approach is that employees won't hear what you're saying until you talk about raises.

- **Eliminating raises from the discussion:** The idea behind this approach is that raises don't belong in the performance appraisal session at all. Instead, these sessions should focus exclusively and extensively on the employees' past performance, while issues such as raises and objectives should be discussed in separate sessions.

Separate sessions for separate purposes

Although some companies still include raises in performance reviews, many employers have separated the goal-setting and development phases from the performance-review phase. One main reason for this separation is that employees who sit through reviews aren't ready to immediately shift gears and start talking about objectives, growth, and development — and neither are their managers.

Plus, if the review has been less than glowing, employees are even less inclined to start thinking and talking about their objectives. They're still licking their wounds from the evaluations and need some time and distance in order to process what they've heard before reopening their minds to goal setting and development.

Finally, the objectives of these meetings are entirely different. Performance appraisals look *backward* and evaluate the employees' past actions, competencies, and outcomes; employees leave these sessions with an understanding of the areas in which they did well and the areas in which they need to improve. Goal-setting and development meetings are designed to look at the *future* and help employees set development plans and objectives to enhance their own growth and performance on the job.

Remember: When holding meetings of any kind, the attendees must literally and figuratively be on the same page. That doesn't happen easily or naturally when performance appraisals and employee development are bundled into one session.

Because there is no uniform agreement on this matter, be sure to have a clear understanding of the way in which your company's raise process is linked to the performance appraisal process. If you're given a choice, opt for separate sessions to discuss raises. Doing so will allow you to focus thoroughly and unequivocally on an employee's performance during the appraisal session, while focusing equally thoroughly on raises in a later session. With this approach, your employees will have a clearer understanding of the most important factors in both of these key areas.

In some companies, managers advise their employees of the dollar amount of the increase they'll be given. In other companies, managers discuss only the percentage increase. In many companies, managers don't provide any final information regarding raises; instead, all they're allowed to do is recommend raises to senior management. In this case, they tell the employees the raise amounts or percentages that they're recommending and explain that they'll provide the employees with the exact amount at a later date.

If your company includes goal setting as part of the performance appraisal session, this would be the point in the evaluation when you and your employees discuss specific objectives and action plans for the coming year. Shifting gears can be difficult for you *and* your employees, so I recommend that you try to set up a separate time with your employees to carry out this very important function. (See the nearby sidebar, "Separate sessions for separate purposes," for more information.)

Providing negative feedback

Many managers have lingering fears about giving negative feedback to their employees during their evaluation sessions. But the negative comments that you provide in these sessions will be less stressful for you because this won't be the first time that you've made them to your employees. By wandering around and spending a good deal of time with your employees (see Chapter 8), you've already provided them with negative feedback when their performance merited it. They already know where they're performing well and where they're performing poorly, and they could just as easily provide themselves with the same negative feedback that you provide in these sessions.

Nonetheless, three strategies can make this process even easier for you:

✔ **Sit down.** Obviously, performance appraisals are sit-down activities, which is a plus because providing negative feedback to your employees is much easier when you're both seated. Why? Because people are far less likely to get heated up when they're sitting down.

Also pay attention to *where* you're seated. A desk that separates you from your employees can be a psychological as well as physical barrier. In order to send a message to your employees that you want to partner with them in the appraisal process, try either sitting next to them or pulling your chair around your desk and sitting face-to-face with no barriers between the two of you. In either setup, you'll be able to give negative feedback more easily, and they'll be able to receive it more easily as well.

✔ **Use *I* not *you*.** When you're providing negative feedback to your employees, one surefire way to generate a harsh reaction is to lace your comments with the word *you*. Frequent use of the word *you* sounds like a combination of accusation and scolding, and employees are likely to become increasingly defensive with each additional *you*.

Try using the word *I* instead of *you* when possible. For example, instead of saying "You didn't complete the project on time," try saying "I'm wondering why the project came in late." In this way, you've centered the issue on yourself and the project, which opens the door for a conversation instead of a confrontation.

✔ **Focus on behaviors.** The essence of performance appraisal is focused on behavior — and that's essential to keep in mind when providing negative feedback. The idea is for your employees to sense that you're concerned or upset with some aspect of their *behavior* but not with them as individuals.

For example, if you asked an employee to give a particular report to certain employees, but she gave it to all the employees, you *could* say, "You made a mistake by giving this report to everyone," but your employee will probably perceive this as a direct attack, and she's likely to react in kind. With some minor tweaking of the wording, you can rephrase and refocus the feedback so that it's targeted on the behavior and perceived as less of an attack: "Giving this report to everyone was a mistake."

Eliminating interruptions

By selecting appropriate venues for the appraisal sessions (see "Selecting the right venue," earlier in this chapter), you've automatically reduced the likelihood of interruptions.

However, when it comes to these sessions, reducing the likelihood of interruptions is not good enough. In order to gain the full measure of value from performance appraisal sessions with your employees, you have to eliminate interruptions, or at least bring them down to the absolute minimum.

Advising the team

Prior to the evaluation session, be sure to let others know that you are not to be disturbed while this meeting is in progress. This means no paging, no one knocking on the office door, and no one opening the door slightly just to peek in and see if you're serious about not being interrupted.

Taking no phone calls

If you have a "do not disturb" function on your phone, set it for this meeting. If not, let all calls go to voicemail.

If you have a caller identification system, don't look over every time your phone rings. Doing so is rude, inconsiderate, and a disruption.

Don't forget to turn off your cellphone during the meeting. Let all calls to your cellphone go to voicemail. You shouldn't be doing anything with your cellphone during this meeting — no texting, no e-mailing, and no talking.

Avoiding your computer

Don't sit at your computer during this meeting. Managers who do so often can't resist the temptation to look over every time a new e-mail arrives, and some can't keep their hands off the keyboard.

Actively listening

As you lead appraisal sessions, your effectiveness will be enhanced if you display solid listening skills. By listening carefully to what your employees are saying, not only will you be able to learn more about their actions and their motivations for taking them, but you'll also be better able to determine whether your employees fully understand the reasons behind the ratings that you provided.

Regardless of ratings, employees feel better about the evaluation process if they truly sense that they're being heard.

As part of the open exchange of ideas that is at the heart of appraisal sessions, you can take some steps to strengthen your listening skills.

- **Focus on what your employees are saying.** Some of the best ways to do this are to restate, rephrase, and summarize what they say — for example, you can say, "Let me make sure I understand," and then put their comments in your own words. Anytime you aren't sure what they mean, ask for clarification.

- **Focus on what they're *not* saying.** Pay extra attention to their body language, such as their facial expressions, whether they're slouched or sitting forward, whether their arms are crossed, and whether they maintain eye contact.

- **Show your employees that you're engaged in the discussion.** Your body language and comments should show your employees that you're interested in this dialogue with them. You can do this by sitting forward, nodding when appropriate, and adding occasional comments and interjections indicating that you're involved and listening (such as, "I see" and even "Uh-huh").

Wrapping up the discussion

If you've fully worked your way through the agenda that you created for a given session and you're satisfied that the objectives you established prior to the session have been met, it's time to bring the session to a close. As you do so, follow these key steps:

1. **Give your employees a recap of their performance, particularly their major areas of strength and success, along with the one or two areas where the most improvement is needed.**

2. **Tell your employees that you'll be meeting again soon to talk about objectives and plans for growth and development for the coming evaluation period.**

   Ask the employees to do some thinking in these areas and to write a draft of their objectives and development plan between now and that next meeting.

If you can do so on the spot, set a specific date and time for that meeting. If you can't finalize a date at this time, let your employees know that you'll be setting a date to meet within two weeks.

3. **If you did not discuss raises during the appraisal sessions, let your employees know that you'll soon be setting up a separate meeting to do so**.

4. **Ask your employees if they have any further questions or if there are any other matters that they want to discuss in this session.**

5. **Sign and date the evaluation forms and ask your employees to do likewise.**

   Be sure to mention that they can add their own comments to the form if they want.

6. **Express your positive expectations as you bring the sessions to an end.**

   Let your employees know that you have confidence in them and their ability to succeed in making the improvements that were discussed during the appraisal sessions.

Chapter 7

Avoiding the Most Common Mistakes

*A*s you work your way through the performance appraisal process with your employees, you need to be on the lookout for the tripping points that can undercut not only *your* effectiveness but the effectiveness of the appraisal process itself. Managers have myriad opportunities to make mistakes in the appraisal process, and sometimes just one slip-up can render the whole process useless.

Fortunately, these pitfalls aren't hidden or camouflaged subtleties. They're far more apparent than that — especially when you know what to look for.

In this chapter, I shine a spotlight on the range of mistakes that *other* managers often make in the evaluation process, so that you don't make the same mistakes yourself.

Managing Your Misperceptions

One of the main errors that managers make in the performance appraisal process is failing to see employees as they truly are. When this happens, managers typically place too much emphasis on matters of minimal importance and too little emphasis on the stuff that matters most.

Managers who misperceive the realities of their employees' behaviors do so as a result of their own needs, biases, expectations, prior experiences, and memories. And no matter what the source of these misperceptions may be, the result is the same: The managers' thinking is distorted, and they end up with evaluations that are equally distorted.

Calibrating recent events

Whether your employees have recently done something great or something that grates, the most likely outcome is that these recent actions and outcomes play a greater role in appraisals than is actually warranted.

Say an employee has been doing a good job throughout the year, consistently meeting her objectives. It wouldn't be surprising to find that her performance appraisal is, fittingly, in the "good" range. But if she makes a mistake toward the end of the evaluation period, her appraisal is likely to suffer in a totally disproportionate way. In fact, even small recent mistakes can trump much greater successes from months ago.

Why? Because recent events are far fresher in your memory than are the distant events that happened early in the evaluation period. With recent events, you can relive the exact feelings of satisfaction or annoyance that you experienced just a few weeks ago — whether your employees leaped over the bar or tripped over it.

At the same time, as you think back to your employees' successes and failures earlier in the year, you can review the facts as spelled out in your notes or log, but the physical and emotional reactions are gone, which reduces their influence on your thinking today.

As you complete your appraisals, make sure you're not placing undue emphasis on the good or bad things that happened in the past month or two — be sure to consider the events of the *entire* evaluation period.

As you're making notes on your employees' performance throughout the year, write down more than just the facts. Whether you're truly excited by your employees' performance or results or you're supremely dissatisfied, try to capture some of your enthusiasm or disappointment in your notes as well. This way, your notes will help you consider the entire year's worth of events — not just the ones that happened in the last couple of months.

Overpowering bias and stereotypes

Another misperception that managers may have about their employees may have nothing to do with the employees at all: I'm talking about biases and stereotypes. *Remember:* Such notions can be favorable or unfavorable, but either way, they're a clear source of inaccurate appraisals.

Biases and stereotypes are really about prejudice, which literally means "to prejudge." Prejudging is particularly problematic in performance appraisals because one central managerial role in the process is to judge the employees' behavior. If the judging component is completed before the process even starts, there's no point in starting the process at all.

If the potential damage that bias and stereotyping heap on the performance appraisal process is not enough to convince you to dispel your prejudicial beliefs, something else just might grab your attention: a lawsuit. That's right: If you allow factors such as race, religion, gender, national origin, sexual orientation, age, or disability to affect your appraisal of your employees, you and your company are likely to face a claim of discrimination.

Beating bias

Managerial bias is a strong preconceived leaning or inclination about a person or situation. Such bias can be positive or negative, and it can cause managers to look at their employees' performance and see accomplishments where there are none and overlook failures where there are many.

One of the most compelling ways to conduct a bias test on yourself is to take a sample of one of your employee's behaviors that you rated as "excellent" and ask yourself if all your other employees would have received the exact same ratings if they had performed at the exact same level. If you would've rated some of them lower, some bias has slipped into your thinking.

The first step in eliminating bias is recognizing it.

Stopping the stereotypes

When it comes to stereotyping, managers take the supposed characteristics of a group and apply them to all its members. Although some stereotypes are positive, most are unflattering, unfair, and inappropriate. When stereotypes enter any phase of the performance appraisal process, the information is instantly tainted, and the credibility of the appraisal drops to zero.

A quick way to see whether stereotyping is entering your own thinking is to pick any particular group of people, whether based on political affiliation, nationality, weight, age, or any other factor. With that group in mind, ask yourself whether you believe that there are any personality traits that are typical of all its members. If you think such characteristics exist, you're also finding the stereotypes that exist in your mind. Whether these stereotypes are positive or negative, they're sure to interfere with your effectiveness in the appraisal process.

When you're aware of the stereotypes you hold, you'll have taken a gigantic step toward eradicating them.

Rethinking "just like me"

When managers sense that they have a lot in common with certain employees, they tend to be extra lenient when appraising the performance of these employees.

If a manager and an employee share common backgrounds and experiences, the manager is likely to feel significantly greater levels of trust, understanding, and familiarity with this employee — which leads to more positive evaluations. For example, say you grew up on a farm in the Midwest, worked your way through college, and married your high school sweetheart. You're going to feel much closer to an employee who has a similar background than you will to an unmarried employee who grew up in a major city, partied through college, and spent his summers traveling around Europe. When it's time for the performance evaluation, that common bond between you and that first employee will generate higher ratings.

By letting the bonds of commonality overpower the facts of performance, you're overlooking three key and costly points:

✔ Although you may have an employee whose background is remarkably similar to yours, there is no reason to assume that her performance is going to be equally remarkable.

✔ Plenty of employees are just like you in many respects, but certainly not in *every* respect. And some of those dissimilar respects just might be their competence, work ethic, loyalty, or honesty.

✔ If an employee senses that you're somehow swayed by a commonality in your backgrounds, that employee may also sense that she has a wild card that will automatically condone marginal work, self-serving behaviors, and flaunting of company policies and standards.

When a manager has a lot in common with an employee and that sense of commonality leaks into the performance evaluations, the rest of the employees have a different term for this: They call it *favoritism*. And if you're looking for an instant way to undercut teamwork, cooperation, loyalty, and productivity, favoritism is right at the top of the list.

Recognizing the halo effect

If you're looking for one of the most common errors in the performance appraisal process, you'll find it in the *halo effect*. The halo effect is the tendency to allow your employees' excellent performance in one area to impact the way you evaluate their performance in all other areas.

When your employees have performed extremely well in one key part of the job, you need to provide them with a very positive rating in that area. But after you've assigned that rating, you need to approach the next item with a clean slate and no lingering positive predispositions from the last item.

The halo effect comes into play when managers don't make a clean break from the rating on that previous item. Instead, their positive rating on one item leads to equally positive ratings on every other item, regardless of actual performance.

For example, say you're a real stickler for detail, and you just finished giving one of your employees an outstanding rating on his thoroughness, detail-mindedness, and accuracy.

However, instead of moving to the next factor and making a merit-based rating, the halo that you just placed on your employee gets in your way, leading you to conclude that because he performed with distinction in one important area, surely he's deserving of equally high ratings in all other areas.

That one halo leads to halos in every category, and that leads to trouble. Here are some of the problems caused by the halo effect:

- ✔ **When employees figure out which category is the key source of all the positive ratings, they focus their behavior only on that category.** For example, if neatness and accuracy are the hot buttons that trigger a vast array of positive ratings, you'll end up with employees who devote all their energy to this area. Of course, this means that they're devoting less energy to other areas, such as productivity, communication, and quality of work, to name just a few.

- ✔ **When employees are provided with positive ratings across the board, they know that many of those ratings were undeserved.** Instead of feeling appreciative for such ratings, they're more likely to view the process as meaningless. If they're going to get a barrage of outstanding ratings that have nothing to do with their performance, sure, they'll accept these ratings, but they won't accept the notion that performance appraisal is a valuable process.

- ✔ **A collection of equally positive ratings across the board actually sends a less flattering message about the manager's attitude — namely, that the manager didn't devote much time, energy, or effort to the appraisal process.** Instead, the manager simply hooked onto one piece of performance and used it as the litmus test for ratings in all other categories. Employees generally believe that their managers' lack of interest and concern in the appraisal process is indicative of a lack of interest and concern for them as individuals. Although recognition has been consistently found to be linked to motivation, that isn't the case for recognition that's perfunctory or undeserved. A string of undeserved positive ratings is more likely to be perceived as insulting, degrading, and even embarrassing.

Dismissing the horns effect

The halo effect (see the preceding section) has an evil twin known as the *horns effect.* With the horns effect, when employees perform poorly in one key performance area, managers give them lower ratings in all areas.

As you may expect, the horns effect generates even more negative reactions than the halo effect. At least with the halo effect, the employees received positive ratings. But with the widespread negative ratings associated with the horns effect, not only are the ratings inaccurate, but they can reduce possibilities for employees to receive raises, promotions, and other pluses that accompany positive ratings.

The horns effect results in some significant problems:

✔ **When employees know that they've at least been performing satisfactorily but they're given uniformly low ratings, they see the entire evaluation process as unbalanced and unfair.** When employees believe that a process that's at the heart of their tenure, earnings, and career is somehow inequitable, their attitude toward their job, their manager, and their work takes a major hit. And their performance and productivity soon do likewise.

✔ **If the employees can figure out which specific behavior contaminated their overall ratings, they'll place undue emphasis in that area, while putting less emphasis in all other areas.** This leads to further gaps in their performance, productivity, and overall satisfaction.

✔ **Most managers actively *say* they treat employees honestly, fairly, and respectfully, but when they let the horns effect horn in on their evaluations, all these pronouncements go down the drain — along with the managers' credibility.** And when you lose credibility with your employees, your potential effectiveness across the board is severely compromised.

✔ **When employees see that their evaluations are inexplicably and unacceptably low, they're disappointed and angry — which comes out in full force in the one-on-one sessions with their managers.** The likelihood of having an open discussion about the employees' performance and development is impossible when the horns effect has tainted the ratings.

Getting beyond first impressions

The shelf-life of first impressions is remarkable. If you think back to the first time that you met the significant others in your work life or personal life, you can probably remember, and in many cases picture, that first encounter. Not only does the image of that first encounter stay with you, but so do many of the initial feelings that you had toward that person.

The problem is, when employees make a positive or negative first impression, it often stays with their managers and leads to an equally positive or negative impression of their work.

For example, think of an employee whose first weeks on the job were filled with questions. Every assignment or request was followed by a barrage of questions befitting an investigative reporter. He filled the air with questions about projects, calendars, meetings, dates, deadlines, styles, and standards. And in some cases, he asked the same question more than once or twice or three times.

After a month or two, he finally settled down, learned the lay of the land, and became a contributing member of the team. But that first impression is still there, lurking in the memory bank of everyone who worked with him in that early period. That first impression is the foundation upon which all other impressions are built.

Even as these early impressions are overshadowed by more recent events, they never totally disappear. And one of the times when they typically reveal themselves is during the performance evaluation process. As managers mull over the data that they've gathered, some of that first-impression data can still leak into the evaluative process.

Instead of ignoring first impressions, try to remember them. By drawing them out, considering them carefully, placing them in the context where they belong, and acknowledging that your employees have come a long way since then, you'll be far less likely to allow them to alter your thinking and ratings.

Countering the contrasts

As part of the performance evaluation process, managers are often tempted to compare employees with each other, instead of comparing them with the standards that have been established for a given position. When this occurs, one employee may have done clearly excellent work, but his work isn't as good as that of an amazing superstar in the department — which can lead to a lower rating for the first employee, who has clearly met all the established criteria for a far better rating.

Making this mistake is particularly easy when you're preparing the evaluation forms. The contrast effect sneaks in when you've just evaluated an absolutely fantastic employee, and now it's time to rate an employee who has performed well, but not quite as well as the previous employee.

A parallel outcome occurs when you complete the evaluation of a marginal employee and then start to work on the evaluation of a very good employee. You're likely to give that latter employee an even higher rating than merited, again just because of her fortuitous placement in the lineup.

Either way, employees feel cheated and angry.

 One of the best ways to prevent the contrast effect from occurring is to take a break between appraisals, especially if you've just completed a great or marginal evaluation. You can stand up and stretch, take care of a quick chore, return a brief phone call, take a quick stroll to the break room and back, or go back and look at several of the evaluations that you've already completed.

By redirecting your thinking to other matters between evaluations, you're better able to clear your head and start each evaluation with an open mind.

Minding your emotions

Your emotions have a major impact on the way you see the world around you. When you're upset, everything looks a little worse; when you're content, everything looks a little better. You're only human, which means your mood fluctuates when you're at work — for reasons related and unrelated to your job. Maybe you just received some major recognition for the way you managed a particular project, or perhaps you just got some bad news about a family member.

Either way, your emotional state affects your thinking, attitudes, and behavior, and that means it also impacts the way you conduct performance evaluations. This doesn't mean that you must be in a particular emotional state in order to oversee the process fairly. Instead, if you sense that you're feeling particularly upbeat or downtrodden when you're about to evaluate one of your employees, honestly accept this state of mind and remember that it can impact the appraisal that you're completing.

Having accepted the fact that you're in a particularly positive or negative state of mind, one way to calibrate the impact is to take out a couple of appraisals that you already completed and cover up the ratings that you provided on two or three items. Look over the performance categories and your written comments, and then decide what the rating should be. When you have them in mind, uncover the ratings that you provided and see how close you are to them now. If you came up with significantly higher or lower ratings than in the completed evaluations, keep that in mind as you continue the process with the upcoming evaluations.

Veering from the center

Another common mistake in the appraisal process is called the *central tendency* — a predisposition to rate all employees in the center of the rating scale, regardless of the fact that their actual performance merits higher or lower ratings.

Managers who employ this questionable strategy ignore yet another fact: namely, that this approach suffers from inaccuracy, inequity, and a total lack of substantiation.

Some managers contend that this approach treats all employees fairly by giving them essentially the same ratings, while also saving the managers time in carrying out the process. Both of these assumptions are highly problematic:

> ✔ **All employees have *not* performed the same, and providing them all with equal ratings isn't going to increase anyone's sense of equity in the workplace.**

To the contrary, employees who believe they deserve better-than-average ratings are going to feel that they haven't been given equitable treatment at all.

✔ **Although it may indeed take you less time to complete an evaluation where all employees are provided with ratings in the middle of the scale, this approach is actually more time-consuming overall.** Why? Because the one-on-one sessions with employees will be long, drawn out, and confrontational. And, after the sessions, you'll need to spend more time dealing with performance problems generated by employees who are dissatisfied with inaccurate ratings and an apparent lack of concern, interest, and support from you.

In many cases, the actual reasons behind this mistaken approach are a combination of questionable energy, lack of commitment to the performance appraisal process, lack of understanding of the process, and a desire to avoid going out on any kind of limb when evaluating employees.

If you notice that all your evaluations indicate that your employees are average through and through, go through the evaluations again.

Avoiding the skews

There are two common mistakes in the appraisal process that are strikingly similar to the central tendency, and these are called the *positive skew* and *negative skew*. Instead of rating all the employees in the middle of the scale, some managers rate all their employees on the positive end of the scale, while other managers rate all their employees negatively.

Going positively skewed

The positively skewed evaluations suffer from several questionable assumptions:

✔ **They lead to fewer, if any, confrontations, disagreements, and denials in the one-on-one sessions.** Sure, the one-on-one sessions will be less stressful because employees won't insist that their evaluations should be lower. Unfortunately, the feedback is useless.

✔ **Positive evaluations are easier and quicker to write.**
This too is correct — it's always easier to write praise
than it is to craft negative feedback. But again, there is no
point in giving positive feedback for behaviors that are
less than positive. In fact, such positive reinforcement
can encourage employees to continue to engage in counterproductive behaviors that should be avoided.

✔ **By bestowing heaps of praise, thanks, and adulation
upon employees, I'll be well liked.** This is a myth.
The reality is that these managers are more likely to be
viewed as needy, weak, and easily manipulated.

✔ **Providing the employees with positive feedback will
encourage them to work hard to continue to improve
their performance.** This is true, as long as the positive feedback is associated with positive performance.
Providing positive feedback for all performance renders
all the feedback meaningless. As noted earlier, it also
rewards behaviors that should be punished.

If an employer ever needs to take disciplinary action
because of the questionable performance of a given
employee, it'll be far more difficult to pursue if the
employee's performance evaluations are filled with positive ratings.

✔ **Positive ratings for employees make managers look
good in the eyes of their *own* managers (hence, making
them more promotable).** After all, if their department is
filled with outstanding people, these managers can be
promoted and one of the outstanding employees in their
department can move into the open position.

The problem is, when the actual performance levels of
the employees become apparent — and sooner or later
this does happen — everybody suffers. If these managers
are promoted, they're removed from their zone of competence, while the employees left behind haven't been
adequately coached to handle their current responsibilities, let alone increased responsibilities.

Going negatively skewed

An equally problematic set of errors occurs when managers
give all their employees' equally low ratings. And the motivations for this approach are equally questionable:

✔ **For some managers, the idea behind the overly negative ratings is to identify the really tough and driven employees.** The contention is that when employees are burdened with negative ratings, only the strong will survive.

This type of macho reasoning doesn't belong in the workplace. Nothing about inequitable evaluations will engender improved performance. When employees perform well and still receive wholly unwarranted negative evaluations, they feel resentment, frustration, dissatisfaction, and distrust.

✔ **These managers may also contend that there simply are no outstanding employees, regardless of the facts.** For such managers, there is a sense of pride in believing that no one is capable of achieving the high standards that they've set for the department. Their stated objective is that their extremely high standards will push employees to work even harder.

These managers may claim that their high standards will inspire employees to leap for that brass ring, but in truth, the managers won't let anyone grasp it. On a deeper level, they may well believe that granting positive ratings to their employees somehow diminishes their own worth to the company. Besides, in order for goals to be motivational, they must be challenging yet attainable. If they're totally out of reach, there is no reason to think of them as motivational.

The term *attribution* refers to the way in which people draw inferences about the causes of various events or behaviors. People make incorrect attributions quite frequently, and some can be found in the performance appraisal process. Frequently described as *attribution errors* or *attribution bias,* the most common example is the tendency of some managers to regard employees' successes as the result of the efforts of the managers themselves, while regarding the source of the employees' failures as being the employees themselves.

Doing Away with Discussion Stoppers

When you're reviewing your employees' performance during the face-to-face evaluation sessions, you may unwittingly do something that brings an open discussion to a grinding halt. And when this happens, the remainder of the conversation is strained, uncomfortable, and incapable of reaping the benefits that performance appraisal offers.

Keeping the discussion stoppers in mind is the best way to stop them from interfering with your evaluation sessions.

Labeling

Managers can easily look at their employees' behaviors and affix labels to the employees themselves. For example, employees who turn in their work late could be called "lazy," employees who clown around could be called "immature," and employees who don't have positive working relationships with some of their peers could be called "nasty."

The problem is, when you label an employee, the most common reactions are defensiveness, anger, vociferous denial, and harsh challenges. Employees typically feel insulted when they're labeled, and most won't just roll over and take it.

You're even likely to see your employees respond with various physical reactions, such as sweating, tightness in the neck or jaw, and shallow breathing, all of which are common reactions to stressful situations. In fact, by using language that your employee will likely interpret as a verbal assault, you're likely to see your employees demonstrate the most common reaction to stress: namely, fight or flight — neither of which is exactly at the top of the list for effective performance appraisals.

The best way to avoid this problem is to avoid labeling employees at any point in the evaluation process. Instead of focusing on a label, focus on the employees' specific behaviors that caused you to come up with a label in the first place.

For example, if you believe that an employee is lazy, focus on specific documented instances in which his behaviors clearly demonstrated laziness. If projects were late, assignments were shabbily completed, or the employee was sleeping on the job, those points are the ones to discuss.

The best way to provide feedback is to focus on your employees' behaviors and not on their traits, characteristics, or personalities. After all, there isn't much your employees can do with a label other than deny it. But by providing specific performance data instead of a catchall label, you're setting the stage to work productively with your employees to implement a plan of correction. Plus, they'll be much more receptive to doing so.

The weaknesses that people identify in others are often their own shortcomings. People are quick to see their own weaknesses in others because they're so familiar with them in their own behavior. As part of the appraisal process, look for any common negative themes that you're identifying among your employees. You may be highlighting your *own* weaknesses, rather than theirs.

Mentioning other employees

Another key mistake during the one-on-one performance evaluation sessions is to talk about your employees' co-workers. Even if a given employee is part of the most amazing team in the company, this isn't the time to be discussing the other players.

This session is the individual employee's special time with you, and all the focus and emphasis should be on him, not on anyone else.

Some managers bring up the names of other employees because they believe that these colleagues can serve as role models and examples. For example, when employees have questions about what it takes to do an outstanding job in a particular performance area, some managers respond by suggesting that the employee take a look at a particular co-worker. This type of response is replete with problems:

- ✔ The employee who is being evaluated doesn't want to hear praise about some other employee — she wants specific insights from the manager regarding the best steps to take in order to generate measurable improvements in performance and future ratings.

  Some employees feel insulted that their manager would use their evaluation time as an opportunity to praise someone else.

- ✔ It is also possible that a manager has an inaccurate impression of a so-called excellent co-worker. Perhaps the named co-worker is quite skilled at presenting a favorable image to the manager but not much more. Maybe there is less to this employee than meets the manager's eye.

✔ If employees believe that there are certain favored employees in the department, this perception is likely to be further reinforced if a manager happens to mention these individuals during the evaluation.

✔ Mentioning other employees during an evaluation session is likely to diminish teamwork and camaraderie within the department. Employees tend to leave this type of session believing that teamwork means very little and that they should take whatever steps they can to step over their co-workers and gain their managers' attention and favor.

Getting defensive

During the course of the appraisal discussion, some employees may make condescending or degrading comments that attack you or the ratings you provided. It's quite normal to react defensively when faced with such comments, but as a manager, you have to remain focused, businesslike, and professional.

If you sense that you're getting upset, take a few deep breaths, let the employee vent, and refrain from instantly responding. When you do say something, use a calm and deliberative style.

Let the employee know that you're actively listening by summarizing, rephrasing, and asking questions. When doing so, be sure to ask rhetorical questions at the end of your statements, such as, "Isn't it?" or "Don't you think?" The idea is to generate several "yes" responses from your employees because this can help bring them into a more agreeable mindset.

If you become defensive in these sessions, the credibility of your ratings becomes highly suspect. And this can lead to more provocative questions and comments from your employees.

Arguing

Some managers make the mistake of getting into arguments with their employees during evaluation sessions. If you argue during these sessions, you'll have automatically entered an argument that you can't win.

If you ultimately prevail on every point, you still lose because your employee was able to drag you into unprofessional and unbusinesslike behavior. All your feedback to the employee from this point on will be overshadowed by this questionable behavior.

And if you somehow fail to prevail on every point in the argument, then you lose in two ways:

- ✔ You obviously lose the argument and the points that you were trying to emphasize.

- ✔ You lose because your employee was able to drag you into this verbal quagmire.

 The best way to avoid an argument is by refusing to engage. If your employee tries to draw you in, tell her that you aren't going to argue over any of this. At the same time, let the employee know that you want to answer all her questions. If the employee expresses concern over ratings in a particular area, calmly respond with facts, figures, dates, and examples.

Creating Problems rather than Solutions

Some managerial behaviors are specifically crafted to avoid problems in the appraisal process, but they end up having the exact opposite impact.

Bargaining

Some managers enter the appraisal sessions with the expectation that they may do some bargaining with the employees before finalizing their ratings. These managers hope that their willingness to negotiate will avoid confrontations in the evaluation sessions, but the outcome is more problematic:

- ✔ **It causes confrontations.** Instead of avoiding confrontations in the evaluation sessions, the bargaining process actually opens the door to a good deal of heated debate and disagreement — and not over one or two points but over every point in the evaluation.

- ✔ **It misses the point.** Performance appraisals, by definition, are the managers' assessments of their employees' work. When employees are able to determine their final ratings, the accuracy, consistency, and fairness of the process suffer a serious decline.

- ✔ **It rewards one behavior.** Instead of basing ratings on performance across a broad range of work-related categories, bargaining ends up with ratings that are based heavily on the employees' negotiating skills.

- ✔ **It undercuts the self-evaluations.** When managers bargain over the evaluations, self-ratings are no longer honest assessments of the employees' own performance. Instead, these assessments are excessively high and resemble the opening offer in a negotiation session.

Talking too much

Another common mistake in the evaluation process occurs when managers spend more time talking than listening. These performance evaluation sessions are a dialogue, a time for you and your employees to openly discuss performance, exchange ideas, review results and goals, and ask and answer questions.

When managers turn these dialogues into monologues, the employees typically stop listening after just a few minutes. At that point, all the managers' comments become background noise, and the performance appraisals fall into the background as well.

When you hold evaluation sessions with your employees, keep a mental stopwatch focused on the amount of time that you're talking. If you sense that you're talking more than half the time, you need to do a lot more listening. Pay careful attention to your employees. Their words as well as their body language can tell you whether you're talking too much.

Postponing the sessions

When a manager's workload gets too intense, he may be tempted to postpone a performance evaluation session. But unless there is a real emergency, postponing an appraisal is a major mistake. Here's why:

- ✔ **It sends an undermining message.** Postponing an appraisal meeting sends an immediate message that the process isn't particularly significant. If you want your employees to be serious about the performance appraisal process, you have to take it seriously, too. And this means making a firm commitment to hold these sessions as scheduled.

- ✔ **It makes it easy for you to postpone the meeting again.** When one performance appraisal session has been postponed, the likelihood of having it postponed in the future increases dramatically. Plus, when you postpone one employee's performance appraisal session, you're more likely to postpone other employees' appraisal sessions.

- ✔ **It's demoralizing to the individual.** If you postpone only one performance appraisal session while holding all the others, the employee whose meeting is postponed is given a negative message — whether you intend it or not. The message is that he isn't as important as the other employees.

Surprising Your Employees

When managers surprise their employees in the performance appraisal sessions by providing ratings that are grossly different from what the employees expected, the managers have made one of the most fundamental errors in the entire process.

Throughout the evaluation period, employees should have a clear and accurate understanding of the effectiveness of their performance in every key area. When you practice managing by wandering around, you're doing more than observing the performance of your employees, documenting what you see, and establishing a log that will be vital when formulating the employees' evaluations at the end of the evaluation period.

Your role when wandering around includes providing ongoing coaching, guidance, and feedback to your employees. You're providing this feedback very close to the employees' behaviors, and you're providing it on a formal, as well as an informal, basis (including sit-down mini-evaluations at several points).

The result is that employees know exactly how they're doing every day, and they have a clear idea of the areas of their performance that are going well, along with those where improvement is needed. As a result of the feedback and guidance that you're regularly providing, your employees are taking regular and continuous steps each day to upgrade their performance and effectiveness on the job.

Chapter 8

Following Up

Some of the most important steps in the performance appraisal process are those that you take *after* you've completed the evaluation sessions with your employees. These follow-up actions are steppingstones to enhance your employees' performance, productivity, and development.

Performance appraisal is no longer an annual stand-alone program. Instead, it's an integral component of the overall process of performance management, functioning as part of a five-step cycle:

1. **Goal setting**

   Managers and employees meet and jointly establish specific performance and developmental goals. These goals are based in part on data and ratings produced in the performance evaluations.

2. **Ongoing coaching**

   Managers provide intermittent formal and informal feedback, guidance, and support to their employees throughout the evaluation period.

3. **Self-evaluations**

   As the time for the annual appraisal approaches, the employees complete their own evaluations, only this time they know exactly how they've performed.

4. **Performance evaluations.**

   Managers review all the performance data and complete the formal evaluations of their employees.

5. **Evaluation sessions.**

   Managers meet with their employees individually to go over the formal performance evaluations, but the tension and apprehension are all but eliminated because there are no surprises.

After these evaluation sessions, the next step is a return to Step 1, goal setting. And the cycle starts anew.

In this chapter, I cover Step 1 of the performance appraisal process — everything that happens *after* you've held your evaluation session and you start all over again.

Setting Goals

There isn't much point in providing your employees with a stack of feedback if nothing is done with it. Simply turning the employees loose and telling them that you expect to see some improvement is tantamount to turning your back on your employees and on the appraisal process itself. When your employees see your lack of involvement and support, they're likely to take that stack of feedback and toss it aside.

If you want to raise an employee's performance to the next level, your most useful and compelling tool is your completed performance appraisal. That completed appraisal opens the door to goal setting, and the goals that you establish with each of your employees are at the heart of their motivation, development, and success.

Looking forward instead of backward

Up to this point in the performance appraisal process, your focus has been on the past. You've gathered reams of data on your employees' successes, failures, strengths, and weaknesses. You've amassed this information by tapping every conceivable source and resource to fill in any blanks from the previous year.

Now it's time to look at the upcoming year, and that's the focus of goal setting. At this point in the process, you're turning around to face the future with your employees. And the notion of turning around is particularly appropriate because these goals can truly help stage a turnaround for any of your employees who may be struggling.

Your employees' futures are filled with opportunities to build their competencies, achieve outstanding results, and take their overall performance to new heights. By working with your employees to help establish their goals, and then providing them with coaching, guidance, and support along the way, you're creating the perfect climate for them to grow, and for their performance and effectiveness to do likewise. And if this happens, it'll be reflected in every aspect of your employees' work, as well as in their appraisals at the end of the next evaluation period.

Managers who keep focusing on their employees' pasts instead of their futures tend to dwell on problems and failures, which sets the stage for repeat performances in the coming year.

Opting for goals over dreams

Say you have an employee who says that his goal is to do a better job in every area next year. That sounds great, except for one little problem: It's not a goal.

Your employee has actually articulated a dream, essentially a general wish or desire for a particular outcome. Nothing is wrong with dreams, but just having a dream doesn't mean it'll come true. If your employees want to turn their dreams into reality, they need to formulate them as goals.

Real goals have several distinct characteristics in common:

- ✔ **Goals are specific.** When your employees have real goals, nothing about them is general. Their goals won't be just to improve performance; instead, their goals will focus directly on the precise aspect or aspects of performance that they're aiming to improve.

- ✔ **Goals are realistic.** Your employees' goals need to be appropriate for their position, responsibilities, and training. Real goals don't impose expectations that are totally unrelated to the employees' knowledge, skills, abilities, or standards.

✔ **Goals are prioritized.** All goals are not the same. Some are clearly critical and high priority, while others are important but lower in priority. As a result, every goal should have a clear and identifiable priority associated with it. Whether it's a numerical or alphabetical ranking makes no difference. What does make a difference is that the employee understands the priority associated with each goal and takes care of the most important goals first.

✔ **Goals are measurable.** As an employee pursues her goals, she and you need to know exactly where she is in the process. And, even more important, you both need to know if and when she's met a particular goal. As a result, true goals have a quantitative quality that allows them to be clearly measured at every point along the way. Because goals are measurable, employees and managers know exactly how the employees are performing every step of the way. At the end of the day, or at the end of the evaluation period, neither you nor your employee has any questions about goal attainment.

✔ **Goals are reachable.** Goals should certainly be challenging, but they should also be attainable. Granted, they should stretch your employees, but people can only stretch so far. If a goal is truly out of an employee's reach, it isn't truly a goal.

✔ **Goals are supported by action plans.** In order for your employees to reach their goals, the goals need to encompass clear planning. Action plans should include dates and deadlines, along with expected levels of project completion or goal attainment associated with each benchmark date. These plans set the path for employees to follow as they pursue their goals. Without action plans, employees may see where they want to go, but they don't know how to get there.

As you work with your employees to establish action plans, think of yourself as a reporter and ask lots of questions that start with *who, what, where, when, why,* and *how.*

If even one of the preceding elements is missing, it's back to dreamland.

The preceding characteristics of goals apply whether you're talking about a performance goal or a personal goal. But when it comes to goal-setting in the workplace, performance goals need to meet the following guidelines, too:

- ✔ **Performance goals should be aligned with the organization's goals.** Performance goals should support the style, standards, ethics, vision, and mission of your company.

- ✔ **Performance goals should be linked to your goals.** The idea is that the employees' goals should support the goals of their manager. As a result, when your employees reach their goals, it should help you meet yours. In turn, the attainment of your goals should help your manager meet her goals. In this way, the employees' goals from level to level are linked together and aligned with the goals of the company's top leadership.

- ✔ **Both you and your employees should agree on their performance goals.** When you've finished helping your employees formulate their goals for the coming year, the process should end with total understanding and agreement. If there are questions, doubts, or concerns, you need to address and resolve them before anything is finalized.

Motivating your employees to meet their goals

Just because you and your employees have been working on setting goals doesn't automatically mean that your employees will be motivated to reach them.

When goals are simply dumped on employees, without any employee involvement or input, and without any consideration of the employees' needs, the goals are likely to be rejected and, thus, void of any motivational impact. One of the key steps in establishing goals that are truly motivational is to establish them *with* your employees, rather than *for* your employees.

The presence of goals doesn't necessarily mean that employees will be motivated, but the lack of goals undercuts the likelihood of *any* significant motivation. After all, motivation energizes employees to take action to move toward a particular goal. If there are no goals to meet down the road, the employees will have no particular drive to get there.

If your employees sense a link between fulfillment of their needs and the goals that you jointly establish with them, the goals are likely to have more of a motivational impact. For example, if the employees' needs are focused on receiving recognition for successful performance, and your policy is to provide recognition for excellent work, your employees are likely to be motivated to do a great job.

Challenging your employees enough but not too much

When establishing goals with your employees, you need to give some extra thought to the level of difficulty of the goals themselves.

Extremely challenging goals

Some managers believe that goals should be as challenging as possible. The hope is that, if goals are extremely difficult or maybe even impossible to reach, employees will be highly motivated to reach them. Such challenging goals will energize employees to push themselves to great lengths, well beyond their normal efforts. And by doing so, they'll have raised their performance and surpassed the milestones and standards associated with less-rigorous goals.

Managers who subscribe to this theory believe that, when faced with impossible goals, some employees will rise to the occasion. Plus, even if employees aren't able to reach these goals, they'll have the satisfaction of truly exerting themselves in the pursuit of goals that would've scared away less-hearty souls.

Here's the reality: When goals are nothing short of impossible, the employees may initially hit the ground running, but as they realize that the goals pose insurmountable barriers, and as their efforts to reach those goals lead to backsliding, the outcome is a motivational meltdown. Most employees reason that if goals absolutely can't be met, there's no point in even trying.

Extremely easy goals

At the other end of the continuum, some managers believe that easily attainable goals are the most motivational. The idea is that, when employees meet their goals, whatever the goals may be, they experience a strong sense of accomplishment, and that's a strong source of motivation.

Plus, when employees reach their goals, they get recognition from their managers, which is yet another motivator. And when employees meet their goals, they experience increases in self-confidence, self-esteem, and self-image, all obviously positive outcomes. Hence, the reasoning goes, because employees are motivated to receive these psychological rewards, it makes sense to provide them with numerous opportunities to do so, and this is just what easy goals will do.

Here's the reality: Easily attained goals don't even register on the motivation scale. When employees can exert little or no effort and reach their goals, the message is that such goals are insignificant and meaningless.

When employees meet too-easy goals, they don't experience feelings of achievement or accomplishment. Instead, the goals are so minor that the employees who reach them believe that they haven't achieved or accomplished much of anything.

When goals can be reached with minimal effort by anyone who strolls into the department, they're void of any of the feelings of success that accompany the attainment of serious and significant goals. In fact, some employees are actually embarrassed when granted recognition for meeting unchallenging goals.

When goals are viewed by the employees as frivolous, simple, insignificant, and meaningless, they contribute more to disinterest and dissatisfaction than they do to motivation. After all, if a basketball hoop is 1 foot high and the size of a swimming pool, there isn't much satisfaction associated with hitting a shot — and there isn't much fun in that either.

Challenging goals

Goals that have a positive motivational impact are challenging, but they must be realistically challenging. They aren't a walk in the park, nor do they call for your employees to walk on Mars. Instead, they require a good deal of work on projects that are demanding, significant, and meaningful.

There is no guarantee that your employees will meet challenging goals, but with serious effort, energy, drive, and focus — along with support, guidance, and feedback from you — there is a chance that your employees will experience a major success. And with that success will come meaningful recognition and a true sense of achievement and accomplishment, which is highly motivational.

Looking at the Types of Goals

When you completed the appraisals of your employees, you gave each individual ratings in a wide range of work-related categories. You can now look back at these evaluations and use each employee's specific ratings as the basis for goal setting.

In fact, these ratings provide the ideal starting point for establishing the two most important types of goals in the workplace: performance goals and developmental goals.

Performance goals

When you create performance goals with your employees, place your emphasis on jointly establishing clear, specific, measurable, and meaningful objectives in three interrelated areas:

- **Output and results goals:** Goals in this area focus on quantitative measures of productivity, yield, and results that the employees are expected to achieve. For example, goals in this area can be targeted at numbers of units produced, hours billed, claims handled, or sales closed.

- **Competency goals:** These goals focus on the way in which your employees carry out their job responsibilities and strive to build their output and productivity. Goals in this arena focus on such measurables as quantity and quality of work, interpersonal skills, leadership effectiveness, job knowledge and expertise, communication skills, planning and administration, and problem solving.

✓ **Behavioral goals:** These goals focus on the specific behaviors that your employees demonstrate every day while carrying out their various job responsibilities. Goals in this area deal with targeted improvements in such areas as attitude, friendliness, dedication, energy, handling pressure, and supporting the company's values and mission.

Developmental goals

As you work with your employees to establish their performance goals, you also need to use this opportunity to establish additional goals that focus on your employees' growth, learning, and development.

In order to set developmental goals that actually enhance your employees' knowledge, skills, abilities, and effectiveness on the job, you need to keep in mind some key points all the way through the goal-setting process.

Identifying each employee's needs

Some of your employees will have individual areas in which their performance falls short. When working with them to create developmental goals, the first step is to identify the areas in which further development is actually needed — for example, in terms of leadership, communication, teamwork, or administrative and planning skills.

The best source of this type of information is each individual employee's evaluation. Take a close look at the areas in which you gave relatively low ratings, consider the significance of each area, and then select those that are most critical for effective performance and success on the job.

This is also an excellent time to review any 360-degree feedback (if your company has such a program). Whether you used this feedback as part of the employees' evaluations or not, 360-degree feedback is very helpful for identifying areas in which further development may be warranted.

A good deal of development is focused on areas in which employee performance needs some improvement, but don't forget to also take a look at the areas in which your employees performed particularly well. These areas may be significant strengths already, and with additional development, they can grow into major assets for the company as well as for the employees themselves.

Building your employees' motivation to learn

If you just take the findings from the evaluations and throw your employees into a training program, the outcome is likely to be underwhelming at best. In order for true learning to occur, the participants in any kind of educational program should be motivated to learn. Without motivation, any efforts to build their skills and upgrade their knowledge will be little more than background noise.

One of the best ways to increase your employees' motivation to learn is to make sure that their thoughts, ideas, and opinions are included in designing their developmental program. Have individual meetings and open discussions with each of your employees to make sure that they have input in their developmental program. As part of these discussions, be sure to let your employees see how they can benefit by meeting their developmental goals.

Establishing developmental goals

With your employees' developmental needs clearly identified, and the employees' inputs included in the process, you're ready to jointly establish developmental goals. Developmental goals clearly outline the performance areas where your employees will pursue development, as well as the specific outcomes they'll be seeking in each. Developmental objectives are held to the same standards of specificity, measurement, challenge, and prioritization as the employees' performance goals.

For example, assume that one of your employees is starting to take on some leadership responsibilities, and she clearly shows potential for advancement. However, she hasn't had any formal leadership training. One developmental goal would be focused on building her leadership skills by having her spend a specific number of hours in leadership training and guided leadership experiences. The action plan for this developmental goal would include specific benchmarks regarding classes and seminars to attend, articles and books to read, predetermined and closely monitored leadership opportunities, and predetermined formal feedback and coaching sessions to review her effectiveness in these leadership roles.

Setting the developmental plan

As soon as you and your employees have agreed on the developmental goals, as in the case of establishing performance goals, the next step is to create a thorough plan to energize and guide the process throughout the evaluation period. This step-by-step plan includes developmental areas to be covered, resources required, programs to attend, training materials needed, commitments from other employees who will help, follow-up meetings, and clearly defined benchmarks and deadlines.

Setting up a developmental training program

As you and your employees review the various developmental options and educational programs, pay attention to seven key factors that are the hallmarks of better programs:

- ✔ The program should emphasize learning by experience.

- ✔ Your employees should have numerous opportunities to practice their newly acquired knowledge and skills.

- ✔ Your employees should receive prompt, accurate, and supportive feedback every step of the way.

- ✔ The educational atmosphere should be open, communicative, and highly receptive to questions and discussions.

- ✔ The material being covered should be directly applicable to what your employees will be doing on the job.

- ✔ There should be varying educational techniques to identify and build on the individual learning styles of your employees.

- ✔ The program should be evaluated on the basis of the actual results that are achieved. For example, if the program is designed to help employees deal more effectively with customers, there should be a decrease in customer complaints.

Some educational programs use questionnaires to evaluate their effectiveness, but the questions miss the mark because they either ask the employees if they enjoyed the program or test the employees on what they learned. The problem is, the employees may enjoy a program but learn absolutely nothing. Or they may learn a laundry list of information but have no idea how to apply any of it.

One of the most effective ways to evaluate the effectiveness of these types of programs is to look at subsequent employee behaviors and performance results.

Employees generate much of their knowledge while on the job, and you're their primary trainer. They're learning not only from the formal sessions that you provide, but also from the example that you're setting every day. You're their central role model, and that makes you their most compelling trainer.

Managing after the Evaluation

As soon as you and your employees have jointly created and agreed upon performance and developmental goals for the current evaluation period, your role as a manager includes ongoing and regular communication, contact, and coaching.

This doesn't mean that you'll be sacrificing any of your core job responsibilities (for example, in terms of planning, organizing, problem solving, or dealing with customers or vendors). Instead, you'll be balancing your more traditional managerial responsibilities with responsibilities that focus on the most important assets in the company — your employees.

Wandering around

Wandering around is one of the best ways to monitor your employees' progress as they strive to reach their goals. If you observe your employees making great strides, you can easily provide some informal feedback that helps them understand how they're doing, while simultaneously encouraging them to continue the same successful behaviors.

At the same time, if you find your employees falling short for any reason, you're literally in an advantageous position to do something about it. Had you not been wandering around, you might have learned about the issue at a later date (when it turned into a crisis), or you might not have learned about it at all.

By wandering around, not only will you be able to quickly spot specific problems early, but you'll also be able to take proactive steps to control and correct them. Plus, your on-site observation will give you much greater insight into the cause or causes of the problems, and that will help you set the stage to prevent recurrences in the future.

While you're wandering around, try also to treat the process as managing by _wondering_ around: Do more than observe and gather data. Try to understand the reasons _behind_ the behaviors and outcomes that you're observing. With such knowledge, you're even better armed to prevent recurrences.

Coaching your employees toward their goals

When you find your employees engaging in particularly productive behaviors, you can take some powerful steps to keep them on this positive track. Plus, when you find your employees engaging in behaviors and outcomes that aren't helping them advance toward their goals, you can take equally powerful steps to help them get back on track. In both cases, you can generate these positive outcomes by playing one of the most important roles in management today: the role of the coach.

Some managers regard coaching as occasional words of encouragement or casual suggestions. Coaches do engage in these behaviors, but there's more to coaching than this.

Coaching is actually an ongoing managerial function in which you work with your employees to build their strengths and competencies, draw out their most effective and productive behaviors, help them identify and surpass obstacles, provide them with counseling for counterproductive behaviors, and keep them on target as they follow their developmental plans and pursue their goals.

When you see your employees engaging in particularly effective behaviors, give them some words of encouragement. This type of positive feedback increases the likelihood that they'll repeat these behaviors.

At the same time, if your employees are engaging in behaviors that appear to be counterproductive, how you respond depends on how serious the problems are. If the employees' actions aren't particularly serious, a few words to the wise, preferably not in front of others, are probably all that is necessary.

However, if the behaviors are more problematic, meet with the employees to review the issue in more detail. When you do so, keep the following key points in mind:

✔ Meet with your employee as close to the problematic behavior as possible.

✔ Hold the meeting in private.

✔ Be specific in describing the questionable performance and the problems that emerged or can emerge as a result.

✔ Provide clear and specific guidance and modeling.

✔ Be sure your employee understands and agrees to change his behavior.

✔ Tell your employee what will happen if the questionable performance continues.

✔ Set a follow-up date, preferably within 30 days, to meet with your employee to discuss the status of the situation.

✔ Document the discussion and place a copy in your employee's file.

✔ In your wandering around, be sure to follow up on this specific aspect of your employee's performance.

Whether you observe your employees taking actions that are outstanding or unacceptable, be sure to enter them in the log that you use when formulating their performance evaluations.

By acting as a coach, you're providing your employees with regular feedback, guidance, and direction, whether for problematic behaviors or productive behaviors. You're helping to build their performance, competencies, and behaviors, while simultaneously helping them advance toward their goals.

Part III
Phrases and Expressions That Work

The 5th Wave   By Rich Tennant

"...faster than a speeding bullet...more powerful than a locomotive...these are just a few of your positive attributes."

In this part . . .

*T*hese chapters contain more than 3,200 appraisal phrases that deal with the most important performance areas in your employees' jobs. The phrases run the gamut from exceptional all the way to unsatisfactory. There are phrases for every occasion, and, no doubt, occasions for every phrase.

The phrases in the positive categories are designed to encourage and motivate your employees to keep up the good work. At the same time, the phrases in the less-than-satisfactory range are designed to identify areas where your employees need to improve, as well as to open the door to productive discussions on this very matter.

Chapter 9

The Best Phrases for Quality and Quantity of Work

● ●

In This Chapter

▶ Building and reinforcing employee output

▶ Identifying and enhancing employee thoroughness

▶ Assessing and rewarding time-management skills

● ●

*T*wo primary areas of emphasis in the performance appraisal process are the quality and quantity of each employee's work. Quality and quantity are two central performance measures for which employees need thorough and accurate feedback. Regardless of performance, when such feedback is questionable, productivity is likely to be questionable, too.

Your written comments are a great opportunity to provide employees with complete and long-lasting feedback on the quality and quantity of their work. On the one hand, writing a general statement indicating that an employee needs to produce more or do a neater job is easy; so is simply writing a statement that there are no quality or quantity problems. But these comments have no impact when it comes to sustaining excellent performance or improving marginal performance.

In order for your written feedback to have a long-lasting impact, you need to focus on the individual performance factors that determine the quality and quantity of your employees' work, such as accuracy, detail-mindedness, productivity, multi-tasking, and setting priorities, to name just a few. The best strategy is to include targeted phrases that energize an employee to keep up the good work in key areas, while also encouraging employees to focus more carefully on the quality and quantity of their work where needed. This chapter provides you with the full spectrum of those phrases.

Accuracy

Exceptional: Consistently exceeds expectations

- ✔ Sets the gold standard for accuracy
- ✔ Produces consistently error-free work
- ✔ Produces work that is 100 percent reliable
- ✔ Has zero tolerance for mistakes

Excellent: Frequently exceeds expectations

- ✔ Has an ongoing focus on accuracy
- ✔ Finds and corrects errors
- ✔ Emphasizes accuracy to others
- ✔ Checks and rechecks for accuracy

Fully competent: Meets expectations

- ✔ Keeps accuracy in mind
- ✔ Expects accuracy in all aspects of the job
- ✔ Maintains detailed and accurate records
- ✔ Does not tolerate sloppy work

Marginal: Occasionally fails to meet expectations

- ✔ Does not spend enough time reviewing
- ✔ Produces documentation that is not consistently reliable
- ✔ Is too tolerant of errors
- ✔ Produces frequently unreliable output
- ✔ Tends to overlook specifications

Unsatisfactory: Consistently fails to meet expectations

- ✔ Produces work that cannot be relied upon
- ✔ Needs constant monitoring
- ✔ Has made errors that have led to significant problems
- ✔ Always falls short of the mark in terms of accuracy

Detail-Mindedness

Exceptional: Consistently exceeds expectations

- ✔ Covers every significant detail from A to Z
- ✔ Takes thoroughness to a new level
- ✔ Energizes others to work carefully
- ✔ Catches critical details missed by others
- ✔ Meticulously manages every key detail
- ✔ Manages the details, and doesn't let the details manage him
- ✔ Possesses uncanny insight into the role and relevance of every detail
- ✔ Can discuss details with anyone at any level
- ✔ Remains unsatisfied until a topic is totally mastered
- ✔ Accurately analyzes and prioritizes details

Excellent: Frequently exceeds expectations

- ✔ Has a great eye for detail
- ✔ Regards the term *minor detail* as an oxymoron
- ✔ Keeps details in perspective
- ✔ Can get down to a microscopic level if needed
- ✔ Never gets mired in minor details
- ✔ Quickly notices when key details are overlooked
- ✔ Digs into the details
- ✔ Has detailed knowledge that is greatly valued by others
- ✔ Supports conclusions with appropriate details
- ✔ Is uncomfortable when details are lacking

Fully competent: Meets expectations

- ✔ Includes all relevant details
- ✔ Discerns relevant from irrelevant details
- ✔ Sweats the small stuff
- ✔ Makes sense of the masses of detail

- Steps up to the challenge of handling details
- Does not miss a major detail
- Stays on top of the details
- Is comfortable with the expected level of detail
- Pushes extra-hard to handle the details

Marginal: Occasionally fails to meet expectations

- Has little concern for details
- Sees the big picture, but overlooks the small picture
- Leaves the details to others
- Struggles with details
- Leaves out points that should be included
- Randomly omits details
- Lets the details slide
- Regards details as a major challenge
- Regards details as a low priority
- Sees details as an inconvenience
- Procrastinates when handling details
- Gets careless with details

Unsatisfactory: Consistently fails to meet expectations

- Does not get down to details
- Overlooks essential details
- Focuses on the fine points and misses the major ones
- Focuses on the major points and misses most others
- Tries to bluff when asked about details
- Omits vital details, but includes insignificant details
- Regards details as fluff
- Is easily distracted when working on details
- Provides details that are sloppy, inaccurate, or incomplete

Meeting Goals

Exceptional: Consistently exceeds expectations

- ✔ Sets challenging goals and surpasses them
- ✔ Is truly inspirational with her goal attainment
- ✔ Establishes increasingly rigorous objectives
- ✔ Is passionate about meeting goals
- ✔ Gives 110 percent, 100 percent of the time
- ✔ Is the ultimate role model for goal setting and attainment
- ✔ Encourages and guides others to surpass their goals
- ✔ Turns obstacles into challenges and then overcomes them
- ✔ Has confidence in his ability to meet challenging goals, and for good reason
- ✔ Is highly knowledgeable about the actual process of setting goals
- ✔ Is a key source of information about goal setting for employees in many departments
- ✔ Shows a high degree of creativity in setting and pursuing goals
- ✔ Consistently seeks out larger and more challenging goals
- ✔ Has a passion for goal attainment that spreads throughout her team

Excellent: Frequently exceeds expectations

- ✔ Meets or exceeds goals every time
- ✔ Has a very strong goal orientation
- ✔ Will not stop until all the goals are met
- ✔ Gives his all to meet all the objectives
- ✔ Helps others meet their objectives
- ✔ Is undaunted by unforeseen disruptions or blockages
- ✔ Stays with the plan, but maintains wiggle room to handle the unexpected

- Never loses sight of the target
- Keeps the communication lines open regarding all goal-related matters
- Reaches goals that elude others
- Focuses on high-impact goals, without losing sight of lesser goals
- Understands the vision, values, and culture of the company, and develops goals with them in mind
- Realistically adjusts the priorities of goals as work situations change
- Approaches goals with energy, enthusiasm, drive, and focus

Fully competent: Meets expectations

- Is energized by demanding goals
- Is fully committed to meeting goals
- Meets both short-term and long-term objectives
- Follows the action plan to achieve goals
- Works around or through obstacles
- Keeps goals in mind throughout the day
- Works diligently to accomplish all the established objectives
- Sets challenging yet reachable goals
- Is highly motivated to meet every goal
- Is receptive to new and different goals that help the company realize its mission
- Shows initiative and self-direction in setting goals
- Works diligently to help establish goals and plans
- Clearly communicates objectives to others
- Tackles every goal tenaciously

Marginal: Occasionally fails to meet expectations

- Rarely devotes adequate attention to goals
- Rushes through the goal-setting process

- ✔ Sets aside the most demanding goals
- ✔ Overlooks the action plan
- ✔ Expects others to meet their goals, while ignoring her own
- ✔ Spends too much time on second-tier objectives
- ✔ Seeks advice in setting and pursuing goals, but rarely follows it
- ✔ Displays random performance in both establishing and pursuing goals
- ✔ Asks questions about goals and plans, but doesn't always listen
- ✔ Avoids discussions about goals
- ✔ Doesn't pay enough attention to the company's goals
- ✔ Thrives on picking the low-hanging fruit
- ✔ Displays more talk than action when it comes to meeting goals

Unsatisfactory: Consistently fails to meet expectations

- ✔ Fails to meet even the most basic objectives
- ✔ Loses sight of goals
- ✔ Establishes routine goals and fails to meet them
- ✔ Is easily distracted from goals, rather than attracted to them
- ✔ Has questionable organizational skills, making all his goals far more difficult to reach
- ✔ Is overwhelmed by the most basic goals
- ✔ Sets goals and ignores them
- ✔ Has yet to establish a truly challenging and productive goal
- ✔ Avoids goal-setting sessions and discussions
- ✔ Fails to fully engage in pursuing her objectives
- ✔ Downsizes goals after committing to pursue them as originally designed
- ✔ Puts goals on a back burner and leaves them there
- ✔ Fails to see the consequences of missing goals

Multi-Tasking

Exceptional: Consistently exceeds expectations

- Deftly juggles several balls at once
- Is energized by additional tasks
- Truly enjoys the challenge of multi-tasking
- Uses strong organizational skills for multi-tasking success
- Has had multiple successes because of his multi-tasking
- Increases attention and focus to successfully complete several tasks simultaneously
- Completes the most important tasks first
- Actively seeks additional tasks
- Switches seamlessly from one project to another
- Takes on and completes a wide range of additional tasks with no loss of quality
- Is able to effectively manage a seemingly unmanageable amount of tasks
- Is the go-to person for additional projects

Excellent: Frequently exceeds expectations

- Can shift gears on a dime
- Approaches multi-tasking with multiple skills
- Always says "yes" to additional responsibilities
- Maintains excellent focus on all projects
- Prioritizes tasks and gets the jobs done
- Manages time to complete multiple tasks in a timely manner
- Prioritizes projects for maximum productivity
- Allocates time effectively to complete a wide range of tasks
- Is highly regarded and respected for her ability to multi-task

Fully competent: Meets expectations

- Readily assumes and completes multiple assignments
- Regards multi-tasking as part of the job
- Accepts additional assignments without hesitation
- Will not stop until the work is done and the deadlines are met
- Realistically adjusts priorities when new work is assigned
- Allocates time effectively on multiple projects
- Maintains efficiency across a broad range of projects
- Regards multi-tasking as a way to add value to the company
- Keeps quality in mind on all tasks

Marginal: Occasionally fails to meet expectations

- Has missed more deadlines because of his multi-tasking
- Sets sights on the easiest tasks
- Agrees to additional assignments, but lets them slide
- Jumps from task to task, while completing few of them
- Engages in multi-tasking but lacks in quality
- Has produced more errors as the tasks have increased
- Tends to decline additional work

Unsatisfactory: Consistently fails to meet expectations

- Is overwhelmed by the expectations of multi-tasking
- Inadequately focuses on any single task
- Is unable to distinguish major from minor tasks
- Stresses out with additional responsibilities
- Regards additional tasks as an intrusion
- Complains when asked to handle additional tasks
- Can handle only a small number of basic tasks at one time
- Looks to others to do the work

Performance Levels

Exceptional: Consistently exceeds expectations

- ✔ Finds the most effective ways to get the job done
- ✔ Creates new strategies to improve performance
- ✔ Improves the performance of others
- ✔ Focuses abundant energy and effort on the job
- ✔ Targets efforts for maximum results, and then achieves them
- ✔ Is motivated to perform at a superior level
- ✔ Maintains the highest personal performance standards
- ✔ Is clearly superior in every measurable area of performance
- ✔ Expects and attains outstanding results
- ✔ Serves as a highly positive role model in all performance areas
- ✔ Took a virtually impossible assignment and turned it into a major winner
- ✔ Set a new high-water mark on the XYZ project
- ✔ Grabs the brass ring on every project
- ✔ Dazzles senior management

Excellent: Frequently exceeds expectations

- ✔ Comes to work ready to excel
- ✔ Sets high personal performance expectations
- ✔ Relentlessly pursues outstanding outcomes
- ✔ Expects more and gets it
- ✔ Refuses to settle for status-quo performance
- ✔ Does not know the word *average*
- ✔ Is energized by the prospect of achieving challenging goals
- ✔ Prioritizes work for maximum results
- ✔ Has a compelling "can-do" attitude

- Is undaunted by difficult challenges, tough obstacles, or frustrating events
- Plans to succeed and does so
- Bounces back from setbacks
- Is frequently mentioned by name whenever the topic of outstanding performance comes up
- Keeps pushing until the desired outcomes are achieved
- Jump-starts stalled projects
- Takes great pride not only in meeting goals but in surpassing them

Fully competent: Meets expectations

- Is open to new strategies to improve results
- Has visibly improved her performance levels
- Is steadily upgrading every performance area
- Actively seeks strategies to improve performance
- Can be counted on for solid performance
- Focuses his priorities on maximum effectiveness and success
- Maintains focus on the main event
- Takes feedback to heart and strives to improve
- Focuses on work, not on the clock
- Is a stable and consistent performer
- Is very interested in suggestions to build performance
- Effectively focuses her energy on the job

Marginal: Occasionally fails to meet expectations

- Is satisfied with his current performance, despite the fact that it isn't satisfactory
- Prefers to slip under the bar instead of leaping over it
- Can be sidetracked by minor obstacles and challenges
- Is tolerant of mediocre performance
- Regards performance measures as unfair

- Has an inflated view of her own work
- Insists that improvements in performance are coming soon
- Feels that others are intentionally trying to make him look bad
- Spends more time as a spectator than as a participant
- Comes up short on long-term projects
- Spends time on low-priority projects
- Is primarily interested in things that have little to do with work
- Is rarely around when it's time for heavy lifting
- Does C-level work on A-level projects
- Misunderstands the priorities of the job

Unsatisfactory: Consistently fails to meet expectations

- Attributes performance problems to other people or circumstances
- Fails to take responsibility for her failures
- Has received complaints from customers
- Has received complaints from management
- Has displayed performance levels that have been declining
- Talks the performance talk, but does not walk the walk
- Has fallen into a habit of questionable performance
- Spends more time socializing than working
- Shows little interest or motivation in upgrading performance
- Doesn't pay enough attention to the work that needs to be done
- Expects others to carry the load
- Regards goals as suggestions
- Always seeks the easy way out
- Is unwilling to accept feedback and guidance
- Steps back when it's time to step up

Productivity

Exceptional: Consistently exceeds expectations

- ✔ Produces a remarkable amount of high-quality work
- ✔ Inspires others with his output
- ✔ Sets a new standard for productivity
- ✔ Puts the "pro" in *productivity*
- ✔ Monitors productivity and implements upgrades as needed
- ✔ Always seeks opportunities to be even more productive
- ✔ Dazzles everyone with the quality and quantity of her work
- ✔ Is productivity minded
- ✔ Regards productivity as a top priority
- ✔ Generates great productivity from others
- ✔ Identifies and implements steps to enhance output
- ✔ Is responsible for a major increase in departmental productivity
- ✔ Always goes the extra mile(s)
- ✔ Fully understands the figures behind productivity
- ✔ Works hard and works smart
- ✔ Streamlines departmental operations
- ✔ Raises the bar for everyone
- ✔ Is energized by challenges that would derail others
- ✔ Offers outstanding suggestions to increase productivity

Excellent: Frequently exceeds expectations

- ✔ Is motivated to be highly productive
- ✔ Has steadily increased personal output
- ✔ Provides suggestions that enhance productivity
- ✔ Serves as an excellent role model of productive behavior
- ✔ Focuses on people as well as productivity

- ✔ Is productive under less-than-perfect conditions
- ✔ Makes others more productive
- ✔ Generates and implements creative ideas
- ✔ Works directly with others to enhance their productivity
- ✔ Is eager to learn about ways to be more productive
- ✔ Quickly incorporates new knowledge to build productivity
- ✔ Turns challenges into opportunities
- ✔ Is a stellar producer
- ✔ Is productive beyond standard requirements
- ✔ Takes on any task
- ✔ Single-handedly led to the success of the XYZ project through his efforts
- ✔ Is regarded as a productivity guru

Fully competent: Meets expectations

- ✔ Produces solid quality and quantity of work
- ✔ Helps others work better
- ✔ Shares insights to improve productivity
- ✔ Works with the team to build output
- ✔ Has been improving her productivity
- ✔ Understands how to produce more
- ✔ Puts in extra hours to get the desired results
- ✔ Builds productivity by being well organized
- ✔ Fully embraces the need for greater productivity
- ✔ Is a storehouse of productivity knowledge
- ✔ Does more than talk about productivity

Marginal: Occasionally fails to meet expectations

- ✔ Is sporadic with his output
- ✔ Is often uneven with her productivity
- ✔ Can work hard, but not consistently
- ✔ Could be far more productive

- Tends to set the bar too low
- Does not exert consistent effort
- Can meet the mark in terms of productivity, but frequently falls short
- Blames productivity problems on others
- Bogs down performance and productivity with his misdirected actions
- Spends too much time on low-priority tasks
- Works reactively rather than proactively
- Tries to do just enough to get by
- Is an amateur in the world of productivity
- Sets aside quality
- Talks about working productively, but rarely does so

Unsatisfactory: Consistently fails to meet expectations

- Is slipping in terms of her personal productivity
- Is distracted by non-work issues
- Doesn't focus enough energy and attention on the work to be done
- Sets low goals and fails to meet them
- Doesn't regard productivity as a priority
- Sees his personal output slipping and does nothing to stop it
- Interferes with the performance of others
- Displays disruptive or distracting behaviors
- Often needs to redo her work
- Rarely gets out of first gear
- Regards productivity as someone else's concern
- Takes inappropriate or reckless shortcuts
- Shows little interest in being more productive
- Fails to fully engage in projects
- Disregards suggestions to build productivity

Setting Priorities

Exceptional: Consistently exceeds expectations

- ✔ Understands and resolves A-level matters before B-level and C-level matters
- ✔ Uses sound judgment and insights when rank-ordering projects
- ✔ Serves as a valuable resource to determine the role and priority of totally different tasks
- ✔ Always knows which projects belong at the top of the list and which belong at the bottom
- ✔ Easily and quickly singles out low-priority tasks
- ✔ Clarifies priorities for employees at any job level
- ✔ Prevents others from pursuing minor projects that superficially appear to be important
- ✔ Quickly and accurately calibrates project priorities

Excellent: Frequently exceeds expectations

- ✔ Is keenly aware of the subtleties that make one project more important than another
- ✔ Places work priorities over personal priorities
- ✔ Adapts his workload and priorities to meet workplace demands
- ✔ Breaks projects into logical pieces to make sure that top priorities are handled first
- ✔ Is able to set priorities when under great pressure
- ✔ Tackles high-value projects first
- ✔ Targets efforts on tasks with the largest payoff
- ✔ Uses multi-tasking to handle low-priority items

Fully competent: Meets expectations

- ✔ Understands priorities and how to establish them
- ✔ Discusses priorities when there is confusion

- Is unafraid to ask questions about priorities
- Shifts priorities as needed
- Clarifies and then correctly handles competing priorities
- Is very cognizant of priorities and adjusts focus as necessary
- Reviews priorities before starting tasks

Marginal: Occasionally fails to meet expectations

- Confuses priorities with preferences
- Starts working before prioritizing
- Uses inappropriate criteria in determining what to do first
- Leaves major projects until the end
- Argues over priorities
- Decides on priorities and rigidly sticks to them, even when situations call for flexibility
- Sees unessential matters as essential and vice versa
- Lacks insight into her own ability to handle priorities
- Is easily sidetracked by low-value tasks

Unsatisfactory: Consistently fails to meet expectations

- Ignores priorities of assigned projects
- Treats all assignments as having essentially the same priorities
- Places no priority on setting priorities
- Randomly prioritizes assignments
- Works on lowest priorities first
- Sees only the small picture
- Spends too much time on low-level priorities and too little time on major priorities
- Wallows in trivial matters

Timeliness

Exceptional: Consistently exceeds expectations

- Is a master of time management
- Is on time and on target with his work
- Generates more than an hour's worth of productivity in each hour
- Is excellent at prioritizing work
- Helps others manage their time
- Builds the time-management skills of fellow employees
- Streamlines tasks and processes
- Has a great sense of time and timing
- Never misses a deadline
- Meets deadlines like clockwork
- Creates and implements timesaving strategies
- Consistently makes the best use of her time
- Plans out the work, and then works the plan
- Has a high degree of expertise in time management, and applies it on every project
- Completes most projects early and all projects on time
- Is sensitive to the time demands and constraints of others
- Produces on-time, high-quality work
- Knows when and how to delegate

Excellent: Frequently exceeds expectations

- Coordinates projects to meet deadlines
- Develops realistic plans and schedules
- Keeps the entire team on time
- Has a keen sense of what to do and when to do it
- Gives top attention to top priorities
- Manages time instead of letting time manage him

- Doesn't procrastinate
- Stays on schedule or ahead of it
- Never loses sight of time constraints
- Is excellent at estimating the time required for projects
- Manages to get more done in less time
- Is punctual in all aspects of the job
- Maintains flexibility to take on additional tasks
- Completes many projects before the due date
- Has yet to miss a deadline
- Delegates work and follows up as needed

Fully competent: Meets expectations

- Completes work on time
- Avoids time wasters
- Establishes appropriate priorities
- Develops workable schedules
- Knows what needs to be done and not done
- Effectively assigns work to others
- Keeps commitments to get work done
- Places a premium on planning
- Keeps projects on schedule
- Delivers results on time
- Tracks projects carefully
- Makes productive use of her time
- Follows a proven time-management system
- Lives by the philosophy that time is money
- Makes commitments to deadlines and keeps them
- Watches the time, not the clock

Marginal: Occasionally fails to meet expectations

- Treats deadlines as if they are optional
- Devotes too much time to second-tier matters

- Rarely completes the assigned tasks on time
- Constantly feels overwhelmed
- Works on many assignments that should be delegated
- Is easily drawn into secondary tasks
- Is too quick to set aside important projects
- Randomly rank-orders projects
- Blames others when work runs late
- Is intermittent, at best, with planning
- Is late with major projects but on time with minor ones
- Surprises others when work is on time
- Occasionally meets deadlines but with questionable quality
- Is too late with too much work

Unsatisfactory: Consistently fails to meet expectations

- Wastes time on low-ticket items
- Places procrastination over performance
- Allows work to stack up
- Constantly falls behind
- Has yet to meet a deadline
- Waits until the last minute
- Ignores coaching
- Doesn't pay enough attention to the needs of those waiting for his work
- Consistently fails to make the best use of time
- Spends too much time crafting excuses
- Regards time management as a waste of time
- Is uninterested in time-management tools or programs
- Feels no sense of urgency
- Manages time like a pinball

Chapter 10

The Best Phrases for Communication and Interpersonal Skills

····································

In This Chapter

▶ Spotlighting communication strengths and areas for improvement

▶ Recognizing and enhancing team building

▶ Rewarding and rebuilding people skills

····································

*I*n order for your employees to effectively carry out their responsibilities and meet their short-term and long-term objectives, they need to know how well they're communicating and dealing with others.

Ironically, some managers have difficulty communicating assessments in these two areas, especially when it comes to written comments. They're concerned that their feedback on communication won't be communicated clearly, and they worry that providing feedback on interpersonal relations will actually strain the working relationships instead of improving them. When written comments focus on vague and general trends and themes, these outcomes are the most likely.

Communication skills and interpersonal skills are actually composed of numerous factors — such as cooperation, teamwork, listening, negotiating, and telephone skills — all of which lend themselves to appraisal. If any one of these factors is overlooked in the appraisal process, opportunities for recognition and personal growth will be diminished. This chapter targets the key factors that determine effectiveness in communications and interpersonal skills and provides the full continuum of performance appraisal phrases for each.

Cooperation

Exceptional: Consistently exceeds expectations

- ✔ Sets an example for the entire company with her cooperation
- ✔ Builds cooperation within the department
- ✔ Builds cooperation among departments
- ✔ Creates a climate of cooperation
- ✔ Is clearly one of the most cooperative employees

Excellent: Frequently exceeds expectations

- ✔ Is always ready to cooperate
- ✔ Has a totally cooperative attitude
- ✔ Is one of the easiest people to work with

Fully competent: Meets expectations

- ✔ Can always be counted on to pitch in
- ✔ Readily cooperates whenever the opportunity arises
- ✔ Is a solid addition to any group
- ✔ Has a strong concern for others

Marginal: Occasionally fails to meet expectations

- ✔ Cooperates, but with strings attached
- ✔ Is too self-absorbed to display much cooperation
- ✔ Manipulates rather than cooperates
- ✔ Does not view cooperation as a priority

Unsatisfactory: Consistently fails to meet expectations

- ✔ Is the last person to offer to help
- ✔ Generates conflict rather than cooperation
- ✔ Cannot be counted upon to cooperate
- ✔ Disrupts even the most cooperative groups

Customer Service

Exceptional: Consistently exceeds expectations

- Is very responsive to the customers' needs
- Provides the maximum in customer service
- Has an upbeat and friendly demeanor
- Knows the product from A to Z
- Is the customers' first choice
- Serves as a great customer service role model
- Understands the customers as individuals
- Treats customers as partners
- Is the go-to person for difficult customers or calls
- Builds excellent relationships with customers
- Regards customer service as a top priority
- Is a regular winner of customer service awards
- Is satisfied only if the customers are satisfied

Excellent: Frequently exceeds expectations

- Puts customers first
- Goes the extra mile for the customers
- Puts customer satisfaction at the top of the list
- Is motivated to meet the customers' needs
- Solves problems and resolves issues
- Is able to satisfy dissatisfied customers
- Makes each customer feel special
- Is highly skilled in handling problem situations

Fully competent: Meets expectations

- Is always pleasant
- Listens carefully
- Gives first-rate service

✔ Provides fast service

✔ Treats every customer with respect

✔ Makes the customers feel important

✔ Knows the customers by name

✔ Builds customer loyalty

✔ Always projects a positive attitude

Marginal: Occasionally fails to meet expectations

✔ Underestimates the importance of the customers

✔ Doesn't have adequate product knowledge

✔ Fails to listen carefully

✔ Is more interested in ending the conversation than ending a problem

✔ Shows no interest in building positive relationships with the customers

✔ Keeps customers waiting

Unsatisfactory: Consistently fails to meet expectations

✔ Puts the customers second rather than first

✔ Interrupts the customers

✔ Does not pay attention to what customers are saying or feeling

✔ Provides incorrect information

✔ Argues with customers

✔ Becomes emotional

✔ Abandons customers

✔ Embarrasses and humiliates customers

✔ Has a condescending attitude

✔ Is rude to the customers

✔ Makes inappropriate comments

✔ Gets too personal

✔ Does nothing to improve his customer service skills

✔ Doesn't care about losing customers

Listening

Exceptional: Consistently exceeds expectations

- ✔ Listens actively to what others are saying
- ✔ Restates, repeats, and rephrases
- ✔ Cares about what others are saying
- ✔ Devotes full attention when speaking with others

Excellent: Frequently exceeds expectations

- ✔ Takes follow-up action on matters that are discussed
- ✔ Does not interrupt
- ✔ Listens to the full story before drawing conclusions
- ✔ Creates a climate that encourages communication
- ✔ Practices two-way communication

Fully competent: Meets expectations

- ✔ Does not make snap judgments
- ✔ Uses dialogues, not monologues
- ✔ Is a patient listener
- ✔ Asks questions if she does not understand

Marginal: Occasionally fails to meet expectations

- ✔ Rarely pays attention
- ✔ Rushes people who try to communicate with him
- ✔ Insists on being heard, but does not listen to others
- ✔ Ignores what others are saying

Unsatisfactory: Consistently fails to meet expectations

- ✔ Is preoccupied when others are talking
- ✔ Does more talking than listening
- ✔ Multi-tasks when she should be listening
- ✔ Repeatedly asks the same questions

Meetings

Exceptional: Consistently exceeds expectations

- ✔ Knows when to meet and when to use other media
- ✔ Establishes an agenda and follows it unless there is a true need to cover additional topics
- ✔ Keeps discussions open, productive, and robust
- ✔ Runs meetings that are known for excellent problem solving and decision making

Excellent: Frequently exceeds expectations

- ✔ Is a valued participant in any meeting
- ✔ Sets up additional meetings if warranted
- ✔ Sends out appropriate pre-meeting information
- ✔ Keeps meetings on track and on target

Fully competent: Meets expectations

- ✔ Conducts meetings that start and end on time
- ✔ Generates participation from all attendees
- ✔ Listens carefully throughout meetings
- ✔ Uses technical media only when necessary

Marginal: Occasionally fails to meet expectations

- ✔ Usually arrives late
- ✔ Constantly asks questions, but ignores the answers
- ✔ Holds far too many meetings
- ✔ Lets meetings run themselves

Unsatisfactory: Consistently fails to meet expectations

- ✔ Brings up irrelevant topics
- ✔ Attends meetings, but remains uninvolved
- ✔ Sends text messages during meetings
- ✔ Sleeps during meetings

Negotiating

Exceptional: Consistently exceeds expectations

✔ Plans thoroughly before entering negotiations

✔ Sets positive expectations

✔ Studies the people with whom he is negotiating

✔ Finds creative solutions

✔ Actively listens throughout the process

✔ Keeps attention on interests rather than positions

✔ Has a great ability to reconcile differences

✔ Focuses on areas of shared interest

✔ Has materials ready to make agreement easier for the other side

✔ Trades concessions instead of giving anything away

✔ Generates win-win outcomes

Excellent: Frequently exceeds expectations

✔ Understands the sources of power in negotiations

✔ Avoids trickery and deceit

✔ Is flexible without being flimsy

✔ Takes a collaborative approach

✔ Focuses on objective factors, not personal factors

✔ Keeps relationships intact, regardless of outcomes

✔ Is very aware of the subtleties of the negotiation process, especially body language

✔ Tries to create a bigger pie, rather than going for a larger slice of the established pie

Fully competent: Meets expectations

✔ Focuses on the people in the negotiation process

✔ Carefully considers all alternatives

✔ Recognizes that there can be more than one acceptable solution

✔ Generates a wide range of options

✔ Avoids a win-lose mindset and strategy

✔ Keeps emotions out of the process

✔ Uses constructive and confident language

✔ Uses empathy

✔ Has a give-and-take attitude

✔ Keeps an open mind

Marginal: Occasionally fails to meet expectations

✔ Demands rather than negotiates

✔ Doesn't understand the needs of others

✔ Focuses too heavily on positions rather than people

✔ Views every session as win-lose rather than win-win

✔ Loses sight of the objectives of the negotiation process

✔ Is more combative than collaborative

Unsatisfactory: Consistently fails to meet expectations

✔ Views negotiation sessions as "take" rather than "give and take"

✔ Uses unethical negotiation tactics

✔ Is more bluff than facts

✔ Is a pushover

✔ Wins negotiations and loses relationships

✔ Takes an adversarial position

✔ Ignores what others have to say

✔ Displays poor listening skills from start to finish

✔ Uses wishy-washy language

✔ Displays a lack of planning and organization

✔ Is overly emotional

✔ Locks into a position and causes others to do likewise

✔ Generates more stalemates than settlements

✔ Enflames situations instead of defusing them

Persuasiveness

Exceptional: Consistently exceeds expectations

- ✔ Is a master of language and persuasion
- ✔ Always knows the right way to say something
- ✔ Persuades others when no one else comes close
- ✔ Is highly effective in bringing others to her way of thinking
- ✔ Increases persuasive impact by adjusting his communication style
- ✔ Has an excellent ability to build trust
- ✔ Has a level of expertise that enhances his ability to persuade others
- ✔ Uses logic and facts at just the right time
- ✔ Uses language, phrasing, and body language that quickly make others feel comfortable and ready to accept her ideas
- ✔ Uses his ability to listen as a powerful persuasion tool
- ✔ Makes others feel that they have truly been heard
- ✔ Uses persuasion but not manipulation
- ✔ Shows others how they win by agreeing with her
- ✔ Has a great deal of personal charisma

Excellent: Frequently exceeds expectations

- ✔ Draws others to his way of thinking
- ✔ Is known as a credible person
- ✔ Views others as partners rather than opponents
- ✔ Takes the time to truly understand other people and their needs
- ✔ Guides others to her way of thinking
- ✔ Uses the input of others to draw them over to his way of thinking
- ✔ Relies on reason and is totally reasonable when trying to persuade others

✔ Is well versed when it comes to handling objections or concerns

✔ Has remarkable diplomatic skills

✔ Is trusted throughout the company

Fully competent: Meets expectations

✔ Has a solid ability to influence others

✔ Persuades without arguing

✔ Uses empathy effectively

✔ Thinks before responding

✔ Knows the facts and uses them to bolster her position

✔ Is always well prepared

✔ Persuades, but never with high-pressure tactics

✔ Understands the players and the situation

Marginal: Occasionally fails to meet expectations

✔ Is more forceful than tactful

✔ Is too impatient to be persuasive

✔ Tries to push her ideas on others

✔ Ignores the subtleties of persuasion

✔ Demands more than persuades

✔ Lets emotions interfere

Unsatisfactory: Consistently fails to meet expectations

✔ Gets upset when others disagree

✔ Gives up when he's unable to persuade others

✔ Resorts to name calling

✔ Resorts to bullying when all else fails

✔ Is primarily interested in taking advantage of others

✔ Is hampered by being distrusted

✔ Persuades by flexing her power

✔ Is not regarded as honest or credible

Sales Skills

Exceptional: Consistently exceeds expectations

- Is regarded by all as a sales superstar
- Prepares thoroughly before any presentation
- Practices and rehearses before presentations
- Identifies possibly difficult questions and scripts the best answers
- Is a master of sales presentations
- Helps build the sales skills of others on the team
- Is a true sales professional
- Provides customers with more service and support than they ever dreamed of
- Uses a collaborative selling style
- Treats customers as partners
- Builds trust rapidly
- Is a major asset at trade shows
- Handles objections skillfully
- Knows when and how to close
- Has an excellent sales closing rate
- Has an excellent close ratio
- Finds creative solutions to customers' problems
- Is regarded by customers as a great problem-solver
- Consistently surpasses sales quotas
- Is the customers' favorite
- Is a great prospector who often finds sales gold

Excellent: Frequently exceeds expectations

- Has a great understanding of customers' needs
- Is regarded as highly credible and trustworthy
- Focuses on meeting customers' needs and not his own
- Treats customers respectfully

- Is a highly effective listener
- Is honest, fair, above-board, and ethical
- Is always striving to build her sales skills
- Works with other sales reps and develops several "best practices" sales techniques
- Is unshaken by rejections
- Knows when to stop talking
- Knows the precise moment to ask for the order
- Has a great ability to turn prospects into customers
- Stays current with the latest customer relationship management systems
- Asks the most effective closing questions

Fully competent: Meets expectations

- Establishes and reaches challenging sales goals
- Easily deals with difficult customers
- Creates and keeps long-term relationships with customers
- Generates solid results when cold calling
- Knows how and when to sell add-ons
- Meets sales quotas
- Makes great use of sales questions
- Builds rapport
- Follows up regularly
- Regularly analyzes his sales performance and makes continual improvements
- Keeps her commitments
- Actively seeks sales leads
- Is persistent without being a pest

Marginal: Occasionally fails to meet expectations

- Is more interested in meeting her own needs than the needs of the customers
- Talks more than listens

- Arrives at sales calls without necessary materials
- Assumes that all customers are alike
- Has a know-it-all strategy
- Is poorly prepared for presentations
- Pushes products that the customer may not need or want
- Makes promises that can't be kept
- Makes negative comments about the competition
- Sees selling as a confrontation, not a collaboration
- Uses a hard sell that pushes customers away
- Has an inflated view of his own sales abilities
- Is overwhelmed by even the most basic objections
- Doesn't pay enough attention to the XYZ account
- Ignores customers after a sale
- Gets minimal repeat business
- Rarely meets the sales quota

Unsatisfactory: Consistently fails to meet expectations

- Doesn't pay attention to customers
- Takes an adversarial position
- Has lost several valuable customers
- Has an unacceptable sales closing rate
- Rarely lets the customers get a word in
- Misses appointments
- Shows up late for sales calls
- Misses sales quotas
- Has used the same sales presentation for years
- Isn't prepared for sales presentations
- Is overly aggressive
- Isn't persistent enough
- Overlooks opportunities to close sales
- Exercises questionable ethics and judgment

Teamwork

Exceptional: Consistently exceeds expectations

- Generates remarkable results through teamwork
- Turns a group into a team
- Applies in-depth knowledge of team building
- Puts "we" before "me"
- Creates teams when there were none
- Is an ideal team member
- Strengthens the bonds of teamwork among all her fellow employees
- Is an essential member of the team
- Is critical to the team's success
- Is vital to the team
- Exemplifies the essence of teamwork
- Recognizes and builds the unique abilities of each member of the team
- Has superb conflict management skills

Excellent: Frequently exceeds expectations

- Builds teamwork within and between departments
- Creates excellence through teamwork
- Makes the whole greater than the sum of the parts
- Creates a climate of teamwork
- Makes every member of the team feel important
- Is a great team player
- Is an asset to any team
- Is a model member of any team
- Holds the team together through tough projects
- Has an infectious cooperative attitude
- Is a true team builder
- Takes any team up a notch

Fully competent: Meets expectations

- ✔ Builds a sense of teamwork
- ✔ Energizes the team
- ✔ Is a key contributor to the team's success
- ✔ Makes the most of the talents of all team members
- ✔ Sets high expectations for everyone on the team
- ✔ Resolves problems and conflicts within the team
- ✔ Works well with all team members
- ✔ Keeps team members well informed

Marginal: Occasionally fails to meet expectations

- ✔ Focuses more on himself than on the team
- ✔ Has personal interests that conflict with team interests
- ✔ Places personal goals above team goals
- ✔ Cooperates only sporadically
- ✔ Won't help unless there is something in return
- ✔ Cooperates begrudgingly
- ✔ Agrees to cooperate, but rarely does
- ✔ Devotes minimal time and energy to helping others

Unsatisfactory: Consistently fails to meet expectations

- ✔ Is a disruptive influence on team operations
- ✔ Undercuts the cooperative efforts of others
- ✔ Has an uncooperative attitude
- ✔ Constantly pushes her own agenda
- ✔ Is always ready to say "no"
- ✔ Is insensitive to the needs of others
- ✔ Puts "me" before "we"
- ✔ Ignores requests for help
- ✔ Is more likely to clash than cooperate
- ✔ Needs constant reminding to be more cooperative

Telephone Skills

Exceptional: Consistently exceeds expectations

- Has remarkable patience
- Is specifically requested by many callers
- Is always professional
- Is customer-centric 24-7
- Has superb telephone etiquette
- Makes every caller feel special
- Follows up with callers until all matters are resolved
- Receives numerous written and verbal compliments
- Is frequently sought to handle problem calls
- Is highly skilled in dealing with outbound as well as inbound calls
- Finishes calls on a positive note
- Enjoys taking the most difficult and problematic calls
- Has a smile that is apparent to all callers
- Has a file filled with compliments from callers
- Serves as an excellent role model for "best practices" telephone techniques

Excellent: Frequently exceeds expectations

- Makes all callers feel welcome
- Has a smile in her voice
- Has a positive and upbeat style
- Maintains a calm demeanor on all calls
- Has an uncanny ability to quickly and easily build trust
- Has a warm and friendly attitude that comes through
- Is polite throughout every call
- Handles the most difficult calls with great skill
- Tirelessly handles tremendous call volume

Fully competent: Meets expectations

- ✔ Develops great relationships with callers
- ✔ Handles complaints promptly and effectively
- ✔ Is always prompt and courteous
- ✔ Listens carefully
- ✔ Goes out of his way to help every caller
- ✔ Continues to upgrade her telephone skills
- ✔ Provides every caller with VIP service
- ✔ Trains others in telephone skills

Marginal: Occasionally fails to meet expectations

- ✔ Rushes calls
- ✔ Talks too quickly
- ✔ Strands callers on hold
- ✔ Doesn't provide adequate follow-up to callers
- ✔ Has insufficient product knowledge
- ✔ Doesn't always speak clearly
- ✔ Takes too long to answer the phone
- ✔ Is quick to say "no," instead of doing some checking

Unsatisfactory: Consistently fails to meet expectations

- ✔ Is discourteous to callers
- ✔ Makes callers feel unwelcome
- ✔ Can be rude to callers
- ✔ Is prone to arguing
- ✔ Treats callers disrespectfully
- ✔ Has been named in formal complaints from callers
- ✔ Gives any answer, even if it's incorrect
- ✔ Enflames problem situations
- ✔ Regards calls as a nuisance
- ✔ Has a complete lack of product knowledge

Written and Verbal Communication

Exceptional: Consistently exceeds expectations

- ✔ Is a master of written communication
- ✔ Is the go-to person when others need help with writing
- ✔ Has the most readable writing in the company
- ✔ Keeps e-mail messages on target and to the point
- ✔ Has clear, direct, and concise writing
- ✔ Writes without grammatical errors
- ✔ Creates reports and documentation that are consistently outstanding
- ✔ Is a compelling speaker
- ✔ Says more by saying less
- ✔ Actively listens to others
- ✔ Thinks before he talks
- ✔ Uses captivating language
- ✔ Gives highly organized presentations
- ✔ Is a superb public speaker
- ✔ Is totally comfortable in front of a group
- ✔ Is known as the company wordsmith
- ✔ Is a great debater
- ✔ Is a great communicator
- ✔ Is an enthralling speaker who easily holds the attention of others
- ✔ Reads other people well
- ✔ Senses when others are on data overload and when they need more information

Excellent: Frequently exceeds expectations

- ✔ Has very readable writing
- ✔ Hits the perfect level of detail

✔ Writes to the point, rather than around it

✔ Is a gifted writer

✔ Has raised the writing in her department to a new level

✔ Sets the standard for excellent business writing

✔ Proofreads carefully

✔ Carefully crafts all his writing

✔ Is always well organized with her written work

✔ Selects the appropriate writing style for different readers and situations

✔ Holds the interest of others in his writing

✔ Is a clear and articulate communicator

✔ Has an outstanding vocabulary, but never overdoes it

✔ Generates a great deal of interest whenever she speaks

✔ Communicates easily with everyone

✔ Is an excellent writing coach

✔ Effectively reads subtle cues and body language

✔ Is smooth without being slick

Fully competent: Meets expectations

✔ Is confident and comfortable with writing projects

✔ Is at ease and effective in front of a group

✔ Prepares thoroughly before making presentations

✔ Communicates easily with employees at all levels

✔ Is not inclined to talk for the sake of talking

✔ Is a good listener

✔ Uses words effectively and economically

✔ Is clear and informative when speaking or writing

✔ Avoids excessive use of jargon

✔ Writes with very few grammatical errors

Marginal: Occasionally fails to meet expectations

- ✔ Uses a writing style that can be difficult to understand
- ✔ Hasn't shown interest in becoming a better writer
- ✔ Procrastinates on projects that involve writing
- ✔ Sends e-mail messages that are unclear
- ✔ Writes too much on every project
- ✔ Has writing that lacks adequate detail and specificity
- ✔ Doesn't listen carefully enough, and communication suffers as a result
- ✔ Speaks without organizing his thoughts
- ✔ Provides too much detail
- ✔ Doesn't provide enough detail
- ✔ Uses e-mail style for formal written business communications
- ✔ Needs to listen more and talk less

Unsatisfactory: Consistently fails to meet expectations

- ✔ Writes with numerous grammatical errors and typos
- ✔ Takes a long time to get to the point
- ✔ Ignores punctuation
- ✔ Is a grammatical nightmare
- ✔ Tends to ramble
- ✔ Tends to mumble
- ✔ Uses inappropriate terms and expressions
- ✔ Is insensitive to others in her comments
- ✔ Is unaware of messages that his body language is sending
- ✔ Produces work that always needs significant editing
- ✔ Often uses the wrong words
- ✔ Rushes when writing, and it shows
- ✔ Doesn't pay attention to the cues and body language of others
- ✔ Doesn't listen

Chapter 11

The Best Phrases for Planning, Administration, and Organization

. . . .

In This Chapter

▶ Recognizing and enhancing managerial behaviors

▶ Highlighting organizational skills and filling the gaps

▶ Identifying and reinforcing goal attainment

. . . .

*A*s employees pursue challenging goals, they may be bursting with energy and enthusiasm, but their performance can fall terribly short because of issues related to planning, administration, and organization. Such matters are often regarded solely as managerial functions, but the truth is that, every day, employees at every job level are taking specific actions in these arenas, along with numerous related actions to keep their work on track, on target, and on time.

In addition to feedback that is targeted on the employees' planning and organizing skills, there is a real need for feedback in such related areas as managing, meeting deadlines, sticking to schedules, watching costs, establishing goals, and adjusting to change. Feedback in each of these areas provides employees with recognition where due, as well as with direction and encouragement where needed.

Because much of the information that employees receive on matters of planning and organizing is in written form, it's particularly important for written feedback in this area to be clear, focused, and functional. Employees have a wide range of planning and organizational responsibilities, and this chapter provides an equally wide range of performance appraisal phrases to cover employees' performance in each.

Adjusting to Change

Exceptional: Consistently exceeds expectations

- ✔ Not only adjusts to change, but is a key source of change
- ✔ Is a positive change agent
- ✔ Is a quick study when it comes to adapting to change
- ✔ Works with employees to help them understand changes and adjust to them
- ✔ Regards the change process as a source of creativity and innovation
- ✔ Holds brainstorming sessions for the sole purpose of generating needed changes
- ✔ Sees change playing a major role in employee growth and development
- ✔ Regards adaptation to change as a survival skill
- ✔ Doesn't view any of the traditional systems, policies, or procedures as being sacred
- ✔ Creates a climate that encourages and supports change

Excellent: Frequently exceeds expectations

- ✔ Helps other employees adapt to changes
- ✔ Reduces resistance to change by openly communicating about it
- ✔ Has a high degree of intellectual curiosity, and uses it to understand and manage change
- ✔ Has made changes that led to creative solutions to departmental problems
- ✔ Adjusts to changes by studying and understanding them
- ✔ Takes one change and uses it as a springboard for further changes
- ✔ Is an active advocate for change
- ✔ Always seeks better ways to do things

Fully competent: Meets expectations

- ✔ Recognizes the rapid pace of change in the workplace and readily adapts to it
- ✔ Is receptive to new ideas
- ✔ Continues to build his personal knowledge base to be ready for change
- ✔ Digs in and understands changes and the reasons for them
- ✔ Serves as a role model for others in her ability to adjust to change
- ✔ Has an open mind when it comes to new ways of doing things

Marginal: Occasionally fails to meet expectations

- ✔ Reacts first by finding fault with any change
- ✔ Looks for ways to avoid change
- ✔ Makes disparaging remarks about changes
- ✔ Shows resistance to change whenever the opportunity arises
- ✔ Tries to influence others to resist change
- ✔ Keeps talking about how things worked in the past

Unsatisfactory: Consistently fails to meet expectations

- ✔ Refuses to give change a chance
- ✔ Makes disparaging remarks about individuals who suggest or implement changes
- ✔ Will not give up his old way of doing things
- ✔ Sabotages new programs, processes, or procedures
- ✔ Makes false claims about specific changes
- ✔ Taunts co-workers who accept changes
- ✔ Becomes visibly upset when changes are discussed
- ✔ Is highly vocal in expressing disdain for changes
- ✔ Refuses to use new methods, strategies, systems, or technologies

Bottom-Line Orientation

Exceptional: Consistently exceeds expectations

- Generates excellent ideas for increasing revenue as well as cutting costs
- Has made suggestions that have clearly had a positive impact on the bottom line
- Makes direct contributions to the company's profit
- Is fully dedicated to the company's success
- Builds a strong bottom-line orientation among her employees
- Creates and implements strategies to enhance the bottom line
- Has taken a wide range of actions to cut wasteful expenditures
- Takes specific actions to improve earnings before interest, taxes, depreciation, and amortization
- Establishes goals that are directly linked to the bottom line

Excellent: Frequently exceeds expectations

- Builds an increased bottom-line understanding and focus among his employees
- Is profit-minded
- Understands and implements solid financial planning
- Takes a wide range of steps to improve profit
- Is very comfortable reading and analyzing financial data
- Has a solid understanding of balance sheets and income statements
- Has turned her area into a profit center
- Has implemented changes in production, design, systems, or strategies that have helped the bottom line
- Implements employee incentives and motivational programs that help increase productivity

Fully competent: Meets expectations

- ✔ Never loses sight of the bottom line
- ✔ Works with employees to streamline operations and save money
- ✔ Discusses bottom-line issues with employees
- ✔ Works with his employees to develop "best practices" strategies
- ✔ Helps employees understand the link between their performance and the company's financial success
- ✔ Is always on the lookout for steps, strategies, and programs to improve profit
- ✔ Helps all employees understand the ways in which they can contribute to the bottom line
- ✔ Stays current with financial news that impacts the company and the industry at large

Marginal: Occasionally fails to meet expectations

- ✔ Takes few steps that actually contribute to the company's profits
- ✔ Talks about her contribution to the bottom line, but the numbers don't show it
- ✔ Does little to build employees' financial knowledge and skills
- ✔ Shows little interest in the company's financial condition
- ✔ Does nothing with financial data when presented with it

Unsatisfactory: Consistently fails to meet expectations

- ✔ Makes unnecessary costly purchases
- ✔ Engages in behaviors that hurt the bottom line
- ✔ Regards the bottom line as someone else's concern
- ✔ Implements new programs without considering their impact on the bottom line
- ✔ Doesn't look at any lines, including the bottom line
- ✔ Is not interested in the bottom line

Controlling Costs

Exceptional: Consistently exceeds expectations

- Is highly cost conscious in every decision
- Is excellent at projecting costs
- Creates highly effective systems and processes to monitor and control costs
- Is financially astute
- Has developed a high degree of cost consciousness among his employees
- Keeps the company's financial goals clearly in mind
- Generates significant savings by implementing sustainability programs
- Encourages and rewards cost-saving suggestions from her employees
- Creates and implements highly productive cost-saving practices, policies, and programs

Excellent: Frequently exceeds expectations

- Develops financial management skills in others
- Places a high priority on cost-benefit analysis in his thinking and decision-making
- Maintains excellent financial control
- Is budget-minded
- Negotiates fees effectively and professionally
- Has an excellent ability to focus on the big financial picture as well as the details
- Digs deeply into the numbers and finds additional ways to control costs
- Is fiscally conservative, but not cheap
- Accurately analyzes costs
- Avoids wasting money, materials, or resources

Fully competent: Meets expectations

- Monitors department expenses daily
- Has a demonstrated ability to control departmental costs
- Carefully monitors and controls costs, and encourages her employees to do the same
- Effectively manages the financial side of the job
- Operates within the budget
- Clearly communicates cost-related issues to his employees

Marginal: Occasionally fails to meet expectations

- Rarely considers cost when making decisions
- Lets costs slip out of control
- Approves invoices without reading them carefully
- Rarely pays attention to costs
- Is too liberal with company money
- Is too quick to cut expenses
- Cuts expenses without adequate consideration of consequences
- Is overly aggressive when cutting costs

Unsatisfactory: Consistently fails to meet expectations

- Lets costs run totally out of control
- Makes purchases without approval
- Overlooks the budget
- Is unable to develop a workable budget
- Ignores the expense reimbursement policy
- Ignores per-diem travel allowance guidelines
- Approves any expense
- Regards the company credit card as a gift card
- Puts a budgetary stranglehold on the department
- Starts cutting costs and doesn't know when to stop
- Cuts expenses to the point that customers suffer

Establishing Goals

Exceptional: Consistently exceeds expectations

- ✔ Sets rigorous goals for herself
- ✔ Builds the employees' goal-setting skills
- ✔ Works with employees to set challenging and motivational goals
- ✔ Establishes a goal-oriented mindset among his employees
- ✔ Jointly creates goals that bring out the best performance in others
- ✔ Works with employees to tailor developmental goals to their needs
- ✔ Has raised the standards for goal setting throughout the department
- ✔ Establishes goals that are aligned with her manager's goals
- ✔ Is an expert in setting goals
- ✔ Develops user-friendly strategies to help employees meet their goals
- ✔ Generates enthusiasm around the goal-setting process

Excellent: Frequently exceeds expectations

- ✔ Approaches goal-setting with positive expectations
- ✔ Establishes checkpoints and deadlines for every goal
- ✔ Has insight into employees as individuals that contributes to their buy-in and commitment
- ✔ Serves as a model for others with his goal-setting strategy
- ✔ Includes well-crafted action plans and strategies in her goal setting

Fully competent: Meets expectations

- ✔ Establishes challenging goals
- ✔ Sets specific and measurable goals

✔ Sets goals for performance and development

✔ Works with employees to set goals

✔ Attaches priorities to every goal

✔ Regards goal setting as a major priority

✔ Sets goals based on facts

✔ Helps employees write and refine their goals

✔ Creates action plans that are clear and functional

Marginal: Occasionally fails to meet expectations

✔ Establishes vague goals

✔ Creates easily attainable goals

✔ Sets reasonable goals, but fails to aggressively pursue them

✔ Primarily establishes low-priority goals

✔ Sets goals at the last minute

✔ Sets goals for employees without their input

✔ Devotes very little time to establishing goals

✔ Regards goal setting as a process for others to carry out

✔ Focuses on goals that have little to do with the company's goals

Unsatisfactory: Consistently fails to meet expectations

✔ Creates goals off the top of his head

✔ Creates goals that pose no significant challenge

✔ Comes up with the same goals every year

✔ Sets goals without any provision for follow-up

✔ Sets goals that lack action plans

✔ Fails to establish clear and measurable goals

✔ Provides employees with no guidance or support in goal setting

✔ Treats goal setting as a cut-and-paste activity

✔ Establishes impossible goals

Management Skills

Exceptional: Consistently exceeds expectations

- ✔ Builds the managerial skills of her peers
- ✔ Develops high-performing teams
- ✔ Selects and hires outstanding individuals
- ✔ Has A-level coaching skills
- ✔ Values the employees' ideas and suggestions
- ✔ Treats all employees with respect and trust
- ✔ Is up-to-date on the latest management practices
- ✔ Is the resident expert on management
- ✔ Maintains ongoing two-way communication with his team
- ✔ Remains calm and steady under pressure
- ✔ Manages by wandering around
- ✔ Has totally transformed a formerly chaotic department

Excellent: Frequently exceeds expectations

- ✔ Stays current on new developments in the field of management
- ✔ Is continuously developing her employees
- ✔ Treats employees as valued resources
- ✔ Has very low turnover in his department
- ✔ Creates highly effective motivational and incentive programs
- ✔ Understands her employees as individuals
- ✔ Encourages and supports employee learning and growth
- ✔ Keeps the employees well informed
- ✔ Has the highest standards of fairness

Fully competent: Meets expectations

- ✔ Listens to his employees
- ✔ Identifies with management

- Is responsive to all employees
- Adheres to company standards and policies
- Reads management books and magazines
- Is more proactive than reactive
- Is team oriented

Marginal: Occasionally fails to meet expectations

- Is rarely accessible
- Relies on antiquated programs and strategies
- Micromanages in every situation
- Hoards responsibilities that should be delegated
- Ignores employees
- Keeps employees uninformed and out of the loop
- Demands respect instead of earning it
- Provides minimal thanks, credit, and recognition

Unsatisfactory: Consistently fails to meet expectations

- Plays favorites
- Demands that everything be done her way
- Takes no steps to train or develop employees
- Is inaccessible
- Blames employees for failures
- Takes credit for the employees' success
- Treats employees as expendable
- Yells at employees
- Has a high rate of turnover
- Has a high rate of accidents
- Has a high rate of absenteeism
- Shows minimal concern for employee health and welfare
- Is overly controlling
- Bullies employees

Meeting Deadlines

Exceptional: Consistently exceeds expectations

- Plans and organizes to beat deadlines, rather than meet them
- Never misses a deadline
- Completes work ahead of deadlines
- Is energized by tight deadlines
- Remains unshaken by demanding deadlines
- Keeps his employees highly focused on the deadlines
- Approaches demanding deadlines with a calm and steady resolve
- Would miss just about anything before missing a deadline

Excellent: Frequently exceeds expectations

- Regards deadlines as a top priority
- Does whatever has to be done to meet deadlines
- Plans work to avoid last-minute crunches
- Meets deadlines without sacrificing quality
- Never loses sight of the deadlines
- Establishes realistic deadlines and meets them
- Plans and organizes work to consistently meet deadlines
- Treats deadlines as goal lines

Fully competent: Meets expectations

- Prioritizes work to meet high-priority deadlines
- Meets every major deadline
- Carefully monitors the progress of her employees to be sure that deadlines are met
- Is deadline oriented
- Communicates openly about deadlines
- Has contingency plans if unexpected obstacles get in the way

✔ Meets deadlines that he commits to

✔ Takes deadlines very seriously

✔ Is highly committed to meeting deadlines

Marginal: Occasionally fails to meet expectations

✔ Meets many deadlines, but with questionable quality of work

✔ Meets lower-priority deadlines, while neglecting major deadlines

✔ Waits until the last minute and then notices deadlines

✔ Makes promises about deadlines but doesn't take them seriously

✔ Turns most deadline situations into crises

✔ Gets sidetracked and misses deadlines

✔ Misses deadlines because of her inadequate planning

✔ Occasionally panics under the pressure of deadlines

✔ Is far too lax when it comes to meeting deadlines

Unsatisfactory: Consistently fails to meet expectations

✔ Has missed every major deadline

✔ Misses more deadlines than he meets

✔ Gets close to many deadlines, but meets few

✔ Makes excuses rather than deadlines

✔ Regards deadlines as suggestions

✔ Loses sight of the deadlines

✔ Misses deadlines and blames others

✔ Causes delays, instead of planning for them

✔ Runs late and tells no one

✔ Sets impossible deadlines

✔ Sets extremely lax deadlines

✔ Shows minimal concern when deadlines are missed

✔ Has no sense of urgency

Organizing

Exceptional: Consistently exceeds expectations

- ✔ Runs a highly organized department
- ✔ Organized a totally chaotic department
- ✔ Organizes for the short term and the long term
- ✔ Brings outstanding organization to all projects

Excellent: Frequently exceeds expectations

- ✔ Is highly regarded for her organizational skills
- ✔ Organizes projects to prevent overlaps or gaps in responsibilities
- ✔ Is always able to access needed items or information
- ✔ Logically organizes his work and work area

Fully competent: Meets expectations

- ✔ Helps co-workers get organized and stay organized
- ✔ Sets aside time regularly to organize work
- ✔ Has her own system for organizing, and it works
- ✔ Uses a highly effective organizing system

Marginal: Occasionally fails to meet expectations

- ✔ Is more concerned with being organized than getting the job done
- ✔ Has an organizing system that is so personalized that it's incomprehensible
- ✔ Has a work area that is a giant mess

Unsatisfactory: Consistently fails to meet expectations

- ✔ Suffers from a lack of organization in every aspect of his work
- ✔ Can spend hours looking for items that should take seconds to find
- ✔ Is the least organized person in the company

Planning

Exceptional: Consistently exceeds expectations

- ✔ Is highly skilled at generating employee buy-in on plans she establishes
- ✔ Is truly a master planner
- ✔ Helps others to develop and implement plans
- ✔ Is well regarded for his planning skills
- ✔ Is systems minded
- ✔ Establishes plans, policies, and practices that improve performance and productivity
- ✔ Establishes contingencies when situations require the plans to be altered or refined
- ✔ Establishes realistic plans
- ✔ Is typically well ahead of plan when it comes to progress and performance
- ✔ Sets plans for success and then effectively implements them
- ✔ Is equally skilled at long-term and short-term planning
- ✔ Involves employees in the planning process

Excellent: Frequently exceeds expectations

- ✔ Sets realistic plans
- ✔ Establishes plans that are down to earth and workable
- ✔ Sets a standard for planning that others are inclined to follow
- ✔ Effectively communicates plans to all who need to know
- ✔ Makes plans, but is never overwhelmed by them
- ✔ Makes the best use of technology to establish and communicate plans

Fully competent: Meets expectations

- ✔ Stays on plan and helps others to do the same
- ✔ Monitors plans and progress every day

✔ Creates plans that are thorough without being cumbersome

✔ Develops strategies, but never loses sight of the goal

✔ Lets others know when plans need to be changed or adjusted

✔ Supports plans with all the necessary documentation

✔ Leaves very little to chance

Marginal: Occasionally fails to meet expectations

✔ Creates plans that are so detailed that they stifle the employees

✔ Tends to make plans at the last minute

✔ Establishes unrealistic plans

✔ Plans for the expected outcome, instead of planning for the unexpected

✔ Makes derogatory comments about the planning process

✔ Waits for problems, instead of anticipating them

✔ Waits until the last minute to determine the necessary resources, which by then are often unavailable

✔ Shows minimal interest in planning

Unsatisfactory: Consistently fails to meet expectations

✔ Leaves everything to chance

✔ Does not believe in planning

✔ Establishes unworkable plans

✔ Creates plans that are skimpy and unusable

✔ Regards planning as a waste of time

✔ Takes a wait-and-see approach on every project

✔ Fails to plan, leading to failure

✔ Relies on yesterday's plans

✔ Believes that she doesn't need to plan

✔ Ignores the established plans

✔ Commits to formulate plans, but then does nothing

Setting and Adhering to Schedules

Exceptional: Consistently exceeds expectations

✔ Maintains the perfect level of detail when scheduling

✔ Has a clear understanding of the projects and the players, which leads to highly effective scheduling

✔ Uses state-of-the-art scheduling systems and technology

✔ Stays ahead of schedule

✔ Works with his team to stay ahead of schedule

✔ Creates schedules that include contingency plans to deal with the unexpected

✔ Solicits employee inputs when establishing schedules

✔ Regularly communicates on scheduling updates, adjustments, and realignments

✔ Carefully balances the needs of the employees with the needs of the company

✔ Is meticulous in establishing schedules

Excellent: Frequently exceeds expectations

✔ Regularly follows up to be sure that work is being performed on schedule

✔ Sets schedules that lead to timely delivery of high-quality work

✔ Establishes schedules that are clear, logical, and reasonable

✔ Builds employee motivation and commitment to stay on schedule

✔ Helps employees to get back on schedule

✔ Creates outstanding scheduling based on outstanding planning

✔ Operates on schedule or ahead of schedule

Fully competent: Meets expectations

- ✔ Consistently upgrades her scheduling skills
- ✔ Creates realistic schedules
- ✔ Keeps his team on schedule
- ✔ Develops the scheduling skills of her employees
- ✔ Gives regular status updates
- ✔ Pays attention to requests for schedule changes

Marginal: Occasionally fails to meet expectations

- ✔ Waits for others to do the scheduling
- ✔ Sets unworkable schedules
- ✔ Schedules at the last minute
- ✔ Sets schedules, but fails to track progress along the way
- ✔ Frequently changes the schedule
- ✔ Changes schedules without communicating with others
- ✔ Uses antiquated scheduling practices
- ✔ Confines his scheduling to scraps of paper
- ✔ Has taken no steps to upgrade her scheduling skills
- ✔ Regards schedules as loose guidelines
- ✔ Has difficulties staying on schedule
- ✔ Has overly rigid scheduling practices

Unsatisfactory: Consistently fails to meet expectations

- ✔ Is inflexible with scheduling
- ✔ Sets schedules at the last minute, if at all
- ✔ Establishes schedules, and then disregards them
- ✔ Is regularly behind schedule
- ✔ Has yet to complete a project ahead of schedule
- ✔ Ignores all schedules
- ✔ Creates schedules that are too vague to be useful
- ✔ Sets schedules that appear to be random

Chapter 12

The Best Phrases for Leadership

*L*eadership is about influencing others to reach established goals. As such, it's one of the most critical roles in any company. Leadership maintains the vision, values, culture, objectives, and standards for the company, and when leadership is in doubt, the company is in trouble.

As a result, accurately appraising the leadership skills of anyone who plays a leadership role is critical. This stretches from upper management all the way to employees who have no formal leadership titles but carry out occasional leadership functions, such as chairing a committee or running an event. If you look at all your employees, you'll see that many of them have leadership responsibilities, regardless of their titles.

Leadership isn't a one-dimensional behavior that's either present or not. Instead, it's an amalgam of many functions — including such leadership-related responsibilities as motivating employees, building employees' skills, providing feedback, screening and hiring, managing conflict, coaching, making decisions, delegating, and more — all of which need to be reviewed as part of a thorough performance appraisal.

In light of the critical role that leadership plays in any organization, choosing the right words in the appraisal process is important — not only for the success of your employees, but for the success of your company as well.

Building a Team

Exceptional: Consistently exceeds expectations

- ✔ Has outstanding team-building skills
- ✔ Builds a team-oriented attitude among all her employees
- ✔ Has taken a marginally functional department and converted it into a highly productive team
- ✔ Uses specific exercises to further strengthen his team
- ✔ Manages a department that is well known for its high level of teamwork
- ✔ Has an extraordinary ability to turn a group into a team
- ✔ Pulls employees together into a cooperative, supportive, and highly successful team
- ✔ Creates a team-oriented environment

Excellent: Frequently exceeds expectations

- ✔ Possesses a strong goal orientation, which contributes to the solidarity and focus of her employees
- ✔ Develops a winning attitude among his employees
- ✔ Structures projects and assignments to further strengthen teamwork among her employees
- ✔ Makes all employees feel that they're valued members of the team
- ✔ Implements a broad range of special activities that further strengthen his team
- ✔ Uses a team approach to develop and utilize the unique talents of each employee

Fully competent: Meets expectations

- ✔ Recognizes and rewards team-oriented behaviors and actions
- ✔ Consistently emphasizes the importance of teamwork in the department and company at large
- ✔ Is highly effective in bonding employees together

- Is a solid team player
- Builds highly productive teams
- Generates positive measurable outcomes as a result of teamwork
- Sets consistently high expectations regarding teamwork among her employees

Marginal: Occasionally fails to meet expectations

- Has minimal concern for teamwork, which is sensed by his employees and evident in their behavior
- Makes public comments that place employees in conflict with each other
- Doesn't differentiate between healthy competition and conflict
- Undercuts teambuilding by providing preferential treatment to certain employees
- Rarely takes action to deal with conflicts or disagreements among her employees
- Makes overlapping assignments that create conflict
- Takes no action to deal with disruptive employees
- Needs to focus less on team activities and more on team productivity

Unsatisfactory: Consistently fails to meet expectations

- Engaged in behaviors that turned a successful team into several splintered factions
- Provides no recognition or rewards for teamwork
- Stays physically removed from his employees
- Never works with the group as a whole
- Communicates to the group primarily through reprimands
- Makes no effort to be part of the team
- Focuses on her own needs, rather than on the needs of the team
- Interrupts team meetings with comments and behaviors that are far off topic

Coaching

Exceptional: Consistently exceeds expectations

- ✔ Works with employees on an individual and group basis to build skills and performance
- ✔ Provides ongoing guidance and training
- ✔ Recognizes outstanding performance
- ✔ Is more inclined to coach than to discipline
- ✔ Is widely regarded as a source of excellent advice
- ✔ Develops formal coaching plans for individual employees as needed
- ✔ Uses a variety of highly productive coaching techniques

Excellent: Frequently exceeds expectations

- ✔ Tailors coaching techniques to best fit his employees
- ✔ Uses coaching techniques that build motivation and enthusiasm
- ✔ Uses a coaching style that bonds employees together
- ✔ Knows when and how to coach in public as well as in private
- ✔ Provides excellent follow-up to monitor the results of her coaching
- ✔ Accurately tracks and measures the effectiveness of his coaching
- ✔ Utilizes a coaching style that involves and energizes her employees

Fully competent: Meets expectations

- ✔ Truly enjoys the coaching side of the job
- ✔ Regards coaching as a key part of his job
- ✔ Has helped employees meet their performance objectives as well as their developmental objectives through coaching
- ✔ Helps employees learn to coach themselves in many areas

- Uses innovative coaching strategies to generate measurable improvements in employee performance
- Is regarded by employees as a first-rate coach
- Creates a winning atmosphere with her coaching style
- Is genuinely committed to working with employees to build skills and solve problems
- Provides employees with the tools and guidance they need to succeed

Marginal: Occasionally fails to meet expectations

- Is more inclined to discipline than coach
- Frequently reprimands and rarely recognizes employees
- Has a sink-or-swim mentality in practically every situation
- Provides employees with far more information than they can absorb
- Acts more like a critic than a coach
- Regards coaching as a one-way process, and rarely listens to employees
- Provides minimal follow-up after coaching
- Quickly becomes impatient when trying to coach
- Uses a one-size-fits-all style of coaching

Unsatisfactory: Consistently fails to meet expectations

- Ignores the coaching side of the job
- Believes that ridicule is part of coaching
- Equates coaching with lecturing
- Focuses coaching on areas that are of secondary interest and importance
- Bases coaching on inadequate data
- Lets favoritism influence his coaching practices and techniques
- Turns coaching into nagging
- Coaches employees as if they were children

Delegating

Exceptional: Consistently exceeds expectations

- ✓ Uses delegating as a means to enhance employee skills
- ✓ Effectively manages her time by delegating work
- ✓ Uses delegation as a method to build employee performance and confidence
- ✓ Provides employees with the tools, resources, and support to successfully complete the projects he delegates
- ✓ Has successfully increased productivity through her delegating practices
- ✓ Builds a stronger team through his delegation strategies
- ✓ Delegates in a way that sends a message of trust and respect to employees

Excellent: Frequently exceeds expectations

- ✓ Carefully reviews projects and personnel prior to delegating
- ✓ Appropriately delegates work to individuals and teams
- ✓ Monitors employee performance without stifling it
- ✓ Has excellent insight into the kinds of projects that should and should not be delegated
- ✓ Understands how much independence and autonomy can be granted to each employee
- ✓ Is able to put faltering delegated projects back on track
- ✓ Includes delegation as part of the employee development program
- ✓ Provides employees with a clear understanding of the standards, expectations, and goals on projects that she delegates

Fully competent: Meets expectations

- ✓ Delegates and follows up
- ✓ Has had considerable success with projects that he has delegated

- Knows when and how to delegate
- Delegates and then provides coaching, guidance, and feedback as needed
- Monitors employee performance after delegating work
- Grants employees authority to get the job done
- Accurately monitors and measures the status of the projects that she delegates
- Understands employees' strengths and weaknesses, and keeps them in mind when delegating

Marginal: Occasionally fails to meet expectations

- Needs to review delegated projects more frequently, instead of waiting until such projects are completed
- Delegates, but then intervenes
- Totally redoes work that he delegates
- Provides inadequate information regarding standards and expectations on work she delegates
- Delegates work, but provides employees with minimal freedom to carry it out
- Delegates projects, but can't really let go of them
- Only delegates the most trivial work

Unsatisfactory: Consistently fails to meet expectations

- Delegates work that he should do himself
- Delegates too much work
- Fails to follow up on delegated work
- Delegates work and essentially never looks at it again
- Refuses to delegate anything
- Is afraid to delegate
- Keeps changing her mind about expectations and objectives after projects have been delegated
- Insists on controlling projects that he delegates

Inspiring Enthusiasm and Commitment

Exceptional: Consistently exceeds expectations

- ✔ Has a genuinely positive attitude that spreads across her department
- ✔ Energizes others with his upbeat outlook
- ✔ Serves as a model for her fellow employees with her energy and expectations
- ✔ Consistently makes extraordinary efforts to achieve extraordinary results
- ✔ Makes major sacrifices to help the company
- ✔ Frequently expresses his appreciation of the opportunities provided by the company
- ✔ Consistently surpasses expectations and standards, leading to similar behaviors from her fellow employees
- ✔ Creates a culture of positive energy and loyalty

Excellent: Frequently exceeds expectations

- ✔ Maintains an upbeat and positive attitude, and draws the same out of others
- ✔ Is bursting with contagious enthusiasm
- ✔ Helps turn around negative situations with his enthusiasm and optimism
- ✔ Is genuinely excited about her work
- ✔ Never misses an opportunity to build goodwill for the company, both internally and externally
- ✔ Is willing to go the extra mile and encourages others to follow his lead

Fully competent: Meets expectations

- ✔ Is able to make any project more interesting and rewarding
- ✔ Makes it difficult for others to slack off because of her sheer enthusiasm, energy, and drive

- Puts in long hours and works hard, inspiring many of his employees to do the same
- Seizes every opportunity to make positive comments about the company
- Generates suggestions rather than complaints
- Is always looking for ways to improve performance, productivity, and the company itself

Marginal: Occasionally fails to meet expectations

- Enflames problematic situations
- Encourages fellow employees to rock the boat
- Regards the company as the opposition
- Does the minimum amount of work
- Frequently talks about how much better things are at other companies
- Is always looking for a reason to miss work
- Frequently says "no," and encourages others to do the same

Unsatisfactory: Consistently fails to meet expectations

- Places job responsibilities a distant second behind other interests and pursuits
- Speaks negatively about the company
- Is indifferent to developments in the company
- Ridicules employees who show energy and enthusiasm
- Looks for problems rather than solutions
- Is a constant source of complaints
- Puts a negative spin on company policies, programs, and developments
- Is always looking for ways to do less for the company
- Fabricates malicious stories about her co-workers and/or the company at large
- Shows the most excitement when the workday is drawing to a close

Making Decisions

Exceptional: Consistently exceeds expectations

- Uses participative decision making when appropriate
- Bases decisions on facts
- Gathers the facts and relies on them
- Is sensitive to time constraints when making decisions
- Approaches decision making with an open mind
- Is well regarded as a first-rate decision maker
- Clearly understands the costs and benefits of his decisions
- Is receptive to innovative ideas and suggestions
- Conducts thorough research prior to making major decisions

Excellent: Frequently exceeds expectations

- Truly values the input of other employees
- Makes difficult decisions that measurably improve operations
- Deliberates on decisions, but never overlooks the time and timing
- Involves employees in many decisions that affect them and their work
- Acts decisively, but not impulsively
- Makes unilateral decisions when needed
- Shares the credit when decisions generate excellent outcomes
- Accepts responsibility if decisions don't yield desired outcomes

Fully competent: Meets expectations

- Separates significant data from insignificant data
- Makes timely decisions
- Is trusted by her employees when it comes to decision making

- Takes decision-making responsibilities seriously
- Is able to clearly explain the rationale behind his decisions
- Relies on facts rather than emotions
- Keeps the good of the company in mind
- Reaches decisions that are fair, ethical, and trusted

Marginal: Occasionally fails to meet expectations

- Turns every decision into a group decision
- Takes too much time to make a decision
- Is overly influenced by insignificant details
- Lets corporate politics play too great a role
- Tends to waver back and forth
- Ignores most input from others
- Makes snap decisions
- Relies on questionable sources
- Is overly influenced by emotions
- Is easily swayed by others
- Procrastinates on important decisions

Unsatisfactory: Consistently fails to meet expectations

- Has difficulty making decisions
- Has made a string of questionable decisions
- Ignores the facts
- Acts impulsively on major decisions
- Labors excessively long on minor decisions
- Asks for input from others, and then ignores it
- Insists that everything be done her way
- Lets bias and stereotypes influence decision making
- Enters decision making with a closed mind
- Ignores ideas that differ from his
- Abandons her decisions at the first sign of a challenge

Managing Conflict

Exceptional: Consistently exceeds expectations

- Creatively resolves conflicts
- Productively guides conflicts to generate innovative ideas
- Understands conflicts and manages them effectively
- Uses team-building strategies to resolve conflicts
- Manages conflict, instead of letting conflict manage him
- Recognizes the inevitability of conflict and applies the most effective strategies to manage it
- Is truly gifted in getting to the heart of the matter and resolving it
- Is known for being fair, level-headed, and honest when dealing with conflicts

Excellent: Frequently exceeds expectations

- Defuses conflict situations before they erupt
- Prevents conflicts from escalating
- Builds conflict management skills among her employees
- Varies his conflict management strategies to best fit the situation
- Has solid mediation and arbitration skills
- Successfully mediates interpersonal conflicts
- Identifies potential conflict situations and takes proactive steps to deal with them
- Is frequently sought to resolve conflicts

Fully competent: Meets expectations

- Remains calm and focused in conflict situations
- Is sensitive to conflict situations and acts promptly to deal with them

✔ Separates causes from symptoms in resolving conflicts

✔ Listens carefully to all disputants

✔ Takes a fair and level-headed approach

✔ Isn't afraid to get involved when conflicts arise

✔ Continuously works to improve her conflict management skills

✔ Has sought out and obtained training in conflict management

✔ Is skilled in preventing, as well as dealing with, conflict

Marginal: Occasionally fails to meet expectations

✔ Creates more conflicts than he solves

✔ Sweeps conflicts under the rug

✔ Insists on having her way in all situations

✔ Tries to impose his will in every conflict situation

✔ Is uncommunicative in conflict situations

✔ Fails to actively address conflict situations

✔ Creates win-lose situations rather than win-win situations

✔ Lets conflicts fester for too long

Unsatisfactory: Consistently fails to meet expectations

✔ Is a source of conflict wherever she goes

✔ Puts employees into conflicts with each other

✔ Implements policies and practices that cause conflicts between departments

✔ Shows favoritism in dealing with conflict situations

✔ Fails to listen carefully to all sides

✔ Argues more than he listens

✔ Develops projects and assignments that create conflicts

✔ Has a management style that generates conflicts

✔ Creates conflicts in situations where there haven't been any

Motivating Employees

Exceptional: Consistently exceeds expectations

- ✔ Successfully implements a broad range of motivational programs
- ✔ Treats employees as individuals and focuses on their unique motivations
- ✔ Establishes programs in which employees meet their needs while pursuing departmental goals
- ✔ Provides employees with opportunities to fulfill their needs for achievement and accomplishment
- ✔ Inspires others with her motivation and drive
- ✔ Relies on different motivators for different employees
- ✔ Is a truly motivational speaker
- ✔ Has outstanding observational skills, which contribute to strong motivational strategies

Excellent: Frequently exceeds expectations

- ✔ Implements creative recognition programs
- ✔ Energizes seemingly unmotivated employees
- ✔ Eliminates key sources of employee dissatisfaction
- ✔ Successfully motivates employees by enriching their jobs
- ✔ Knows when and how to use money as a motivator
- ✔ Builds employee motivation by building the employees' skills
- ✔ Has a great deal of insight and understanding when it comes to employee motivation
- ✔ Has raised employee motivation to new heights

Fully competent: Meets expectations

- ✔ Links meaningful rewards to desired behaviors
- ✔ Energizes others with his enthusiasm
- ✔ Continues to develop her motivational skills

✔ Offers a variety of programs to tap employees' individual motivations

✔ Has creative ideas regarding new ways to motivate employees

✔ Uses positive feedback as a powerful motivator

✔ Creates an energizing and uplifting work atmosphere

✔ Builds self-motivation in his employees

Marginal: Occasionally fails to meet expectations

✔ Treats employees as if they all have the same motivations

✔ Asks for employee ideas and suggestions on motivational programs, and then ignores them

✔ Establishes motivational programs that fit her needs rather than the employees' needs

✔ Uses outdated motivational practices

✔ Provides employees with random rewards

✔ Uses overly competitive motivational programs that undermine unity and teamwork

✔ Has only a minimal understanding of what truly motivates his employees

Unsatisfactory: Consistently fails to meet expectations

✔ Uses fear as a motivator

✔ Creates an aura of fear that dissatisfies her employees

✔ Has caused highly motivated employees to shut down

✔ Has a lack of self-motivation, which interferes with the motivation of his employees

✔ Undermines employee motivation with arbitrary treatment

✔ Provides employees with feedback on their performance only after long delays

✔ Has no interest in learning about motivation or being a better motivator

✔ Has a motivational style based primarily on bullying

Proactive Behaviors

Exceptional: Consistently exceeds expectations

- Anticipates problems and takes steps to prevent them
- Is always thinking two steps ahead
- Made the XYZ project successful because of her proactive thinking

Excellent: Frequently exceeds expectations

- Prepares for the unexpected
- Has an eye for potential barriers and blockages
- Creates strategies today that prevent problems tomorrow
- Builds a proactive mindset among his employees

Fully competent: Meets expectations

- Establishes contingency plans
- Has a proactive mindset
- Acts on situations before they turn into problems
- Works with associates to prevent future problems

Marginal: Occasionally fails to meet expectations

- Only plans for expected outcomes
- Takes a wait-and-see approach
- Is frequently caught off-guard by unexpected outcomes
- Acts more like a spectator than a participant

Unsatisfactory: Consistently fails to meet expectations

- Is reactive instead of proactive
- Waits until tomorrow to plan for tomorrow
- Moves from one preventable crisis to another
- Contributed to the failure of the XYZ project because she wasn't proactive

Providing Feedback

Exceptional: Consistently exceeds expectations

- ✔ Provides feedback as close as possible to the behavior in question
- ✔ Makes excellent use of positive feedback
- ✔ Is always constructive when providing negative feedback
- ✔ Includes specific examples in his feedback
- ✔ Provides a great deal of recognition when merited
- ✔ Provides positive feedback in public, and negative feedback in private
- ✔ Uses feedback as a powerful tool to educate her employees
- ✔ Makes employees feel coached rather than disciplined
- ✔ Always concludes negative feedback with positive expectations

Excellent: Frequently exceeds expectations

- ✔ Doesn't create a lengthy delay between performance and feedback
- ✔ Teaches others how to provide effective feedback
- ✔ Provides performance-based negative feedback without destroying the employees or his working relationship with them
- ✔ Takes extra steps to be sure that her employees understand the feedback
- ✔ Provides constructive feedback that helps employees learn, grow, and improve their performance
- ✔ Consistently gives feedback that is fair and factual
- ✔ Displays a great deal of empathy when designing and delivering feedback

Fully competent: Meets expectations

- ✔ Provides appropriate feedback based on employee performance

✔ Is sensitive to employees and situations when providing feedback

✔ Gives feedback that is clear and specific

✔ Picks the right venues for providing feedback

✔ Includes corrective actions when providing negative feedback

✔ Is becoming increasingly effective in providing feedback

✔ Listens to employees while providing them with feedback

✔ Goes to great lengths to provide constructive feedback

Marginal: Occasionally fails to meet expectations

✔ Waits too long to provide feedback

✔ Rarely provides thanks, credit, or recognition

✔ Misses too many opportunities to provide feedback

✔ Gives feedback that is too general to be useful

✔ Tends to be more destructive than constructive in the feedback he gives

✔ Is reluctant to provide negative feedback

✔ Tends to label employees during feedback sessions

✔ Is long on negative feedback and short on positive feedback

Unsatisfactory: Consistently fails to meet expectations

✔ Gives feedback that is unnecessarily harsh

✔ Gives feedback based more on impressions than facts

✔ Reprimands employees in public

✔ Ignores employees' comments or explanations

✔ Never recognizes her employees' successes

✔ Is quick to provide negative feedback

✔ Is overly harsh with certain employees

✔ Gives feedback that has a degrading and insulting tone

✔ Avoids providing negative feedback

Screening and Hiring

Exceptional: Consistently exceeds expectations

- Identifies, screens, and selects outstanding employees
- Always adheres to all pre-employment rulings, guidelines, and laws
- Attracts outstanding job candidates
- Bases decisions on thorough and complete job-related information
- Only asks job-related pre-employment questions
- Treats all job applicants extremely well
- Listens and observes carefully during the interview process
- Spends more time listening than talking during job interviews
- Bases job requirements on skills and abilities that are truly required to perform the job well

Excellent: Frequently exceeds expectations

- Makes every applicant feel welcome
- Treats all applicants fairly
- Knows when to talk and when to listen
- Bases decisions on the applicant's work history
- Is fully committed to maintaining diversity
- Has full knowledge of equal employment opportunity guidelines
- Uses a structured interview format
- Takes time to prepare before every interview
- Never loses outstanding applicants

Fully competent: Meets expectations

- Treats all applicants fairly and equally
- Takes notes during the interview process

✔ Gathers thorough and complete information

✔ Clearly explains job responsibilities to each applicant

✔ Effectively answers all questions about the company

✔ Delves into every gap in the applicants' work histories

✔ Avoids interruptions during job interviews

✔ Takes job-related references prior to offering employment

Marginal: Occasionally fails to meet expectations

✔ Asks "pet questions" that are unrelated to the job

✔ Conducts totally unstructured interviews that generate questionable information

✔ Makes snap decisions

✔ Bases hiring decisions more on feelings than facts

✔ Ignores appointments and keeps applicants waiting

✔ Rushes applicants through the interviews

✔ Fails to fully prepare before interviews

✔ Settles for superficial answers, instead of probing deeper

✔ Takes no notes during job interviews

Unsatisfactory: Consistently fails to meet expectations

✔ Asks personal questions

✔ Lets personal bias and stereotypes influence his thinking

✔ Has no understanding of equal employment opportunity rulings or guidelines

✔ Has exhibited behaviors in the hiring process that have led to complaints against the company

✔ Tries to upset applicants to see how they react

✔ Makes offers of employment prior to completing all the steps in the screening process

✔ Loses excellent candidates

✔ Argues with applicants

✔ Makes promises that cannot be kept

Chapter 13

The Best Phrases for Job Knowledge and Expertise

*Y*our employees' knowledge, expertise, and skills are central to success on the job, and they require specific attention in the performance appraisal process. But there's more to these factors than meets the eye.

When appraising your employees in this area, you may be tempted to focus on the amount of information they've amassed, and then appraise them solely on this factor. However, such appraisals are more appropriate for computer chips than for human beings.

In addition to appraising your employees' overall levels of knowledge, you need to appraise the degree to which they are able to productively *apply* this knowledge to the job. After all, an employee may be a storehouse of wisdom, but if he keeps the storehouse locked, there isn't much value to it.

The most powerful phrases in this area focus not only on employees' knowledge, expertise, and technical skills, but also on the ways in which employees apply these factors to their work. With this in mind, phrases focus on such behaviors as sharing knowledge, building employees' skills, mentoring, researching, serving as a positive role model, and more.

In light of the key role played by job knowledge, you want to make sure to use knowledgeable phrases when providing feedback in this area.

Ability to Apply Expertise to the Job

Exceptional: Consistently exceeds expectations

- Handles every technical challenge skillfully, thoroughly, and effectively
- Has applied her expertise to save the company a substantial amount of money
- Has used his technical knowledge to generate numerous improvements in processes, procedures, and operations
- Applied her expertise to the XYZ project and contributed directly to the project's success
- Transformed the XYZ project from a failure to a success by applying his expertise
- Makes highly technical information interesting and understandable
- Enhances the effectiveness of group meetings by sharing her expertise on issues or questions that arise

Excellent: Frequently exceeds expectations

- Presents complicated information in understandable chunks
- Uses expertise appropriate to the situation or problem
- Creatively applies her expertise
- Enhances the expertise of her fellow employees
- Is able to take theoretical information and make practical use of it on the job
- Has helped find solutions to several problems through his technological insights
- Provides technical information in user-friendly language

Fully competent: Meets expectations

- Shows a high degree of intellectual effectiveness
- Easily absorbs and applies new information

✔ Communicates effectively with technical and nontechnical employees

✔ Uses her expertise to raise the quality and quantity of work

✔ Shows tenacity in solving technical problems

✔ Always seeks ways to use his knowledge to make improvements on the job

✔ Focuses on causes rather than symptoms

Marginal: Occasionally fails to meet expectations

✔ Relies on outdated knowledge

✔ Is impatient with nontechnical employees

✔ Is more interested in quick answers than the right answer

✔ Goes into far too much detail when asked a question

✔ Uses so much technical jargon that she is difficult to understand

✔ Provides information that is not regarded as credible

✔ Starts providing an answer before hearing the entire question

✔ Provides too many answers that are either fluff or bluff

Unsatisfactory: Consistently fails to meet expectations

✔ Pushes out-of-date solutions on employees, and then becomes defensive if employees raise questions

✔ Provides inaccurate technical information

✔ Responds to technical questions with an arrogant, degrading, and demeaning style

✔ Ignores requests for help

✔ Is more interested in his field than in getting the job done

✔ Lacks expertise in areas in which it is most needed on the job

✔ Provides solutions that have created larger problems

Acting as a Mentor

Exceptional: Consistently exceeds expectations

- ✔ Always makes time to mentor others
- ✔ Genuinely enjoys helping others learn
- ✔ Takes great pride in seeing employees build their skills, productivity, and personal effectiveness
- ✔ Has generated major improvements in employee performance through his mentoring
- ✔ Is comfortable and effective working side-by-side with employees to help them learn
- ✔ Targets her mentoring efforts on areas in which critical skills need upgrading
- ✔ Provides mentoring on a scheduled basis, as well as spontaneously when needed

Excellent: Frequently exceeds expectations

- ✔ Organizes his time to allow mentoring
- ✔ Conducts two-way communication that serves as a powerful mentoring tool
- ✔ Shows employees what to do and how to do it, and then provides opportunities for hands-on practice
- ✔ Serves as a mentor without being asked to do so
- ✔ Mentors new employees and brings them up to speed quickly
- ✔ Regards mentoring as an ongoing process rather than an intermittent task
- ✔ Consistently receives great praise and appreciation from employees whom she mentors

Fully competent: Meets expectations

- ✔ Readily volunteers to mentor others
- ✔ Is undergoing training to improve his mentoring skills
- ✔ Is able to complete all her work while still providing first-rate mentoring to others

- ✔ Provides information that adheres to all company standards and guidelines when he mentors
- ✔ Develops employees to the point that they can help in the mentoring process
- ✔ Includes a high degree of support and positive feedback in her mentoring
- ✔ Approaches mentoring with positive expectations every step of the way
- ✔ Has an excellent base of knowledge and shares it effectively in the mentoring process

Marginal: Occasionally fails to meet expectations

- ✔ Has outdated knowledge in various areas in which he is mentoring
- ✔ Provides brief answers to questions that require more thorough responses
- ✔ Mentors employees at inconvenient or inopportune times
- ✔ Doesn't consistently follow up
- ✔ Ends mentoring sessions abruptly, even when employees have additional questions
- ✔ Is uninterested in mentoring, and it shows
- ✔ Rushes through mentoring from start to finish

Unsatisfactory: Consistently fails to meet expectations

- ✔ Provides information on shortcuts and workarounds that violate standards and compromise quality
- ✔ Focuses on employee mistakes, and then provides inadequate corrective information
- ✔ Makes far more negative comments than positive ones
- ✔ Has a threatening undercurrent in her mentoring
- ✔ Places unrealistic expectations on employees, and then reprimands employees who fall short
- ✔ Focuses more on discipline than on development
- ✔ Has no patience with employees who are struggling
- ✔ Is more of a tormentor than a mentor

Acting as a Positive Role Model

Exceptional: Consistently exceeds expectations

✔ Models the most effective behaviors

✔ Is a highly respected and productive individual whose behaviors are emulated by his employees

✔ Is highly conscious of the impact that her behaviors have on the actions of other employees

✔ Consistently aligns her behavior with the company's standards, ethics, values, and objectives

✔ Recognizes that one of the most powerful training tools is the example that he sets

✔ Has built a high level of respect and trust with employees, causing them to model her behaviors

✔ Has developed his employees to the point that they, too, exhibit model behaviors

✔ Is a true example of what it means to "walk the walk"

Excellent: Frequently exceeds expectations

✔ Takes specific steps to model the behaviors that she expects from employees

✔ Has a positive impact on employee performance through his enthusiasm, upbeat attitude, and energy

✔ Sets an example that has helped improve the productivity of all her employees

✔ Never asks employees to adhere to standards that he doesn't demand of himself

✔ Sets an example that has contributed to an atmosphere of excellence within the department

✔ Maintains and demonstrates excellence in all aspects of her work

Fully competent: Meets expectations

✔ Sets a clear example of behaviors for his employees to follow

✔ Is always aware of the impact that her behaviors are having on the performance of others

✔ Provides appropriate positive reinforcement when he sees employees emulating his behavior

✔ Is comfortable and successful as a role model

✔ Shows employees what to do and how to do it, and does so without showing off

✔ Is genuinely committed to demonstrating model behavior

Marginal: Occasionally fails to meet expectations

✔ Doesn't always remember that her behaviors serve as a model for other employees

✔ Occasionally overlooks the impact that his actions are having on other employees

✔ Inconsistently adheres to company policies, sending a mixed message to employees

✔ Has engaged in some questionable behaviors that are now being displayed by her employees

✔ Tries to serve as a positive role model, but frequently falls short of the mark

✔ Underestimates the impact of his behaviors on the performance others

Unsatisfactory: Consistently fails to meet expectations

✔ Demonstrates questionable behaviors that negatively influence the actions of her employees

✔ Ignores standards that he imposes on others

✔ Gets upset with employees when they emulate her questionable behaviors

✔ Cuts corners while expecting perfection from his employees

✔ Is uncomfortable with the notion that she is a role model

✔ Advises employees to look to other individuals as role models

✔ Lives by the adage "Do as I say, not as I do"

Applying Analytical Skills

Exceptional: Consistently exceeds expectations

- Has a problem-solving style that is both analytical and creative
- Conducts credible, thorough, and reliable analyses
- Has come up with new problem-solving strategies and solutions in his department by thinking analytically
- Quickly sees through specious arguments
- Has successfully used her analytical skills to solve several long-term problems
- Effectively uses analytical skills to solve technical as well as nontechnical problems
- Has raised the standards of analytical thinking among his peers
- Makes high-quality decisions that measurably contribute to the bottom line

Excellent: Frequently exceeds expectations

- Bases conclusions on thorough analyses of all relevant data
- Supports conclusions with solid reasoning
- Identifies and focuses on relevant details
- Is a highly analytical problem solver
- Breaks problems into their individual parts and solves them piece by piece
- Is a clear and logical thinker
- Includes listening as a key part of her analytical approach
- Has business sense and analytical skills that are a powerful combination

Fully competent: Meets expectations

- Uses a logical and orderly problem-solving approach
- Relies on specifics, not generalizations

- Has a deliberative problem-solving style, but never loses sight of deadlines
- Discerns relevant data from irrelevant data
- Is able to separate hype from facts
- Helps fellow employees build their analytical skills
- Asks the right questions at the right time
- Is receptive to ideas that differ from his own
- Is a tenacious investigator

Marginal: Occasionally fails to meet expectations

- Bases decisions more on opinions than analyses
- Uses analytical skills, but relies on limited data
- Is more interested in a quick solution than a thorough analysis
- Quickly becomes defensive when asked about the reasoning behind her decisions
- Relies on less-than-credible sources
- Has a disorganized strategy that has led to lost documentation
- Is overly involved in the analysis process and loses sight of the objectives

Unsatisfactory: Consistently fails to meet expectations

- Manipulates facts to reach conclusions that he prefers
- Produces results that lack credibility
- Draws conclusions based on inadequate analysis
- Uses antiquated data to support her conclusions
- Lets personal bias influence his analyses
- Is consistently superficial in her analyses
- Overlooks critical data and developments
- Focuses on one idea and refuses to consider others
- Criticizes rather than analyzes

Building Employees' Skills

Exceptional: Consistently exceeds expectations

- Varies training styles to meet employees' learning styles
- Is highly successful in developing employees' expertise and skills
- Provides training that is readily applicable to work that needs to be done on the job
- Has measurably improved performance and productivity by training others
- Has had a positive impact on the bottom line through her efforts to build employees' skills
- Creates a true learning environment
- Creates and implements outstanding on-the-job and off-the-job employee development programs
- Has provided training and guidance to prepare several of her employees for promotions

Excellent: Frequently exceeds expectations

- Provides timely feedback to reinforce learning
- Gives employees plenty of opportunities to practice
- Automatically gravitates toward training roles
- Is approached by many employees who want to learn about "best practices"
- Ensures that employees in her department are always well trained
- Regards employee development as a key part of his job
- Follows up regularly on all training
- Quickly identifies and addresses areas in which employees need further training and development

Fully competent: Meets expectations

- Gladly helps and guides her fellow employees
- Takes no shortcuts when training

- ✔ Builds employee skills through two-way communication rather than one-way communication
- ✔ Is always looking for ways to improve his own training skills
- ✔ Is open and communicative when teaching
- ✔ Never turns down an opportunity to train
- ✔ Takes great pride in the growth and development of her employees
- ✔ Conducts highly successful training programs

Marginal: Occasionally fails to meet expectations

- ✔ Does little more than lecture his employees
- ✔ Plays favorites in selecting employees for training
- ✔ Has employees who emerge from her department with no additional skills
- ✔ Provides no follow-up after training
- ✔ Waits for employees to fail before taking any steps to train them
- ✔ Builds his employees' skills in areas that have little to do with successful performance
- ✔ Expects employees to train themselves

Unsatisfactory: Consistently fails to meet expectations

- ✔ Shows no interest in building her employees' knowledge, skills, or abilities
- ✔ Never has time to train his employees
- ✔ Retaliates against employees who complain about the quality of training that she provides
- ✔ Typically provides training that is out-of-date
- ✔ Is unresponsive to employee questions
- ✔ Has taken no recent steps to upgrade his own skills
- ✔ Fails to build employees' skills, but reprimands employees for questionable performance in areas that require such skills

Computer Skills

Exceptional: Consistently exceeds expectations

- Has expert-level knowledge regarding a wide range of computer programs, databases, and languages
- Has finely tuned technical troubleshooting skills
- Helps fellow employees build their computer skills
- Is directly responsible for changes in company computer systems that have led to measurable improvements across several performance areas
- Has in-depth knowledge of several operating systems
- Sets the standard for outstanding Web and Internet skills and usage
- Is able to create upgrades, patches, and functionality improvements

Excellent: Frequently exceeds expectations

- Is continuously upgrading her computer knowledge and skills
- Quickly learns and applies new programs
- Has a wide range of knowledge regarding hardware and software
- Creates tailor-made training programs to help employees learn new systems
- Has an outstanding intuitive sense of computer operations
- Helps keep company computers at state-of-the-art levels
- Is always on the lookout for new cost-effective systems and applications

Fully competent: Meets expectations

- Is highly receptive to new computer programs and software upgrades
- Helps fellow employees with computer problems

✔ Follows company policies regarding computer usage

✔ Is familiar with a broad range of computer hardware and software

✔ Has well-developed word processing skills

✔ Uses graphics effectively

✔ Has made several successful slide-show presentations

✔ Makes excellent use of e-mail

✔ Stays current on computer technologies relevant to his work

✔ Is comfortable with spreadsheets and databases

Marginal: Occasionally fails to meet expectations

✔ Is slow to adjust to new or upgraded computer programs

✔ Is unmotivated to increase her computer knowledge

✔ Doesn't take advantage of many features available on company computers

✔ Tends to copy too many employees on e-mail messages

✔ Frequently interrupts others with basic computer questions

✔ Relies on manual processes that should be managed on his computer

✔ Uses e-mail for personal messages

✔ Flags routine e-mail messages as urgent

Unsatisfactory: Consistently fails to meet expectations

✔ Downloads programs in violation of company policy

✔ Is resistant to computer upgrades

✔ Forwards inappropriate e-mail messages

✔ Wastes time visiting Web sites unrelated to her job

✔ Doesn't always read his e-mail

✔ Doesn't respond to e-mail that requires a response

✔ Contacts the IT department for technical support on matters that she should be able to handle herself

Researching Skills

Exceptional: Consistently exceeds expectations

- Has cutting-edge online research skills
- Generates excellent data from the best sources and resources
- Has state-of-the-art skills in designing, administering, and interpreting surveys
- Produces high-quality and reliable research projects
- Uses a broad range of appropriate statistical measurements and tests
- Has an outstanding ability to differentiate relevant data from less significant data
- Produces research reports that are well reasoned, well written, and well received

Excellent: Frequently exceeds expectations

- Is thorough and well organized in his research methods
- Builds the research skills of her employees
- Develops a solid research plan while remaining open to further data gathering and analyses if the findings warrant such actions
- Differentiates between trustworthy and untrustworthy sources
- Digs through and analyzes a vast array of data before reaching any conclusions
- Has a solid understanding of statistical analyses, and is able to see through questionable statistical methodologies
- Takes full advantage of the most appropriate technologies when conducting research
- Continuously conducts relevant research in his field, independent of assignments to do so

Fully competent: Meets expectations

- Has expertise in the field that provides her with a jump-start on research projects

- Doesn't waste time with questionable sources
- Uses a variety of search engines to check and cross-check sources and gather additional useful information
- Is comfortable and effective in handling research-oriented projects
- Begins research projects with an open mind
- Completes research projects on time
- Continues to build his research skills

Marginal: Occasionally fails to meet expectations

- Conducts research randomly and jumps from one resource to another
- Spends too much time with marginal sources of data and too little time with valuable sources of data
- Can get sidetracked during the research process
- Rushes through research projects
- Is more focused on gathering data than analyzing it
- Uses outmoded data analysis techniques and technologies
- Asks for advice when conducting research, but rarely follows it
- Relies on summaries and overviews, rather than facts and figures

Unsatisfactory: Consistently fails to meet expectations

- Actively avoids projects that require research
- Reacts first by trying to delegate research assignments
- Is easily influenced by small amounts of data
- Tends to rely on questionable resources
- Is more influenced by the appearance of Web sites than by their content
- Is unfamiliar and uncomfortable with most search engines
- Relies on outdated materials and sources
- Produces research reports that lack clarity and credibility

Sharing Knowledge

Exceptional: Consistently exceeds expectations

- ✔ Genuinely enjoys sharing her expertise to help build employee productivity, performance, and confidence
- ✔ Is approached by many employees with questions, and always makes time to answer them
- ✔ Manages to complete his work with distinction while always making time to share knowledge

Excellent: Frequently exceeds expectations

- ✔ Is generous with her time and ideas
- ✔ Holds informal discussion sessions with interested employees on numerous workplace questions
- ✔ Lives by the philosophy that "anything worth knowing is worth sharing"

Fully competent: Meets expectations

- ✔ Seeks opportunities to share insights and information with other employees
- ✔ Has raised employee performance and satisfaction by sharing his knowledge
- ✔ Runs training sessions that are regarded as valuable perks

Marginal: Occasionally fails to meet expectations

- ✔ Doesn't have much up-to-date knowledge to share
- ✔ Regards questions as an intrusion on her time
- ✔ Spends a minimal amount of time sharing his knowledge

Unsatisfactory: Consistently fails to meet expectations

- ✔ Refuses to make time to share insights and information
- ✔ Makes employees feel unwelcome if they come to her with questions
- ✔ Uses an arrogant and condescending tone when responding to inquiries

Technical Knowledge

Exceptional: Consistently exceeds expectations

- Keeps his technical skills on the cutting edge
- Is the go-to person for technical questions
- Offers comments, suggestions, and answers that are widely respected and carry a great deal of weight
- Has made important technical contributions to her field
- Is passionate about continuing to learn
- Can discuss technical issues with anyone at any level
- Reads for pleasure in his field
- Has technical expertise that has contributed directly to the success of the company
- Is regarded as an expert's expert

Excellent: Frequently exceeds expectations

- Has a high degree of intellectual curiosity
- Is on top of new developments in her field
- Is truly an expert in his field
- Maintains state-of-the-art knowledge
- Is one of the resident experts in the company
- Knows it all without being a know-it-all
- Is highly regarded as a technically savvy individual
- Has great knowledge, but never shows off

Fully competent: Meets expectations

- Digs in and finds the right answers to complex technical questions
- Has a solid grasp of the entire field
- Has thorough knowledge from A to Z
- Asks questions when stumped
- Listens carefully instead of jumping in with an answer

✔ Takes active steps to build her expertise both on and off the job

✔ Is continuously upgrading his knowledge base

✔ Always takes advantage of learning situations, whether on or off the job

✔ Keeps all licenses and certifications current

Marginal: Occasionally fails to meet expectations

✔ Has let her expertise fall behind

✔ Gives superficial answers to detailed questions

✔ Has no interest in continuing education

✔ Builds technical expertise in areas that have little to do with the needs of the company

✔ Has in-depth knowledge in too narrow of an area

✔ Has impressive credentials, but spends too much time talking about them

✔ Relies on information that has since been updated

✔ Shows declining interest in his area of expertise

✔ Focuses more on yesterday's knowledge than tomorrow's challenges

Unsatisfactory: Consistently fails to meet expectations

✔ Bases decisions on knowledge that is out of date

✔ Shows no interest in upgrading her technical knowledge

✔ Turns away from opportunities to build his expertise

✔ Lets licenses and certifications lapse

✔ Is unfamiliar with the latest developments in her field

✔ Gets caught up in the technical details and fails to see the larger issues

✔ Becomes argumentative when his facts are questioned

✔ Hasn't taken a class or attended a seminar in years

Chapter 14

The Best Phrases for Attitude

· ·

In This Chapter

▶ Recognizing and encouraging enthusiasm toward the job

▶ Identifying and rewarding steady and consistent performance

▶ Targeting and fortifying behaviors that demonstrate loyalty

· ·

*O*ne of the most common themes in performance appraisals is focused on employee attitude. Unfortunately, much of the feedback concerning attitude is marginally useful at best. The problem is that *attitude* is a term that has many components, and simply advising an employee that she has a great attitude or a poor attitude is not particularly helpful.

Overarching positive comments about super attitudes provide no information regarding behaviors for an employee to continue, while overarching negative comments about terrible attitudes provide no information regarding behaviors for the employee to eliminate. Plus, vague or general feedback in this area can actually chip away at the employees' attitudes.

As a result, the most effective way to provide meaningful feedback in this area is to use descriptive phrases that focus directly on the most compelling behaviors that reflect employee attitudes at work, such as attendance, dedication, commitment, reliability, initiative, energy, handling of pressure and stress, and more.

When providing feedback in this area, keep in mind that, as an employee improves his performance, his attitude improves as well.

Accepting Assignments

Exceptional: Consistently exceeds expectations

- ✔ Reaches out for additional assignments
- ✔ Has increased departmental productivity as a result of her willingness to assume additional assignments
- ✔ Enjoys the challenge and learning opportunities that accompany his assignments

Excellent: Frequently exceeds expectations

- ✔ Accepts assignments without hesitation
- ✔ Reorganizes her work to carry out all assignments as needed
- ✔ Completes every assignment thoroughly and on time

Fully competent: Meets expectations

- ✔ Is always willing to do extra work
- ✔ Approaches all assignments seriously and energetically
- ✔ Discusses assignments and clarifies expectations and priorities in advance
- ✔ Effectively prioritizes and completes assignments

Marginal: Occasionally fails to meet expectations

- ✔ Begrudgingly accepts assignments
- ✔ Frequently claims that he's too busy to handle assignments
- ✔ Regards assignments as punishments
- ✔ Asks for assignments, and then ignores them

Unsatisfactory: Consistently fails to meet expectations

- ✔ Continuously looks for reasons to refuse an assignment
- ✔ Becomes exasperated when offered an assignment
- ✔ Instantly looks for other people to do the work
- ✔ Fails to complete her assigned work

Attendance

Exceptional: Consistently exceeds expectations

- ✔ Has had perfect attendance since day one
- ✔ Schedules personal appointments during non-work hours
- ✔ Has not used any sick leave
- ✔ Attends all work-related sessions, including those held after hours, during the evening, and on the weekend
- ✔ Is a model of excellent attendance

Excellent: Frequently exceeds expectations

- ✔ Always arrives on time or a few minutes early
- ✔ Has only had *x* days of absence during the year
- ✔ Has significantly improved attendance in her department
- ✔ Is absent only when he's truly unable to work

Fully competent: Meets expectations

- ✔ Gets right to work as soon as she arrives
- ✔ Follows the company's policies on breaks
- ✔ Promptly advises management if he's unable to work

Marginal: Occasionally fails to meet expectations

- ✔ Regularly makes personal appointments in the middle of the workday
- ✔ Spends the last hour of work preparing to leave
- ✔ Is frequently late to work
- ✔ Looks for ways to miss work and still get paid

Unsatisfactory: Consistently fails to meet expectations

- ✔ Has used up all her sick time in the first *x* weeks
- ✔ Takes sick days when he isn't sick
- ✔ Abuses the company's break policy
- ✔ Stays home and doesn't notify anyone

Can-Do Attitude

Exceptional: Consistently exceeds expectations

- Has a can-do attitude, plus a will-do attitude
- Actively seeks opportunities to take on the most demanding and difficult tasks
- Focuses on what can be done, rather than on what can't be done

Excellent: Frequently exceeds expectations

- Has had a positive impact on the attitudes and performance of his fellow employees through his can-do approach to work
- Is certain of her ability to get any job done and done right
- Has yet to encounter a project that he can't handle

Fully competent: Meets expectations

- Is always ready to jump in and get the job done
- Seeks opportunities to show what she can do
- Actively seeks the more challenging tasks
- Rarely if ever says "I can't"

Marginal: Occasionally fails to meet expectations

- Has a can-do attitude, but falls short with his performance
- Focuses more on what can't be done rather than on what can be done
- Talks about having a can-do attitude, but her behavior rarely reflects it

Unsatisfactory: Consistently fails to meet expectations

- Initially responds to any request by saying that it can't be done
- Has a "can't-do" attitude
- Is more likely to undo a project than do it
- Says "no" before hearing all the facts

Dedication and Commitment

Exceptional: Consistently exceeds expectations

- ✔ Put in astounding hours on the XYZ project to help make it a major success
- ✔ Foregoes personal opportunities to keep work commitments
- ✔ Shows unwavering dedication to the company and its mission

Excellent: Frequently exceeds expectations

- ✔ Puts in extra hours without being asked to do so
- ✔ Works nights and weekends whenever needed
- ✔ Fully immerses himself in the job

Fully competent: Meets expectations

- ✔ Is always willing to accept extra assignments
- ✔ Takes pride in demonstrating her dedication to the company
- ✔ Has a strong personal commitment to the company's goals

Marginal: Occasionally fails to meet expectations

- ✔ Is dedicated to the company whenever it's convenient
- ✔ Gives his work intermittent attention, rather than concentrated attention
- ✔ Claims she is dedicated to the company, but takes no significant steps to show it

Unsatisfactory: Consistently fails to meet expectations

- ✔ Speaks negatively about the company but positively about the competition
- ✔ Is critical of the company's vision, values, and goals
- ✔ Uses time at work to advance his personal agenda rather than the company's agenda

Emphasizing Safety

Exceptional: Consistently exceeds expectations

- ✔ Keeps the issue of safety on her employees' minds at all times
- ✔ Has taken highly effective actions in his department to maintain the lowest accident rate in the company
- ✔ Regards safety as one of her top priorities
- ✔ Regards personal and group safety as a major concern
- ✔ Has dramatically reduced accidents in his area
- ✔ Has received awards for her steps and suggestions to improve safety in the workplace
- ✔ Always takes the safest approach in carrying out all responsibilities

Excellent: Frequently exceeds expectations

- ✔ Continuously building his employees' awareness of safety issues
- ✔ Has measurably improved safety ratings in her department
- ✔ Recognizes and rewards employees for safe actions and safety-related suggestions
- ✔ Has brought in experts to discuss safety with employees
- ✔ Adheres to high personal standards of safety
- ✔ Leads classes on workplace safety
- ✔ Has implemented several programs to improve safety
- ✔ Has played an active role in designing and implementing the company's emergency preparedness programs
- ✔ Is an active member of the company's safety committee
- ✔ Has not had one accident in his years with the company

Fully competent: Meets expectations

- ✔ Follows all company policies on safety
- ✔ Keeps safety in mind in all her work and non-work activities each day

✔ Serves as a model of safe behavior

✔ Never puts himself or other employees in risky or dangerous situations

✔ Promptly and thoroughly investigates all accidents

✔ Is decreasing the accident rate in her area

✔ Participated in the company's programs on safety training, CPR, and first aid

✔ Participated in additional training in emergency preparedness

Marginal: Occasionally fails to meet expectations

✔ Spends a minimal amount of time talking about safety

✔ Produces vague and general write-ups of employee accidents and safety incidents

✔ When accidents occur, is primarily interested in blaming someone

✔ Shows little concern for the increasing rate of accidents in his area

✔ Has been involved in x accidents during the year

✔ Provides no significant training on safety

Unsatisfactory: Consistently fails to meet expectations

✔ Overlooks the fact that her area has the highest accident rate in the company

✔ Pushes production at the expense of safety

✔ Engages in risky behaviors on the job

✔ Ignores the company's policies on safety

✔ Places the issue of safety toward the bottom of his list of priorities on the job

✔ Ridicules employees who insist on working safely

✔ Covers up accidents when they occur

Energy

Exceptional: Consistently exceeds expectations

- Has remarkable energy throughout the day
- Has a boundless energy level
- Brings an unending supply of energy to the job

Excellent: Frequently exceeds expectations

- Is still energized when most others are exhausted
- Energizes those who work with her
- Maintains a high degree of energy during extended business travel
- Is never at a loss for energy

Fully competent: Meets expectations

- Is always ready to do more work
- Productively channels his energy to the job
- Is highly productive all day long
- Actively seeks challenging and demanding projects

Marginal: Occasionally fails to meet expectations

- Consistently focuses on less rigorous projects
- Frequently diverts her energy to nonproductive pursuits
- Becomes less productive as the day progresses
- Starts projects with a good deal of energy, but runs out of gas quickly

Unsatisfactory: Consistently fails to meet expectations

- Falls asleep during the workday
- Waits for others to do the heavy lifting
- Never exerts extra effort
- Devotes more energy to non-work activities than to his job

Flexibility

Exceptional: Consistently exceeds expectations

- ✔ Has an open mind and carefully considers all new ideas, strategies, and approaches
- ✔ Has generated creative solutions to complicated problems by maintaining an open mind
- ✔ Encourages and actively listens to new ideas

Excellent: Frequently exceeds expectations

- ✔ Has contributed to an open and communicative climate in the department by demonstrating flexibility
- ✔ Regards employees as valued resources, and carefully considers all their ideas
- ✔ Is genuinely interested in ideas that differ from the established way of doing things

Fully competent: Meets expectations

- ✔ Is receptive to change, but only if it makes sense
- ✔ Is flexible without being wishy-washy
- ✔ Increases her employees' receptiveness to new ideas

Marginal: Occasionally fails to meet expectations

- ✔ Hardly considers ideas that differ from his current thinking and understanding
- ✔ Regards ideas that differ from hers to be marginally valuable at best
- ✔ Is too flexible and easily influenced by others

Unsatisfactory: Consistently fails to meet expectations

- ✔ Is totally resistant to ideas that differ from his
- ✔ Insists on doing things the way she has done them before
- ✔ Regards employees who offer alternatives to his way of doing things as troublemakers

Focus

Exceptional: Consistently exceeds expectations

- ✓ Directs laser-like attention on every project
- ✓ Has amazing powers of concentration
- ✓ Focuses equally well on big-picture items and details
- ✓ Keeps her team focused on the work to be done

Excellent: Frequently exceeds expectations

- ✓ Productively focuses energy and effort on major projects
- ✓ Has an unbending focus on his work
- ✓ Never loses sight of the objectives
- ✓ Locks her attention on the goals to be met, and then tenaciously pursues them

Fully competent: Meets expectations

- ✓ Is a persistent problem solver who keeps digging until he finds the answer
- ✓ Stays focused on her projects from start to finish
- ✓ Directs his full attention to work-related matters throughout the day

Marginal: Occasionally fails to meet expectations

- ✓ Directs too much attention to issues of secondary importance
- ✓ Drifts from one project to another, without closure on any
- ✓ Is easily distracted

Unsatisfactory: Consistently fails to meet expectations

- ✓ Fails to fully direct her attention and efforts on the work to be done
- ✓ Focuses attention on lower-level projects
- ✓ Focuses attention on non-work projects
- ✓ Takes an excessive number of breaks

Following Company Policies and Procedures

Exceptional: Consistently exceeds expectations

- ✔ Clearly understands and adheres to the company's policies, procedures, standards, and expectations
- ✔ Understands policies and procedures, along with the spirit and intent behind them
- ✔ Offers valuable and viable suggestions if he disagrees with specific policies or procedures

Excellent: Frequently exceeds expectations

- ✔ Keeps employees up-to-date regarding changes in policies and procedures that impact their work
- ✔ Explains and clarifies policies and procedures
- ✔ Applies polices fairly

Fully competent: Meets expectations

- ✔ Understands most policies and procedures and is able to quickly find answers when in doubt
- ✔ Takes policies and procedures seriously
- ✔ Follows company policies and sets an expectation for her employees to do likewise

Marginal: Occasionally fails to meet expectations

- ✔ Is always looking for ways to work around the policies
- ✔ Regards the policies and procedures as loose suggestions
- ✔ Can apply company policies inequitably

Unsatisfactory: Consistently fails to meet expectations

- ✔ Follows his own procedures rather than company procedures
- ✔ Picks and chooses the policies and procedures that she will follow
- ✔ Demands that others follow policies that he ignores

Going the Extra Mile

Exceptional: Consistently exceeds expectations

✔ Puts in extra time, energy, and effort to produce the highest-quality work

✔ Is always ready to do more for the company, regardless of the time, place, or demands

✔ Seeks out the most demanding and challenging projects

✔ Won't settle for average performance, whether from herself or from anyone else

Excellent: Frequently exceeds expectations

✔ Strives to deliver more than whatever is expected

✔ Puts in extra energy, effort, and time to generate excellent results

✔ Willingly takes on the most demanding tasks at any time

Fully competent: Meets expectations

✔ Works extra hours when extra work is needed

✔ Never complains when projects require additional time and effort

✔ Is always ready to step up and do more work

Marginal: Occasionally fails to meet expectations

✔ Is unwilling to go the extra mile for anyone but himself

✔ Begrudgingly goes the extra mile, and then complains at every step

✔ Typically comes up with excuses for why she can't help out

Unsatisfactory: Consistently fails to meet expectations

✔ Is never available when extra help is needed

✔ Frequently responds by saying, "That's not my job"

✔ Is unwilling to do anything beyond the bare minimum

Handling Pressure and Stress

Exceptional: Consistently exceeds expectations

- ✔ Maintains composure and focus in high-pressure situations
- ✔ Is a calming influence during stressful periods
- ✔ Has truly remarkable stress management skills and abilities
- ✔ Helps build his employees' stress management skills
- ✔ Improves her performance as the pressure increases
- ✔ Is extra-energized in high-pressure situations
- ✔ Helps others remain calm and focused by continuing his own excellent performance in stressful situations
- ✔ Remains unfazed by the pressures of a heavy workload and highly demanding deadlines

Excellent: Frequently exceeds expectations

- ✔ Remains positive and confident when under severe pressure
- ✔ Adjusts schedules, priorities, and strategies to effectively handle increased job pressures
- ✔ Tolerates high levels of pressure with no slippage in her performance
- ✔ Prevents or reduces the severity of pressure situations through his planning skills
- ✔ Remains calm, steady, and focused as pressure increases
- ✔ Never falters when under pressure
- ✔ Takes steps to remove unnecessary sources of stress on the job
- ✔ Manages stress, rather than letting stress manage her

Fully competent: Meets expectations

- ✔ Goes into high gear when the pressure is on
- ✔ Puts in extra energy and hours when job pressures increase

- ✔ Is building his stress management skills
- ✔ Keeps up her productivity under stressful circumstances
- ✔ Copes with stress by working even harder
- ✔ Maintains wide-open communication in high-pressure periods
- ✔ When stress levels increase, uses stress management techniques to help calm himself as well as fellow employees

Marginal: Occasionally fails to meet expectations

- ✔ Tends to lose focus during periods of high pressure
- ✔ Experiences high levels of stress in situations that are not particularly stressful
- ✔ Creates even more pressure and stress for herself by falling behind on projects
- ✔ Is outwardly nervous and jumpy when under pressure
- ✔ Lets productivity slide as pressure increases
- ✔ Becomes overly emotional when under pressure
- ✔ Loses patience in direct proportion to increases in pressure

Unsatisfactory: Consistently fails to meet expectations

- ✔ Displays significant declines in performance with the slightest increases in pressure
- ✔ Misses work when the pressure increases
- ✔ Constantly complains about the pressures of the job
- ✔ Is unable to perform effectively when under pressure
- ✔ Tends to shut down when stressed
- ✔ Becomes short-tempered when pressure increases
- ✔ Starts to panic at the first sign of pressure
- ✔ Increases stress instead of managing it

Initiative

Exceptional: Consistently exceeds expectations

- ✔ Is a true self-starter
- ✔ Appropriately identifies work that needs to be done, and then takes action
- ✔ Takes action on projects, issues, or concerns whenever and wherever needed

Excellent: Frequently exceeds expectations

- ✔ Shows consistently high levels of initiative, self-reliance, and independence
- ✔ Needs the absolute minimum amount of supervision
- ✔ Seeks assignments instead of waiting for them

Fully competent: Meets expectations

- ✔ Steps up when there is work to be done
- ✔ Once given an assignment, works autonomously and effectively
- ✔ Helps foster a spirit of initiative among his employees

Marginal: Occasionally fails to meet expectations

- ✔ Waits for work to come her way
- ✔ Shows initiative primarily on minor tasks and assignments
- ✔ Is slow to take action on projects that truly need his attention
- ✔ Takes initiative, but fails to provide adequate communication regarding the steps that she's taking

Unsatisfactory: Consistently fails to meet expectations

- ✔ Needs constant prodding to get the job done
- ✔ Does very little unless given a specific directive
- ✔ Actively avoids assignments that require initiative and drive

Level of Supervision Required

Exceptional: Consistently exceeds expectations

- ✔ Has surpassed goals on numerous projects that included virtually no direct supervision
- ✔ Works without supervision and delivers consistently outstanding work
- ✔ Is highly effective in managing his own projects from start to finish

Excellent: Frequently exceeds expectations

- ✔ Can be trusted to deliver outstanding work with an absolute minimum of supervision
- ✔ Displays excellent judgment, decision making, and problem solving when working on her own
- ✔ Independently handled the XYZ project from inception to its highly successful conclusion

Fully competent: Meets expectations

- ✔ Knows when to ask for additional guidance and direction
- ✔ Is steadily earning increased levels of independence
- ✔ Actively seeks opportunities to work autonomously

Marginal: Occasionally fails to meet expectations

- ✔ Only devotes full effort when closely monitored
- ✔ Doesn't know when to ask for help
- ✔ Tends to focus on questionable priorities when turned loose

Unsatisfactory: Consistently fails to meet expectations

- ✔ Without ongoing supervision, slips to unacceptable performance levels
- ✔ Needs regular reminders to stay on track
- ✔ Becomes nervous and stressed out when working independently

Reliability and Dependability

Exceptional: Consistently exceeds expectations

- ✔ Displays exceptional performance day after day
- ✔ Keeps his word under all circumstances
- ✔ Regardless of the situation, will do everything possible to make sure that her performance is steady and strong
- ✔ Is unstopped by obstacles, pressures, and demands that would justifiably derail others

Excellent: Frequently exceeds expectations

- ✔ Can be counted on to give 110 percent under all circumstances
- ✔ Keeps his commitments and works with fellow employees to help them keep theirs
- ✔ Automatically works extra hours if that's what it takes to get the job done right

Fully competent: Meets expectations

- ✔ Can be counted upon for steady performance
- ✔ Demonstrates consistently solid performance in all aspects of her work
- ✔ Handles projects conscientiously from start to finish

Marginal: Occasionally fails to meet expectations

- ✔ Demands reliability from others, but not from himself
- ✔ Has energy, drive, and performance levels that are inconsistent and unpredictable
- ✔ Talks about deliverables, but does not consistently deliver

Unsatisfactory: Consistently fails to meet expectations

- ✔ Disappoints employees who depend on her
- ✔ Makes promises that he doesn't keep
- ✔ Guarantees that deadlines will be met, but consistently misses them

Understanding and Supporting Company Values and Mission

Exceptional: Consistently exceeds expectations

- Represents the best in company values with her actions
- Takes a wide range of actions that help support and fulfill the company's mission
- Frequently articulates and reinforces company values for other employees
- Consistently demonstrates a full and unwavering commitment to the company's mission
- Establishes and pursues goals that help the company advance toward its mission
- Believes that the company is pursuing a worthy mission
- Takes a wide range of actions that encourage other employees to focus more clearly on the company's mission

Excellent: Frequently exceeds expectations

- Helps other employees understand and act in accordance with the company's values and mission
- Has values that are in direct alignment with the company's values
- Establishes and follows specific plans and strategies to help the company realize its vision and fulfill its mission
- Regards the company's mission as his mission
- Takes immediate action to deal with behaviors that contradict company values
- Recognizes and rewards employees whose outstanding behaviors help move the company closer to its mission

Fully competent: Meets expectations

- Fully understands and accepts the company's values and mission
- Consistently performs in line with company's vision and values

- ✓ Clearly reflects the company's values in his actions
- ✓ Keeps company values in mind at all times
- ✓ Has great faith in the company's mission and ability to fulfill it
- ✓ Demonstrates a high degree of respect for the company's values
- ✓ Takes pride in the company's mission

Marginal: Occasionally fails to meet expectations

- ✓ Occasionally engages in behaviors that ignore the values of the company
- ✓ Hasn't taken the time to understand the company's mission
- ✓ Ignores all communications and meetings that present information on the company's values and mission
- ✓ Doesn't regard the mission of the company as being particularly significant
- ✓ Provides other employees with misinformation regarding the company's mission and values
- ✓ Doesn't believe that issues related to the company's values or mission are her concern

Unsatisfactory: Consistently fails to meet expectations

- ✓ Often behaves in ways that are in direct conflict with the company's values
- ✓ Has personal values that are significantly different from those of the company
- ✓ Actively disagrees with the company's mission
- ✓ Speaks negatively about the company's mission
- ✓ Has turned his employees against the company's mission
- ✓ Places her mission above the mission of the company
- ✓ Acts as if company values don't apply to him
- ✓ Manipulates company values to justify questionable behaviors

Volunteering

Exceptional: Consistently exceeds expectations

- ✔ Always the first one to volunteer for committees, task forces, and extra responsibilities
- ✔ Not only volunteers, but plays an active role as a volunteer
- ✔ Doesn't turn down opportunities to volunteer

Excellent: Frequently exceeds expectations

- ✔ Senses a high degree of personal satisfaction by assuming voluntary responsibilities at work
- ✔ Has made many valuable contributions to the company through her various roles as a volunteer
- ✔ Has taken actions that directly led to increased interest in volunteering in several areas of the company

Fully competent: Meets expectations

- ✔ Regards volunteering as part of his job
- ✔ Devotes serious time and energy to voluntary roles
- ✔ Has personally recruited several volunteers

Marginal: Occasionally fails to meet expectations

- ✔ Joins voluntary committees, but then shows very little involvement or support
- ✔ Volunteers to help, but complains about doing so
- ✔ Spends too much time on voluntary functions at the expense of her other responsibilities

Unsatisfactory: Consistently fails to meet expectations

- ✔ Hasn't volunteered for anything
- ✔ Signs up to volunteer, but doesn't show up
- ✔ Always has a reason to avoid volunteering
- ✔ Volunteers opinions rather than time

Chapter 15

The Best Phrases for Ethics

*E*thical issues in the workplace have always been important. They bring down individuals as well as companies. Most people are aware of the damages that ethical shortcomings can wreak on a company, but many people don't realize that a strong performance appraisal system can play a critical preventive role.

Performance appraisals, accompanied by ongoing coaching and feedback, have the potential to identify and arrest unethical behaviors before they lead to a different kind of arrest. With feedback and guidance from solid performance appraisal systems, unethical behaviors are likely to be identified and stopped in their earliest stages.

In order to stop these breaches of ethics, appraisals need to do more than merely advise an employee that he's been acting unethically. In order for feedback regarding unethical behavior to have a lasting impact, it needs to target specific unethical acts.

This chapter focuses on the broad range of written comments that deal with the broad range of unethical behaviors. These phrases focus on employee behaviors in such areas as equal employment opportunity, diversity, sustainability, honesty, integrity, fairness, and more.

With strong feedback in each of these specific areas, you can prevent unethical behaviors from expanding and contaminating your company.

Diversity

Exceptional: Consistently exceeds expectations

- Truly values diversity
- Shows great respect for individual differences
- Approaches programs, policies, and decisions with a highly inclusive mindset
- Works with a diverse team to generate highly creative ideas, suggestions, and outcomes
- Transformed a group of diverse employees into a highly creative, cohesive, and productive team
- Conducts diversity training programs
- Encourages, supports, and utilizes the unique talents of each of her employees
- Achieves consistently outstanding results by building diverse work groups and task forces

Excellent: Frequently exceeds expectations

- Highly effective in leading diverse teams
- Encourages and supports diverse problem-solving strategies
- Always looking for ways to include all his employees in tasks, projects, and programs
- Maintains a high degree of two-way communication with all employees
- Identifies and breaks down barriers that separate her employees
- Creates, implements, and supports diversity policies and programs
- Continuously monitors the level of diversity

Fully competent: Meets expectations

- A strong supporter of diversity in the workplace
- Develops and maintains diverse teams
- Treats all employees with a high degree of respect and trust

- ✔ Continues to attend training sessions on diversity
- ✔ Understands how to prevent and deal with discrimination
- ✔ Supports company actions and practices to increase diversity
- ✔ Has a great deal of interest in the ideas, inputs, and suggestions from all his employees
- ✔ A strong advocate of diversity training and diversity programs

Marginal: Occasionally fails to meet expectations

- ✔ Tends to exclude rather than include
- ✔ Allows stereotypes and bias to influence her dealings with others
- ✔ Has a diverse team, but plays favorites
- ✔ Takes minimal steps to draw upon the individual talents of his employees
- ✔ Is demonstrating decreased willingness to abide by the company's diversity policies
- ✔ Is slow to adjust to diversity
- ✔ Is increasingly resistant to the company's diversity efforts
- ✔ Shows passive resistance to all efforts to increase diversity

Unsatisfactory: Consistently fails to meet expectations

- ✔ Is unsupportive of any efforts to increase diversity
- ✔ Has sidestepped every opportunity for diversity training
- ✔ Takes actions that undermine the company's diversity efforts and programs
- ✔ Avoids taking any steps that support diversity
- ✔ Makes derogatory and divisive comments
- ✔ Has made discriminatory comments that have led to complaints from co-workers
- ✔ Is uncommunicative and untrusting when dealing with a diverse group of employees

Equal Employment Opportunity

Exceptional: Consistently exceeds expectations

- ✔ Understands and follows all Equal Employment Opportunity (EEO) rulings, laws, and guidelines
- ✔ Keeps employees current on EEO rulings, laws, and guidelines
- ✔ Has helped strengthen her fellow employees' commitment and awareness of EEO
- ✔ Takes swift and appropriate corrective actions when employees deviate from established EEO standards
- ✔ Regards EEO as a top priority
- ✔ Plays a leading role in developing the company's EEO programs
- ✔ Is continuously upgrading his EEO knowledge and expertise
- ✔ Is the company's resident expert on EEO matters

Excellent: Frequently exceeds expectations

- ✔ Leads formal and informal training sessions on EEO
- ✔ Makes all decisions independent of race, color, religion, gender, national order, disability, age, or sexual orientation
- ✔ Actively and vocally supports EEO guidelines and expectations
- ✔ Keeps EEO in mind when creating and implementing new programs
- ✔ Monitors company compliance with EEO guidelines and regulations
- ✔ Has developed a climate in which there have been no claims of discrimination filed against the company
- ✔ Plays an ongoing role in upgrading the company's EEO policies and programs

Fully competent; Meets expectations

- ✔ Is genuinely committed to EEO
- ✔ Is fully aligned with the company's standards, values, and expectations regarding EEO
- ✔ Demonstrates a high degree of insight and sensitivity on EEO issues
- ✔ Has upgraded her fellow employees' knowledge and understanding of EEO issues
- ✔ Adheres to all the company's policies on EEO
- ✔ Has made suggestions to improve or clarify the company's EEO policies
- ✔ Actively solicits employees' ideas and suggestions regarding the company's EEO policies and programs

Marginal: Occasionally fails to meet expectations

- ✔ Shows minimal interest in EEO policies, practices, and programs
- ✔ Only attends required EEO training sessions
- ✔ Has a basic understanding of EEO guidelines, but often overlooks them
- ✔ Ignores most communication regarding EEO
- ✔ Has an inadequate understanding of EEO guidelines
- ✔ Provides inaccurate information on EEO matters
- ✔ Looks for ways to get around EEO policies

Unsatisfactory: Consistently fails to meet expectations

- ✔ Ignores EEO laws and rulings
- ✔ Engages in sexually harassing behaviors
- ✔ Makes offensive comments based on race, color, religion, gender, national order, disability, age, or sexual orientation
- ✔ Lets bias and stereotyping enter his decision making
- ✔ Creates artificial barriers to exclude or hold back individuals whose backgrounds are different from hers
- ✔ Has engaged in behaviors that led to formal complaints against the company

Fairness

Exceptional: Consistently exceeds expectations

✔ Places major importance on fair treatment of all employees

✔ Has a solid reputation as a fair and equitable leader

✔ Has helped others truly understand fairness and how to implement it

✔ Has made significant changes in polices and programs to eliminate unfair elements

✔ Has a strong sense of fairness that is apparent in all decisions that he makes

✔ Keeps fairness at the core of her decision making

✔ Takes immediate action to remedy inequitable situations

Excellent: Frequently exceeds expectations

✔ Treats all of his employees in a fair and just manner

✔ Regards fairness as one of the most important criteria in all of her decision making

✔ Leads a department that is widely regarded as a bastion of fairness

✔ Listens carefully to employees' concerns about fairness, and takes corrective actions where warranted

✔ Clearly communicates standards and expectations regarding equitable treatment of all employees

✔ Has a great deal of expertise on legal guidelines regarding equitable treatment of employees

Fully competent: Meets expectations

✔ Ascertains that all employees are treated fairly

✔ Takes prompt action to counsel employees who engage in unfair behaviors

✔ Has obtained training that specifically focused on equity in the workplace

✔ Provides employees with ongoing coaching to increase their understanding of the role and importance of fairness at work

✔ Keeps employees fully aware of company standards, expectations, and values regarding fair treatment

✔ Has widened the reach of many programs to provide fair access for all employees

Marginal: Occasionally fails to meet expectations

✔ Has been advised of his unfair behaviors, but continues to repeat them

✔ Implements activities and programs without adequate consideration of their fairness

✔ Provides inadequate attention to inequities in the workplace

✔ Treats workplace inequities as minor matters that do not require prompt attention

✔ Treats the symptoms of unfair treatment, instead of treating the causes

✔ Makes pronouncements about fairness on the job, but does not take action when issues arise

Unsatisfactory: Consistently fails to meet expectations

✔ Plays favorites

✔ Rationalizes that unfair treatment will make employees stronger

✔ Treats employees unfairly, which has led to formal complaints

✔ Is unresponsive to employees' concerns regarding unfair treatment

✔ Reprimands employees who voice concern about inequities at work

✔ Makes decisions without considering how fair or unfair they may be

✔ Is unconcerned about the unfair impact of her actions

Giving Back to the Community

Exceptional: Consistently exceeds expectations

- ✔ Truly values the opportunity to help those in need
- ✔ Is actively involved in volunteer activities in the community
- ✔ Plays a leadership role in various community organizations
- ✔ Helps raise substantial contributions for nonprofit organizations
- ✔ Has taken actions that increased volunteerism among her fellow employees
- ✔ Serves as a model of the company's values, focusing on helping and serving the community
- ✔ Has been singled out for awards from community organizations that she serves
- ✔ Has led various drives to help disaster victims

Excellent: Frequently exceeds expectations

- ✔ Always makes time to help community organizations
- ✔ Consistently supports causes, events, and organizations that help those in need
- ✔ Is truly committed to helping those who are less fortunate
- ✔ Has generated increased company-wide support for important causes and organizations
- ✔ Has a genuine sense of compassion toward the less fortunate
- ✔ Has built goodwill for the company through his civic-minded actions

Fully competent: Meets expectations

- ✔ Has strong personal values focused on voluntarism
- ✔ Takes actions to increase employee awareness of the value of community service
- ✔ Encourages employee involvement in community activities, but never pressures anyone

✔ Is able to effectively balance community service with the demands of her job

✔ Is highly regarded in the company for his work in the community

✔ Serves as an excellent role model for other employees when it comes to volunteerism

✔ Actively supports company policy regarding community service

Marginal: Occasionally fails to meet expectations

✔ Is slow to support company-wide efforts to help those in need

✔ Makes comments that discourage employees from participating in volunteer activities in the community

✔ Ignores company policy on community service

✔ Keeps pushing the company to do more for his favorite charity and less for other charities

✔ Uses many company resources and materials for charity work, and does so without permission

✔ Solicits contributions for her favorite charity during work hours rather than during breaks

Unsatisfactory: Consistently fails to meet expectations

✔ Is quick to disparage the volunteer activities of others

✔ Provides no scheduling flexibility for employees who engage in community service

✔ Resists aligning his behavior with company values and policies regarding community service

✔ Is overly involved in community activities and lets her job responsibilities falter

✔ Provides favorable treatment for employees who participate in his favorite volunteer activities

✔ Misses too much work as a result of volunteer activities

✔ Pressures employees to give time or money for her favorite charities

Honesty

Exceptional: Consistently exceeds expectations

- Is 100 percent trustworthy
- Is widely respected for his honesty
- Is regarded as totally credible by all who work with her
- Completes projects that are based on honest data gathering and analysis
- Is above-board, straightforward, and candid
- Displays intellectual honesty in all aspects of his work
- Is the go-to person for honest answers and opinions
- Signs off on projects only when the work is 100 percent reliable

Excellent: Frequently exceeds expectations

- Digs in and finds the right answers to difficult questions, instead of trying to bluff her way through
- Has established a high degree of personal trust
- Keeps her word on all matters
- Is fully trusted in all she says and does
- Regards honesty as a top priority in dealings with his fellow employees
- Has fostered a climate of honesty within her department

Fully competent: Meets expectations

- Doesn't stray from the truth
- Is a person of his word
- Gives credit where credit is due
- Is willing to make serious sacrifices in order to keep her commitments
- Successfully establishes honest and open two-way communication with his employees
- Provides honest feedback in order to help employees learn, grow, and develop

✔ Uses honest facts, figures, and data to support her conclusions

Marginal: Occasionally fails to meet expectations

✔ Believes that there is no problem in having a "fudge factor" in every project

✔ Holds back highly pertinent data

✔ Rarely gives the full story

✔ Is inclined to bend the truth

✔ Provides misleading updates on his projects

✔ Excessively embellishes her accomplishments

✔ Makes promises that he knows cannot be kept

✔ Will say anything to get her way

✔ Is widely regarded as being less than credible

Unsatisfactory: Consistently fails to meet expectations

✔ Makes comments that always must be taken with a grain of salt

✔ Gives different people different stories regarding the same situation

✔ Caused the XYZ project to fail because of her lack of forthright behavior

✔ Has a basic lack of honesty that has garnered numerous complaints

✔ Produces projects and reports that always need extra scrutiny and fact checking because of questionable analyses and misleading conclusions

✔ Takes credit for work done by others

✔ Generates questionable results by manipulating the numbers

✔ Is held in questionable regard by his employees because of issues regarding honesty and trust

✔ Is frequently caught in lies

✔ Makes up facts to support her position

Integrity

Exceptional: Consistently exceeds expectations

- ✔ Maintains the highest standards of personal integrity
- ✔ Displays exemplary behavior in every aspect of his work
- ✔ Is highly regarded for her integrity both within and outside the company
- ✔ Is a true embodiment of the company's values regarding integrity
- ✔ Sets the high-water mark for integrity
- ✔ Identifies the most worthy steps and then takes them
- ✔ When given a choice, always opts for the reputable route
- ✔ Finds and implements the sterling way to handle any ethically challenging situation

Excellent: Frequently exceeds expectations

- ✔ Sets very high personal standards of integrity, which his employees emulate
- ✔ Will not consider less-than-honorable plans, strategies, or behaviors
- ✔ Consistently engages in meritorious behavior
- ✔ Can be counted upon to act honorably in all situations
- ✔ Builds a climate of integrity in her department
- ✔ Demonstrates the highest levels of integrity in all dealings with employees
- ✔ Handles all dealings with his customers with the highest levels of integrity
- ✔ Has a strong sense of integrity that underlies dealings with vendors

Fully competent: Meets expectations

- ✔ Is well-intentioned in all her workplace behaviors
- ✔ Consistently takes the high road

✔ Appropriately counsels employees who engage in disingenuous behaviors

✔ Has a strong sense of right and wrong, and consistently strives to do what's right

✔ Maintains high standards of integrity across his department

✔ Makes decisions that consistently reflect her strong commitment to acting reputably

✔ Quickly dismisses less-than-exemplary options

Marginal: Occasionally fails to meet expectations

✔ Lets expedience trump integrity

✔ Sets integrity aside when pursuing his goals

✔ Rationalizes her less-than-meritorious behaviors

✔ Does not rank integrity particularly high on his list of priorities

✔ Always expects integrity from others, but doesn't always display it herself

✔ Intermittently demonstrates acceptable levels of integrity

✔ Has had several recent lapses in integrity

Unsatisfactory: Consistently fails to meet expectations

✔ Violates company standards and expectations regarding employee integrity

✔ Has put the company at risk with his untoward actions

✔ Engages in underhanded behaviors

✔ Has taken actions that have caused his employees to question his integrity

✔ Has generated complaints from customers because of issues with his integrity

✔ Has been the cause of concern from vendors because of her integrity

✔ Has cost the company customers and money because of his disingenuous behavior

✔ Has engaged in questionable behaviors that have led to corporate embarrassment

Judgment

Exceptional: Consistently exceeds expectations

- ✔ Is highly regarded for her judgmental ability
- ✔ Keeps company values, standards, and ethics in mind in any situation requiring his judgment
- ✔ Is comfortable with transparency in any stage of the judgmental process

Excellent: Frequently exceeds expectations

- ✔ Makes decisions when fully informed with reliable data
- ✔ Includes significant others in significant decisions
- ✔ Has nothing to hide when making decisions

Fully competent: Meets expectations

- ✔ Has a commitment to ethics that underlies his judgments
- ✔ Immediately counsels employees who display questionable judgment
- ✔ Has conducted formal sessions with employees to further educate them on business ethics

Marginal: Occasionally fails to meet expectations

- ✔ Occasionally displays questionable judgment and engages in arguably unethical business practices
- ✔ Shrouds much of his decision making in secrecy
- ✔ Shows a disconnect between her personal ethics and the company's ethical standards

Unsatisfactory: Consistently fails to meet expectations

- ✔ Makes decisions without consideration of company ethics and values
- ✔ Brags about business conquests that clearly contradict the company's ethical standards
- ✔ Has damaged the company's image, goodwill, and reputation through his ethical lapses

Maintaining Professionalism

Exceptional: Consistently exceeds expectations

- Is passionate about using her professional skills and expertise to help others
- Has a strong commitment to his field
- Is continuously building her skills and knowledge base
- Is regarded by other professionals in the field as a true expert
- Stays at the cutting edge of knowledge in his field
- Is highly effective in applying her professional expertise to the job
- Adheres to a strong code of ethics regarding professional behavior
- Gives advice, analyses, and recommendations that are 100 percent trustworthy

Excellent: Frequently exceeds expectations

- Places a great deal of emphasis on providing valuable professional services to others
- Is known for sound decision making
- Attends numerous formal training programs and classes to continue to augment his professional expertise
- Gravitates into formal and informal leadership roles based on her expertise
- Takes time to educate others in his field
- Generates a wide range of new and creative ideas that contribute to her field and the company at large

Fully competent: Meets expectations

- Maintains ties to his field, professional association, and professional peers
- Demonstrates a high degree of pride in all of his work

✔ Actively seeks opportunities to enhance her professional training

✔ Is able to effectively apply his professional skills to the job

✔ Continues to expand her professional expertise

✔ Is truly passionate about his field

Marginal: Occasionally fails to meet expectations

✔ Has let her professional expertise slide

✔ Appears to be burning out

✔ Has stopped reading professional journals and magazines

✔ Has lost his enthusiasm and passion for the field

✔ Is becoming increasingly involved in peripheral interests instead of focusing on her areas of expertise

✔ Takes no time to help his employees learn about the field

✔ Is uninterested in discussing new trends and developments in her field

✔ Has lost contact with most of his professional peers

Unsatisfactory: Consistently fails to meet expectations

✔ Ignores her professional code of ethics

✔ Has caused serious productivity problems because of his out-of-date knowledge

✔ Uses outmoded problem-solving techniques and strategies

✔ Has let her professional designations, certifications, and licensing expire

✔ Has been expelled from his professional association

✔ Has had her license revoked by a regulatory agency

Sustainability

Exceptional: Consistently exceeds expectations

- Is truly committed to sustainability and doing what is best for the environment
- Is the prime force behind the company's award-winning sustainability program
- Has saved the company thousands of dollars through his sustainability efforts
- Has built companywide awareness about sustainability
- Has inspired her employees to take a wide range of sustainable steps
- Has devised systems and measurements to track the company's sustainability programs and practices
- Has an expert level of knowledge of sustainable practices

Excellent: Frequently exceeds expectations

- Encourages and supports employee suggestions regarding sustainability
- Has fostered a department-wide climate of sustainability
- Played a key role in saving the company x gallons of water per year
- Is the driving force behind an x percent reduction in the use of paper
- Is directly responsible for an x percent increase in the amount of recycled trash
- Is responsible for an x percent reduction in the use of electricity
- Led the company's effort to buy environmentally friendly products
- Established and runs the sustainability committee

Fully competent: Meets expectations

- Provides employees with appropriate recognition for actions that help sustainability

✔ Is steadily building his knowledge of sustainability

✔ Supports the company's sustainable policies and practices

✔ Monitors her employees' performance to be sure that sustainability guidelines are being followed and standards are being met

✔ Works with vendors and customers to help them with sustainability efforts

✔ Focuses efforts on recycling, using less, buying recycled goods, and reusing products where possible

✔ Is a member of the sustainability committee

✔ Circulates important articles on sustainability and the actions employees can take to help reduce waste

✔ Is a source of outstanding ideas for sustainability

Marginal: Occasionally fails to meet expectations

✔ Pays passing attention to sustainability, but does not demonstrate serious commitment in this area

✔ Asks employees for their suggestions on sustainability, but then does nothing with them

✔ Has made no effort to understand the company's sustainability programs, policies, and objectives

✔ Ignores requests to attend company sessions that deal with sustainability

✔ Takes minimal sustainability steps, but believes that he is already doing enough

Unsatisfactory: Consistently fails to meet expectations

✔ Is unconcerned with issues of sustainability

✔ Makes no effort to reuse or recycle

✔ Ignores company polices and guidelines on sustainability

✔ Refuses to take even the most basic sustainability steps

✔ Regards sustainability as a fad

✔ Continues to engage in behaviors that contradict the company's sustainability programs and policies

✔ Shows a lack of concern for the amount of paper, electricity, and water that she wastes every day

Chapter 16

The Best Phrases for Creative Thinking

In This Chapter

▶ Sharpening the tools that build creative thinking

▶ Creating a climate that supports innovative ideas

▶ Overcoming the barriers that prevent creative problem solving

*O*ne of the hallmarks of successful employees is their ability to think creatively and develop innovative solutions to the vast number of problems they encounter on the job. Companies that support this type of thinking are not only better able to cope with today's myriad challenges, but also to predict and prepare for tomorrow's challenges.

Identifying, enhancing, and reinforcing your employees' efforts to engage in creative thinking is critical. You should be doing this informally throughout the evaluation period, and you should specifically target this area during the formal reviews.

Your appraisal will do more than provide your employees with specific and accurate feedback regarding their efforts to apply and support creativity on the job. It will also provide them with tools to build their skills in this area, along with guidance and support to help them do so.

You need to appraise key behaviors that relate to creative thinking on the job, such as generating new ideas, being receptive to new ideas, thinking outside the box, encouraging and supporting innovation from others, and more.

The phrases in this chapter are designed to reflect and encourage creative thinking.

Brainstorming

Exceptional: Consistently exceeds expectations

- Uses brainstorming sessions to generate a large number of creative ideas, many of which have been implemented
- Encourages employees to present as many ideas as possible
- Takes appropriate follow-up action on all ideas generated in brainstorming sessions

Excellent: Frequently exceeds expectations

- Lets employees know that there is no such a thing as a bad idea in brainstorming sessions, and she means it
- Conducts brainstorming sessions that are both playful and productive
- Sets positive expectations ahead of these sessions, which helps lead to consistently positive results

Fully competent: Meets expectations

- Picks interdepartmental topics and includes employees from other departments
- Leads discussions that are free of criticism and reprisals
- Has motivated other managers to implement brainstorming because of the success of his sessions

Marginal: Occasionally fails to meet expectations

- Provides no follow-up after brainstorming sessions
- Does most of the talking during brainstorming
- Cuts discussions short during brainstorming sessions

Unsatisfactory: Consistently fails to meet expectations

- Refuses to hold brainstorming sessions
- Criticizes employees for their suggestions
- Takes reprisals against employees if he does not agree with their suggestions and new ideas

Embracing Change

Exceptional: Consistently exceeds expectations

- ✔ Creates a dynamic environment in which productive change is sought, implemented, and embraced

- ✔ Sees herself as a change agent, and regards this role as a key component of her position

- ✔ Utilizes a high degree of two-way communication when implementing change

- ✔ Includes employees in the change process

- ✔ Keeps employees involved at every step of the change process

- ✔ Solicits and incorporates employee input in the change process

- ✔ Identifies areas in which changes are needed, and then generates enthusiasm for these changes

- ✔ Uses excellent business insight and judgment in determining which changes to implement

- ✔ Introduces many changes to keep the company at the forefront of new strategies, technologies, and programs

Excellent: Frequently exceeds expectations

- ✔ Builds employees' abilities to adjust to change

- ✔ Avoids change for the sake of change

- ✔ Excels at analyzing proposed changes and implementing the changes that are most likely to be effective

- ✔ Regards change as a key force behind learning, growth, and development

- ✔ Helps employees see how they'll benefit from changes that are being implemented

- ✔ Keeps employees involved in the change process and treats them with trust and respect at every step

- ✔ Introduces changes that contribute to measurable improvement in employee performance

- ✔ Has created an atmosphere that is highly supportive of change

Fully competent: Meets expectations

✔ Adjusts to most changes quickly and easily

✔ Works directly with his employees to help them adjust to change

✔ Is a highly effective change agent

✔ Maintains a receptive attitude to proposed changes

✔ Reacts to change initially by learning more about it

✔ Reacts to most change in a positive, upbeat, and supportive manner

✔ Maintains positive expectations toward changes that are being implemented

✔ Uses ongoing formal and informal communication with her employees to reduce resistance to change

✔ Enjoys playing an active role in the change process

✔ Carefully considers the potential impact of the changes that he proposes

✔ Focuses on the gains associated with changes that are being implemented

Marginal: Occasionally fails to meet expectations

✔ Becomes nervous and anxious at the first sign of change

✔ Accepts change in a half-hearted manner that is emulated by other employees

✔ Avoids discussions to determine changes, but then complains about the changes that are made

✔ Pushes for changes that are likely to create confusion and dissention

✔ Only embraces self-serving changes

✔ Doesn't provide adequate analysis, reasoning, or documentation behind the changes that she proposes

✔ Pushes for changes without adequately considering their potential outcomes

✔ Frequently introduces changes that are neither necessary nor productive

- ✔ Has caused widespread productivity problems among his employees because he introduces one change after another, many of which are questionable at best

- ✔ Places more attention on making changes than making products

Unsatisfactory: Consistently fails to meet expectations

- ✔ Campaigns against proposed changes without fully understanding them

- ✔ Regards most changes as personal threats

- ✔ Only embraces changes that she suggests

- ✔ Introduces major changes without prior discussion or approval

- ✔ Indicates that he operates in accord with recent changes, but then ignores them

- ✔ Is unwilling to even discuss the prospect of various changes

- ✔ Offers her ideas for changes in other areas, but never for her own area

- ✔ Is unwilling to listen to his employees' suggestions for changes

- ✔ Excludes her employees from discussions regarding change in her area

- ✔ Makes his decisions about proposed changes without hearing any of the facts

- ✔ Generates a climate of resistance to change among her employees

- ✔ Initially reacts to change by rejecting it

- ✔ Initially reacts to change by fighting it

- ✔ Becomes upset with his employees who support proposed changes

- ✔ Continuously brings up changes that have failed in the past

- ✔ Approaches proposed changes with negative expectations

- ✔ Takes actions to undermine newly introduced changes

Encouraging and Supporting Innovation from Others

Exceptional: Consistently exceeds expectations

✔ Is widely regarded as an someone who seriously encourages innovative thinking

✔ Provides significant tangible and intangible rewards to employees who try to create new ideas, solutions, or suggestions

✔ Helps encourage innovative thinking by practicing it

✔ Holds frequent discussions on innovative problem-solving techniques to enhance employee awareness and effectiveness in this area

✔ Works directly with her employees to help build their skills in generating innovative ideas

✔ Shares his creative thinking expertise with his employees

✔ Provides her employees with coaching and encouragement when their efforts at innovative thinking fall short

Excellent: Frequently exceeds expectations

✔ Provides employees with significant recognition for their efforts as well as their successes at innovation

✔ Works with employees to analyze and improve their innovative ideas

✔ Maintains an open mind regarding employee attempts at innovation

✔ Initially reacts to employees' innovative ideas by listening rather than judging

✔ Provides employees with feedback and follow-up on the innovative ideas that they've discussed with him

Fully competent: Meets expectations

✔ Provides employees with constructive criticism of the their innovative ideas and suggestions

- Provides employees with ongoing feedback and encourages them to continue to develop their innovative ideas
- Supports educational programs to build her employees' skills in this area
- Holds frequent brainstorming sessions with employees
- Regularly communicates with his employees to discuss their new ideas

Marginal: Occasionally fails to meet expectations

- Lets employees present new ideas, but only on relatively unimportant matters
- Rarely has time to discuss new ideas
- Expects minimal innovation from her employees, which is exactly what she receives
- Expresses interest in meeting with his employees to brainstorm, but never does so
- Speaks of her interest in hearing innovative ideas from employees, but provides a lackluster response to all of them

Unsatisfactory: Consistently fails to meet expectations

- Convinces employees that they aren't creative
- Ignores employees' innovative comments, ideas, or suggestions
- Only provides negative feedback on employees' innovative ideas
- Is quick to reprimand employees if their efforts at innovative problem-solving strategies fall short
- Regards innovative thinking and problem solving as playing and fooling around
- Frequently advises employees that they aren't paid to be creative
- Ridicules employees' attempts at innovation
- Doesn't fully understand his employees' new ideas, but reacts negatively nonetheless

Generating New Ideas

Exceptional: Consistently exceeds expectations

- ✔ Is a constant source of outstanding new ideas
- ✔ Takes good ideas and turns them into outstanding ideas
- ✔ Finds new and better ways to get things done in her department and in many other areas as well
- ✔ Continuously generates ideas that improve performance and productivity
- ✔ Generates numerous creative approaches to problems that appear to be unapproachable
- ✔ Looks at old problems in new ways and solves many of them
- ✔ Is highly regarded as a major source of new ideas and creative thinking
- ✔ Demonstrates remarkable creativity on any assignment that he takes on

Excellent: Frequently exceeds expectations

- ✔ Generates ideas that are innovative and practical
- ✔ Comes up with ideas that consistently show insight and foresight
- ✔ Keeps chipping away at problems until she finds a new pathway to solve them
- ✔ Is a source of creative ideas for employees in many different areas
- ✔ Consistently finds ways to work smarter
- ✔ Doesn't merely generate new ideas, but generates new ideas that are practical, functional, and productive
- ✔ Revisits old ideas in new ways and gets excellent outcomes

Fully competent: Meets expectations

- ✔ Is always on the lookout for new and better ways to handle job responsibilities

- Enjoys working on projects that call for new ideas
- Has used innovative thinking to solve several complicated problems
- Pushes himself to come up with new ideas
- Regards creative thinking as an important part of her job
- Seeks challenging problems that call for innovative solutions
- Strives to apply innovative thinking to all of his projects

Marginal: Occasionally fails to meet expectations

- Comes up with new ideas that have little applicability to work
- Is more interested in the quantity than the quality of ideas that she generates
- Generates new ideas but does nothing with them
- Focuses on generating new ideas to solve insignificant problems
- Takes his old ideas, slightly rewraps them, and then insists that they're entirely new
- Becomes overly upset if her new ideas are questioned

Unsatisfactory: Consistently fails to meet expectations

- Hasn't taken any steps to generate new ideas
- Is uninterested in seeking new ways to handle responsibilities or solve problems
- Isn't inclined to push himself to come up new ideas
- Insists on implementing her new ideas without adequate analysis or planning
- Has implemented new ideas that led to serious productivity problems
- Doesn't regard innovative thinking as part of his job
- Insists on pushing her old ideas
- Takes credit for new ideas that aren't his

Presenting New Ideas for Company Policies and Procedures

Exceptional: Consistently exceeds expectations

✔ Has created several new policies that have had a measurably positive impact on employee performance

✔ Is always looking for ways to improve departmental operations

✔ Has taken several highly productive steps to streamline numerous procedures

✔ Stays aware of best-practices approaches to a wide range of policies and procedures, and consistently makes solid suggestions for improvement

✔ Has implemented new cost-saving procedures

✔ Reviewed current policies and removed language that was either out of date or out of compliance with current regulations

✔ Has designed and implemented new policies in several important emerging areas

✔ Generates ideas to improve policies or procedures that are always appropriate, well researched, and a clear improvement over current practices

Excellent: Frequently exceeds expectations

✔ Listens to her employees for recommendations regarding policies and procedures

✔ Has reduced the company's legal exposure through his recommended policy changes

✔ Is always looking for ways to upgrade operations that directly impact the bottom line

✔ Carefully studies the flow of work before presenting her ideas for improved procedures

✔ Finds conflicting and overlapping policies and procedures and recommends specific steps to correct them

- Includes an appropriate level of detail when presenting his ideas for changes in policies and procedures

- Is systems-minded and consistently presents state-of-the-art methods to upgrade a wide range of company systems

- Has outstanding systems expertise and is frequently sought for advice when it comes to writing or revising policies and procedures

Fully competent: Meets expectations

- Recommends improvements to company policies or procedures, instead of complaining about them

- Always provides clear and well written documentation to support his recommended changes in company policies or procedures

- Continues to study and take classes to build her expertise in this area

- Keeps an open mind when presenting his ideas to upgrade policies and procedures

- Takes a creative look at company policies and procedures and focuses on changes and upgrades that will last well into the future

- Provides a broad range of viable options when making suggestions to improve policies or procedures

- Is directly responsible for new policies that have led to improvements in employee morale and satisfaction

Marginal: Occasionally fails to meet expectations

- Recommends new procedures without fully understanding current procedures

- Recommends policy or procedural changes without adequate analysis or understanding of their potential impact

- Makes suggestions for new policies or procedures that are often out of date

- Has ideas for changes in policies and procedures that tend to be too general

- Makes recommendations for new policies and procedures that lack adequate documentation

✔ Gives presentations on new policies and procedures that are filled with far too much detail

✔ Disregards concerns about potential problems associated with her suggested changes in policy

✔ Ignores questions regarding his suggested improvements to polices and procedures

✔ Rarely considers costs when recommending changes in policies or procedures

✔ Suggests changes in policies and procedures that tend to focus only on the short term

✔ Refuses to consider input from others regarding her proposed changes to policies and procedures

✔ Tends to complain about policies and procedures rather than recommend specific improvements

✔ Believes that policies and procedures being used in other companies will automatically work here

Unsatisfactory: Consistently fails to meet expectations

✔ Continues to fixate on changing one particular policy because it directly impacts his work

✔ Recommends changes in policies or procedures that are far too costly to implement

✔ Becomes defensive when asked to provide more detail on the rationale behind her recommended changes

✔ Insists on having his recommendations implemented, regardless of their value

✔ Pressures her employees to support her recommended policy changes

✔ Continues to recommend implementation of policies that have failed in the past

✔ Takes it personally when his suggested changes in policies or procedures are not implemented

✔ Hasn't offered one suggestion to improve policies or procedures

✔ Shows no interest in improving company policies or procedures

Problem Solving

Exceptional: Consistently exceeds expectations

- Uses an arsenal of creative strategies to productively solve a wide range of problems

- Consistently generates outstanding solutions to the most demanding problems

- Focuses on solving problems, not on symptoms

- Has powerful analytical skills that she applies to every stage of the problem-solving process

- Establishes workable, prioritized, and highly effective problem-solving plans for each problem, instead of instantly jumping in and trying to solve them all

- Varies his problem-solving style to meet the nature and demands of the problem itself

- Approaches all problems with confidence and the expectation that she will generate solid and innovative solutions

- Actively seeks out problems that require the most creative thinking

Excellent: Frequently exceeds expectations

- Is a highly effective problem solver from start to finish

- Comes up with creative strategies when other employees are stuck

- Is frequently sought for a second look at problems that have stumped other employees

- Takes a fresh look at problems and identifies new inroads to solve them

- Creatively uses state-of-the-art technology to help in the problem-solving process

- Finds solutions that have eluded many others

Fully competent: Meets expectations

- Defines and understands problems before attempting to solve them

✓ Is a tenacious problem solver

✓ Has a broad range of problem-solving skills that he applies effectively to all problems and problem situations

✓ Is confident in her creative methods and unafraid to take a stand

✓ Creatively works his way around, over, under, or through obstacles in the problem-solving process

✓ Solves problems before they become crises

Marginal: Occasionally fails to meet expectations

✓ Gets stumped on the more challenging problems and quickly moves on to others that are easier to solve

✓ Generates average solutions to problems that could yield far more positive results if approached more creatively

✓ Is uninterested in new problem-solving strategies

✓ Focuses excessively on superficial issues, while often overlooking the deeper cause of the problem

✓ Identifies problems, but takes inadequate steps to resolve them

✓ Rushes through problems that require more thorough analysis

✓ Is reluctant to make recommendations based on her findings

Unsatisfactory: Consistently fails to meet expectations

✓ Employs problem-solving techniques that end up generating even more problems

✓ Creates more problems than he solves

✓ Overlooks or underestimates problems until they've become major issues

✓ Analyzes minor issues and lets larger problems fester and grow

✓ Decides on the solution to a problem before starting her analysis

✓ Comes up with solutions that are incorrect, insufficient, and invalid

Receptiveness to New Ideas

Exceptional: Consistently exceeds expectations

- ✔ Consistently demonstrates a high degree of interest in ideas and suggestions from his employees

- ✔ Has a totally open mind when it comes to hearing new ideas

- ✔ Encourages innovative thinking from others

- ✔ Regards new ideas as an essential component of personal growth

- ✔ Is not only receptive to new ideas, but also works with employees to further shape and refine them

- ✔ Emphasizes that great individual and corporate success emanate from new ideas

- ✔ Truly believes that excellent ideas can come from anyone at any level of the organization

Excellent: Frequently exceeds expectations

- ✔ Always makes time to listen to the employees' new ideas

- ✔ Is seen by employees as being truly interested in their innovative thinking

- ✔ Follows up with employees after discussing their creative ideas with them

- ✔ Takes appropriate action on employees' ideas

- ✔ Actively solicits new ideas from her employees

- ✔ Always provides thanks, credit, and recognition for new ideas, regardless of whether the ideas can be used

Fully competent: Meets expectations

- ✔ Is open to ideas and suggestions that differ from his thinking or way of doing things

- ✔ Rewards employees for suggestions that are implemented

- ✔ Implements employee ideas and suggestions whenever possible

- ✔ Lets the employees know that she has high expectations regarding their innovative thinking

✔ Never misses an opportunity to ask for new ideas and suggestions from the employees

✔ Is seen by employees as being interested in their ideas

✔ Has created an atmosphere in which all employees are totally comfortable presenting their ideas to him

Marginal: Occasionally fails to meet expectations

✔ Talks about her ideas when employees want to discuss their ideas

✔ Goes through the motions of listening to employees' new ideas, but doesn't really pay attention

✔ Rarely takes steps to do anything with the employees' new ideas

✔ Believes that employees lack the expertise and insight to come up with useful suggestions on significant matters

✔ Is satisfied with current operations and doesn't see the need for suggestions

✔ Believes that the employees' innovative ideas highlight his own lack of such ideas

Unsatisfactory: Consistently fails to meet expectations

✔ Is uninterested in hearing ideas from employees

✔ Advises employees to do their work and stop bringing their ideas to her

✔ Tells employees that all their ideas have been tried, and they don't work

✔ Regards employees' ideas as an interruption

✔ Is brief and abrupt when employees try to present their ideas to him

✔ Doesn't listen when employees present new ideas to her

✔ Repeatedly cancels meetings with employees to discuss their ideas

✔ Chastises employees whose ideas differ from his

✔ Lives by the philosophy that employees should "stop thinking and start doing"

Seeking Improvements

Exceptional: Consistently exceeds expectations

- Pushes for improvements on a wide range of issues, ranging from the most detailed matters all the way to global developments that offer major opportunities for the company

- Has presented several outstanding ideas to reduce costs

- Comes up with excellent ideas to build revenues

- Is responsible for operational improvements that are having a positive impact on the bottom line

- Carefully scans the marketplace for new opportunities

- Uses her solid knowledge of business operations to help streamline operations company-wide

Excellent: Frequently exceeds expectations

- Continuously seeks specific steps, strategies, and programs that will make the company more effective

- Is highly observant of all company operations and works with key employees to discuss and implement improvements

- Meets formally and informally with his employees to openly discuss ways to make improvements to the company

- Is able to find creative applications for ideas that others may have overlooked

- Reads a great deal about customer service and provides viable suggestions to build the company's effectiveness in this area

Fully competent: Meets expectations

- Interprets her responsibilities broadly and looks beyond her assigned tasks for ways to improve the company

- Is always on the lookout for ways to build the company's success

✔ Provides his employees with support and recognition for their efforts to make improvements to the company

✔ Is never satisfied with the status quo

Marginal: Occasionally fails to meet expectations

✔ Occasionally comes up with new ideas for improvement, but does nothing with them

✔ Rarely devotes serious attention to seeking and creating improvements

✔ Shows minimal interest in hearing about planned improvements for the company

✔ Continuously focuses on the need for improvements in areas that are of minimal importance to the success of the company

✔ Attends strategy sessions, but doesn't participate in the discussions

✔ Encourages her employees to make suggestions for improvements, and then ignores them

✔ Doesn't focus on improvements beyond his department

Unsatisfactory: Consistently fails to meet expectations

✔ Has an "it's not my job" attitude when it comes to seeking improvements for the company

✔ Hardly focuses on her own job, let alone looking for larger improvements

✔ Suggests strategies that contradict the company's values and ethics

✔ Solicits improvement ideas from his employees and then presents them as his own

✔ Discourages her employees from seeking any improvements

✔ Changes the subject when employees start talking about the ways to make improvements to the company

✔ Shows complete disinterest in trying to find ways to make any significant improvements

Thinking outside the Box

Exceptional: Consistently exceeds expectations

- Approaches problems with an open mind and without preconceived notions
- Questions assumptions regarding the significance of each piece of data and reassesses the value of each
- Looks at issues, questions, and dilemmas from every angle and generates entirely new ways to resolve them
- Is unrestrained by traditional problem-solving approaches, strategies, or expectations
- Generates productive outcomes by including unlikely people or resources in the problem-solving process
- Is unconcerned with others' opinions regarding the approach or style that he's using
- Keeps an ongoing log of her creative ideas in order to continuously enhance them
- Thinks outside the box by moving out of his workstation or office in order to literally look at a problem in a different light

Excellent: Frequently exceeds expectations

- Productively integrates people, processes, and systems that seemingly don't go together at all
- Takes concepts that are cast in stone and then shatters, reshapes, or redefines them to generate more productive ideas and solutions
- Excludes seemingly essential components to open the door to a wider range of creative solutions
- Is open to totally different ideas, assumptions, and strategies
- Isn't afraid to make mistakes
- Doesn't give up in the face of doubtful comments by others who observe her unorthodox style

Fully competent: Meets expectations

- Avoids yesterday's problem-solving strategies
- Enjoys working on projects that require creative thinking and solutions
- Has attended training sessions that focus on creative thinking and problem solving
- Uses his excellent observational skills to find overlooked pieces of data that can open up entirely new ways to solve problems
- Has an unconventional problem-solving style that yields better-than-conventional results
- Is always looking for new and productive ways to use everyday items

Marginal: Occasionally fails to meet expectations

- Overly satisfied with the status quo
- Is afraid of making a wrong decision
- Regards unconventional thinking as too risky
- Has negative feelings and expectations when engaged in thinking that is slightly different from her traditional approach
- At the first sign of a problem, immediately reverts from creative thinking to overly structured thinking
- Believes that he is already thinking outside the box, but his actions indicate otherwise

Unsatisfactory: Consistently fails to meet expectations

- Is far more comfortable thinking inside the box
- Rarely challenges assumptions
- Is unwilling to change her thinking style, regardless of recent questionable decisions
- Refuses to attend programs that focus on creative thinking
- Only takes on projects that can be handled with very conventional thinking
- Avoids projects that call for creative thinking
- Regards the concept of thinking outside the box as a fad

Chapter 17

The Best Phrases for Self-Development and Growth

*O*ne of the major objectives of performance appraisals is to provide employees with targeted feedback and guidance to help them learn, grow, and develop. Without a developmental component, performance appraisals would be relegated to the role of a mirror, showing employees how their performance looks but providing no help, support, or guidance to do anything about it.

The developmental comments that you include in your performance appraisals will ultimately help your employees experience the satisfaction associated with increased personal growth and increased personal productivity. Plus, as employees become more effective and productive, the effectiveness and productivity of the company will be enhanced.

Employee self-development is not a one-dimensional concept. Instead, in order for feedback in this area to have its intended positive impact, it needs to focus on the key components of development and growth. You need to include instructive phrases on such topics as training, personal goals, career planning, seeking learning opportunities, building problem-solving skills, widening one's knowledge base, and more.

Employees and employers alike seek growth and development, and your phrases in this area will help both of them meet this goal.

Becoming a Value-Added Employee

Exceptional: Consistently exceeds expectations

- ✔ Makes measurable contributions far beyond expectations
- ✔ Has stepped far beyond his performance expectations and taken actions that have generated major opportunities for the company
- ✔ Provides guidance that raises the competence, performance, and output of her fellow employees
- ✔ Has held costs constant while measurably improving his output as well as the output of his employees
- ✔ Has played a central role in generating additional revenue for the company because of her broad base of knowledge and experience
- ✔ Is able to integrate information and draw highly profitable conclusions
- ✔ Is clearly one of the company's best investments
- ✔ Continues to keep his base of knowledge at expert levels
- ✔ Is widely regarded as one of the company's most valuable resources

Excellent: Frequently exceeds expectations

- ✔ Is sought out by employees in many departments outside of her own because of her knowledge and expertise
- ✔ Is a major asset to the department and the company at large because of his skills mix
- ✔ Builds the skills and productivity of her employees
- ✔ Is one of the company's major assets
- ✔ Has skills that are unique to the department and central to its success
- ✔ Has built his expertise in areas that directly impact the bottom line
- ✔ Takes a wide range of actions that enhance the reputation of the company

✔ Has played a key role in attracting several outstanding individuals to this company because of her expertise and stature in the industry

✔ Has made efforts that have contributed to a significant drop in the unit cost of each item

✔ Generates maximum productivity from company resources

✔ Is always willing and able to take on additional projects

✔ Raises the quality of the decisions that are made in meetings just by being there

Fully competent: Meets expectations

✔ Has a direct and positive impact on the quantity and quality of his fellow employees' work because of the quality and quantity of his own work

✔ Continues to make increasingly valuable suggestions

✔ Continues to develop specific skills that increase her productivity

✔ Takes steps to build knowledge, skills, and abilities that directly lead to increases in the quality and quantity of work

✔ Brings a continuously expanding set of unique skills that enhance performance and productivity in his department

✔ Continues to expand her technology skills in areas that are valued by the company

✔ Has a proactive mindset

✔ Uses his solid planning skills to complete work on time and prevent crises and crunches along the way

✔ Strives to exceed expectations on all of her projects

Marginal: Occasionally fails to meet expectations

✔ Does his job and nothing more

✔ Contributes to the company in ways that tend to be minimal and of slight value at best

✔ Has allowed her value to the company to decrease over the years

✔ Sets goals to increase his value to the company but then sets them aside

✔ Rarely challenges herself to pursue rigorous work that would truly increase her value to the company

✔ Doesn't exert enough energy or effort to truly increase his value to the company

✔ Believes that she adds more value than is actually the case

✔ Focuses his energy in areas of minimal importance

Unsatisfactory: Consistently fails to meet expectations

✔ Has taken no steps to enhance her skills and value to the company

✔ Has taken actions that actually decrease his value to the company

✔ Takes actions without considering the value that they add to or subtract from the company

✔ Demonstrates no significant value-added behaviors due in great part to her lack of interest in self-development

✔ Acts in ways that discourage or diminish value-added behaviors from his employees

✔ Does the minimum amount of work, leading to the minimum amount of added value

✔ Makes negative comments about the company

✔ Shows a complete disregard over the impact that her actions can have on the company's reputation and goodwill

✔ Rejects all opportunities to assume additional responsibilities

✔ Fails to seize opportunities to develop skills that would increase his value to the company

Building Problem-Solving Skills

Exceptional: Consistently exceeds expectations

- ✔ Has established and surpassed goals that focus on improving her problem-solving skills

- ✔ Does a great deal of independent reading to continue to strengthen his problem-solving skills

- ✔ Further enhances her problem-solving skills by helping other employees build theirs

- ✔ Seeks and seizes opportunities to strengthen his problem-solving skills

- ✔ Models her problem-solving skills on those of the best problem-solvers in the company

- ✔ Has outstanding problem-solving skills and continues to take steps to make them even stronger

- ✔ Has actively pursued training programs to enhance his problem-solving skills

Excellent: Frequently exceeds expectations

- ✔ Devotes extra time, energy, and effort to building her problem-solving skills

- ✔ Is open to new ideas and suggestions to further build his problem-solving skills

- ✔ Clearly demonstrated her improved problem-solving skills in handling the XYZ project

- ✔ Has made and kept commitments to upgrade his problem-solving skills

- ✔ Has transformed her previously weak problem-solving skills into strong problem-solving skills

- ✔ Continues to attend educational programs and seminars that focus on problem-solving skills

Fully competent: Meets expectations

- ✔ Is steadily improving his ability to solve problems

- ✔ Has solid problem-solving skills that she continues to develop

✔ Is highly interested in feedback from others to help build his ability to solve problems

✔ Applies suggestions and strategies from others to help strengthen her problem-solving abilities

✔ Has demonstrated a marked improvement in his problem-solving skills since his last performance appraisal

✔ Seeks and accepts feedback on her problem-solving skills

Marginal: Occasionally fails to meet expectations

✔ Agrees to take steps to improve his problem-solving ability, but fails to do so

✔ Is satisfied with her problem-solving skills, even though they have consistently fallen short

✔ Uses problem-solving strategies that no longer apply to workplace issues

✔ Doesn't take advantage of company-sponsored programs to build his problem-solving abilities

✔ Is unresponsive to offers of help from fellow employees who have excellent mentoring skills in several areas, including problem-solving

Unsatisfactory: Consistently fails to meet expectations

✔ Has taken no steps to upgrade her problem-solving skills

✔ Is unwilling to listen to feedback to upgrade his problem-solving abilities

✔ Has shown no improvement in her problem-solving skills since her last performance appraisal

✔ Has shown a decline in his ability to solve problems

✔ Actively avoids opportunities to bolster her problem-solving ability

✔ Has caused smaller issues to turn into major problems as a result of his refusal to build his problem-solving skills

✔ Refuses to acknowledge the problems that have been caused by her current problem-solving skills

Career Planning

Exceptional: Consistently exceeds expectations

- ✔ Is taking all the right steps to meet his career goals
- ✔ Applies her strong goal orientation to the career planning process
- ✔ Monitors his career plans and makes appropriate adjustments and upgrades
- ✔ Continues to set increasingly higher career goals for herself
- ✔ Accompanies all career goals with solid career planning
- ✔ Has set planning and goals that allow him to be on a fast track in his career
- ✔ Combines her career goals with the energy, drive, and focus to meet them
- ✔ Has built a strong team under him as part of his plan to continue to advance
- ✔ Adapts career plans appropriately to capitalize on unforeseen career opportunities

Excellent: Frequently exceeds expectations

- ✔ Is receptive to career guidance
- ✔ Builds on the career advice that she receives
- ✔ Monitors his career plans and progress and takes active steps to stay on course
- ✔ Obtains appropriate training required for short-term and long-term career goals
- ✔ Treats career goals as seriously as performance goals and works equally diligently to meet them
- ✔ Has serious career goals but never loses sight of the performance goals that she has also established
- ✔ Takes courses and attends seminars to help him guide and manage his career
- ✔ Does a good deal of reading in the area of career planning
- ✔ Is serious, thorough, and committed in planning her career

Fully competent: Meets expectations

- ✔ Has established clear career plans and goals for himself
- ✔ Continues to meet her near-term career goals
- ✔ Establishes career plans but does not over-plan
- ✔ Sets career plans and sticks with them
- ✔ Sets challenging yet realistic career goals and the plans that are needed to meet them
- ✔ Is undeterred by career setbacks or disappointments
- ✔ Takes advantage of the career-building opportunities available within the company
- ✔ Utilizes the company's resources to continue to advance his career
- ✔ Has learned a great deal by formulating her own career goals and has used this experience to establish solid expertise to help other employees set their career goals and plans
- ✔ Attends career planning seminars and applies what he learns

Marginal: Occasionally fails to meet expectations

- ✔ Has done no serious career planning
- ✔ Takes a reactive mode when it comes to career planning
- ✔ Sets career goals but lacks career plans
- ✔ Is so locked into her career plans that she instantly rejects other career options
- ✔ Has career plans, but they lack specificity
- ✔ Has set career goals without adequate consideration of the planning required to meet them
- ✔ Puts career plans ahead of performance plans
- ✔ Fails to track the progress that he is making in pursuing his career goals
- ✔ Focuses more on the format than the content of her career plan
- ✔ Has established a career direction but no career goals

- Talks a great deal about the importance of career planning but has done very little for his own career

- Has set career goals but ignores opportunities to move closer to them

- Takes advantage of none of the company's resources to help develop and solidify her career plan

- Attends career planning sessions but doesn't apply any of the training

Unsatisfactory: Consistently fails to meet expectations

- Ignores the career plans that he establishes

- Devotes no time to career planning

- Assumes that she has no responsibility for setting career plans or goals

- Takes no steps to build knowledge, skills, and abilities required for the next step in his career

- Has unrealistic career goals and equally unrealistic career plans

- Has not engaged in career planning in the past and demonstrates no interest in doing so now

- Has set career goals but takes steps that directly contradict them

- Has intentionally missed individual and group meetings to discuss career goals and planning

- Waits for others to tell her where her career should go from this point

- Instantly rejects any advice or coaching that deals with his career

- Takes no initiative in seeking the training that she needs in order to reach her personal goals

- Expresses regret about his career options but takes no action to do anything about them

- Has landed in her present position without any career planning and has no interest in starting now

Personal Goals

Exceptional: Consistently exceeds expectations

- ✔ Has a clear vision of his future and works diligently to make it a reality
- ✔ Has a strong personal goal orientation, which has inspired fellow employees to follow suit
- ✔ Strives to attain personal goals that easily elude others
- ✔ Takes responsibility for her personal growth and development
- ✔ Consistently meets his personal objectives and then sets new ones that are even more challenging
- ✔ Establishes clear and challenging short-term and long-term personal goals
- ✔ Demonstrates great initiative and energy in pursuing her personal goals

Excellent: Frequently exceeds expectations

- ✔ Establishes clear, specific, and measurable personal goals
- ✔ Has attained his personal goals, which has led to markedly improved performance
- ✔ Sets goals that are all accompanied by well-designed action plans
- ✔ Devotes major effort to reaching her personal goals
- ✔ Is able to meet his personal goals while also meeting his performance goals
- ✔ Continues to set increasingly challenging personal goals
- ✔ Shows great confidence regarding her ability to meet personal goals

Fully competent: Meets expectations

- ✔ Takes his personal goals seriously
- ✔ Listens to counsel from others regarding her personal goals and the best strategies to meet them

✔ Sets challenging yet realistic goals regarding his skills, education, and career

✔ Has established personal goals and a path to meet them

✔ Obtains the training that is needed to achieve her personal goals

✔ Helps other employees determine their personal goals

✔ Shows a high degree of tenacity in pursuing his personal goals

Marginal: Occasionally fails to meet expectations

✔ Sets personal goals, but none that would enhance her performance on the job

✔ Takes no serious steps to meet his personal goals

✔ Sets very general personal goals

✔ Sets unchallenging personal goals

✔ Hasn't made a serious commitment to meeting her personal goals

✔ Sets lofty personal goals but has no plans or strategies to meet them

✔ Demonstrates very little persistence in the pursuit of personal goals

Unsatisfactory: Consistently fails to meet expectations

✔ Has established no goals to further develop his skills, abilities, or expertise

✔ Accepts no responsibility for setting her own personal goals

✔ Has had the same personal goals for an extended period of time and has failed to meet any of them

✔ Gives up easily in the pursuit of his personal goals

✔ Jumps from one personal goal to another but reaches none

✔ Pursues personal goals at the expense of performance goals

Responding to Performance Appraisals and Coaching

Exceptional: Consistently exceeds expectations

- ✔ Fully commits herself to following specific action plans to make improvements noted in her performance appraisal
- ✔ Accepts constructive feedback positively and is highly oriented toward making improvements in areas discussed with him
- ✔ Makes immediate corrective action based on the coaching that she receives
- ✔ Actively seeks coaching and uses it wisely
- ✔ Carefully considers every point in his performance appraisal and takes specific steps to deal with each

Excellent: Frequently exceeds expectations

- ✔ Appreciates coaching and acts on the feedback that she receives
- ✔ Uses the feedback from his performance appraisal and coaching to fine-tune his skills
- ✔ Has been taking highly effective steps to upgrade her performance in areas that were noted in her last performance appraisal
- ✔ Accepts feedback in his performance appraisal with an open mind and readiness to take action
- ✔ Has taken her skills to an entirely new level by focusing on the coaching that she has received

Fully competent: Meets expectations

- ✔ Takes performance appraisal feedback seriously and has made many improvements based on it
- ✔ Pays careful attention to the coaching that he receives and has upgraded his performance as a result
- ✔ Takes appropriate steps to follow the action plan and improve her performance in areas noted in her performance appraisal

✔ Has taken actions as a result of his most recent performance appraisal, which have led to marked improvements in performance

✔ Is highly receptive to coaching and managerial feedback

Marginal: Occasionally fails to meet expectations

✔ Reacts defensively to feedback on her performance

✔ Appears to listen to coaching but then makes no changes in his behavior

✔ Needs frequent prodding before taking any action on feedback in her performance appraisal

✔ Makes a few quick and easy changes after being coached but ignores the larger issues

✔ Asks no questions during the coaching sessions and then heads off in the wrong direction

✔ Immediately reacts to any constructive feedback with denial

✔ Commits to taking corrective action after his performance appraisal but then fails to do so

✔ Takes some corrective actions immediately after her performance appraisal but then slides back to her old ways

Unsatisfactory: Consistently fails to meet expectations

✔ Doesn't listen to the coaching provided to him

✔ Ignores feedback that she receives in her performance appraisal

✔ Has taken no action based on the feedback and guidance that he received in his last performance appraisal

✔ Has received coaching on the same issue several times and has yet to show any signs of improvement

✔ Spends more time arguing than listening in performance appraisals

✔ Ignores her appointments for coaching sessions

✔ Is unreceptive to constructive feedback or coaching

Seeking Learning Opportunities

Exceptional: Consistently exceeds expectations

- ✔ Seeks out and attends seminars and training programs in his specialty
- ✔ Is an avid reader of magazines and journals in her field
- ✔ Has outstanding observation skills that allow him to learn details that others are likely to miss
- ✔ Is consistently acquiring new skills and building existing skills
- ✔ Regards the acquisition of knowledge as one of her highest priorities
- ✔ Quickly reaches a high level of expertise in new areas
- ✔ Brings a high degree of intellectual curiosity to the job
- ✔ Genuinely enjoys working in challenging situations that require major amounts of learning
- ✔ Is highly motivated to maintain cutting-edge expertise

Excellent: Frequently exceeds expectations

- ✔ Puts in extra hours for the sole purpose of building his skills and abilities
- ✔ Frequently engages in informal discussions to upgrade her knowledge base
- ✔ Seeks feedback from others in order to build and enrich his knowledge base
- ✔ Recognizes gaps in her knowledge base and takes active steps to fill them
- ✔ Turns most work situations into learning opportunities
- ✔ Is always in a learning mode
- ✔ Has continued to expand his expertise across a broad range of areas
- ✔ Enjoys work situations in which successful performance requires additional learning and new skills

🗸 Has positively influenced many of her fellow employees through her enthusiasm toward learning

🗸 Consistently has a fast start-up on highly difficult projects because of his active pursuit of knowledge

Fully competent: Meets expectations

🗸 Regards performance appraisals as a learning opportunity

🗸 Takes advantage of the company's mentoring program

🗸 Truly learns from her mistakes

🗸 Is always taking steps to gain more than a superficial understanding of new information that is relevant to his work

🗸 Is currently attending a formal educational program

🗸 Has completed all courses in a formal educational program and received her certification

🗸 Asks questions if he doesn't understand

🗸 Makes good use of the company's educational benefits

🗸 Actively participates in the company's educational programs

Marginal: Occasionally fails to meet expectations

🗸 Rarely takes advantage of the company's educational benefits

🗸 Begrudgingly attends required educational programs and sessions

🗸 Rarely attends in-house educational programs

🗸 Shows no interest in accessing the learning resources available at the company

🗸 Attends educational programs but doesn't actively engage in them

🗸 Is a vocal critic of company training programs, even though she rarely attends any

🗸 Doesn't take the time to read written information that is provided prior to major projects

✔ Hasn't applied any of the information, techniques, or strategies that were emphasized in the training programs that he attended

✔ Rarely devotes enough time to fully mastering new skills that are required for her projects

✔ Enters learning programs with the expectation that he will learn nothing — and that is typically what he learns

✔ Rarely shows enough interest to ask questions

✔ Fails to take advantage of widespread learning opportunities offered by her associates

Unsatisfactory: Consistently fails to meet expectations

✔ Takes no active steps to enhance his expertise

✔ Is invited to many training programs but refuses to attend

✔ Rejects educational opportunities offered to her

✔ Regards additional education as unnecessary

✔ Doesn't believe that seeking additional educational opportunities is his responsibility

✔ Never seeks out educational opportunities and rejects those that are offered to her

✔ Takes no action on his own to pursue learning opportunities

✔ Immediately dismisses information on new techniques, strategies, or approaches, instead of listening to any of it

✔ Continues to rely on outmoded skills and outdated information, even after receiving specific coaching on newer approaches

✔ Avoids assignments and projects that require the acquisition of new knowledge or skills

✔ Prefers to do her work the old way rather than learn new technologies, processes, or procedures

Training

Exceptional: Consistently exceeds expectations

- ✔ Regards training as one of his highest personal priorities
- ✔ Devotes a high degree of energy and effort to getting the most out of all training programs and sessions
- ✔ Offers insightful comments that help herself and others learn during training sessions
- ✔ Is a positive influence in all training programs
- ✔ Builds a great deal of interest in training across his department
- ✔ Attends training sessions and then informally trains others
- ✔ Actively participates in training programs

Excellent: Frequently exceeds expectations

- ✔ Takes all training seriously
- ✔ Shows immediate interest in new topics for training
- ✔ Asks excellent questions
- ✔ Adjusts easily and quickly to new training technologies
- ✔ Is a valuable participant in all training programs and sessions
- ✔ Quickly applies new knowledge to the job
- ✔ Continues to review training materials after the sessions have ended

Fully competent: Meets expectations

- ✔ Genuinely enjoys the learning process
- ✔ Is an active and eager learner

✔ Is never late to training sessions

✔ Completes all required preparation prior to training sessions

✔ Pays careful attention throughout the training process

✔ Is highly appreciative of the training that she receives

✔ Strives to apply whatever he has learned in training

Marginal: Occasionally fails to meet expectations

✔ Comes up with numerous excuses to avoid training

✔ Rarely participates in discussions during training sessions

✔ Is late to most training sessions

✔ Attends training sessions but fails to pay attention

✔ Claims that she doesn't need training, even though her performance contradicts this assertion

✔ Believes that his skills and knowledge are greater than they really are

✔ Signs up for training programs but rarely attends

Unsatisfactory: Consistently fails to meet expectations

✔ Shows no interest in additional training

✔ Is quick to criticize the training that is provided

✔ Misses training sessions

✔ Engages in disruptive behaviors during training sessions

✔ Fails to apply new information to the job

✔ Insists on using her former practices, instead of applying new practices in which she has been trained

✔ Makes no effort to educate himself

✔ Believes her current training is sufficient, even though it is not

✔ Makes derogatory comments during training sessions

✔ Fails to attend required classes

Widening One's Knowledge Base

Exceptional: Consistently exceeds expectations

- ✔ Is consistently among the first to learn new strategies or technologies

- ✔ Makes an ongoing effort to remain at the cutting edge of his field

- ✔ Actively pursues a broad range of opportunities to enhance her knowledge base

- ✔ Consistently seeks opportunities — both on and off the job — to build his knowledge base

- ✔ Anticipates new business trends and takes steps to widen her knowledge base to capitalize on them

- ✔ Sets challenging goals regarding the breadth of his knowledge base and then takes serious steps to surpass them

- ✔ Reads a vast array of books, journals, and magazines to further widen her range of knowledge

Excellent: Frequently exceeds expectations

- ✔ Places a great deal of emphasis on building his knowledge base in areas that directly and indirectly impact his ability to do the job

- ✔ Takes ongoing steps to build her knowledge base as well as the knowledge bases of her employees

- ✔ Maintains a continuously widening knowledge base

- ✔ Serves as an excellent model for other employees because of the steps he has taken to widen his knowledge base

- ✔ Maintains an open mind when dealing with information that challenges her current state of knowledge

- ✔ Continues to expand his already broad base of knowledge

- ✔ Has significantly widened her base of knowledge since her last performance appraisal

Fully competent: Meets expectations

- Made and kept a commitment to widen his knowledge base
- Frequently attends programs, classes, and seminars to build her knowledge base
- Uses a wide range of online and offline resources to widen his knowledge base
- Takes proactive steps to build her knowledge base
- Wisely uses company resources to continue to expand his knowledge base
- Has continued to widen her knowledge base since her last performance appraisal

Marginal: Occasionally fails to meet expectations

- Sets personal goals to widen his knowledge base but fails to meet them
- Has allowed her base of knowledge to fall increasingly out of date with the passage of time
- Continually uses outmoded strategies, highlighting his lack of interest in widening his knowledge base
- Waits for others to present her with opportunities to widen her knowledge base
- Demonstrates little initiative when it comes to widening his knowledge base
- Is uninterested in learning about new strategies and technologies that differ from what she is doing today

Unsatisfactory: Consistently fails to meet expectations

- Has taken no productive steps to widen his knowledge base
- Actively resists new information that contradicts what she already knows
- Ignores company-sponsored opportunities to build and widen his knowledge base
- Ignores suggestions to take specific classes that would help build her knowledge base
- Has established neither goals nor plans to widen his knowledge base

Part IV
The Part of Tens

The 5th Wave   By Rich Tennant

In this part . . .

In the well-established tradition of *For Dummies* books, the chapters in this part provide you with the ten most powerful, persuasive, and motivational words that you can use in the performance appraisal process, along with ten outstanding employee behaviors that merit special recognition. Communication plays a compelling role throughout the appraisal process, and these chapters provide you with extra communication tools that generate and sustain highly positive and productive performance from your employees.

That's a powerful punch for such a pithy part!

Chapter 18

The Top Ten Words to Include in a Performance Appraisal

. . . .

In This Chapter

▶ Choosing words that energize your employees

▶ Interspersing words that establish positive expectations

▶ Including words that inspire feelings of confidence and self-worth

. . . .

*O*ne of the most effective ways to enhance the impact of the appraisals you provide is to select words that have a strong positive emotional charge. You may think that as long as you somehow get your message across, your word choice isn't all that important. After all, the message is what counts, right? The truth is, some words hit home far more quickly and compellingly than others.

In this chapter, I fill you in on ten positively charged words that pack a punch. By including them in your feedback, you greatly increase the likelihood that your comments will actually be heard and that your employees' performance will actually improve.

The Employee's Name

A person's name is one of the most powerfully charged words that she knows. If it wasn't the first word she ever heard, it's certainly among the very earliest.

When someone hears her own name, she reacts. She may turn, jump, flinch, or smile, but regardless of the specific action, she's not likely to ignore it, nor is she likely to ignore what happens after her name is called. By saying your employee's name before providing her with feedback, you're improving her readiness to listen carefully to your next words — and to act on them.

Achievement

Numerous studies have found the word *achievement* to be one of the premier sources of employee motivation. When employees hear the word *achievement* in your feedback, they're better able to sense the significance of their accomplishments.

Your employees can certainly experience feelings of achievement as they carry out their work, and they can give themselves any number of positive messages. However, when they hear you use the word *achievement,* its true motivational impact is released. After all, you can tell yourself that you achieved an important landmark, but this feedback is far more compelling when voiced by your manager.

Providing your employees with feedback that incorporates the word *achievement* has another benefit: When your employees encounter future opportunities that offer the possibility of achievement-oriented feedback, they're more likely to push themselves to go for the gold.

Build

The word *build* is literally and figuratively one of the most constructive words to use in the performance appraisal process. It has a strong positive connotation — the word *build* inherently assumes that something positive is going to be designed, created, and brought to life. In this way, the word *build* sets off positive emotions as soon as it's heard or seen.

The word *build* also has a strong visual component. In fact, when most people see or hear the word *build,* it isn't simply filed away with most other words. The more common tendency is to mentally envision completed structures, such as buildings and bridges. Because your employees are automatically linking *build* with the successful completion of major projects, the word has a positive emotional charge.

The word *build* also implies an orderly, structured, and well-planned process with a real foundation. As a result, it connotes organized growth and development, and not a quick or superficial set of steps. Plus, most building projects are carried out by teams, which means that the word sends a subtle message that you'll be teaming up with your employees to help them along their paths of development.

In light of the compelling and memorable impact associated with the word *build,* you should include it across the broad spectrum of employee performance — for example, when you're talking about building productivity, output, relationships, knowledge, skills, strengths, teamwork, performance, and profits.

Can

By using the word *can* when appraising your employees, you're sending a subtle message — not only in terms of positive expectations but also in terms of your confidence in the employees' abilities to perform successfully. The more your employees hear what they *can* do, the more likely they are to do it. When you lace your comments with *can,* you're literally reinforcing your employees' can-do attitude.

As important as it is to emphasize what your employees' can do, it's equally important to avoid the word *can't.* The word *can't* sends a negative message about your employees' potential and can easily undermine their expectations and efforts.

Growth

There is no question that employees aspire to experience growth at work. However, growth is such a slow process that many employees aren't sure whether it's happening at all. In fact, because growth occurs in such minuscule snippets, some employees can miss it altogether.

By working with your employees each day, you can see growth when it occurs. In fact, you probably see more of your employees' growth than anyone they know. That fact, in combination with the role that you play as their manager, provides you with extra insight and credibility when it comes to recognizing their growth.

However, if you don't mention the word *growth,* your employees can still miss it, even if you glowingly describe their accomplishments. Employees want to know whether and how they've been growing, and by including the word *growth* in your comments, you can provide them with an answer that is clear, meaningful, and energizing. Plus, the use of this word continues to encourage your employees to repeat the behaviors that have helped them grow to this point.

Profit

The word *profit* has a strong emotional impact for employees at all levels of a company. As a result, it's a very important word to use in the appraisal process. In fact, when profit is minimized in performance appraisals, it's likely to be minimized in other ways as well.

There are actually two key reasons to use the word *profit:*

- ✔ **Employees at all levels should be thinking about it.** By keeping profit in mind, any employee becomes far more likely to take small or large steps to help the company be more successful.

- ✔ **When employees hear your feedback and consider changing their behavior, they need to understand how they'll benefit personally by making such changes.** Many employees make decisions about changing their behavior as a result of performance appraisal feedback by asking themselves, "What's in it for me?" One of the most effective ways to answer this question is to clearly show your employees how they will "profit" by taking the actions that you're suggesting.

Promotion

Every employee remembers his first promotion with pride, and simply hearing the word *promotion* brings back at least a hint of those positive feelings. Plus, promotions have long been found to be a strong source of employee motivation. The result is that both of these factors contribute to the long-lasting positive emotional charge associated with the word *promotion.*

In light of these two factors, plus the role that performance appraisal plays in the promotion process, using the word *promotion* is particularly important when appraising your employees' performance.

The best time to use this word is when you're discussing performance in areas that directly relate to advancement, such as your employees' leadership abilities, technical knowledge, and communication skills. By specifically using *promotion* in this context, your employees are given a clearer understanding of the link between outstanding work in specific performance areas and advancement in the company.

Although using the word *promotion* is important, it's equally important to avoid making any promises or commitments about promotions. Managers who make such promises to their employees may soon find that they've walked right into a contract.

Success

When providing positive feedback, you may be tempted to focus on numbers, dates, facts, and figures. However, the best way to make this type of information memorable and motivational is to include the word *success* in the process.

By including *success* as you review your employees' successful attainment of hard numbers, your words will have a more compelling impact. Although your feedback will still have its share of rates, ratios, and percentages, such data will be wrapped in a motivational package that gives your employees a strong sense of recognition and personal competence.

Employees may or may not take the numbers with them after your review session, but the powerful psychological impact of this type of recognition will stay with them for a long time. Plus, because recognition is such a strong motivator, your use of the word *success* increases the likelihood that your employees will repeat their excellent behaviors in the future.

Thanks

In light of the large amount of ground that you have to cover in performance appraisals, one powerful word that you can easily overlook is *thanks*. If you forget to use the word *thanks,* you're losing a valuable and cost-effective opportunity to raise an employee's spirits, morale, and sense of self-worth.

As you prepare your performance appraisals for each employee, try to single out one major accomplishment that made a truly positive difference in the department or company at large. During the appraisal session, after you discuss this particular achievement, pause for a second or two and then thank your employee. Don't be surprised if your employee pauses for a second or two in return. She'll probably be shocked, and that fact alone will allow your thanks to have a deep and lasting positive impact.

Yes

Most people are conditioned to react positively to the word *yes* because it's associated with favorable outcomes in most areas of their lives. The word *yes* is particularly powerful because it plays a critical role in building mutual understanding and agreement. You want your employees to listen to your comments and act on them, and the more they hear the word *yes,* the more likely they are to do exactly that.

Some managers give the word *yes* a good deal of play but then undo all its power and effectiveness by attaching one little word to it — namely, the word *but.* When employees hear "Yes, but . . ." the word *yes* becomes a prelude to a rejection. As a result, that *yes* may as well be *no,* which is another word to avoid in the appraisal process.

The best way to benefit from the power of *yes,* and still add some points afterwards, is to say "Yes, and. . . ."

You can further strengthen the impact of your feedback by giving your employees more opportunities to say *yes.* One of the best ways to generate a *yes* is to end a sentence with a rhetorical question that can only generate a *yes.* For example, you're reading this book right now, aren't you?

Chapter 19

The Top Ten Behaviors Meriting Special Recognition

In This Chapter

▶ Identifying special behaviors that deserve special attention

▶ Reinforcing behaviors that add value to the employee and to the company

▶ Increasing the likelihood that outstanding behaviors will be repeated

*R*ecognition is one of the most powerful sources of employee motivation, and performance appraisals offer a perfect opportunity to formally identify and recognize your employees' successes and achievements, whether in terms of their job performance or their personal growth and development. Although recognizing all of your employees' accomplishments is important, ten behaviors jump off the chart and merit *special* recognition.

The common theme shared by these behaviors is that they demonstrate particularly high levels of dedication, commitment, and energy — all of which add significant value to the company. Plus, when one employee engages in these behaviors, some of her co-workers will likely follow suit because they, too, will be interested in receiving recognition from you.

If you want your employees to repeat these outstanding behaviors, the best step is to recognize them as you manage by wandering around and as you conduct performance appraisals.

Your employees learn from you every day, not only as a result of your direct guidance and mentoring but also as a result of your actions. So, another powerful way to draw out the top ten behaviors from your employees is to engage in them yourself.

Exceeding Expectations

Employees have the opportunity to exceed expectations in virtually every aspect of their jobs. They can exceed tangible and measurable expectations (such as the quality and quantity of their work), as well as intangible expectations (such as their attitude or energy).

When employees exceed expectations, they don't necessarily do so as a result of your guidance or direction — they do it more as a result of their own initiative, drive, and personal standards of performance. Employees who exceed expectations typically derive a great deal of personal satisfaction out of doing so — and this satisfaction is enhanced and reinforced by the positive feedback that you provide, especially in your performance appraisals.

Mentoring Co-Workers

Employees who mentor others are actually demonstrating several excellent behaviors simultaneously, all of which are worthy of special recognition. First, in order to serve as a mentor, an employee must have a high degree of expertise, along with a full understanding of the company's performance standards in the area in which he is mentoring.

Mentors also send clear messages about the company's values, ethics, and mission. As a result, employees who serve as mentors are key purveyors of the company's values — and that's easily as important as their specific mentoring responsibilities.

In addition, mentors must have solid training abilities that build and reinforce other employees' skills. Plus, mentors must have solid organizational skills, allowing them to train other employees while simultaneously maintaining excellent levels of performance in carrying out their other responsibilities.

One of the most desirable characteristics of any employee is the ability to add value to the company, and mentors are able to do this in two ways:

✔ In order to mentor successfully, they must develop their own skills to expert levels, which clearly adds value to the company.

✔ When employees are mentored, *their* value to the company increases as well.

Taking Classes

When an employee takes classes, she's demonstrating her strong desire not only to continue her learning, growth, and development but also to increase the value that she brings to her job and the company at large. In addition, the fact that she can take classes while successfully carrying out her job responsibilities is a testimony to her energy, drive, persistence, and organizational ability.

There is no question that your employees' value to the company increases as they build their knowledge, skills, and abilities. Plus, their emphasis on learning indicates that these employees have maintained their intellectual curiosity and in no way see themselves slowing down, burning out, or topping out. Their desire to further their education is a clear sign that they continue to be motivated to achieve, advance, and play increasingly important roles in the company.

Although education is its own reward, the special recognition that you provide to your employees in this area *literally* makes education more rewarding.

Coming Up with a Great New Idea

Great new ideas merit great recognition. When your employees come up with truly outstanding ideas, such as those that save money, generate money, highlight better ways to get a job done, or build significant goodwill, you should give them special recognition — not only when they come up with the idea but also during the performance appraisal.

In order for your recognition to have the maximum impact, be sure to focus not only on the outstanding idea but also on the underlying factors that brought it to life. These ideas are actually the result of a combination of creative thinking, persistence, dedication, self-direction, and a strong need to achieve.

When your employees generate great ideas, the message to your *own* manager is that you've created a climate that focuses on innovation and creative thinking — which can lead to some great recognition for *you,* too!

Taking Self-sacrificing Actions

Providing recognition to your employees who place their own needs and priorities behind those of the company is particularly important. These employees are willing to set aside their own plans and step up to work on serious situations that are spinning out of control, such as rescuing a difficult and demanding project, taking care of an unhappy customer, calming a volatile situation, or handling emergencies.

The recognition that you provide for self-sacrificing behaviors should encompass more than the behaviors themselves. Your special recognition should also focus upon your employees' expertise in the situations that called for such sacrifices, as well as upon your employees' loyalty, commitment, and strong sense of responsibility.

Solving a Long-term Problem

Some of the toughest problems to solve in a company are resistant to efforts of some of the best problem solvers. These problems can exist in any area and include any aspect of company operations. They can be as varied as turnover, slow-paying customers, product design, system glitches, and turf wars between departments, to name just a few.

However, at some point or another, someone comes up with a perfect solution to one of these problems. If one of your employees is the problem solver, she clearly merits special recognition from you.

The bulk of your recognition should naturally focus on excellent problem-solving skills, but you should provide equally compelling recognition for the behaviors that accompanied your employee's problem-solving success, including her persistence, inquisitiveness, innovative problem-solving style, and refusal to give up.

Volunteering

When employees volunteer to serve on committees, help with special events and programs, or undertake additional projects, they're demonstrating behaviors that contribute to their own growth and development, while also helping the company — and both of these actions merit special recognition.

As companies solicit volunteers for various projects, employees who step up are demonstrating their desire to be part of the team and take hands-on actions to help the company meet its objectives. Underneath each act of volunteerism is a strong sense of loyalty, dedication, and a desire to make a contribution to the company.

Plus, when employees perform successfully in various voluntary roles, while performing equally well in carrying out their formal job responsibilities, they're demonstrating solid planning and organizing skills. Such skills are worthy not only of special recognition but also of special consideration when supervisory positions open up.

Building Goodwill

At some point, one of your employee's actions in the company or in the community will generate major positive recognition for the company itself. Perhaps this employee will reach a particularly important landmark. Maybe he'll head a highly successful fundraising effort. Or perhaps he'll play a central role in spearheading company support for victims of a natural disaster.

Regardless of the specific achievement, your employee's actions, leadership, or service will give the company's reputation, stature, and image a significant boost. And when company goodwill gets a boost, the value of the company gets a boost as well.

When you have an employee who successfully engages in extraordinary behaviors that enhance goodwill — whether such actions are part of his job description or not — he clearly merits extraordinary recognition from you.

Surpassing Goals

As you work with your employees, monitor their progress, and provide them with coaching and guidance, you'll find a select few who surpass their challenging performance goals or developmental goals. This achievement is one of the most revealing indicators of your employees' work ethic, personal standards, and drive, and it's clearly worthy of special recognition in the performance appraisal process.

Employees who surpass their goals know that they've done so, and they're likely to sense high levels of personal satisfaction, competence, and effectiveness as a result. You can elevate these positive feelings to even higher levels during the performance review by specifically recognizing your employees' success in exceeding their challenging goals.

Some employees' overall goals are to exceed their goals. The more special the recognition you provide for doing so, the more likely they are to continue their special goal-oriented performance.

Going the Extra Mile

As you review the broad range of behaviors displayed by your employees during the course of the evaluation period, be sure to look for steps that your employees have taken to do something extra to help their co-workers, customers, or the company at large. Often, these extra steps — large or small — make the difference between a good employee and a great employee, and, as such, they deserve special recognition.

Employees who go the extra mile are demonstrating an ongoing willingness to do whatever they can to help others, and they're willing to do so with high-level assignments as well as with minor chores.

These kinds of supportive and dedicated behaviors by some of your employees not only reflect highly positive attitudes but also help build such attitudes among their co-workers. In light of the widespread positive impact associated with going the extra mile, you should go the extra mile yourself in providing extra recognition to these employees.

Index

• *Q* •

• *R* •

JSINESS, CAREERS & PERSONAL FINANCE

:counting For Dummies,
∎ Edition*
∎-0-470-24600-9

∎okkeeping Workbook
r Dummies†
∎-0-470-16983-4

∎mmodities For Dummies
∎-0-470-04928-0

∎ing Business in China For Dummies
∎-0-470-04929-7

E-Mail Marketing For Dummies
978-0-470-19087-6

**Job Interviews For Dummies,
3rd Edition*†**
978-0-470-17748-8

**Personal Finance Workbook
For Dummies*†**
978-0-470-09933-9

Real Estate License Exams For Dummies
978-0-7645-7623-2

Six Sigma For Dummies
978-0-7645-6798-8

**Small Business Kit For Dummies,
2nd Edition*†**
978-0-7645-5984-6

Telephone Sales For Dummies
978-0-470-16836-3

JSINESS PRODUCTIVITY & MICROSOFT OFFICE

:ess 2007 For Dummies
∎-0-470-03649-5

:el 2007 For Dummies
∎-0-470-03737-9

Fice 2007 For Dummies
∎-0-470-00923-9

tlook 2007 For Dummies
∎-0-470-03830-7

PowerPoint 2007 For Dummies
978-0-470-04059-1

Project 2007 For Dummies
978-0-470-03651-8

QuickBooks 2008 For Dummies
978-0-470-18470-7

Quicken 2008 For Dummies
978-0-470-17473-9

**Salesforce.com For Dummies,
2nd Edition**
978-0-470-04893-1

Word 2007 For Dummies
978-0-470-03658-7

IUCATION, HISTORY, REFERENCE & TEST PREPARATION

ican American History
r Dummies
∎-0-7645-5469-8

ebra For Dummies
∎-0-7645-5325-7

ebra Workbook For Dummies
∎-0-7645-8467-1

: History For Dummies
∎-0-470-09910-0

ASVAB For Dummies, 2nd Edition
978-0-470-10671-6

British Military History For Dummies
978-0-470-03213-8

Calculus For Dummies
978-0-7645-2498-1

**Canadian History For Dummies,
2nd Edition**
978-0-470-83656-9

Geometry Workbook For Dummies
978-0-471-79940-5

**The SAT I For Dummies,
6th Edition**
978-0-7645-7193-0

Series 7 Exam For Dummies
978-0-470-09932-2

World History For Dummies
978-0-7645-5242-7

OD, HOME, GARDEN, HOBBIES & HOME

idge For Dummies, 2nd Edition
∎-0-471-92426-5

in Collecting For Dummies,
d Edition
∎-0-470-22275-1

oking Basics For Dummies,
∎ Edition
∎-0-7645-7206-7

Drawing For Dummies
978-0-7645-5476-6

**Etiquette For Dummies,
2nd Edition**
978-0-470-10672-3

Gardening Basics For Dummies*†
978-0-470-03749-2

Knitting Patterns For Dummies
978-0-470-04556-5

Living Gluten-Free For Dummies†
978-0-471-77383-2

**Painting Do-It-Yourself
For Dummies**
978-0-470-17533-0

:ALTH, SELF HELP, PARENTING & PETS

ger Management For Dummies
∎-0-470-03715-7

xiety & Depression Workbook
r Dummies
∎-0-7645-9793-0

ting For Dummies, 2nd Edition
∎-0-7645-4149-0

g Training For Dummies,
d Edition
∎-0-7645-8418-3

Horseback Riding For Dummies
978-0-470-09719-9

Infertility For Dummies†
978-0-470-11518-3

**Meditation For Dummies
with CD-ROM, 2nd Edition**
978-0-471-77774-8

**Post-Traumatic Stress Disorder
For Dummies**
978-0-470-04922-8

**Puppies For Dummies,
2nd Edition**
978-0-470-03717-1

**Thyroid For Dummies,
2nd Edition†**
978-0-471-78755-6

Type 1 Diabetes For Dummies*†
978-0-470-17811-9

eparate Canadian edition also available
eparate U.K. edition also available

lable wherever books are sold. For more information or to order direct: U.S. customers visit www.dummies.com or call 1-877-762-2974.
:customers visit www.wileyeurope.com or call (0) 1243 843291. Canadian customers visit www.wiley.ca or call 1-800-567-4797.

INTERNET & DIGITAL MEDIA

AdWords For Dummies
978-0-470-15252-2

**Blogging For Dummies,
2nd Edition**
978-0-470-23017-6

**Digital Photography All-in-One
Desk Reference For Dummies,
3rd Edition**
978-0-470-03743-0

**Digital Photography For Dummies,
5th Edition**
978-0-7645-9802-9

**Digital SLR Cameras & Photography
For Dummies, 2nd Edition**
978-0-470-14927-0

**eBay Business All-in-One Desk
Reference For Dummies**
978-0-7645-8438-1

eBay For Dummies, 5th Edition*
978-0-470-04529-9

eBay Listings That Sell For Dummies
978-0-471-78912-3

Facebook For Dummies
978-0-470-26273-3

**The Internet For Dummies,
11th Edition**
978-0-470-12174-0

**Investing Online For Dummies,
5th Edition**
978-0-7645-8456-5

**iPod & iTunes For Dummies
5th Edition**
978-0-470-17474-6

MySpace For Dummies
978-0-470-09529-4

Podcasting For Dummies
978-0-471-74898-4

**Search Engine Optimization
For Dummies, 2nd Edition**
978-0-471-97998-2

Second Life For Dummies
978-0-470-18025-9

**Starting an eBay Business
For Dummies, 3rd Edition**
978-0-470-14924-9

GRAPHICS, DESIGN & WEB DEVELOPMENT

**Adobe Creative Suite 3 Design
Premium All-in-One Desk Reference
For Dummies**
978-0-470-11724-8

**Adobe Web Suite CS3 All-in-One
Desk Reference For Dummies**
978-0-470-12099-6

AutoCAD 2008 For Dummies
978-0-470-11650-0

**Building a Web Site For Dummies,
3rd Edition**
978-0-470-14928-7

**Creating Web Pages All-in-One Desk
Reference For Dummies,
3rd Edition**
978-0-470-09629-1

**Creating Web Pages For Dummies,
8th Edition**
978-0-470-08030-6

Dreamweaver CS3 For Dummies
978-0-470-11490-2

Flash CS3 For Dummies
978-0-470-12100-9

Google SketchUp For Dummies
978-0-470-13744-4

InDesign CS3 For Dummies
978-0-470-11865-8

**Photoshop CS3 All-in-One
Desk Reference For Dummies**
978-0-470-11195-6

Photoshop CS3 For Dummies
978-0-470-11193-2

**Photoshop Elements 5
For Dummies**
978-0-470-09810-3

SolidWorks For Dummies
978-0-7645-9555-4

Visio 2007 For Dummies
978-0-470-08983-5

**Web Design For Dummies
2nd Edition**
978-0-471-78117-2

**Web Sites Do-It-Yourself
For Dummies**
978-0-470-16903-2

**Web Stores Do-It-Yourself
For Dummies**
978-0-470-17443-2

LANGUAGES, RELIGION & SPIRITUALITY

Arabic For Dummies
978-0-471-77270-5

Chinese For Dummies, Audio Set
978-0-470-12766-7

French For Dummies
978-0-7645-5193-2

German For Dummies
978-0-7645-5195-6

Hebrew For Dummies
978-0-7645-5489-6

Ingles Para Dummies
978-0-7645-5427-8

Italian For Dummies, Audio Set
978-0-470-09586-7

Italian Verbs For Dummies
978-0-471-77389-4

Japanese For Dummies
978-0-7645-5429-2

Latin For Dummies
978-0-7645-5431-5

Portuguese For Dummies
978-0-471-78738-9

Russian For Dummies
978-0-471-78001-4

Spanish Phrases For Dummies
978-0-7645-7204-3

Spanish For Dummies
978-0-7645-5194-9

**Spanish For Dummies,
Audio Set**
978-0-470-09585-0

The Bible For Dummies
978-0-7645-5296-0

Catholicism For Dummies
978-0-7645-5391-2

**The Historical Jesus
For Dummies**
978-0-470-16785-4

Islam For Dummies
978-0-7645-5503-9

**Spirituality For Dummies,
2nd Edition**
978-0-470-19142-2

NETWORKING AND PROGRAMMING

ASP.NET 3.5 For Dummies
978-0-470-19592-5

C# 2008 For Dummies
978-0-470-19109-5

Hacking For Dummies, 2nd Edition
978-0-470-05235-8

**Home Networking
For Dummies, 4th Edition**
978-0-470-11806-1

Java For Dummies, 4th Edition
978-0-470-08716-9

**Microsoft® SQL Server™ 2008
All-in-One Desk Reference For Dummies**

3 1901 04242 1711

978-0-7645-9939-2

**Networking For Dummies
8th Edition**
978-0-470-05620-2

**SharePoint 2007
For Dummies**
978-0-470-09941-4

**Wireless Home Networking
For Dummies, 2nd Edition**
978-0-471-74940-0

Praise for Sudhir Venkatesh's *Gang Leader for a Day*

"Venkatesh offers an eye-opening account into an underserved city within the city."
—Kyra Kyles, *Chicago Tribune*

"The achievement of *Gang Leader for a Day* is to give the dry statistics ['of unemployment, crime, and family hardship'] a raw, beating heart."
—Matthew Shaer, *The Boston Globe*

"[A] riveting account of life in a hope-deprived hell."
—Wook Kim, *Entertainment Weekly*

"A rich portrait of the urban poor, drawn not from statistics but from vivid tales of their lives and his, and how they intertwined."   —*The Economist*

"A sensitive, sympathetic, unpatronizing portrayal of lives that are usually ignored or lumped into ill-defined stereotype."
—Loma Campbell, *Financial Times*

"Truly remarkable . . . Venkatesh recounts scenes of a sort that one would be hard-pressed to find in any other book."   —Ted Conover, *The Nation*

"A compelling portrait of life in the projects."   —Laura Miller, *Salon*

"Mr. Venkatesh is to be applauded for his pathbreaking work and his compelling exposition."   — Tyler Cowen, *The New York Sun*

"An almost thrillerlike tale."   —Michael Agger, *Mother Jones*

"Venkatesh is . . . a rising star."   —Charles Leroux, *Chicago Tribune*

"Eloquent . . . chilling."   —Alex Kotlowitz, *Slate*

"It's an insightful and entertaining read."   —Bloomberg.com

"Sudhir Venkatesh was born with two abnormalities . . . an overdeveloped curiosity and an underdeveloped sense of fear. . .   ʿwriting about the poor tends to reduce living, breathing, jokin~   ual, moral human beings to dupes who are shoved about ᵗ   ʰook . . . shows, day by day and dollar by dollar ᵗ   ʲders . . . cops, and Venkatesh himself trⁱ   standard materials."   ᵣ of *Freakonomics*

PENGUIN BOOKS

GANG LEADER FOR A DAY

Sudhir Venkatesh is William B. Ransford Professor of Sociology at Columbia University. He has written extensively about American poverty and is currently working on a project comparing the urban poor in France and the United States. His writings, stories, and documentaries have appeared in *The American Prospect, This American Life,* and *The Source* and on PBS and National Public Radio.

GANG LEADER FOR A DAY

A Rogue Sociologist
Takes to the Streets

SUDHIR VENKATESH

PENGUIN BOOKS

PENGUIN BOOKS

Published by the Penguin Group

Penguin Group (USA) Inc., 375 Hudson Street, New York, New York 10014, U.S.A.

Penguin Group (Canada), 90 Eglinton Avenue East, Suite 700, Toronto,
Ontario, Canada M4P 2Y3 (a division of Pearson Penguin Canada Inc.)

Penguin Books Ltd, 80 Strand, London WC2R 0RL, England

Penguin Ireland, 25 St Stephen's Green, Dublin 2, Ireland (a division of Penguin Books Ltd)

Penguin Group (Australia), 250 Camberwell Road, Camberwell,
Victoria 3124, Australia (a division of Pearson Australia Group Pty Ltd)

Penguin Books India Pvt Ltd, 11 Community Centre,
Panchsheel Park, New Delhi – 110 017, India

Penguin Group (NZ), 67 Apollo Drive, Rosedale, North Shore 0632,
New Zealand (a division of Pearson New Zealand Ltd)

Penguin Books (South Africa) (Pty) Ltd, 24 Sturdee Avenue,
Rosebank, Johannesburg 2196, South Africa

Penguin Books Ltd, Registered Offices:
80 Strand, London WC2R 0RL, England

First published in the United States of America by the Penguin Press,
a member of Penguin Group (USA) Inc. 2008
Published in Penguin Books 2008

5   7   9   10   8   6   4

Copyright © Sudhir Venkatesh, 2008
All rights reserved

THE LIBRARY OF CONGRESS HAS CATALOGED THE HARDCOVER EDITION AS FOLLOWS:
Venkatesh, Sudhir Alladi.
Gang leader for a day : a rogue sociologist takes to the streets / Sudhir Venkatesh.
p.   cm.
Includes index.
ISBN 978-1-59420-150-9 (hc.)
ISBN 978-0-14-311493-2 (pbk.)
1. Gangs—Illinois—Chicago.   2. African Americans—Illinois—Chicago.
3. Chicago (Ill.)—Social conditions.   4. Venkatesh, Sudhir Alladi.   I. Title.
HV6439.U7C46   2008
364.1'0660977311—dc22
2007040170

Printed in the United States of America
Designed by Claire Vaccaro

To Autry Harrison

CONTENTS

FOREWORD
Stephen J. Dubner

I believe that Sudhir Venkatesh was born with two abnormalities: an overdeveloped curiosity and an underdeveloped sense of fear.

How else to explain him? Like thousands upon thousands of people, he entered graduate school one fall and was dispatched by his professors to do some research. This research happened to take him to the Robert Taylor Homes in Chicago, one of the worst ghettos in America. But blessed with that outlandish curiosity and unfettered by the sort of commonsensical fear that most of us would experience upon being held hostage by an armed crack gang, as Venkatesh was early on in his research, he kept coming back for more.

I met Venkatesh a few years ago when I interviewed him for *Freakonomics,* a book I wrote with the economist Steve Levitt. Venkatesh and Levitt had collaborated on several academic papers about the economics of crack cocaine. Those papers were interesting, to be sure, but Venkatesh himself presented a whole new level of fascination. He is soft-spoken and laconic; he doesn't volunteer much information. But every time you ask him a question, it is like tugging a thread on an old tapestry: the whole thing unspools and falls at your feet. Story after story, marked by lapidary detail and hard-won insight: the rogue cop who terrorized the neighborhood, the jerry-built network through which poor families hustled to survive, the time Venkatesh himself became gang leader for a day.

Although we wrote about Venkatesh in *Freakonomics* (it was many readers' favorite part), there wasn't room for any of these stories. Thankfully, he has now written an extraordinary book that details all his adventures and misadventures. The stories he tells are far stranger than fiction, and they are also more forceful, heartbreaking, and hilarious. Along the way he paints a unique portrait of the kind of neighborhood that is badly misrepresented when it is represented at all. Journalists like me might hang out in such neighborhoods for a week or a month or even a year. Most social scientists and do-gooders tend to do their work at arm's length. But Venkatesh practically lived in this neighborhood for the better part of a decade. He brought the perspective of an outsider and came away with an insider's access. A lot of writing about the poor tends to reduce living, breathing, joking, struggling, sensual, moral human beings to dupes who are shoved about by invisible forces. This book does the opposite. It shows, day by day and dollar by dollar, how the crack dealers, tenant leaders, prostitutes, parents, hustlers, cops, and Venkatesh himself tried to construct a good life out of substandard materials.

As much as I have come to like Venkatesh, and admire him, I probably would not want to be a member of his family: I would worry too much about his fearlessness. I probably wouldn't want to be one of his research subjects either, for his curiosity must be exhausting. But I am very, very happy to have been one of the first readers of Venkatesh's book, for it is as extraordinary as he is.

PREFACE

I woke up at about 7:30 A.M. in a crack den, Apartment 1603 in Building Number 2301 of the Robert Taylor Homes. Apartment 1603 was called the "Roof," since everyone knew that you could get very, very high there, even higher than if you climbed all the way to the building's actual rooftop.

As I opened my eyes, I saw two dozen people sprawled about, most of them men, asleep on couches and the floor. No one had lived in the apartment for a while. The walls were peeling, and roaches skittered across the linoleum floor. The activities of the previous night—smoking crack, drinking, having sex, vomiting—had peaked at about 2:00 A.M. By then the unconscious people outnumbered the conscious ones—and among the conscious ones, few still had the cash to buy another hit of crack cocaine. That's when the Black Kings saw diminishing prospects for sales and closed up shop for the night.

I fell asleep, too, on the floor. I hadn't come for the crack; I was here on a different mission. I was a graduate student at the University of Chicago, and for my research I had taken to hanging out with the Black Kings, the local crack-selling gang.

It was the sun that woke me, shining through the Roof's doorway. (The door itself had disappeared long ago.) I climbed over the other stragglers and walked down to the tenth floor, where the Patton family lived. During the course of my research, I had gotten to know the Pattons—a law-abiding family, it should be said—and they treated me kindly, almost like a son. I said good morning to Mama Patton, who was cooking breakfast for her husband, Pops, a seventy-year-old retired factory worker. I washed my face, grabbed a slice of cornbread, and headed outside into a breezy, brisk March morning.

Just another day in the ghetto.

Just another day as an outsider looking at life from the inside. That's what this book is about.

GANG LEADER FOR A DAY

ONE

How Does It Feel to Be Black and Poor?

During my first weeks at the University of Chicago, in the fall of 1989, I had to attend a variety of orientation sessions. In each one, after the particulars of the session had been dispensed with, we were warned not to walk outside the areas that were actively patrolled by the university's police force. We were handed detailed maps that outlined where the small enclave of Hyde Park began and ended: this was the safe area. Even the lovely parks across the border were off-limits, we were told, unless you were traveling with a large group or attending a formal event.

It turned out that the ivory tower was also an ivory fortress. I lived on the southwestern edge of Hyde Park, where the university housed a lot of its graduate students. I had a studio apartment in a ten-story building just off Cottage Grove Avenue, a historic boundary between Hyde Park and Woodlawn, a poor black neighborhood. The contrast would be familiar to anyone who has spent time around

an urban university in the United States. On one side of the divide
lay a beautifully manicured Gothic campus, with privileged students,
most of them white, walking to class and playing sports. On the
other side were down-and-out African Americans offering cheap
labor and services (changing oil, washing windows, selling drugs) or
panhandling on street corners.

I didn't have many friends, so in my spare time I started taking
long walks, getting to know the city. For a budding sociologist, the
streets of Chicago were a feast. I was intrigued by the different ethnic neighborhoods, the palpable sense of culture and tradition. I
liked that there was one part of the city, Rogers Park, where Indians, Pakistanis, and Bangladeshis congregated. Unlike the lily-white
suburbs of Southern California where I'd grown up, the son of immigrants from South Asia, here Indians seemed to have a place in the
ethnic landscape along with everyone else.

I was particularly interested in the poor black neighborhoods
surrounding the university. These were neighborhoods where nearly
half the population didn't work, where crime and gang activity were
said to be entrenched, where the welfare rolls were swollen. In the
late 1980s, these isolated parts of the inner cities gripped the nation's
attention. I went for many walks there and started playing basketball
in the parks, but I didn't see any crime, and I didn't feel particularly
threatened. I wondered why the university kept warning students to
keep out.

As it happened, I attracted a good bit of curiosity from the locals. Perhaps it was because these parks didn't attract many nonblack
visitors, or perhaps it was because in those days I dressed like a Dead-
head. I got asked a lot of questions about India—most of which I
couldn't answer, since I'd moved to the States as a child. Sometimes
I'd come upon a picnic, and people would offer me some of their

soul food. They were puzzled when I turned them down on the grounds that I was a vegetarian.

But as alien as I was to these folks, they were just as alien to me.

As part of my heavy course load at the U of C, I began attending seminars where professors parsed the classic sociological questions: How do an individual's preferences develop? Can we predict human behavior? What are the long-term consequences, for instance, of education on future generations?

The standard mode of answering these questions was to conduct widespread surveys and then use complex mathematical methods to analyze the survey data. This would produce statistical snapshots meant to predict why a given person might, say, fail to land a job, or end up in prison, or have a child out of wedlock. It was thought that the key to formulating good policy was to first formulate a good scientific study.

I liked the questions these researchers were asking, but compared with the vibrant life that I saw on the streets of Chicago, the discussion in these seminars seemed cold and distant, abstract and lifeless. I found it particularly curious that most of these researchers didn't seem interested in meeting the people they wrote about. It wasn't necessarily out of any animosity—nearly all of them were well intentioned—but because the act of actually talking to research subjects was seen as messy, unscientific, and a potential source of bias.

Mine was not a new problem. Indeed, the field of sociology had long been divided into two camps: those who use quantitative and statistical techniques and those who study life by direct observation, often living among a group of people.

This second group, usually called ethnographers, use their firsthand approach to answer a particular sort of question: How do people survive in marginal communities? for instance, or What makes a government policy work well for some families and not for others?

The quantitative sociologists, meanwhile, often criticized the ethnographers' approach. They argued that it isn't nearly scientific enough and that the answers may be relevant only to the particular group under observation. In other words, to reach any important and generalizable conclusion, you need to rely on the statistical analyses of large data sets like the U.S. Census or other massive surveys.

My frustration with the more scientific branch of sociology hadn't really coalesced yet. But I knew that I wanted to do something other than sit in a classroom all day and talk mathematics.

So I did what any sensible student who was interested in race and poverty would do: I walked down the hallway and knocked on the door of William Julius Wilson, the most eminent living scholar on the subject and the most prominent African American in the field of sociology. He had been teaching at the U of C for nearly twenty years and had published two books that reshaped how scholars and policy makers thought about urban poverty.

I caught Wilson just in time—he was about to go to Paris for a sabbatical. But he was also about to launch a new research project, he said, and I could participate if I liked.

Wilson was a quiet, pensive man, dressed in a dark blue suit. Although he had stopped smoking his trademark pipe long ago, he still looked like the kind of professor you see in movies. If you asked him a question, he'd often let several long moments of silence pass—he could be more than a little bit intimidating—before offering a thoughtful response.

Wilson explained that he was hoping to better understand how young blacks were affected by specific neighborhood factors: Did growing up as a poor kid in a housing project, for instance, lead to worse educational and job outcomes than if a similarly poor kid grew up outside the projects? What about the difference between growing up in a neighborhood that was surrounded by other poor areas and growing up poor but near an affluent neighborhood? Did the latter group take advantage of the schools, services, and employment opportunities in the richer neighborhoods?

Wilson's project was still in the planning stages. The first step was to construct a basic survey questionnaire, and he suggested I help his other graduate students in figuring out which questions to ask. This meant going back to earlier studies of black youth to see what topics and questions had been chosen by earlier sociologists. Wilson gave me a box of old questionnaires. I should experiment, he said, by borrowing some of their questions and developing new ones as needed. Sociologists liked to use survey questions that their peers had already used, I learned, in order to produce comparable results. This was a key part of the scientific method in sociology.

I thanked Wilson and went to the library to begin looking over the questionnaires he'd given me. I quickly realized I had no idea how to interview anyone.

Washington Park, situated just across Cottage Grove Avenue from the U of C, is one of Chicago's stateliest parks. Designed in the 1870s by Frederick Law Olmsted and Calvert Vaux, it has a beautiful swimming pool, indoor and outdoor basketball courts, dazzling flower gardens, and long, winding paths that crisscross its nearly four hundred acres. I liked to go running on the clay track that encircled the park, a track that decades earlier had hosted horse and auto races. Until the 1940s the surrounding neighborhood was mainly Irish, but when black families started buying homes nearby, most of the white families moved away. I was always surprised that the university actively dissuaded its students from spending time in Washington Park. I failed to see the danger, at least in the daylight.

After my run I sometimes stopped by the broad, marshy lagoon in the middle of the park. The same group of old black men, usually a half dozen or so, congregated there every day—playing cards, drinking beer, fishing for bass and perch in the lagoon. I sat and listened to them for hours. To this point I had had little exposure to African-American culture at all, and no experience whatsoever in an urban ghetto. I had moved to Chicago just a year earlier from California, where I'd attended a predominantly white college situated on the beach, UC San Diego.

I had been reading several histories of Chicago's black community, and I sometimes asked these men about the events and people of which I'd read. The stories they told were considerably more animated than the history in the books. They knew the intricacies of machine politics—whom you had to befriend, for instance, to get a job or a building permit. They talked about the Black Panther Party of their youth and how it was radically different from today's gangs. "The Panthers had breakfast programs for kids, but these gangs just shoot 'em and feed 'em drugs," one man lamented. I already knew a bit about how the Panthers operated in Chicago during the civil-rights era. What little I knew about modern gangs, however, came from the movies and newspapers—and, of course, the constant cautions issued by the U of C about steering clear of certain neighborhoods.

I was particularly intrigued by the old men's views on race, which boiled down to this: Whites and blacks would never be able to talk openly, let alone live together. The most talkative among them was Leonard Combs, a.k.a. Old Time. "Never trust a white man," he told me one day, "and don't think black folk are any better."

Old Time came to Washington Park every day with his fishing

gear, lunch, and beer. He wore a tired beige fishing hat, and he had lost so many teeth that his gums smacked together when he spoke. But he loved to talk, especially about Chicago.

"We live in a city within a city," he said. "They have theirs and we have ours. And if you can understand that it will never change, you'll start understanding how this city works."

"You mean whites and blacks will never get along?" I asked.

A man named Charlie Butler jumped in. "You got two kinds of whites in this city," he said, "and two kinds of blacks. You got whites who'll beat you if you come into their neighborhood. They live around Bridgeport and on the Southwest Side. Then you got another group that just won't invite you in. They'll call the police if you come in their neighborhood—like where *you* live, in Hyde Park. And the police *will* beat you up."

Charlie was a retired factory worker, a beefy man with tattooed, well-developed arms, a college football star from long ago. Charlie sometimes came to Hyde Park for breakfast or lunch at one of the diners where other blacks hung out, but he never stayed past sundown and he never walked on residential streets, he said, since the police would follow him.

"What about blacks?" I asked.

"You got blacks who are beating their heads trying to figure out a way to live where *you* live!" Charlie continued. "Don't ask me why. And then you got a whole lot of black folk who realize it ain't no use. Like us. We just spend our time trying to get by, and we live around here, where it ain't so pretty, but at least you won't get your ass beat. At least not by the police."

"That's how it's been since black folk came to the city," Old Time said, "and it's not going to change."

"You mean you don't have *any* white friends?" I asked.

"You have any *black* friends?" Old Time countered with a sly grin. I didn't need to answer. "And you may want to ask your professors if *they* have any," he said, clearly pleased with his rebuke.

From these conversations I started to gain a bit of perspective on what it was like to be black in Chicago. The overriding sentiment was that given how the city operated, there was little chance for any significant social progress.

This kind of fatalism was foreign to me. When you grew up in affluent Southern California, even for someone as politically disengaged as I, there was a core faith in the workings of American institutions and a sustaining belief that people can find a way to resolve their differences, even racial ones. I was now beginning to see the limits of my narrow experience. Nearly every conversation with Old Time and his friends wound up at the intersection of politics and race. I couldn't follow all the nuances of their arguments, especially when it came to local politics, but even I could see the huge gap between how they perceived the world and how sociologists presented the life of urban poor people.

One day I asked Old Time and his friends if they'd be willing to let me interview them for Professor Wilson's survey. They agreed, and I tried for a few days. But I felt I wasn't getting anywhere. Most of the conversations ended up meandering along, a string of interruptions and half-finished thoughts.

Charlie could see I was dejected. "Before you give up," he said, "you should probably speak to the people who you really want to talk to—*young* men, not us. That's the only way you're going to get what you need."

So I set out looking for young black men. At the U of C library, I checked the census records to find a tract with poor black families with people between the ages of sixteen and twenty-four.

The Lake Park projects looked good, at least on paper, and I randomly chose Building Number 4040, highlighting on my census printout the apartments where young people lived. Those were the doors I'd be knocking on. Old Time told me that I could go any day I wanted. "Most black folk in the projects don't work," he said, "so they don't have nowhere else to be." Still, I thought a weekend would be the best time to find a lot of people.

On a brisk Saturday afternoon in November, I went looking for 4040 South Lake Park, one of several high-rise projects in Oakland, a lakefront neighborhood about two miles north of the U of C. Oakland was one of the poorest communities in Chicago, with commensurately high rates of unemployment, welfare, and crime. Its population was overwhelmingly black, dating back to the early-twentieth-century southern migration. The neighborhood surrounding the Lake Park projects wasn't much of a neighborhood at all. There were few people on the streets, and on some blocks there were more vacant lots than buildings. Aside from a few liquor stores and broken-down bodegas, there wasn't much commerce. It struck me that most housing projects, even though they are built in cities, run counter to the very notion of urban living. Cities are attractive because of their balkanized variety: wandering the streets of a good city, you can see all sorts of highs and lows, commerce and recreation, a multitude of ethnicities and just as many expressions of public life. But housing projects, at least from the outside, seemed to be a study in joyless monotony, the buildings clustered tightly together but set apart from the rest of the city, as if they were toxic.

Up close, the buildings looked like tall checkerboards, their dull yellow-brick walls lined with rows of dreary windows. A few of the windows revealed the aftermath of an apartment fire, black smudges spreading upward in the shape of tombstones. Most of the buildings had only one entrance, and it was usually clogged with young people.

By now I was used to being observed carefully when I walked around a black neighborhood. Today was no different. As I approached one of the Lake Park projects, five or six young men stared me down. It should be said here that I probably deserved to be stared at. I was just a few months removed from a long stretch of time I'd spent following the Grateful Dead, and I was still under the spell of Jerry Garcia and his band of merrymakers. With my ponytail and tie-dyed shirt, I must have looked pretty out of place. I tended to speak in spiritually laden language, mostly about the power of road trips; the other grad students in my department saw me as a bit naïve and more than a little loopy. Looking back, I can't say they were wrong.

But I wasn't so naïve that I couldn't recognize what was going on in the lobby of the building that I now approached. Customers were arriving, black and white, by car and on foot, hurrying inside to buy their drugs and then hurrying back out. I wasn't sure if this building was Number 4040, and I couldn't find the number anywhere, so I just walked inside. The entryway smelled of alcohol, soot, and urine. Young men stood and crouched on plastic milk crates, a couple of them stomping their feet against the cold. I put my head down, took a breath, and walked past them quickly.

Their eyes felt heavy on me as I passed by. One huge young man, six foot six at least, chose not to move an inch as I passed. I brushed up against him and nearly lost my balance.

There was a long row of beaten-up metal mailboxes, many of them missing their doors. Water was dripping everywhere, puddling on the ground. Shouts and shrieks cascaded down from the higher floors, making the whole building feel like some kind of vibrating catacomb.

Once I got past the entryway, it was darker. I could make out the elevator, but I seemed to be losing any peripheral vision, and I couldn't find the button. I sensed that I was still being watched and that I ought to press the button fast, but I groped around in vain. Then I started looking for the stairwell, but I couldn't find that either. To my left was a large barrier of some kind, but I was too nervous to go around it. To my right was a corridor. I decided to go that way, figuring I'd come across a stairwell or at least a door to knock on. As I turned, a hand grabbed my shoulder.

"What's up, my man, you got some business in here?" He was in his twenties, about as tall and dark as I was. His voice was deep and forceful but matter-of-fact, as if he asked the same question regularly. He wore baggy jeans, a loose-fitting jacket, and a baseball cap. His earrings sparkled, as did the gold on his front teeth. A few other young men, dressed the same, stood behind him.

I told them that I was there to interview families.

"No one lives here," he said.

"I'm doing a study for the university," I said, "and I have to go to Apartments 610 and 703."

"Ain't nobody lived in those apartments for the longest," he said.

"Well, do you mind if I just run up there and knock on the door?"

"Yeah, we do mind," he said.

I tried again. "Maybe I'm in the wrong building. Is this 4040?"

He shook his head. "No one lives here. So you won't be talking to anybody."

I decided I'd better leave. I walked back through the lobby, bag and clipboard in hand. I crossed in front of the building, over an expansive patch of dead grass littered with soda cans and broken glass. I turned around and looked back at the building. A great many of the windows were lit. I wondered why my new friend had insisted that the building was uninhabited. Only later did I learn that gang members routinely rebuffed all sorts of visitors with this line: "No one by that name lives here." They would try to prevent social workers, schoolteachers, and maintenance personnel from coming inside and interrupting their drug trade.

The young men from the building were still watching me, but they didn't follow. As I came upon the next high-rise, I saw the faint markings on the pale yellow brick: Number 4040. At least now I was in the right place. The lobby here was empty, so I quickly skirted past another set of distressed mailboxes and passed through another dank lobby. The elevator was missing entirely—there was a big cavity where the door should have been—and the walls were thick with graffiti.

As I started to climb the stairs, the smell of urine was overpowering. On some floors the stairwells were dark; on others there was a muted glow. I walked up four flights, maybe five, trying to keep count, and then I came upon a landing where a group of young men, high-school age, were shooting dice for money.

"Nigger, what the fuck are you doing here?" one of them shouted. I tried to make out their faces, but in the fading light I could barely see a thing.

I tried to explain, again. "I'm a student at the university, doing a survey, and I'm looking for some families."

The young men rushed up to me, within inches of my face. Again someone asked what I was doing there. I told them the numbers of the apartments I was looking for. They told me that no one lived in the building.

Suddenly some more people showed up, a few of them older than the teenagers. One of them, a man about my age with an oversize baseball cap, grabbed my clipboard and asked what I was doing. I tried to explain, but he didn't seem interested. He kept adjusting his too-big hat as it fell over his face.

"Julio over here says he's a student," he told everyone. His tone indicated he didn't believe me. Then he turned back to me. "Who do you represent?"

"Represent?" I asked.

"C'mon, nigger!" one of the younger men shouted. "We know you're with somebody, just tell us who."

Another one, laughing, pulled something out of his waistband. At first I couldn't tell what it was, but then it caught a glint of light and I could see that it was a gun. He moved it around, pointing it at my head once in a while, and muttered something over and over— "I'll take him," he seemed to be saying.

Then he smiled. "You do *not* want to be fucking with the Kings," he said. "I'd just tell us what you know."

"Hold on, nigger," another one said. He was holding a knife with a six-inch blade. He began twirling it around in his fingers, the handle spinning in his palm, and the strangest thought came over me: *That's the exact same knife my friend Brian used to dig a hole for our tent in the Sierra Nevadas.* "Let's have some fun with this boy," he said. "C'mon, Julio, where you live? On the East Side, right? You don't look like the West Side Mexicans. You flip right or left? Five or six? You run with the Kings, right? You know we're going to find out, so you might as well tell us."

Kings or Sharks, flip right or left, five or six. It appeared that I was Julio, the Mexican gang member from the East Side. It wasn't clear yet if this was a good or a bad thing.

Two of the other young men started to search my bag. They pulled out the questionnaire sheets, pen and paper, a few sociology books, my keys. Someone else patted me down. The guy with the too-big hat who had taken my clipboard looked over the papers and then handed everything back to me. He told me to go ahead and ask a question.

By now I was sweating despite the cold. I leaned backward to try to get some light to fall on the questionnaire. The first question was one I had adapted from several other similar surveys; it was one of a set of questions that targeted young people's self-perceptions.

"How does it feel to be black and poor?" I read. Then I gave the multiple-choice answers: "Very bad, somewhat bad, neither bad nor good, somewhat good, very good."

The guy with the too-big hat began to laugh, which prompted the others to start giggling.

"Fuck you!" he told me. "You got to be fucking kidding me."

He turned away and muttered something that made everyone laugh uncontrollably. They went back to quarreling about who I was. They talked so fast that I couldn't easily follow. It seemed they were as confused as I was. I wasn't armed, I didn't have tattoos, I wasn't wearing anything that showed allegiance to another gang—I didn't wear a hat turned toward the left or right, for instance, I wasn't wearing blue or red, I didn't have a star insignia anywhere, either the five- or six-point variety.

Two of them started to debate my fate. "If he's here and he don't get back," said one, "you know they're going to come looking for him."

"Yeah, and I'm getting the first shot," said the other. "Last time I had to watch the crib. Fuck that. This time I'm getting in the car. I'm *shooting* some niggers."

"These Mexicans ain't afraid of shit. They kill each other in prison, over *nothing*. You better let me handle it, boy. You don't even *speak* Mexican."

"Man, I met a whole bunch of them in jail. I killed three just the other day."

As their claims escalated, so did their insults.

"Yeah, but your mama spoke Mexican when I was with her."

"Nigger, your *daddy* was a Mexican."

I sat down on a cold concrete step. I struggled to follow what they were talking about. A few of them seemed to think that I was an advance scout from a Mexican gang, conducting reconnaissance for a drive-by attack. From what I could glean, it seemed as if some black gangs were aligned with certain Mexican gangs but in other cases the black gangs and Mexican gangs were rivals.

They stopped talking when a small entourage entered the stairwell. At the front was a large man, powerfully built but with a boyish face. He also looked to be about my age, maybe a few years older, and he radiated calm. He had a toothpick or maybe a lollipop in his mouth, and it was obvious from his carriage that he was the boss. He checked out everyone who was on the scene, as if making a mental list of what each person was doing. His name was J.T., and while I couldn't have known it at this moment, he was about to become the most formidable person in my life, for a long time to come.

J.T. asked the crowd what was happening, but no one could give him a straight answer. Then he turned to me. "What are you doing here?"

He had a few glittery gold teeth, a sizable diamond earring, and deep, hollow eyes that fixed on mine without giving away anything. Once again, I started to go through my spiel: I was a student at the university, et cetera, et cetera.

"You speak Spanish?" he asked.

"No!" someone shouted out. "But he probably speaks Mexican!"

"Nigger, just shut the fuck up," J.T. said. Then someone mentioned my questionnaire, which seemed to catch his interest. He asked me to tell him about it.

I explained the project as best as I could. It was being overseen by a national poverty expert, I said, with the goal of understanding the lives of young black men in order to design better public policy.

My role, I said, was very basic: conducting surveys to generate data for the study. There was an eerie silence when I finished. Everyone stood waiting, watching J.T.

He took the questionnaire from my hand, barely glanced at it, then handed it back. Everything he did, every move he made, was deliberate and forceful.

I read him the same question that I had read the others. He didn't laugh, but he smiled. *How does it feel to be black and poor?*

"I'm not *black,*" he answered, looking around at the others knowingly.

"Well, then, how does it feel to be *African American* and poor?" I tried to sound apologetic, worried that I had offended him.

"I'm not African American either. I'm a nigger."

Now I didn't know what to say. I certainly didn't feel comfortable asking him how it felt to be a *nigger.* He took back my questionnaire and looked it over more carefully. He turned the pages, reading the questions to himself. He appeared disappointed, though I sensed that his disappointment wasn't aimed at me.

"*Niggers* are the ones who live in this building," he said at last. "*African Americans* live in the suburbs. African Americans wear ties to work. Niggers can't find no work."

He looked at a few more pages of the questionnaire. "You ain't going to learn shit with this thing." He kept shaking his head and then glanced toward some of the older men standing about, checking to see if they shared his disbelief. Then he leaned in toward me and spoke quietly. "How'd you get to do this if you don't even know who we are, what we're about?" His tone wasn't accusatory as much as disappointed, and perhaps a bit bewildered.

I didn't know what to do. *Perhaps I should get up and leave?* But then *he* turned quickly and left, telling the young men who stayed behind to "watch him." Meaning me.

They seemed excited by how things had turned out. They had mostly stood still while J.T. was there, but now they grew animated. "Man, you shouldn't mess with him like that," one of them told me. "See, you should've just told him who you were. You might have been gone by now. He might have let you go."

"Yeah, you fucked up, nigger," another one said. "You really fucked this one up."

I leaned back on the cold step and wondered exactly what I had done to "fuck up." For the first time that day, I had a moment to ponder what had been happening. Random thoughts entered my mind, but, oddly, none of them concerned my personal safety: *What the hell is Bill Wilson going to do if he finds out about this? How am I supposed to know whether to address an interview subject as black, African American, or Negro? Did every Ph.D. student have to go through this? Can I go to the bathroom?* The sun had set, and it was getting colder. I pulled my jacket tighter and bent over, trying to keep out of the wintry draft.

Yo! Freeze, you want one?"

An older man walked in with a grocery bag full of beers and offered a bottle to one of the young men guarding me. He passed out beers to everyone there. Pretty soon they were all in a better mood. They even gave me a bottle.

By now it was well into the evening. No one seemed to have anywhere to go. The young men just sat in the stairwell telling one another all kinds of stories: about sexual conquests, the best way to smoke a marijuana cigarette, schoolteachers they'd like to have sex with, the rising cost of clothing, cops they wanted to kill, and where they would go when their high-rise building was torn down. This last fact surprised me. Nothing in our records at the university suggested that these projects were closing.

"You have to leave?" I asked. "What kind of neighborhood will you be going to?"

"Nigger, did someone tell you to talk?" one of them said.

"Yeah, Julio," said another, moving in closer. "You ain't got no business here."

I shut my mouth for a while, but some other men stopped by, and they were more talkative. I learned that the Chicago Housing Authority (CHA) was indeed tearing down the Lake Park projects in order to build condominiums and town houses. Some residents were staying on as squatters, and the gang was helping them by pirating electricity.

It was clear to me at this point that the young men I'd stumbled upon in this stairwell were junior members of a broad-based gang, the Black Kings, that sold crack cocaine. The older members explained that the gang was trying to forestall demolition but that it wasn't a pure act of charity: When this building was torn down, they would lose one of their best drug-selling locations.

Once in a while, I tried to interject a research question—What kinds of jobs did the people who lived here have? Why weren't the police in the building?—but they seemed less interested in answering me than in talking among themselves about sex, power, and money.

After a few hours, J.T. returned with a few other men, each of them carrying a grocery bag. More beer. It was late, and everyone seemed a little punchy. The air was stale, and some of the young men had been wondering when they might be able to leave. For the moment, however, the beer seemed to settle them down.

"Here," J.T. said, tossing me another bottle. Then he came closer. "You know you're not supposed to be here," he said quietly. He seemed to feel sorry for me and, at the same time, curious about my presence. Then he, too, began talking about the scheduled demolition of the Lake Park projects. He explained that he and his men had holed up in this building partly out of protest, joining the residents to challenge the housing authority's decision to kick them out.

Then he asked me where I was from.

"California," I said, surprised at the change in topic. "Born in India."

"Hmm. So you don't speak Spanish."

"Actually, I do."

"See! I told you this nigger was a Mexican," said one young gangster, jumping up with a beer in his hand. "We should've beat his ass back then, man! Sent him back to his people. You know they're coming around tonight, you know they *will* be here. We need to get ready—"

J.T. shot the young man a look, then turned back to me. "You're not from Chicago," he said. "You should really not be walking through the projects. People can get hurt."

J.T. started tossing questions at me. What other black neighborhoods, he asked, was I going to with my questionnaire? Why do researchers use multiple-choice surveys like the one I was using? Why don't they just *talk* with people? How much money can you make as a professor?

Then he asked what I hoped to gain by studying young black people. I ticked off a few of the pressing questions that sociologists were asking about urban poverty.

"I had a few sociology classes," he said. "In college. Hated that shit."

The last word I expected to exit this man's mouth was "college." But there it was. I didn't want to push my luck, so I thought I'd just keep listening and hope for a chance to ask about his background.

By now everyone seemed fairly drunk and, more alarmingly, excited at the prospect of a gang war with the Mexicans. Some of the older men started talking logistics—where to station the gang members for the fighting, which vacant apartments could be used as lookout spots, and so on.

J.T. dismissed their belief that something was going to happen that night. Once again he ordered two of the younger men to stay with me. Then he left. I returned to my seat, sipping a beer now and then. It looked like I would be spending the night with them, so I tried to accept my fate. I was grateful when they said I could go to the bathroom—which, as it turned out, was another stairwell a few floors up. Considering that water, and probably urine, were constantly dripping onto our own landing, I wondered why they didn't use a lower floor instead.

The young men stayed up in the stairwell all night, drinking and smoking. Some of them strayed out to the balcony once in a while to see if any cars had pulled up to the building. One of them threw an empty beer bottle to the ground six stories down. The sound of broken glass echoing through the stairwell gave me a fright, but no one else even flinched.

Every so often a few new people came in, always with more beer. They talked vaguely about gang issues and the types of weapons that different gangs had. I listened as attentively as I could but stopped asking questions. Occasionally someone asked me again about my background. They all at last seemed convinced that I was not in fact a Mexican gang member, although some of them remained concerned that I "spoke Mexican." A few of them dozed off inadvertently, sitting on the concrete floor, their heads leaning against the wall.

I spent most of the night sitting on the cold steps, trying to avoid the protruding shards of metal. I would have liked to sleep also, but I was too nervous.

Finally J.T. came back. The early-morning sun was making its way into the stairwell. He looked tired and preoccupied.

"Go back to where you came from," he told me, "and be more careful when you walk around the city." Then, as I began gathering up my bag and clipboard, he talked to me about the proper way to study people. "You shouldn't go around asking them silly-ass questions," he said. "With people like us, you should hang out, get to know what they do, how they do it. No one is going to answer questions like that. You need to understand how young people live on the streets."

I was astounded at what a thoughtful person J.T. appeared to be. It seemed as if he were somehow invested in my succeeding, or at least considered himself responsible for my safety. I got up and headed for the stairs. One of the older men reached out and offered me his hand. I was surprised. As I shook his hand, he nodded at me. I glanced back and noticed that everyone, including J.T., was watching.

What are you supposed to say after a night like this? I couldn't think of anything worthwhile, so I just turned and left.

As I walked back to my apartment in Hyde Park, everything seemed fundamentally different. Crossing from one neighborhood to the next, I speculated about gang boundaries. When I saw a group of people huddled on a corner, I wondered if they were protecting their turf. I had a lot of questions: Why would anyone join a gang? What were the benefits? Didn't they get bored hanging out in stairwells—and how could anyone possibly stand the smell of urine for that long? The surveys in my bag felt heavy and useless. I began to worry about my relationship with Professor Wilson. He certainly wouldn't approve of my experimental journey, done without his approval, and I wondered whether he would pull me off the project if he found out what I'd done. The voice of my father—a professor himself—entered my head. He had always given me advice about education. Throughout my college years, he stressed the need to listen to my teachers, and when I shipped off to Chicago, he told me that the key to success in graduate school would be to develop a good relationship with my advisers.

I took a shower and thought about the rest of my day. I had books to read, papers to write, some laundry to do. But none of that seemed very significant. I tried to sleep, but the rest was fitful. I couldn't get the previous night out of my head. I thought of calling someone, but whom? I wasn't close with any other members of Wilson's research team—and they, too, would probably be upset to find out what I'd done. I realized that if I truly wanted to understand the complicated lives of black youth in inner-city Chicago, I had only one good option: to accept J.T.'s counsel and hang out with people. So I headed back to the Lake Park projects to see if I could once again find J.T. and his gang.

I wasn't really scared as I walked north along Cottage Grove Avenue. A little nervous, certainly, but I was pretty sure that J.T. didn't see me as any kind of a threat. Worst-case scenario? Embarrassment. He and his gang would ask me to leave or they'd laugh at my desire to get to know them better.

It was maybe two o'clock in the afternoon when I arrived. This time I came bearing a six-pack of beer. There were about a dozen young men out front of Number 4040, standing around their cars.

Some of them began to point at me. A few others were playing handball by throwing a tennis ball against the building. As I drew close, all of them turned to watch me.

"You got to be kidding me," I heard someone say. Then I saw J.T., leaning back against a car, smiling and shaking his head.

"Beer?" I said, tossing him a bottle. "You said I should hang out with folks if I want to know what their life was like."

J.T. didn't answer. A few of the guys burst out laughing in disbelief. "He's crazy, I told you!" said one.

"Nigger thinks he's going to hang out with us!"

"I still think he's a Latin King."

Finally J.T. spoke up. "All right, the brother wants to hang out," he said, unfazed. "Let him hang out!"

J.T. grinned and opened up his bottle. Others came around and quickly grabbed the rest of the beers. Then, surprisingly, they all went back to their business. They didn't seem to be discussing anything very pressing, nor were they talking about any criminal activities. They mainly talked about what kind of rims to put on their cars. A few of them took care of the drug customers, handing vials of crack to the people who walked over from nearby buildings or drove up in run-down cars. In the distance I could see a few churchgoers on a Sunday stroll. A handful of gang members stood guard in front of Number 4040, and after a time some of the guys hanging out near the cars relieved them.

J.T. had a lot of questions for me: *You always use those surveys? Can you get a good job after you finish with this research? Why don't you study your own people?*

This last one would become one of his favorites. I felt a strange kind of intimacy with J.T., unlike the bond I'd felt even with good friends. It would have been hard to explain then and is just as hard now, but we had somehow connected in an instant, and deeply.

I tried to act nonchalant when J.T. asked me these questions, but inside I was overjoyed that he was curious about my work. I had a feeling that I was talking to someone about whom most people probably knew little. I didn't know exactly where our conversations might lead, but I sensed I was getting a unique perspective on life in a poor neighborhood. There were plenty of sociological studies on economically disenfranchised youth, but most relied on dry statistics of unemployment, crime, and family hardship. I had joined Bill Wilson's team in hopes of getting closer to the ground. My opportunity to do just that was standing right in front of me.

Every now and then, J.T. went inside the building to meet in private with someone who had driven up in a car.

I played a little handball and, showing off my hard-won suburban soccer skills, bounced the tennis ball off my head a few dozen times. Some of the older gang members were curious about my identity, my role at the university, and of course the reason I had returned. They all looked as tired as I was, and it felt as if we were all taking some welcome comic relief in one another's presence.

In general, I said very little. I asked no "meaningful" questions—mostly about their cars, why they were jacked up so high and whether they changed their own oil—and quickly saw that this strategy might actually work. I had learned the night before that they weren't very receptive to interview questions; they probably had plenty of that from cops, social workers, and the occasional journalist. So I just made small talk, trying to pass the time and act as if I'd been there before.

When J.T. returned from a trip into the building, everyone straightened up a bit.

"Okay!" he shouted. "They're ready, let's go over there." He ordered a few younger members into the building's lobby and motioned the others to get into their cars. He looked at me in a funny way. He smiled. I could tell that he was wondering what to say to me. I hoped he was going to invite me along to wherever they were going.

"You got balls," he said. "I'll give you that. We have to run. Why don't you meet me here next week. Early morning, all right?"

This offer took me by surprise. But I certainly wasn't going to turn him down. J.T. put out his hand, and I shook it. I tried again to think of something witty to say. "Yeah, sure," I said, "but you're buying next time."

He turned and hustled toward his car, a shiny purple Malibu Classic with gold rims. All of a sudden, there was no one left standing around but me.

TWO

First Days on Federal Street

I began spending time with J.T. We'd usually hang out for a little while with some of the more senior members of his gang, and then we'd go for a ride around the South Side.

Although it would take me a few years to learn about J.T.'s life in detail, he did tell me a good bit during our first few weeks together: He had grown up in this neighborhood, then gone to college on an athletic scholarship and found that he loved reading about history and politics. After college he took a job selling office supplies and industrial textiles at a midsize corporation in downtown Chicago. But he felt that his chances of success were limited because he was black; he got angry when he saw white people with lesser skills get promoted ahead of him. Within two years he left the mainstream to return to the projects and the gang life.

J.T. loved to talk about black Chicago as we drove around—the history of the neighborhood, the gangs, the underground economy. Like Old Time and the others who frequented Washington Park, J.T.

had his own personal version of history, replete with stories about great gang leaders and dramatic gang wars. He took me to his favorite restaurants, most of which had their own lively histories. One of them, Gladys's, was a soul-food restaurant where elected community and political leaders used to meet in private. Another marked the spot where two gangs once signed a legendary truce. J.T. always offered to pay for our meals and I, out of appreciation and a student's budget, always accepted.

J.T. once asked me what sociologists had to say about gangs and inner-city poverty. I told him that some sociologists believed in a "culture of poverty"—that is, poor blacks didn't work because they didn't value employment as highly as other ethnic groups did, and they transmitted this attitude across generations.

"So you want me to take pride in the job, and you're only paying me minimum wage?" J.T. countered. "It don't sound like you think much about the job yourself." His tone was more realistic than defensive. In fact, his rejoinder echoed the very criticisms that some sociologists applied to the "culture of poverty" view.

J.T. and I often passed time together at a diner. He might sit quietly, working through the details of his gang's operations, while I read for my sociology classes. Since he didn't want to generate tangible evidence of his enterprise, J.T. didn't write down very much, but he could keep innumerable details straight in his mind: the wages of each one of his two hundred members, the shifts each of them worked, recent spikes in supply or demand, and so on. Occasionally he drifted off, muttering calculations to himself. He didn't share many details with me, but he did sometimes give me a sort of quiz.

"Okay, I got something for you," he said one day over breakfast. "Let's say two guys are offering me a great deal on raw product." I knew enough to know that "raw product" meant powdered cocaine, which J.T.'s gang cooked up into crack. "One of them says if I pay twenty percent higher than the usual rate, he'll give me a ten percent discount a year from now, meaning that if the supply goes down, he'll sell to me before the other niggers he deals with. The other guy says he'll give me a ten percent discount now if I agree to buy from him at the regular price a year from now. What would you do?"

"This all depends on whether you think the supply will be affected a year from now, right?" I said.

"Right, so . . . ?"

"Well, I don't have any idea how this market works, so I'm not sure what to do."

"No, that's not how you need to think. You always take the sure bet in this game. *Nothing* can be predicted—not supply, not anything. The nigger who tells you he's going to have product a year from now is lying. He could be in jail or dead. So take your discount now."

As fascinating as I found such conversations, I rarely took notes in front of J.T., because I didn't want to make him cautious about what he said. Instead I waited until I got back to my apartment to write down as much as I could recall.

We often met a few times a week, but only when he wanted. He would phone me to arrange our meetings, sometimes just a few minutes in advance. J.T. didn't like to talk on the phone. In his soft voice, he'd tell me where and when to meet, and then he'd hang up. Once in a while, I didn't even have time to answer that I couldn't meet because I had a class—and then I'd cut class and meet him anyway. It was pretty thrilling to have a gang boss calling me up to go hang out with him. There were times I wanted to tell my professors the real reason I missed class now and then, but I never did.

Occasionally I hinted to J.T. that I would really, really like to learn more about gang life. But I was too meek to ask for any kind of formalized arrangement. Nor did he offer. Every time he dropped me off in front of my apartment building, he'd just stare out the window. I didn't know whether to say "Good-bye," "Hope to see you again," or "Call me sometime."

One morning, after I'd been hanging out with him for perhaps eight months, J.T. said we'd be visiting a different housing development, the Robert Taylor Homes. I had heard of Robert Taylor; *everybody* had heard of Robert Taylor. It was the largest public housing project in the United States, about ten times bigger than the Lake Park projects, with twenty-eight drab high-rise buildings stretched along a two-mile corridor. It lay a few miles away from the U of C, but since it ran alongside the Dan Ryan Expressway, one of Chicago's main arteries, pretty much everyone in the city drove past Robert Taylor at one time or another.

"I'm going to take you to meet somebody," J.T. said, "but I don't want you to open your mouth. Do you think you can do that?"

"Do I ever open my mouth?" I asked.

"No, but every so often you get a little excited, especially after you drink all that coffee. You open your mouth today, and that's it—we're through. Okay?"

Only once before had I heard such insistence in J.T.'s voice, and that was the night we first met in the stairwell of Building Number 4040 in the Lake Park projects. I finished my breakfast quickly, and then we jumped into his Malibu. The late-morning sky was overcast. J.T. was quiet except for asking me once in a while to see if any cops were following him. He had never asked this before. For the first time, I became fully conscious of just what I was doing: tagging along with the leader of a major crack-selling gang.

But I still hadn't admitted to myself that the man I sat next to

was, at bottom, a criminal. I was too caught up in the thrill of observing the thug life firsthand. In the halcyon suburb where I grew
up, people didn't even wash their cars on the street. In front of me
here was a movie come to life.

There was something else, too, that helped me ignore the questionable morality of the situation. The University of Chicago scholars who helped invent the field of sociology, back when it first
became a legitimate academic discipline, did so by venturing into the
murkier corners of the city. They became famous through their up-
close study of the hobo, the hustler, the socialite; they gained access
to brothels and speakeasies and the smoky back rooms where politicians plied their art. Lately I'd been reading the works of these scholars. So even though I was hanging out with drug traffickers and
thieves, at heart I felt like I was just being a good sociologist.

The street leading into the Robert Taylor Homes was lined with
old, beat-up cars. A school crossing guard leaned on the hood of
a car, her morning duty done, looking as if she'd been through a war.
She waved knowingly at J.T. as we drove past. We pulled up in front
of a high-rise, the lobby populated by a bunch of young men who
seemed to stand at attention when they saw J.T.'s car. Unlike the Lake
Park projects, which were nearly abandoned, Robert Taylor was
thrumming with life. I could hear rap music blasting from a stereo.
People stood around smoking cigarettes and, from the smell of it,
marijuana. Every so often a parent and child passed through the
loose crowd.

J.T. parked his Malibu and strode toward the building like a bad-
ass cowboy swaggering into a bar. He stopped just short of the entrance, surveying the area and waiting as people came to greet him.
As each young man made his way over, J.T. extended his hand gra-

ciously. Few words were spoken; most of the communication was in the form of subtle nods, signals familiar to everyone but me.

"When you gonna come and see me, baby?" one woman called out, and then another: "You gonna take me for a ride, sweetheart?" J.T. smiled and waved them off, playfully tapping their young children on the head as he passed. Two older women in bright blue jackets that read TENANT PATROL came up and hugged J.T., asked him why he didn't come around more often. J.T. was obviously well known in these parts, although I had no idea why.

Just then someone emerged from the lobby. He was obese, roughly J.T.'s age, and he was breathing heavily. His name was Curly, and—as if in mockery of my stereotypical preconceptions—he was a ringer for Rerun from *What's Happening!!* He and J.T. clasped hands, and then J.T. motioned for me to follow them.

"Your mama's house or mine?" Curly asked.

"Mama's pissed at me," J.T. said. "Let's go to your place."

I followed them up a few flights of stairs. We stepped inside an apartment furnished with couches and a few reclining chairs that faced a big TV. There was a Christian show playing. The walls were hung with family photos and a painting of Jesus Christ. Toys were strewn about the floor, and the kitchen counter was crowded with boxes of cereal and cookies. I could smell chicken and rice on the stove. Balls of yarn and knitting needles sat atop a drab glass table. The domestic scene surprised me a bit, for I had read so much about the poverty and danger in Robert Taylor, how children ran around without parents and how drugs had overtaken the community.

J.T. gestured for me to sit on the sofa, and then he and Curly sat down to talk. J.T. didn't introduce me, and before long I was forgotten entirely. Between their fast talk and the gangster vocabulary, I couldn't understand much of what they were saying, but I did manage to pick out some key words: "tax," "product," "monthly dues,"

"Cobras," "Kings," "police," "CHA security." They talked quickly and earnestly. After a while they began throwing numbers at each other in some kind of negotiation. A few times a young man arrived at the screen door and interrupted them, shouting "Five-Oh on Federal" or "Five-Oh in 26." Later J.T. would explain that that's how they communicated the whereabouts of the police: "Five-Oh" meant police, "26" was a building number in Robert Taylor, and "Federal" was a busy street flanking the projects. Cell phones hadn't yet arrived—the year was 1989—so gang members had to pass along such information manually.

I felt a sudden urge to go to the bathroom, but I didn't feel comfortable asking to use the one in the apartment. After some squirming I decided to stand up and walk around. As I made a move to get up, J.T. and Curly looked at me disapprovingly. I sat back down.

Their meeting had lasted at least two hours. "That's it," J.T. finally said. "I'm hungry. Let's pick it up tomorrow."

Curly smiled. "It'll be good to have you back," he said. "Ain't the same since you left."

Then J.T. glanced at me. "Oh, shit," he said to Curly. "I forgot about him. This is Sudhir. He's a cop."

The two of them began laughing. "You can go ahead and take a piss now," J.T. said, and they both laughed even harder. I began to sense that in exchange for access I was meant to serve as a source of entertainment for J.T.

On the car ride back to Hyde Park, J.T. told me what had just happened. He explained that he had grown up in the very Robert Taylor building we'd just visited. For the past couple of years, he'd been working out of the Lake Park projects because the Black Kings' citywide leaders had wanted to increase productivity there. But since the Lake Park projects were now slated for demolition, J.T. was returning to Robert Taylor, where he would be merging his own

Black Kings gang with the local BK faction, which was run by Curly. This merger was being executed at the behest of the gang's higher-ups. Curly had been installed as a temporary leader when J.T. was sent to turn around the Lake Park operation. Curly apparently wasn't a very good manager, which made the gang bosses' decision to bring J.T. back a simple one.

Robert Taylor and the other projects on State Street, J.T. told me, were "easy money," partly since thousands of customers lived nearby but also because of "the white folks who drive over to buy our shit." They came from Bridgeport, Armour Square, and other predominantly white ethnic neighborhoods on the far side of the Dan Ryan Expressway, buying mostly crack cocaine but also some heroin and marijuana. In his new assignment, J.T. told me, he hoped to earn "a hundred times" what he currently earned and buy a house for his mother, who still lived in Robert Taylor. He also said he hoped to buy an apartment for his girlfriend and their children. (In fact, he mentioned several such girlfriends, each of whom apparently needed an apartment.)

At the Lake Park projects, J.T.'s income had been dropping from a peak of about thirty thousand dollars a year. But he told me that now, in Robert Taylor, he stood to make as much as seventy-five thousand dollars or a hundred thousand if business was steady, which would put him nearly in the same league as some of the gang's higher-ups.

He made a few references to the gang's hierarchy and his effort to rise within it. There were a few dozen Black Kings officers above him, spread throughout Chicago, who earned their money by managing several gang factions like J.T.'s. These men were known as "lieutenants" and "captains." Above *them* was another level of gangsters who were known as the "board of directors." I had had no idea how much a street gang's structure mirrored the structure of just about any other business in America.

J.T. made it clear that if you rose high enough in the Black Kings dynasty, and lived long enough, you could make an awful lot of money. As he discussed his move up the ladder, I felt a knot in my stomach. Since meeting him I had entertained the notion that my dissertation research might revolve around his gang and its drug trafficking. I had spoken with him not only about his own gang "set" but about all the Black Kings sets in the city—how they collaborated or fought with one another over turf, how the crack-cocaine economy was fundamentally altering the nature of the urban street gang. Although there was a great deal of social-science literature on gangs, very few researchers had written about the actual business dealings of a gang, and even fewer had firsthand access to a gang's leadership. As we pulled up to my apartment, I realized that I had never formally asked J.T. about gaining access to his life and work. Now it seemed I might be getting shut out just as things were heating up.

"So when you do you think you'll be moving over to Robert Taylor?" I asked.

"Not sure," he said absentmindedly, staring out at the panhandlers who worked the gas station near my apartment.

"Well, I'm sure you'll be busy now—I mean, even busier than you've been. So listen, I just wanted to thank you—"

"Nigger, are we breaking up?" J.T. started laughing.

"No! I'm just trying to—"

"Listen, my man, I know you have to write a term paper—and what are you going to write it on? On me, right?" He giggled and stuck a cigar in his mouth.

It seemed that J.T. craved the attention. It seemed that I was more than just entertainment for him: I was someone who might take him seriously. I hadn't thought about the drawbacks of having my research dependent on the whims of one person. But now I turned giddy at the prospect of continuing our conversations. "That's right," I said. " 'The Life and Times of John Henry Torrance.' What do you think?"

"I like it, I like it." He paused. "Okay, get the fuck out, gotta run."

He offered his hand as I opened the car door. I shook it and nodded at him.

My short walk north to the Lake Park projects would now be replaced by a longer commute, usually by bus, to the Robert Taylor Homes. But as a result of his relocation, J.T. reported that he'd be out of touch for a few weeks. I decided to use that time to do some research on housing projects in general and the Robert Taylor Homes in particular.

I learned that the Chicago Housing Authority had built the project between 1958 and 1962, naming it after the agency's first African-American chairman. It was the size of a small city, with forty-four hundred apartments housing about thirty thousand people. Poor blacks had arrived in Chicago en masse from the South during the great migrations of the 1930s and 1940s, which left a pressing need for the city to accommodate them.

In the beginning, the project was greeted with considerable optimism, but it soon soured. Black activists were angry that Chicago politicians put the project squarely in the middle of an already crowded black ghetto, thereby sparing the city's white ethnic neighborhoods. Urban planners complained that the twenty-eight buildings occupied only 7 percent of the ninety-six-acre plot, leaving huge swaths of vacant land that isolated the project from the wider community. Architects declared the buildings unwelcoming and practically uninhabitable from the outset, even though the design was based upon celebrated French urban-planning principles.

And, most remarkably, law-enforcement officials deemed Robert Taylor too dangerous to patrol. The police were unwilling to provide protection until tenants curbed their criminality—and stopped hurling bottles or shooting guns out the windows whenever the police showed up.

In newspaper headlines, Robert Taylor was variously called "Congo Hilton," "Hellhole," and "Fatherless World"—and this was when it was still relatively new. By the end of the 1970s, it had gotten worse. As the more stable working families took advantage of civil-rights victories by moving into previously segregated areas of Chicago, the people left behind lived almost uniformly below the poverty line. A staggering 90 percent of the adults in Robert Taylor reported welfare—cash disbursements, food stamps, and Medicaid—as their sole form of support, and even into the 1990s that percentage would never get lower. There were just two social-service centers for nearly twenty thousand children. The buildings themselves began to fall apart, with at least a half dozen deaths caused by plunging elevators.

By the time I got to Chicago, at the tail end of the 1980s, Robert Taylor was habitually referred to as the hub of Chicago's "gang and drug problem." That was the phrase always invoked by the city's media, police, and academic researchers. They weren't wrong. The poorest parts of the city were controlled largely by street gangs like the Black Kings, which made their money not only dealing drugs but also by extortion, gambling, prostitution, selling stolen property, and countless other schemes. It was outlaw capitalism, and it ran hot, netting small fortunes for the bosses of the various gangs. In the newspapers, gang leaders were commonly reported as having multimillion-dollar fortunes. This may have been an exaggeration, but it was true that some police busts of the leaders' homes netted hundreds of thousands of dollars in cash.

For the rest of the community, the payout of this outlaw economy—drug addiction and public violence—was considerably less appealing. Combine this menace with decades of government neglect, and what you found in the Robert Taylor Homes were thousands of families struggling to survive. It was the epitome of an "underclass" urban neighborhood, with the poor living hard and virtually separate lives from the mainstream.

But there was surprisingly little reportage on the American inner city—and even less on how the gangs managed to control such a sprawling enterprise, or how a neighborhood like Robert Taylor managed to cope with these outlaw capitalists. Thanks to my chance meeting with J.T. and his willingness to let me tag along with him, I felt as if I stood on the threshold of this world in a way that might really change the public's—if not the academy's—understanding.

I wanted to bring J.T. to Bill Wilson's attention, but I didn't know how. I was already working on some of Wilson's projects, but these were large, survey-based studies that queried several thousand people at a time. Wilson's research team included sociologists, economists, psychologists, and a dozen graduate students glued to their computers, trying to find hidden patterns in the survey data that might reveal the causes of poverty. I didn't know anyone who was walking around talking to people, let alone gang members, in the ghetto. Even though I knew that my entrée into J.T.'s life was the stuff of sociology, as old as the field itself, it still felt like I was doing something unconventional, bordering on rogue behavior.

So while I devoted time to hanging out with J.T., I told Wilson and others only the barest details of my fieldwork. I figured that I'd eventually come up with a concrete research topic that involved J.T., at which point I could share with Wilson a well-worked-out set of ideas.

In late spring, several weeks after his meeting with Curly, J.T. finally summoned me to Robert Taylor. He had moved in with his mother in her apartment, a four-bedroom unit in the northern end of the complex. J.T. usually stayed in a different neighborhood, in one of the apartments he rented for various girlfriends. But now, he said, he needed to be in Robert Taylor full-time to get his gang firmly transplanted into its new territory. He told me to take the bus from Hyde Park down Fifty-fifth Street to State Street, where he'd have a few gang members meet me at the bus stop. It wasn't safe to walk around by myself.

Three of J.T.'s foot soldiers picked me up in a rusty Caprice. They were young and affectless and didn't have anything to say to me. As low-ranking members of the gang, they spent a lot of their time running errands for J.T. Once, when J.T. was a little drunk and getting excited about my writing his biography, he offered to assign me one of his gang members as a personal driver. I declined.

We drove up State Street, past a long stretch of Robert Taylor high-rises, and stopped at a small park in the middle of the complex. It was the sort of beautiful spring day, sunny, with a fresh lake breeze, that Chicagoans know will disappear once the brutal summer settles in. About fifty people of all ages were having a barbecue. There were colorful balloons printed with HAPPY BIRTHDAY CARLA tied to picnic tables. J.T. sat at one table, surrounded by families with lots of young children, playing and eating and making happy noise.

"Look who's here!" J.T. shouted. "The Professor. Welcome back."

His hands were sticky with barbecue sauce, so he just nodded, then introduced me to everyone at the table. I said hi to his girlfriend, whom I knew as Missie, and the young son they had together, Jamel.

"Is this the young man you've been telling me about?" said an older woman, putting her arm on my shoulder.

"Yes, Mama," J.T. said between bites, his voice as obedient as a young boy's.

"Well, Mr. Professor, I'm J.T.'s mother."

"They call her Ms. Mae," J.T. said.

"That's right," she said. "And you can call me that, too." She led me to another table and prepared a large plate of food for me. I told her I didn't eat meat, so she loaded me up with spaghetti, mac and cheese, greens, and cornbread.

We sat around for a few hours while the kids played. I spoke mostly to J.T.'s mother, and we forged a bond immediately. Sensing my interests, she began talking about the challenges of raising a family in public housing. She pointed to different people at the barbecue and filled in their stories. Carla, the birthday girl, was a one-year-old whose father and mother were both in jail for selling drugs. The adults in her building had decided to raise the child. This meant hiding her from the Department of Child and Family Services, which would have sent Carla into foster care. Different families took turns keeping Carla, shifting her to a new apartment whenever they caught wind that the social workers were snooping around. Ms. Mae talked about how teenage girls shouldn't have children so early, about the tragedy of kids getting caught up in violence, the value of an education, and her insistence that J.T. attend college.

J.T. came over to tell me about a big party the Black Kings were hosting later that afternoon. His gang had won a South Side basketball tournament, and everyone would be celebrating. He and I took a walk toward his building. Again I had so many questions: What did his mother think of the life he had chosen? How much did she even know? What did the typical Robert Taylor resident think about his organization?

Instead I asked a pretty tame one: "Why is everyone partying with you tonight? I thought you said it was a *gang* tournament."

"See, around here each building has an organization," he said.

"Organization," I knew, was one of the words that gang members sometimes used to refer to the gang; other words were "set" and "folks."

"And we don't just fight each other. We have basketball tournaments, softball tournaments, card games. Sometimes it's just people in the organization who play, but sometimes we find the best people in the building—like, we sometimes call Darryl, who used to play ball for Wisconsin, but he's not in the organization. So it's a building thing."

"So people in your building actually root for you?" I was puzzled as to how non–gang members viewed the Black Kings.

"Yeah! I know you think this sounds funny, but it's not like everyone hates us. You just have to see, it's a community thing."

He wasn't kidding. The party was held in a courtyard surrounded by three buildings, and several hundred people showed up to eat, drink beer, and party to the music of a DJ. All expenses were paid by the Black Kings.

I stayed close to J.T., sitting on the hood of his car, taking in all the activity. I watched young black men drive up in expensive sports cars, trailed by posses and girlfriends. They all greeted J.T. and congratulated him on winning the tournament.

J.T. explained that it was courtesy for leaders of some of the losing gangs to drop by. "The ones that are shooting at us won't come anywhere near us," he said, "but sometimes you got other organizations that you don't fight, that you just have a rivalry with." He told me that the various gangs' higher-ranking leaders tended to interact peacefully, since they often did business together—unlike the teenagers, or "shorties," he said. "They mostly just beat the shit out of each other in high school or at parties."

J.T. didn't introduce me to many people who stopped by, and I didn't feel comfortable leaving my spot. So I just sat and watched until the beers began making me drowsy. By dusk the party was dying down. That's when J.T. had one of his "shorties" drive me back to my apartment.

After about a month of commuting to his building, I managed to convince J.T. that I didn't need an escort to meet me at the bus stop. If the weather was okay, I'd even walk, which gave me a chance to see some of the neighborhoods that surrounded Robert Taylor. They were all poor, but even with their mixture of dilapidated homes and abandoned lots, not nearly as intimidating.

I always got nervous as I approached Robert Taylor, especially if J.T. wasn't there to meet me. But by now I was known to the gang members stationed out front. So instead of searching me—which they often did to strangers, even if it was an ambulance driver or a utility worker—they let me go up to Ms. Mae's apartment on the tenth floor. She'd fix me a plate of food, and then we would sit and talk.

I felt self-conscious that Ms. Mae had to entertain me while I waited for J.T. I also figured she couldn't really afford to feed another mouth. I once tried to give her a few dollars for my meal. "Young man, don't ever do that again," she scolded, pushing the bills back at me. "Let me tell you something about us. We may be poor, but when you come over here, don't pity us, don't pardon us, and don't hold us to a lower standard than you hold yourself up to."

Ms. Mae was a heavyset woman in her late fifties who, unless she was off to church, always wore an apron. She always seemed to be in the middle of housework. Today's apron was flowery, yellow and pink, with MS. MAE and GOD BLESS printed on it. She wore thick glasses and a warm, inviting look on her face. "You know, I came here with the clothes on my back," she said. "Arkansas. Mother said there was no life for me down there no more. She said, 'Go see your auntie in Chicago, get yourself a man and a job, and don't turn around.' And I didn't. I raised six children in Chicago. Never looked back."

I sat and ate as she spoke, trying to keep up with the stories she was telling as well as the food she kept heaping on my plate.

"We live in a *community,* understand? Not the *projects*—I hate that word. We live in a *community.* We need a helping hand now and then, but who doesn't? Everyone in this building helps as much as they can. We share our food, just like I'm doing with you. My son says you're writing about his life—well, you may want to write about this community, and how we help each other. And when I come over to *your* house, you'll share with me. You'll cook for me if I'm hungry. But when you're here, you're in my home and my community. And we'll take care of you."

I felt nervous as she spoke. Her warmth and her notion of community certainly challenged what I had read about Robert Taylor. Ms. Mae spoke to me as though she were teaching a child about life, not giving an academic researcher answers to scientific questions. Indeed, the time I was spending with families felt less and less like research. People who knew nothing about me nevertheless took me inside their world, talked to me with such openness, and offered me the food that they had probably budgeted for their own children.

No one back at the U of C had prepared me to feel such strong emotional connections to the people I studied. None of the ethno-

graphic studies I'd read offered much guidance about the relationships a researcher formed during fieldwork and how to manage
them. The books talked about the right way to ask a question or address a respondent during an interview, but little about managing relationships with the people you hung out with. In time I would
meet the anthropologist Jean Comaroff, who taught me about the
benefits and dangers of getting personally attached to sources, but
that was still a few years away.

Nor was Ms. Mae's description of "community" something I
was accustomed to from my own background. I don't think I could
name more than a few people who lived on the nearby streets in the
suburb where I grew up, and we certainly never borrowed from one
another or planned activities together. Suddenly I envisioned Ms.
Mae coming to my apartment someday for a visit and eating bland
pasta and steamed vegetables, the only meal I could conceivably
cook for her.

She and I kept speaking. I learned that Ms. Mae was the daughter of sharecroppers, had spent two decades as a nanny and a domestic
worker, and was forced to move into public housing when her husband, J.T.'s father, died of heart disease. He had been a quiet, easy-
going man who worked for the city's transportation department.
Moving into Robert Taylor, she said, was her last-ditch effort to
keep the family intact.

Finally J.T. walked into the apartment. He took one look at me
and laughed. "Is that *all* you do around here?" he said. "I'm beginning to think the only reason you come over here is to eat!"

His mother told him to hush and brought over some more sweet
potato pie for me.

"C'mon, Mr. Professor, finish your food," J.T. said. "I need to survey the building."

J.T. had by now firmly established his reign over a group of three buildings, one on State Street and two on Federal, each of which he liked to walk through at least once a week. "You have the CHA, the landlord, but then we also try to make sure that people are doing what they're told," he explained as we walked. "We can't have this place go crazy with niggers misbehaving. Because that's when police come around, and then customers stop coming around, and then we don't make our money. Simple as that."

As we entered the lobby of one of his buildings, 2315 Federal Street, he grabbed a few of his foot soldiers and told them to follow us. The August heat made the lobby's concrete walls sweat; they were cool to the touch but damp with humidity, just like all the people hanging around.

"I always start with the stairwells," J.T. said. There were three stairwells per building, two on the sides and one running up the middle, next to the elevator. "And I usually have my guys with me, just in case." He winked, as if I should know what "just in case" meant. I didn't, but I kept quiet. The foot soldiers, high-school kids with glittery, cheap necklaces and baggy tracksuits, walked quietly about five feet behind us.

We began climbing. It was only eleven on a weekday morning, but already the stairwells and landings were crowded with people drinking, smoking, hanging out. The stairwells were poorly lit and unventilated, and they smelled vile; there were puddles whose provenance I was happy to not know. The steps themselves were dangerous, many of the metal treads loose or missing. Who were all these people? Everybody we passed seemed to know J.T., and he had a word or a nod for each of them.

On the fifth floor, we came upon three older men, talking and laughing.

J.T. looked them over. "You all staying on the eleventh floor, right?" he asked.

"No," said one of them without looking up. "We moved to 1206."

"To 1206, huh? And who said you could do *that*?" None of them answered. "You need to settle up if you're in 1206, because you're *supposed* to stay in 1102, right?"

The men just cradled their beer cans, heads down, stung by the scolding.

J.T. called out to one of his foot soldiers, "Creepy, get these niggers over to T-Bone." T-Bone, I knew, was one of J.T.'s close friends and senior officers.

As we resumed our climbing, I asked J.T. what had just happened.

"Squatters," he said. "See, a lot of people who live around here don't have a lease. They just hang out in the stairs 'cause it's too cold outside, or they just need a safe place—maybe they're running from the police, or maybe they owe somebody money. We provide them protection. Sometimes they get out of hand, but most of them are pretty quiet. Anyway, they're here to stay."

"The gang protects the squatters?"

"Yeah, no one fucks with them if they're in here. I make sure of that. But we can't have two million of these niggers, so we have to keep track. They pay us."

As we continued our climb, we occasionally passed an older woman wearing a blue Tenant Patrol jacket. There were about a dozen of these women in each building, J.T. said. "They make sure that old folks are doing okay, and sometimes we help them." Somewhere around the thirteenth floor, J.T. stopped when he saw a Tenant Patrol woman bent over a man who was squirming on the floor.

"Morning, Ms. Easley," J.T. said. The man looked like he was just waking up, but I could also smell vomit, and he seemed to be in pain. He lay right outside the incinerator room, and the garbage smelled terrible.

"He's coming down," Ms. Easley told J.T. "He said someone sold him some bad stuff."

"Hmm-hmm," J.T. said disapprovingly. "They all say that when something goes bad. Always blaming it on us."

"Can one of your boys take him to the clinic?"

"Shit, he'll probably just be back tonight," J.T. said, "doing the same thing."

"Yeah, baby, but we can't have him sitting here."

J.T. waved over the remaining foot soldier, Barry, who was trailing us. "Get a few niggers to take this man down to Fiftieth." Barry started in on his task; "Fiftieth" referred to the Robert Taylor medical clinic, on Fiftieth Street.

"All right, Ms. Easley," J.T. said, "but if I see this nigger here tomorrow and he's saying the same shit, Creepy is going to beat his ass." J.T. laughed.

"Yes, yes, I know," she said. "And let me talk to you for a second." She and J.T. took a short walk, and I saw him pull out a few bills and hand them over. Ms. Easley walked back toward me, smiling, and set off down the stairwell. "Thank you for this, sweetheart," she called to J.T. "The kids are going to be very happy!"

I followed J.T. out to the "gallery," the corridor that ran along the exterior of the project buildings. Although you entered the apartments from the gallery, it was really an outdoor hallway, exposed to the elements, with chain-link fencing from floor to ceiling. It got its name, I had heard, because of its resemblance to a prison gallery, a metal enclosure meant to keep inmates in check. J.T. and I leaned up against the rail, looking out over the entire South Side and, beyond it, Lake Michigan.

Without my prodding, J.T. talked about what we had just seen. "Crackheads. Sometimes they mix shit—crack, heroin, alcohol, medicine—and they just can't see straight in the morning. Someone on the Tenant Patrol finds them and helps."

"Why don't you just call an ambulance?" I asked.

J.T. looked at me skeptically. "You kidding? Those folks almost never come out here when we call, or it takes them an hour."

"So you guys bring them to the hospital?"

"Well, I don't like my guys doing shit for them, but once in a while I guess I feel sorry for them. That's Creepy's decision, though. He's the one who runs the stairwell. It's up to him—usually. But this time I'm doing Ms. Easley a favor."

The stairwells, J.T. explained, were the one public area in the building where the gang allowed squatters to congregate. These areas inevitably became hangout zones for drug addicts and the homeless. J.T.'s foot soldiers, working in shifts, were responsible for making sure that no fights broke out there. "It ain't a pretty job," J.T. told me, laughing, "but that's how they learn to deal with niggers, learn to be tough on them."

The gang didn't charge the squatters much for staying in the building, and J.T. let the foot soldiers keep most of this squatter tax. That was one of the few ways foot soldiers could earn any money, since they held the lowest rank in the gang's hierarchy and weren't even eligible yet to sell drugs. From J.T.'s perspective, allowing his foot soldiers to police the stairwells served another important function: It let him see which junior members of his gang showed the potential for promotion. That's why he let guys like Creepy handle this kind of situation. "Creepy can take the man to the clinic, or he can just drag his ass out of the building and let him be," J.T. said. "That's on him. I try not to interfere, unless he fucks up and the police come around or Ms. Easley gets pissed."

I realized this was what J.T. had done the night I first stumbled upon his foot soldiers and was held overnight in the stairwell. He had wanted to see how they handled this stranger. Did they remain calm? Did they ask the right questions? Or did they get out of control and do something to attract the attention of tenants and the police?

"So what was going on with Ms. Easley?" I asked.

"You mean why did I give her money?" J.T. said. "That's what you want to know, right?"

I nodded, a little embarrassed that he could see through my line of indirect questioning.

"Tenant Patrol runs after-school parties for kids, and they buy school supplies. I give them money for that. It keeps them off our ass."

This was the first time J.T. had mentioned having to deal with tenants who might not like his gang's behavior. I asked what Ms. Easley might not like about his gang.

"I wouldn't say that she doesn't *like* us," he said. "She just wants to know that kids can walk around and not get hurt. And she just wants to keep things safe for the women. Lot of these crackheads are looking for sex, too, and they beat up women. It gets wild up in here at night. So we try to keep things calm. That's about it. We just help them, you know, keep the peace."

"So she lets you do what you want as long as you help her deal with people causing trouble? It's a give-and-take? There's nothing that you guys do that pisses her off?"

"We just keep the peace, that's all," he muttered, and walked away.

J.T. sometimes spoke vaguely like this, which I took as a sign to stop asking questions. At times he could be extraordinarily open about his life and his business; at other times he gave roundabout or evasive answers. It was something I'd learn to live with.

We kept climbing until we reached the top floor, the sixteenth. I followed J.T. down the hallway till we came to an apartment without a front door. J.T. told our foot soldier escort to stand guard outside. The young man nodded obediently.

Following J.T. inside, I was hit by a noxious odor of vomit, urine, and burned crack. It was so dark that I could barely see. There were several mattresses spread about, some with bodies on them, and piles of dirty clothing and fast-food wrappers. The holes in the walls were stuffed with rags to keep out the rats.

"Sudhir, come over here!" J.T. shouted. I followed a dim light that came from the rear of the apartment. "See this?" he said, pointing to a row of beat-up refrigerators. "This is where the squatters keep their food." Each fridge was draped with a heavy chain and padlock.

"Where do they get the fridges?" I asked.

"From the housing authority!" J.T. said, laughing. "The CHA managers sell fridges to the squatters for a few bucks instead of taking them back to get them fixed. *Everyone* is in on it. That's one thing you'll learn about the projects."

J.T. explained that this apartment was a "regular" squat, which meant that the people sleeping there paid the gang a rental fee and were therefore allowed to keep food and clothes inside. Ten people stayed in this apartment. A squatter known as C-Note, who had been in the community for more than two decades, was their leader. It was his duty to screen other squatters who wanted to take up quarters, help them find food and shelter, and make sure they obeyed all J.T.'s rules. "We let him run things inside," J.T. said, "as long as he pays us and does what we say."

There were other, less stable squats in the building, J.T. explained.

"We got a lot of apartments that are just basically for the hos and the crackheads. They get high and spend a few nights and then they leave. They're the ones that end up causing trouble around here. That's when the police come by, so we have to be tight with them."

Outside the squat I sat down on the gallery floor, finally able to take a clear breath. I felt overwhelmed by all the new information hitting me. I told J.T. I needed a rest. He smiled, seeming to understand, and told me he'd survey the other two buildings by himself. When I started to resist, worried I might not have this chance again, J.T. read my mind. "Don't worry, Mr. Professor. I do this every week."

"Yeah, you're right," I said. "I'm beat. I'll meet you back at your place. I've got to go write some of this down."

My heart froze after I realized what I'd just said. I had never actually told J.T. that I was keeping notes on all our conversations; I always waited until we split up before writing down what had transpired. Suddenly I feared he would think about everything we'd just witnessed and discussed, including all the illegal activities, and shut me down.

But he didn't even blink.

"Shorty, take Sudhir back to Mama's place," he told the young man who'd been standing guard outside the squat. "I'll be over there in an hour."

I quietly walked down the sixteen flights of stairs and over to Ms. Mae's building. The elevators in Robert Taylor worked inconsistently at best, so the only people who bothered to wait for them were old people and mothers with small children. The foot soldier accompanied me all the way to Ms. Mae's door, but we didn't talk; I tended never to talk to foot soldiers, since they never talked to me—which led me to think they'd probably been told not to.

I wound up sitting at the living room table in Ms. Mae's apartment, writing up my notes. In a short time the apartment had become the place I went whenever I needed a break or wanted to write up some field notes. J.T.'s family grew comfortable with my sitting quietly by myself or even napping on the couch if J.T. was busy.

Sometimes the apartment was peaceful and sometimes it was busy. At the moment J.T.'s cousin and her two children were staying there, as was one of J.T.'s sisters. But the living arrangements were very fluid. Like a lot of the more established households in the projects, Ms. Mae's apartment was a respite for a network of poor and needy relatives who might stay for a night, a month, or longer. Some of them weren't actually relatives at all but were "strays" who just needed a place to stay. It could be hard to sort out J.T.'s relatives from the strays. Several of his uncles, I learned, were high-ranking gang members. But I didn't even know how many siblings he had. I'd often hear him talk about "my sister" or "a brother of mine on the West Side," but I couldn't tell if these people were blood relatives or just friends of the family.

Still, they all seemed content to let me hang out at Ms. Mae's. And they all knew that J.T. didn't want me wandering through the neighborhood by myself. Sometimes Ms. Mae would wordlessly set down a plate of food for me as I wrote, her Christian radio station playing in the background. No one in the family, including J.T., ever asked to see my notes—although once in a while he'd stand over me and joke about whether I was describing him as "handsome." He loved the idea that I might be writing his biography. But in general everyone respected my privacy and let me do my work.

Eventually Ms. Mae even cleared out a space for me in the apartment to keep some clothes and books. Often, during a break from writing up my notes, I would start conversations with Ms. Mae and others in her apartment. They all seemed hesitant to answer specific questions—I'd already witnessed how tenants shied away from interviews with journalists or social workers—but they were more than willing to explain basic aspects of their lives and their community. Like Old Time and his friends in Washington Park, they talked openly about their family histories, Chicago politics, the behavior of the CHA and other city agencies, and life in the projects. As long as I didn't get too nosy—say, by asking about their income or who was living in an apartment illegally—they talked my head off. Just as important, I found I didn't have to hide my ignorance—which wasn't hard, since I was quite naïve about politics and race in urban America. My naïveté about these basic issues actually seemed to endear me to them.

In my brief exposure to J.T. and others in his building, I had already grown dismayed by the gap between their thoughtfulness and the denigrating portrayals of the poor I'd read in sociological studies. They were generally portrayed as hapless dupes with little awareness or foresight. The hospitality that Ms. Mae showed and the tenants' willingness to teach me not only surprised me but left me feeling extraordinarily grateful. I began to think I would never be able to repay their generosity. I took some solace in the hope that if I produced good, objective academic research, it could lead to social policy improvements, which might then better their living conditions. But I also wondered how I might pay them back in a more direct fashion. Given that I was taking out student loans to get by, my options were fairly limited.

Once J.T. saw how much I enjoyed accompanying him on his surveys of the buildings, he took me along regularly. But he often had other work to do, work he didn't invite me to see. And he wasn't ready yet to turn me loose in the buildings on my own, so I generally hung out around Ms. Mae's apartment. I felt a bit like a child, always in need of a baby-sitter, but I could hardly complain about the access I'd been granted into a world that was so radically different from anything I'd ever seen.

Ms. Mae introduced me to the many people who stopped by to visit. In their eyes I was just a student, a bit of an oddball to be sure; sometimes they jokingly called me "Mr. Professor," as they'd heard J.T. say. Several of J.T.'s aunts and cousins also lived in the building, and they warmed to me as well. They all seemed fairly close, sharing food and helping one another with errands or hanging out together on the gallery during the hot summer days.

Life on the gallery tended to be pretty lively. In the evenings families often set up a barbecue grill, pulling chairs or milk crates from their apartments to sit on. I probably could have made friends a lot more quickly if I hadn't been a vegetarian.

Little kids and teenage girls liked to tug my ponytail when I walked past. Others would chant "Gandhi" or "Julio" or "Ay-rab" in my direction. I was still enamored of the view of the city, and still nervous about the fencing that ran around the gallery.

Whenever a child ran toward the railing, I'd instinctively jump up and grab him. Once, a little boy's mother laughed at me. "Take it easy, Sudhir," she said. "Nothing's going to happen to them. It's not like the old days." In "the old days," I found out, some children did fall to their deaths off the Robert Taylor galleries, prompting the CHA to install a safety fence. But it was obvious that the first mistake had been building exterior hallways in windy, cold Chicago.

After dinner parents sent their kids inside the apartments and brought out tables and chairs, cards and poker chips, food and drink. They turned the galleries into dance floors and gambling dens; it could become carnivalesque.

I loved the nightlife on the galleries. And the tenants were generally in a good mood at night, willing to tell me about their lives if they weren't too high or too busy trying to make money. It was getting easier for me to determine when people were high. They'd stagger a bit, as if they were drunk, but their eyes sank back in their heads, giving them a look that was both dreamy and sinister.

It was hard to figure out the extent of crack use among the tenants. A lot of people pointed out that *other* people smoked crack—calling them "rock star" or "user" or "hype"—while insinuating that they themselves never did. Aside from a few older women, like J.T.'s mother, just about everyone was accused of smoking crack at one time or another.

After a while it became clear to me that crack use in the projects was much like the use of alcohol in the suburbs where I grew up: there was a small group of hard-core addicts and a much larger group of functional users who smoked a little crack a few days a week. Many of the crack users in Robert Taylor took care of their families and went about their business, but when they saved up ten or twenty dollars, they'd go ahead and get high. Over time I'd learn enough to estimate that 15 percent of the tenants were hardcore addicts while another 25 percent were casual users.

One of the first people I got to know on the gallery was named Clarisse. She was in her mid-thirties but looked considerably older. Beneath her worn and bruised skin, you could see a beautiful and thoughtful woman who nearly always had a smile ready. She worked as a prostitute in the building—"hustler" was the standard euphemism—and called herself "Clarisse the Mankiller," because, as she put it, "my love knocks 'em dead." Clarisse often hung around with J.T.'s family on their gallery. This surprised me, since I had heard J.T. and Ms. Mae openly disparage the prostitutes in their building.

"That's part of life around here," Ms. Mae had said, "but we keep

away from them and I keep the kids away from them. We don't so-
cialize together."

One quiet evening, as J.T.'s family was getting ready to barbecue,
I was leaning against the gallery fence, looking out at the dusk, when
Clarisse came up beside me. "You never tell me about the kind of
women you like," she said, smiling, and opened a beer. By now I was
used to Clarisse teasing me about my love life.

"I told you," I said, "my girlfriend is in California."

"Then you must get lonely! Maybe Clarisse can help."

I blushed and tried to change the subject. "How long have you
been in the building, and how did you get to know J.T.?"

"They never told you!" Clarisse yelped. "I knew it! They just embarrassed, they don't like to admit I'm family."

"You're part of their family?"

"Man, I'm J.T.'s cousin. That's why I'm around. I live upstairs on
the fifteenth floor with my man. And I work in the building, too.
I'm the one in the family they don't like to talk about, because I'm
open about what I do. I'm a *very* open person—I don't hide nothing from nobody. Ms. Mae knows that. Shit, *everyone* knows it. But,
like I said, they don't always come clean about it."

"How can you live *and* work in the building?" I asked.

"You see these men?" Clarisse pointed at some of the tenants
along the galley, hanging out in front of their own apartments. "You
should see how they treat women." I didn't understand what Clarisse
meant; when she saw my face blank, she laughed. "Oh! We have a
lot to talk about. Clarisse will educate you."

She then gestured toward a few women sitting on chairs. "See,
all of them are hos. They all hustle. It's just that they do it quietly,
like me. We have regulars, *and* we live here. We're not hypes who just
come and go."

What's the difference, I asked her, between a "hype" and a "regular"?

"Regulars like me, we hustle to make our money, but we only go with guys we know. We don't do it full-time, but if we have to feed our kids, we may make a little money on the side. I got two kids I need to feed, and my man don't always help out. Then you got hypes that are just in it for the drugs. They don't live around here, but J.T. lets them work here, and they give him a cut. I don't hang around with them. They're the ones that cause trouble. Some of them have pimps, some of them work for the gang, but they're all in it for the drugs. Clarisse don't mess with drugs. And that's why a lot of people accept us—even if they say things behind our back. They know we're only trying to take care of our families, just like them."

"Are you working now?" I said.

"Baby, I'm always working if the price is right!" She laughed. "But J.T. probably don't want me working tonight, so I won't be hustling."

This confused me, since J.T. had specifically told me that his gang didn't run a prostitution racket. Most gangs didn't, he explained, since there wasn't much money to be made. Prostitutes were hard to manage and required a great deal of attention: They were constantly getting beat up and arrested, which meant long periods without income. They needed to be fed and clothed, and the ones who used drugs were notoriously unpredictable. They were also prone to stealing money.

"What do you mean?" I asked. "You mean J.T. controls you?"

"No, but he told me once that if I wanted to hang out with his family, I had to play by his rules: no hustling when there's a family thing going on. Like tonight. And he runs things around here, so I *have* to play by the rules."

Even though J.T.'s gang didn't actually control the prostitutes in his buildings, Clarisse explained that he did extract a monthly fee from both the hypes and the regulars. The regulars usually paid a flat fee (anywhere from fifteen to seventy-five dollars a month), and in return the gang would beat up any johns who abused the women. The hypes, meanwhile, turned over a cut of their income (ranging from 10 to 25 percent) to J.T.'s foot soldiers, who tried to keep track of how many tricks each woman turned. Clarisse said that J.T. was actually one of the nicer gang leaders on the South Side. He regularly lent money to women, helped them get medical care, even kept a few vacant apartments for them to use as brothels. So although J.T. didn't technically run a prostitution ring, he certainly controlled the flow of prostitution on his turf and profited from it.

The conversation with Clarisse that night made me realize that I was hardly the only person in the projects whose movements were dictated by J.T.

Whenever he took me on a survey of his buildings, I'd watch him deal with the various people who hung out in lobbies, stairwells, galleries, parking lots, and playgrounds. He warned a prostitute not to hustle out in the open. He told a man selling sneakers—they looked like counterfeit Nikes—to move away from the lobby where J.T.'s gang members were selling drugs. J.T. often forbade homeless men from hanging out in the playground, especially if they were drinking. And if he spotted a stranger on the premises, he'd have one of his senior officers interrogate that person to learn his business. J.T. hardly knew every single person out of the roughly five thousand in his domain, but he usually managed to figure out whether someone was a local, and if he couldn't figure it out, he had plenty of people to ask.

All of this was accomplished with little drama. "You folks need to move this activity somewhere else," he'd say matter-of-factly. Or,

"What did I tell you about hustling in the park when kids are playing?" Or, "You can't stay in this apartment unless you deal with Creepy first." I saw a few people resist, but none for any great length of time. Most of them seemed to respect his authority, or at least fear it.

In most of the sociological literature I'd read about gangs—they had been part of the urban fabric in the United States since at least the late nineteenth century—the gang almost always had heated relationships with parents, shopkeepers, social workers, and the police. It was portrayed as a nuisance at best, and more typically a major menace.

J.T.'s gang seemed different. It acted as the de facto administration of Robert Taylor: J.T. may have been a lawbreaker, but he was very much a lawmaker as well. He acted as if his organization truly did rule the neighborhood, and sometimes the takeover was complete. The Black Kings policed the buildings more aggressively than the Chicago police did. By controlling lobbies and parking lots, the BKs made it hard for tenants to move about freely. Roughly once a month, they held a weekend basketball tournament. This meant that the playgrounds and surrounding areas got thoroughly spruced up, with J.T. sponsoring a big neighborhood party—but it also meant that other tenants sometimes had to call off their own softball games or picnics at J.T.'s behest.

Over time J.T. became less reluctant to leave me alone in Robert Taylor. Occasionally he'd just go off on an errand and shout, "Hey, shorty, watch out for Sudhir. I'll be back." I generally didn't stray too far, but I did start up conversations with people outside the gang. That's how I first began to understand the complicated dynamic between the gang and the rest of the community.

One day, for instance, I ran into C-Note, the leader of the squatters, installing an air conditioner in Ms. Mae's apartment. C-Note was a combination handyman and hustler. For five or ten dollars, he'd fix a refrigerator or TV. For a few dollars more, he'd find an ingenious way to bring free electricity and gas into your home. When it came to home repair, there didn't seem much that C-Note couldn't, or wouldn't, do.

After he finished work at Ms. Mae's, I sat with C-Note on the gallery and had a beer. He told me that he had lived in the building for years and held various legitimate blue-collar jobs, but after being laid off several times he had lost his lease and become a squatter. He always found a little work and a place to sleep in J.T.'s building. He stayed out of people's way, he told me. He didn't make noise, didn't use drugs, and wasn't violent. He got his nickname, he explained, because "I got a hundred ways to make a hundred bucks."

I learned that a lot of tenants welcomed C-Note into their homes for dinner, let him play with their children, and gave him money for medicine or a ride to the hospital if he was hurt. But this began to change once J.T. moved his operations back into Robert Taylor. J.T. saw squatters as a source of income, not as charity cases. Nor was he pleased that C-Note was in the good graces of tenants, some of whom lobbied J.T. not to tax C-Note's earnings. Even J.T.'s mother was on C-Note's side in this matter.

But J.T. wasn't one to compromise when it came to money. He had to pay for the upkeep of a few cars as well as several girlfriends, each of whom needed her own apartment and spending allowance. J.T. also liked to go gambling in Las Vegas, and he took no small amount of pride in the fact that he owned dozens of pairs of expensive shoes and lots of pricey clothing. But instead of acting charitably toward someone like C-Note, J.T. was openly resentful of the idea that he was getting a free ride.

One hot Sunday morning, I was hanging out with C-Note and

some other squatters in the parking lot of J.T.'s building, across the street from a basketball court. The men had set up an outdoor auto-repair shop—changing tires, pounding out dents, performing minor engine repairs. Their prices were low, and they had lined up enough business to keep them going all day. Cars were parked at every angle in the lot. The men moved to and fro, hauling equipment, swapping tools, and chattering happily at the prospect of so much work. Another squatter had set up a nearby stand to sell soda and juice out of a cooler. I bought a drink and sat down to watch the underground economy in full bloom.

J.T. drove up, accompanied by four of his senior officers. Three more cars pulled up behind them, and I recognized several other gang leaders, J.T.'s counterparts who ran the other local Black Kings factions.

J.T. walked over to C-Note, who was peering into a car engine. J.T. didn't notice me—I was sitting by a white van, partially hidden from view—but I could see and hear him just fine.

"C-Note!" J.T. yelled. "What the fuck are you doing?"

"What the fuck does it look like I'm doing, young man?" C-Note barked right back without looking up from his work. C-Note wasn't usually quarrelsome, but he could be a hard-liner when it came to making his money.

"We have games running today," J.T. said. He meant the gang's monthly basketball tournament. "You need to get this shit out of here. Move the cars, get all this stuff off the court."

"Aw, shit, you should've told me." C-Note threw an oily cloth to the ground. "What the fuck can I do? You see that the work ain't finished."

J.T. laughed. He seemed surprised that someone would challenge him. "Nigger, are you kidding me?! I don't give a fuck about your work. Get these cars out of here." J.T. looked underneath the cars. "Oh, shit! And you got oil all over the place. You better clean that up, too."

C-Note started waving his hands about and shouting at J.T. "You're the only one who can make money, is that right? You own all this shit, you own all this land? Bullshit."

He pulled out a cigarette, lit it, and kept muttering, "Bullshit." The other squatters stopped working to see what would happen next. C-Note was drenched in sweat and angry, as if he might lose control.

J.T. looked down at his feet, then waved over his senior officers, who had been waiting by the car. A few of the other gang members also got out of their cars.

Once his henchmen were near, J.T. spoke again to C-Note: "I'm asking you one more time, nigger. You can either move this car or—"

"That's some bullshit, boy!" C-Note yelled. "I ain't going any-where. I been here for two hours, and I told you I ain't finished working. So fuck you! Fuck you! Fuck you!" He turned to the other squatters. "This nigger do this every time," he said. "Every time. Fuck him."

C-Note was still chattering when J.T. grabbed him by the neck. In an instant two of J.T.'s officers also grabbed C-Note. The three of them dragged him toward a concrete wall that separated Robert Taylor from the tracks where a commuter train ran. C-Note kept shouting, but he didn't physically resist. The other squatters turned to watch. The gang leaders nonchalantly took some sodas from the cooler without paying.

"You can't do this to us!" C-Note shouted. "It ain't fair."

J.T. pushed C-Note up against the concrete wall. The two offi-cers, their muscular arms plastered with tattoos, pinned him in.

"I told you, nigger," J.T. said, his face barely an inch away from C-Note's, "but you just don't listen, do you?" He sounded exasperated, but there was also a sinister tone to his voice I'd never heard before. "Why are you making this harder?"

He started slapping C-Note on the side of the head, grunting with each slap, C-Note's head flopping back and forth like a toy.

"Fuck you!" C-Note shouted. He tried to turn to look J.T. in the eye, but J.T. was so close that C-Note butted the side of J.T.'s head with his own. This only irked J.T. more. He cocked his arm and pounded C-Note in the ribs. C-Note held his gut, coughing violently, and then J.T.'s henchmen pushed him to the ground. They took turns kicking him, one in the back and the other in the stomach. When C-Note curled up, they kicked him in the legs. "You should've listened to the man, fool!" one of them shouted.

C-Note lay in a fetal position, struggling to catch his breath. J.T. rolled him over and punched him in the face one last time. "Dumb nigger!" he shouted, then walked back toward us, head down, flexing his hand as if he had hurt it on C-Note's skull.

J.T. reached into the squatter's cooler for a soda. That's when he finally noticed me standing there. He frowned when our eyes met. He quickly moved away, going toward the high-rise, but his look gave me a chill. He was clearly surprised to see me, and he seemed a little peeved.

I had been hanging around J.T. and his gang for several months by now, and I'd never seen J.T. engage in violence. I felt like his scribe, tailing a powerful leader who liked to joke with the tenants and, when he needed to be assertive, did so quietly. I was naïve, I suppose, but I had somehow persuaded myself that just because I hadn't seen any violence, it didn't exist. Now I *had* seen a different side of his power, a far less polished presentation.

In the weeks afterward, I began to contemplate the possibility that

I would see more beatings, perhaps even fatal incidents. I still felt exhilarated by my access to J.T.'s gang, but I was also starting to feel shame. My conviction that I was merely a sociological observer, detached and objective, was starting to feel false. Was I really supposed to just stand by while someone was getting beat up? I was ashamed of my desire to get so close to the violence, so close to a culture that I knew other scholars had not managed to see.

In reality I probably had little power to stop anyone from getting abused by the gang. And for the first time in my life, I was doing work that I truly loved; I was excited by my success. Back at the university, my research was starting to attract attention from my professors, and I certainly didn't want to let that go. I told Wilson about the young men I had met and their involvement with gangs. I kept things pretty abstract; I didn't tell him every detail about what I saw. He seemed impressed, and I didn't want to lose his support, so I figured that if I could forget about the shame, maybe it would simply go away.

As time passed, I pretty much stopped talking about my research to friends and family. I just wrote down my notes and tried not to draw attention to myself, except to tell my advisers a few stories now and then.

When I went home to California on vacations or holidays and saw my parents, I told them relatively little about my work in the projects. My mother, who worked as a hospital records clerk, was already worried about my living so far from home, so I didn't want to heighten her concern with stories of gang beatings. And I knew that my father would be upset if he learned that I hid things from my advisers. So I hid my fieldwork from him as well. Instead I just showed them my grades, which were good, and said the least I could get away with.

In retrospect the C-Note beating at least enabled me to view my relationship with J.T. more realistically. It made me appreciate just how deeply circumscribed my interactions with the Black Kings had been. What I had taken to be a fly-on-the-wall vantage point was in fact a highly edited view. It wasn't that I was seeing a false side of the gang, but there was plainly a great deal I didn't have access to. I knew that the gang made a lot of money in a lot of different ways— I had heard, for instance, that they extorted store owners—but I knew few details. All I saw was the flashy consumption: the jewelry, the cars, the parties.

And the gang obviously had an enormous impact on the wider community. It went well beyond telling residents they couldn't hang out in the lobby. The C-Note beating made that clear. But if I was really going to write my dissertation on gang activity, I'd have to learn an awful lot more about how the gang affected everyone else in the community. The problem was figuring the way out from under J.T.'s grip.

THREE

Someone to Watch Over Me

C-Note's friends took him to the hospital, where he received treatment for bruised ribs and cuts on his face. He spent the next couple of months recuperating in the apartment of a friend who lived nearby. Eventually he moved back into Robert Taylor. The building was as much his home as J.T.'s, and no one expected the beating to drive him away for good.

I wondered how J.T. would react the next time I saw him. Up to that point, he was always happy to have me follow him around, to have a personal biographer. "He's writing about my life," he'd boast to his friends. "If you-all could read, you'd learn something." He had no real sense of what I would actually be writing—because, in truth, I didn't know myself. Nor did I know if he'd be upset with me for having seen him beat up C-Note, or if perhaps he'd try to censor me.

I didn't return to Robert Taylor for a week, until J.T. called to invite me to a birthday party for his four-year-old daughter, Shuggie. She was one of two daughters that J.T. had with his girlfriend Joyce; the other girl, Bee-Bee, was two. J.T. and Joyce seemed pretty close. But then again J.T. also seemed close with Missie and their son, Jamel. As much as J.T. seemed to trust me and let me inside his world, he was fiercely protective of his private life. Except for benign occasions like a birthday party, he generally kept me away from his girlfriends and his children, and he often gave me blatantly contradictory information about his family life. I once tried asking why he was so evasive on that front, but he just shut me down with a hard look.

I was nervous as I rode the bus toward Robert Taylor, but my reunion with J.T. was anticlimactic. The party was so big, with dozens of friends and family members, that it was split between Ms. Mae's apartment and another apartment upstairs where J.T.'s cousin LaShona lived. Ms. Mae had cooked a ton of food, and there was a huge birthday cake. Everyone was having a good, loud time.

J.T. strode right over and shook my hand. "How you feel?" he asked—one of his standard greetings. He stared me down for a moment but said nothing more. Then he winked, handed me a beer, and walked away. I barely saw him the rest of the party. Ms. Mae introduced me to some of her friends—I was "Mr. Professor, J.T.'s friend," which conferred immediate legitimacy upon me. I stayed a few hours, played some games with the kids, and then took the bus home.

J.T. and I resumed our normal relationship. Even though I couldn't stop thinking about the C-Note beating, I kept my questions to myself. Until that incident I had seen gang members selling drugs, tenants taking drugs, and plenty of people engaged in small-time hustles to make money. While I was by no means comfortable watching a drug addict smoke crack, the C-Note affair gave me greater pause. He was an old man in poor health; he could hardly be expected to defend himself against men twice his size and half his age, men who also happened to carry guns.

What was I, an impartial observer—at least that's how I thought of myself—supposed to do upon seeing something like this? I actually considered calling the police that day. After all, C-Note had been assaulted. But I didn't do anything. I am ashamed to say that I didn't even confront J.T. about it until some six months later, and even then I did so tentatively.

The confrontation happened after I witnessed another incident with another squatter. One day I was standing outside the building's entryway with J.T. and a few other BKs. J.T. had just finished his weekly walk-through of his high-rise. He was having a quick meeting with some prostitutes who'd recently started working in the building, explaining the rules and taxes. The tenants, meanwhile, went about their business—hauling laundry, checking the mail, running errands.

A few of J.T.'s junior members came out to tell him that one of the squatters in the building, a man known as Brass, refused to pay the gang's squatting fee. They had brought Brass with them down to the lobby. I could see him through the entryway. He looked to be in his late forties, but it was hard to say. He had only a few teeth and seemed in pretty bad shape. I'd heard that Brass was a heroin addict with a reputation for beating up prostitutes. He was also known for moving around from building to building. He wasn't a regular squatter like C-Note, who was on familiar terms with all the tenants. Brass would anger the tenants in one building and then pack up and move along.

J.T. dispatched Price, one of his senior officers, to deal with Brass. Unlike C-Note, who offered only a little resistance, Brass decided to fight back. This was a big mistake. Price was generally not a patient man, and he seemed to enjoy administering a good beating. I could see Price punching Brass repeatedly in the face and stomach. J.T. didn't flinch. Everyone, in fact—gang members and tenants alike—just stood and watched.

Brass started to crawl toward us, making his way outside to the building's concrete entryway. Price looked exhausted from hitting Brass, and he took a break. That's when some rank-and-file gang members took over, kicking and beating Brass mercilessly. Brass resisted throughout. He kept yelling "Fuck you!" even as he was being beaten, until he seemed unconscious. A drool of blood spilled from his mouth.

Then he began flailing about on the ground in convulsion, his spindly arms flapping like wings. By now his body lay just a few feet from us. I groaned, and J.T. pulled me away. Still no one came to help Brass; it was as if we were all fishermen watching a fish die a slow death on the floor of a boat.

I leaned on J.T.'s car, quivering from the shock. He took hold of me firmly and tried to calm me down. "It's just the way it is around here," he whispered, a discernible tone of sympathy in his voice. "Sometimes you have to beat a nigger to teach him a lesson. Don't worry, you'll get used to it after a while."

I thought, *No, I don't want to get used to it.* If I did, what kind of person would that make me? I wanted to ask J.T. to stop the beating and take Brass to the hospital, but my ears were ringing, and I couldn't even focus on what he was telling me. My eyes were fixed on Brass, and I felt like throwing up.

Then J.T. grabbed me by the shoulders and turned me away so I couldn't watch. But out of the corner of my eye, I could see that a few tenants finally came over to help Brass, while the gang mem-

bers just stood over him doing nothing. J.T. held me up, as if to comfort me. I tried instead to support my weight on his car.

That's when C-Note slipped into my thoughts.

"I understand that Brass didn't pay you the money he owed, but
you guys beat up C-Note and he wasn't doing anything," I said impatiently. "I just don't get it."

"C-Note was challenging my authority," J.T. answered calmly. "I
had told him months before he couldn't do his work out there, and
he told me he understood. He went back on his word, and I had to
do what I had to do."

I pushed a little harder. "Couldn't you just punish them with
a tax?"

"Everyone wants to kill the leader, so you got to get them first."
This was one of J.T.'s trademark sayings. "I had niggers watching me,"
he said. "I had to do what I had to do."

I recalled that on the day C-Note challenged him, J.T. had driven
up to the building with a few Black Kings leaders from other neighborhoods. J.T. was constantly worried—practically to the point of
paranoia, it seemed to me—that his own members and fellow leaders wanted to dethrone him and claim his territory. So he may have
felt he couldn't afford to have his authority challenged in their presence, even by a senior citizen whose legs probably couldn't buy him
one lap around a high-school track. Still, J.T.'s explanation seemed
so alien to me that I felt I was watching a scene from *The Godfather.*

By now it was nearly a year since I'd started hanging out with J.T.'s
gang. It was 1990, which was roughly the peak of the crack epidemic in Chicago and other big U.S. cities. Black and Latino gangs
including the Kings, the Cobras, the Disciples, the Vice Lords, the

MCs (Mickey Cobras), and even the Stones, which had been temporarily dismantled a few years earlier, were capitalizing on a huge demand for crack and making a lot of money.

In the old days, a teenager with an appetite for trouble might have gotten involved in vandalism or shoplifting; now he was more likely to be involved in the drug trade. And the neighbor who might have yelled at that misbehaving teenager in the old days was less likely to do so, since that kid might well be carrying a gun.

Politicians, academics, and law-enforcement officials all offered policy solutions, to little avail. The liberal-minded deployed their traditional strategies—getting young people back into school and finding them entry-level jobs—but few gang members were willing to trade in their status and the prospect of big money for menial work. Conservatives attacked the crack epidemic by supporting mass arrests and hefty prison sentences. This certainly took some dealers off the streets, but there was always a surplus of willing and eager replacements.

The national mood had grown increasingly desperate—and punitive. Prosecutors won the right to treat gangs as organized criminal groups, which produced longer prison sentences. Judges gave the police permission to conduct warrantless searches and to round up suspected gang members who were hanging out in public spaces. In schools, mayors ruled out the wearing of bandannas and other clothing that might signal gang affiliation. With each day's newspaper bringing a fresh story about gang violence, these efforts met little political resistance, even if they weren't all that effective.

From J.T.'s perspective the real crisis was that all these measures conspired to make it harder to earn as much money as he would have liked.

Because crack was sold on street corners, with profits dependent on high volume and quick turnover, J.T. had to monitor a round-the-clock economic operation. He loved the challenge of running a business and making money. From all indications his transition to the Robert Taylor Homes was an unqualified success. This had won the attention of his superiors, a group of several dozen people in prison and on the streets known collectively as the Black Kings' board of directors. They had begun inviting J.T. to high-level meetings to discuss the big picture of their enterprise. Pleased with his managerial prowess and attention to detail, they rewarded J.T. with extra responsibilities. He had just been asked, for instance, to help the gang with its foray into Chicago politics.

"Even the gang needs friends with connections," J.T. told me. "And we're getting more successful, so we need more friends."

"I don't see why a gang wants to deal with politicians," I said. "I don't see what they get out of it. It seems they'd have a greater chance of getting caught if they started hanging out with politicos, no?"

He reminded me that his Black Kings gang was just one of about two hundred BK gangs around the city that were making money selling crack. With that much money, the citywide BK leadership needed to think about investing and laundering.

"Let's say, Sudhir, that you're making only a hundred bucks," he explained. "You probably don't have a lot of real headaches. You don't need to worry about niggers stealing it from you. You don't need to worry that when you go into a store, they'll ask you where you got the money. But let's say you got a thousand bucks. Well, you can't really carry it around, and you're a street nigger so you don't have a bank account. You need to keep it somewhere. So you start to have things to think about.

"Now let's say it's ten thousand. Okay, now you got niggers who are watching you buy a few things: a new TV, a new car. They say, 'Oh, Sudhir, he's got a new necklace. And he's a student. He don't work? So where'd he get the money? Maybe he has cash in his house.' So now you have more things to worry about.

"Now let's say it's a hundred thousand. You want to buy a car, but the car dealer has to report to the government when people pay for a car with thirty thousand dollars in cash. So what are you going to do? You may have to pay him a thousand bucks to keep his mouth shut. Then maybe you need to hire security, 'cause there's always some nigger that's going to take the chance and rob you. That's another few thousand, and you got to trust the security you hired, 'cause they know where you keep the money.

"Now let's say you got five hundred thousand or a million. Or more. That's what these niggers above me are worrying about. They need to find ways to clean the money. Maybe they hide it in a friend's business. Maybe they tell their sisters to open up bank accounts. Or they get their church to take a donation. They have to constantly be thinking about the money: keeping it safe, investing it, protecting themselves from other niggers."

"But I still don't understand why you need to deal with politicians."

"Well, see, an alderman can take the heat off of us," J.T. said with a smile. "An alderman can keep the police away. He can make sure residents don't get too pissed off at us. Let's say we need to meet in the park. The alderman makes sure the cops don't come. And the only thing they want from us is a donation—ten thousand dollars gets you an alderman for a year. Like I keep telling you, our organization is about helping our community, so we're trying to get involved in what's happening."

J.T.'s monologue surprised me on two fronts. Although I'd heard about corrupt aldermen in the old days—denying building permits to political enemies, for instance, or protecting a gang's gambling

racket—I had a hard time believing that J.T. could buy off a politi-
cian as easily as he described. Even more surprising was J.T.'s claim
about "helping our community." Was this a joke, I wondered, or did
he really believe that selling drugs and bribing politicians would
somehow help a down-and-out neighborhood pick itself up?

Besides the Black Kings' relationships with various aldermen,
J.T. told me, the gang also worked with several community-based organizations, or CBOs. These groups, many of them created with
federal funding during the 1960s, worked to bring jobs and housing
to the neighborhood, tried to keep kids off the street with recreation
programs, and, in places like the South Side, even enacted truces between warring gangs.

Toward the end of the 1980s, several CBOs tried instilling civic
consciousness in the gangs themselves. They hired outreach workers (most of whom were former gangsters) to persuade young gang
members to reject the thug life and choose a more productive path.
These reformers held life-skills workshops that addressed such issues
as "how to act when you go downtown" or "what to do when a lady
yells at you for drinking beer in the park." They also preached the
gospel of voting, arguing that a vote represented the first step toward
reentry into the social mainstream. J.T. and some other gang leaders
not only required their young members to attend these workshops
but also made them participate in voter-registration drives. Their
motives were by no means purely altruistic or educational: they knew
that if their rank-and-file members had good relationships with local
residents, the locals were less likely to call the police and disrupt the
drug trade.

J.T.'s ambitions ran even higher. What he wanted, he told me, was
to return the gang to its glory days of the 1960s, when South Side
gangs worked together with residents to agitate for improvements in

their neighborhoods. But he seemed to conveniently ignore a big dif-ference: Gangs back then didn't traffic in drugs, extort money from businesses, and terrorize the neighborhood with violence. They were not innocent kids, to be sure. But their worst transgressions tended to be street fighting or intimidating passersby. Because J.T.'s gang *was* involved in drugs and extortion (and more), I was skeptical that he could enjoy much more support from the local residents than he cur-rently had.

One cold November night, J.T. invited me to a meeting at a small storefront Baptist church. An ex-gangster named Lenny Duster would be teaching young people about the rights, responsibilities, and power of voting. The next election, while a full year away, would place in office a great many state legislators as well as city aldermen.

Lenny ran a small organization called Pride, which helped me-diate gang wars. About a hundred young Black Kings attended the meeting, held in a small room at the rear of the church. They were quiet and respectful, although they had the look of teenagers who'd been told that attendance was mandatory.

Lenny was about six foot four, built lean and muscular. He was about forty years old, with streaks of blond hair, and he walked with a limp. "You-all need to see where the power is!" Lenny shouted to the assembly, striding about like a Caesar. "J.T. went to college, I earned a degree in prison. You-all are dropping out of school, and you're ignorant. You can't read, you can't think, you can't understand where the power comes from. It don't come from that gun you got—it comes from what's in your head. And it comes from the vote. You can change the world if you get the niggers that are com-ing down on you out of power. Think about it: No more police stopping you, no more abandoned buildings. You control your destiny!"

He talked to the young men about how to "work" responsibly. It was understood among gang members that "work" meant selling drugs—a tragic irony in that they referred to working in the legitimate economy as "getting a job," not "work."

"You-all are outside, so you need to respect who else is around you," he said. "If you're in a park working, leave the ladies alone. Don't be working around the children. That just gets the mamas mad. If you see kids playing, take a break and then get back to work. Remember, what you do says a lot about the Black Kings. You have to watch your image, take pride in yourself.

"You are not just foot soldiers in the Black Kings," he continued. "You are foot soldiers in the *community*. You will register to vote today, but then you must all go out and register the people in your buildings. And when elections come around, we'll tell you who to vote for and you'll tell them. That's an important duty you have when you belong to this organization."

For my classes at the U of C, I'd been reading about the history of the Chicago political machine, whose leaders—white and black alike—were famous for practicing the dark arts of ballot stuffing, bribery, and yes, predelivered voting blocs. Like his predecessors, Lenny did give these young men a partial understanding of the right to vote, and why it was important, but it seemed that the main point of the meetings was to tell them how to be cogs in a political machine. He held up a small placard with the names of candidates whom the gang was supporting for alderman and state legislator. There was no discussion of a platform, no list of vital issues. Just an insistence that the young men round up tenants in the projects and tell them how to vote.

When Lenny finished, J.T. told his young members they could leave. I sat for a while with J.T. and Lenny. Lenny looked drained. As he drank a Coke, he said he'd been speaking to at least four or five groups every day.

Lenny was careful to explain that his fees came from personal donations from gang members or their leaders. He wanted to distinguish these monies from the profits the gang made from selling drugs. In theory, I understood that Lenny was trying to convince me that he didn't accept drug money, but I found the distinction almost meaningless. Moreover, the gang leaders had a lot of incentive to pay Lenny to keep their gangs from fighting one another. After all, it was hard to conduct commerce in the midst of a gang war. Younger gang members, however, often wanted to stir things up, mostly to distinguish themselves as fighters. That's why some gang leaders even paid Lenny to discipline their own members. "*Disciplination* is an art form," Lenny said. "One thing I like is to hang a nigger upside down over the freeway as the cars come. Ain't never had a nigger misbehave after I try that one."

J.T. and Lenny talked in nostalgic terms about the gang's recent political engagement. Lenny proudly recalled his own days as a Black King back in the 1970s, describing how he helped get out the vote for "the Eye-talians and Jews" who ran his community. He then described, with equal pride, how the gangs "kicked the Eye-talian and Jewish mafia" out of his ward. Lenny even managed to spin the black takeover of the heroin trade as a boon to the community: it gave local black men jobs, albeit illegal ones, that had previously gone to white men. Lenny also boasted that black drug dealers never sold to children, whereas the previous dealers had exercised no such moral restraint. With all his bombast, he sounded like an older version of J.T.

I asked Lenny about his talk that night, how he could simultaneously preach the virtues of voting and the most responsible way to deal drugs. He said he favored a "nonjudgmental approach" with the gang members. "I tell them, 'Whatever you do, try to do it without pissing people off. Make everything a community thing.' "

A bout two weeks later, I got to witness this "community thing" in action. I followed four young Black Kings as they went door-to-door in J.T.'s building to register voters.

Shorty-Lee, a twenty-one-year-old gang member, was the head of the delegation. For about an hour, I trailed him on his route. Most of his knocks went unanswered. The few tenants who did sign their names looked as if they just wanted to make the gang members leave as quickly as possible.

At one apartment on the twelfth floor, a middle-aged woman answered the door. She was wearing an apron and wiping her wet hands on a dish towel; she looked surprised to see Shorty-Lee and the others. Door-to-door solicitation hadn't been practiced in the projects for a long time. "We're here to sign you up to vote," Shorty-Lee said.

"Young man, I *am* registered," the woman said calmly.

"No, we didn't say *register!*" Shorty-Lee shouted. "We said *sign up*. I don't care if you're registered."

"But that's what I'm saying." The woman eyed Shorty-Lee curiously. "I already signed up. I'm going to vote in the next primary."

Shorty-Lee was puzzled. He looked over to the three other BKs. They were toting spiral-bound notebooks in which they "signed up" potential voters. But it seemed that neither Lenny nor J.T. had told them that there was an actual registration form and that registrars had to be licensed.

"Look, you need to sign right here," Shorty-Lee said, grabbing one of the notebooks. He was clearly not expecting even this minor level of resistance. "And then we'll tell you who you're going to vote for when the time comes."

"Who I'm going to vote for!" The woman's voice grew sharp. She approached the screen door to take a better look. As she glanced at me, she waved—I recognized her from several parties at J.T.'s mother's apartment. Then she turned back to Shorty-Lee. "You can't tell me who to vote for," she said. "And I don't think that's legal anyway."

"Black Kings say who you need to vote for," Shorty-Lee countered, but he was growing tentative. He turned to his fellow gang members. "Ain't that right? Ain't that what we're supposed to do?" The others shrugged.

"Young man," the woman continued, "have *you* ever voted?"

Shorty-Lee looked at the others, who seemed quite interested in his answer. Then he looked at me. He seemed embarrassed. "No," he said. "I ain't voted yet. But I will."

"Did you know that you can't take anyone in the voting booth with you?" the woman asked him.

"Naw, that's a lie," Shorty-Lee said, puffing out his chest. "They told me that we'll all be voting together. Black Kings vote together. I told you that we'd be telling you who—"

"No, no, no—that's not what I mean," she interrupted. "I mean, first *you* vote. Then your friend votes, and then he votes—if he's old enough." She was staring now at the youngest boy in the group, a new gang member who looked about twelve years old.

"I'm old enough," the boy said, insulted.

"You have to be eighteen," the woman said with a gentle smile. "How old *are* you?"

"I'm Black Kings!" he cried out. "I can vote if I want to."

"Well, you'll probably have to wait," the woman said, by now exasperated. "And, boys, I got food cooking, so I can't talk to you right now. But if you come back, I can tell you all about voting. Okay? It's probably the most important thing you'll do with your life. Next to raising a family."

"Okay." Shorty-Lee shrugged, defeated.

The others also nodded. "Yes, ma'am," one of them muttered, and they walked off. I waved good-bye to the woman, who smiled as if she'd won the victory of a small-town schoolteacher: a promise that her children would learn.

I followed Shorty-Lee and the others down the gallery. None of them seemed to know what should happen next. Shorty-Lee looked pained, struggling to muster some leadership capacity and perhaps save face.

"You know you can't register people until five o'clock?" I said, wanting to break the silence. I was only a few years older than Shorty-Lee, but I found myself feeling strangely parental. "That's what J.T. told me."

J.T. hadn't told me to say this. But I felt so bad for Shorty-Lee that I wanted to give him an out. I figured I could talk to him later, when we were alone, and explain how registration actually worked.

Shorty-Lee gazed out silently through the gallery's chain-link fence.

"It's about two-thirty," I said. "That's probably why the woman said what she said. You should wait awhile before knocking some more. You'll get more people signed up if you wait. Why don't we go to Ms. Turner's and get some hamburgers? You can start again later."

"Yeah, that's cool," Shorty-Lee said, looking relieved. "I'm hungry, too!" He started barking out commands. "Blackie, you got to get back home, though. We'll get you some food. Kenny, hold my shit. Follow me. I'm getting a cheeseburger, if she still has any cheese left."

They ran off toward Ms. Turner's apartment, a makeshift store on the seventh floor where you could buy food, candy, soda, cigarettes, and condoms. I headed back to Ms. Mae's apartment, trying to think of how to tell J.T. about this "voter-registration drive" without laughing.

The door-to-door canvassing was thankfully just a small part of J.T.'s strategy to politicize the gang. I began attending dozens of rallies in high schools and social-service centers where politicians came to encourage young black men and women to get involved in politics. Newspaper reporters often attended these events. I'm sure they were interested in the gang's involvement, but their curiosity was also piqued by the participation of politicians like the Reverend Jesse Jackson, who urged young people to "give up the gun, pick up the ballot."

J.T. told me he never wanted to run for office, but he was certainly attracted to the new contacts he was gaining through the Black Kings' political initiatives. He talked endlessly about the preachers, politicians, and businesspeople he'd been meeting. J.T. knew that Chicago's gangs were politically active in the 1960s and 1970s, pushing for desegregation and housing reform. He told me more than a few times that he was modeling his behavior on those gang leaders'. When I asked for concrete examples of his collaboration with his new allies, he'd vaguely say that "we're working together for the community" or "we're just trying to make things right."

Perhaps, I thought, he didn't trust me yet, or perhaps there *wasn't* anything concrete to talk about. One of the few political activities I saw him directly manage was a series of educational meetings between Lenny Duster of Pride and various high-ranking Chicago gang leaders. Because the police rarely came around to Robert Taylor, it provided a relatively secure site for such meetings. This kept J.T. busy with providing security, keeping tenants out of the way, and otherwise ensuring a safe climate.

He firmly believed that the community would be stronger when the Black Kings entered the mainstream. "You need to talk about our political activities in your work," he told me. "It's part of who I am."

But he also admitted that the "legit" image was vital to the gang's underlying commercial mission: if law-abiding citizens viewed the gang as a politically productive enterprise, they might be less likely to complain about its drug sales. So J.T. continued to order his rank-and-file members to attend these political rallies, and he donated money to social organizations that called for gang members to turn their lives around. More than anything, I realized, J.T. was desperate to be recognized as something other than just a criminal.

I wasn't sure that I believed him. I had trouble seeing exactly how the Black Kings were a useful group to have around. But they did seem to have a few noncriminal ventures, and perhaps, I thought, I would see more down the line. By this point I had gotten a reputation around the U of C as "the Indian guy who hangs out with the gangs." In general this was a positive image, and I saw little reason to change things.

The more time J.T. spent with the citywide Black Kings leadership and their newfound political allies, the less time he had to escort me through the projects. This presented me with the opportunity I'd hoped for: getting to learn a bit more about the community for myself without J.T. watching over me.

Since I still wasn't very familiar with the neighborhood, I didn't stray too far from J.T.'s building. He had repeatedly told me that I wouldn't be safe walking around other parts of Robert Taylor. The longer I hung around the projects, he said, the more likely that I would be associated with his gang. So I would do well to keep to the gang's areas.

Strangely, while most people think of a gang as a threat, for me—an uninitiated person in the projects—the gang represented security. The courtyard in the middle of the three buildings that J.T. controlled was a closely guarded space. His gang members were everywhere: sitting in cars, leaning out of apartments, hanging around the playground and the parking lot. I didn't know most of them well enough to strike up a conversation, but I was familiar enough to receive the local sign for "friend"—a slight nod of the head, perhaps a raised eyebrow.

I wanted to learn more about the gang's influence on the greater community. C-Note and Clarisse had both suggested to me that the gang was simultaneously a nuisance, a source of fear, and an ally. But they were always a bit cagey.

"Oh, you know how J.T. is," Clarisse once said to me. "He's family, and you know what family is like."

"Them niggers are wearing me out, but I ain't gonna be the one to say nothing," C-Note told me, " 'cause they keep things safe around here."

They tended to look at me as if I knew exactly what they meant, which I didn't. But I was eager to figure it out.

I met the Johnson brothers, Kris and Michael, two Robert Taylor tenants known as expert car mechanics and consummate hustlers. They were both in their late thirties, skinny, with boyish faces, and they always had a positive outlook. Kris had been a promising baseball player until his career was ended by injury. Michael was a musician who'd never gained the level of success he sought. Now they both wanted good full-time jobs but couldn't find steady work. Their lives had been an odyssey of drug addiction, street hustling, jail time, and homelessness. For them, and other underemployed men like them, the projects were a refuge: a familiar home turf with at least a few slivers of opportunity.

These days the Johnson brothers repaired cars in various parking lots around the Robert Taylor Homes. Although J.T. was the ultimate authority in the neighborhood, Kris and Michael also had to strike a deal with C-Note, who was the nominal ruler of the local auto-repair trade. Sometimes C-Note did repair work himself. When he was too tired, he subcontracted it out to people like the Johnson brothers. In return he took a small cut of their profits and let the gang know that the Johnsons were operating with his blessing.

Kris and Michael had set up shop on Federal Street, in the corner of a parking lot littered with garbage and broken glass. About twenty yards down the street, next to an open fire hydrant, they were also running a car wash. The Johnson brothers always attracted a crowd.

"You want me to talk?" Kris asked me. "Then you need to find me some work, find me a customer!"

I was happy to oblige. Walking into the middle of Federal Street, I helped them flag down cars. Then Kris would approach the driver. "You need a wash?" he'd ask. Or, "Looks like your brakes are squeaking, ma'am. Why don't you step outside and let me take a look." Kris and Michael would charm the drivers until they broke down and agreed to have their cars looked at. If that failed, one brother would let the air out of the tires while the other brother occupied the driver. The more beer they drank, the more creative they became.

Toward the end of one hot summer day, T-Bone, one of J.T.'s senior officers, drove up to the car wash in a bright green Chevy Malibu. The Malibu seemed to be the thug's car of choice. Behind

T-Bone was a line of cars waiting for a wash, most of them classic gang vehicles—Malibus, Caprices, Lincoln Town Cars—all with shiny rims and bright paint jobs.

"Every week we need to wash their shit," Michael muttered. "What can you do?" The gang apparently taxed the brothers in the form of free car washes. He grabbed a bucket of soapy water and shouted for Kris to come help. But Kris, his head buried in the hood of a customer's car, shouted back that he was busy. So I offered to help.

When T-Bone saw me jog over with some clean rags, he nearly fell down laughing. "Oh, shit! Next thing he'll be moving in with them!" he said. "Hey, Sweetness, how much you paying the Professor?"

"Ain't paying nothing," answered Michael (a.k.a. Sweetness, apparently). "I'm giving him an education."

This made T-Bone laugh even harder. T-Bone and I got along pretty well, and unlike other members of the gang, he would routinely strike up a conversation with me. He was attending Kennedy-King College, a South Side community college, majoring in accounting. That's why J.T. had put him in charge of the gang's finances. T-Bone had two talkative, precocious children and the appearance of a nerd: he wore big, metal-framed glasses, always carried a notebook (which contained the gang's financial records, I would later learn), and constantly asked me about life at the U of C. "Hope it's harder than where I'm at," he'd say. "I'm getting A's, and I haven't had to pay nobody off yet!"

A commotion rose up from the parking lot where Kris was working: he had gotten into a fight with a customer. Even from afar I could see the veins popping on Kris's face. He kept trying to grab the other man's neck, and the other man kept pushing Kris backward. The other man kneed Kris in the stomach, sending him to the ground, and then Kris picked up a rock and hit his combatant in the head. Now both of them were on the ground, writhing and yelling.

Michael and T-Bone hurried over. "Nigger, not around here!" T-Bone said, laughing at the fairly pathetic display of fighting. "I told you about keeping this shit peaceful."

"It will be peaceful as long as he pays up," Kris said.

"Pays up?" the other man said. "He can finish, then I'll pay. Twenty bucks to fix my radiator? Fuck that! He got to do more than that for twenty."

"Nigger, I already washed the damn car," Kris said. He stood up, wincing. "You took this shit too far. I'm not doing nothing else for twenty bucks." Kris picked up a wrench and hit the man in the leg. The man groaned in pain, his face swollen with anger, and it looked as if he was going to go after Kris.

T-Bone grabbed Kris, even though he could barely keep himself from laughing. "Damn! What did I tell you? Lay that shit down. Now come over here."

T-Bone walked the two men over to the edge of the parking lot. They were both limping. Soon after, Kris started washing T-Bone's car while the other man sat on the ground, nursing his leg.

"I'll teach that nigger!" Kris said to himself loudly. "No one messes with me."

T-Bone walked over to Michael and me. "Nigger was right," he said, pointing to Kris. "He washed the man's car and fixed the radiator. And that costs twenty dollars. He don't need to do nothing else. I got the money for you. And five bucks extra for the hassle."

T-Bone handed Michael the money, slapped my face gently, winked, and hummed a song as he walked off. Michael didn't say anything.

That night, once it was too dark to work on cars, I sat with Michael and Kris by their beat-up white Subaru, and we drank some beers. Michael told me that T-Bone often settled customer disputes for them.

"Why would he do that?" I asked.

"Because we pay him to!" Michael said. "I mean, we don't have a choice."

Michael explained that he and Kris paid T-Bone 15 percent of their weekly revenue. Just as J.T.'s foot soldiers squeezed a little money from squatters and prostitutes, his higher-ranked officers supplemented their income with more substantial taxes. In return, the gang brought Kris and Michael customers and mediated any disputes. This occasionally included beating up a customer who became recalcitrant or abusive. "That happens once a month," Kris said with satisfaction. "Best way to teach people not to fuck with us."

I asked Michael and Kris whether beating one customer might in fact deter other customers. The reply taught me a lot about the Black Kings.

"When *you* got a problem, I bet you call the police, right?" Michael said. "Well, we call the Kings. I call T-Bone because I don't have anyone else to call."

"But you *could* call the police," I said. "I don't understand why you can't call them if something goes wrong."

"If I'm out here hustling, or if you're in the building hustling, there's no police officer who's going to do what T-Bone does for us," Michael said. "Every hustler tries to have someone who offers them protection. I don't care if you're selling socks or selling your ass. You need someone to back you up."

"See, we were both Black Kings when we were younger," Kris said. "Most of the people you see, the older ones who live right here? They were Kings at one time. So it's complicated. I mean, if you own a business on Forty-seventh Street, you pay taxes and you get protection—from the police, from the aldermen—"

I interrupted Kris to ask why they'd need protection from the *aldermen*. He looked at me as if I was naïve—which I was—and explained that the aldermen's line workers, or "precinct captains," liked to tax any off-the-books entrepreneurial activity. "So instead we pay the gang, and the gang protects us."

"But it's more than that," Michael said. "I mean, you're stuck. These niggers make your life hell, but they're family. And you can't choose your family!" He started to laugh so hard that he nearly spilled his beer.

"Just imagine," Kris prodded me. "Let's say another gang came by and started shooting. Or let's say you got a bunch of niggers that get into the building and go and rob a bunch of people. Who's going to take care of that? Police? They never come around! So you got J.T. and the Kings. They'll get your stuff back if it was stolen. They'll protect you so that no niggers can come and shoot up the place."

Kris and Michael really seemed to believe, although with some reservations, that the gang was their extended family. Skeptical as I may have been, the gang plainly *was* looked upon as something other than a purely destructive force. I remembered what J.T. had told me a while back, a pronouncement that hadn't made much sense at the time: "The gang and the building," he had said, "are the same."

One hot afternoon, while hanging out in the lobby of J.T.'s building with some tenants and a few BKs, I saw another side of the relationship between the gang and the community. Outside the building a car was blasting rap music. A basketball game had just finished, and to combat the heat a few dozen people were drinking beer and enjoying the breeze off the lake.

I heard a woman shouting, maybe fifty yards away, in a small grove of oak trees. It was one of the few shady areas on the premises. The trees predated Robert Taylor and would likely be standing long after the projects were gone. The music was too loud for me to make out what the woman was saying, and so I—along with quite a few other people—hurried over.

Several men were physically restraining the woman, who looked to be in her forties. "Let go of me!" she screamed. "I'm going to kick his ass! Just let me at him. Let go!"

"No, baby," one of the men said, trying to calm her down. "You can't do it that way, you can't take care of it like that. Let us handle it."

"Hey, Price!" another man shouted. "Price, come over here."

Price had been a Black Kings member for many years and had a wide range of expertise. At present he was in charge of the gang's security, which matched up well with his love of fighting. He was tall and lanky, and he took his job very seriously. He strode over now to the screaming woman, trailed by a few Black Kings foot soldiers. I waved at Price, and he didn't seem to mind that I had put myself close to the action.

"What's going on?" he asked the men. "Why is Boo-Boo screaming like that?"

"She said the Ay-rab at the store fucked her baby," one man told him. "He gave her baby some disease."

Price spoke softly to her, trying to calm her down. I asked a young woman next to me what was going on. She said that Boo-Boo thought the proprietor of a nearby corner store had slept with her teenage daughter and given her a sexually transmitted disease. There were several such stores in the neighborhood, all of them run by Arab Americans. "She wants to beat the shit out of that Ay-rab," the woman told me. "She was just on her way over to the store to see that man."

By now about a hundred people had gathered around. We all

watched Price talking to Boo-Boo while one of the men locked
Boo-Boo's arms behind her back. Suddenly he let her go, and Boo-
Boo marched off toward the store, with Price beside her and a pack
of tenants following behind. "Kick his ass, Boo-Boo!" someone
hollered. There were other riled shouts: "Don't let them Ay-rabs do
this to us!" and "Price, kill that boy!"

We arrived at a small, decrepit store known as Crustie's. The
name wasn't posted anywhere, but the usual signs were: CIGARETTES
SOLD HERE and FOOD STAMPS WELCOME and PLEASE DO NOT LOITER.
By the time I arrived, Boo-Boo was already inside yelling, but it was
hard to hear what she was saying. I moved closer to the entrance.
Now I could see Boo-Boo taking boxes and cans of food off the
shelves and throwing them, but I couldn't see her target. Price leaned
against the refrigerator case, wearing a serious look. Then Boo-Boo
reached for a big glass bottle, and Price grabbed her before she could
throw it.

A few minutes later, a man ran outside. He looked to be Middle
Eastern; he waved his arms and shouted in what I assumed was Arabic. He was in his early forties, clean-cut, with a short-sleeved, col-
lared shirt. He broke through the crowd, pushing people aside. Some
pushed back, but he managed to unlock his car and get inside.

But Boo-Boo followed him. She started throwing liquor bottles
at the car. One burst on the hood, another missed entirely. The
crowd started hooting, and some of the men grabbed her. We all
watched as the car sped off, with Boo-Boo falling down in the middle of the street, still screaming, "You raped my baby girl! You raped
her, you Ay-rab!"

Price walked slowly out of the store, accompanied by an older
man I recognized as the store's manager. He also looked Middle
Eastern and wore a striped dress shirt and khakis. He had a weary
look about him, as if running a store in this neighborhood had taken

a grave toll. He was talking quietly while Price stared straight ahead, nodding once in a while; the manager appeared to be pleading his case. Finally they shook hands, and Price moved aside, his foot soldiers trailing him.

Then the manager started to carry out cases of soda and beer, leaving them on the sidewalk. The crowd pounced. Most people grabbed just a few cans or bottles, but some were tough enough to wrest away a six-pack or two. The manager hauled out more and more cases, and these disappeared just as fast. He set them down with little emotion, although occasionally he'd glance at the crowd, as if he were feeding birds in a park, and wipe the sweat off his brow. When our eyes met, he just shook his head, shrugged, and walked back inside.

Price watched from a distance. I saw him speaking with Ms. Bailey, a woman in her late fifties who was the tenant president of the building where J.T. lived. I had met Ms. Bailey a few times already. She smiled now as I approached, then grabbed my hand and pulled me into a hug. She turned back to Price.

"We can't have people treat women like that, baby," she said to him. "You-all know that."

"I know, Ms. Bailey," Price said, exasperated. "Like I said, I'm taking care of it. But if *you* want to do it, go ahead!"

"I'll deal with it in my own way, but for now I want you to talk with him tomorrow, okay?"

"Okay, Ms. Bailey, we're on it," Price said matter-of-factly. "J.T. or I will take care of it."

Ms. Bailey started yelling at a few women who stood arguing with the store manager. "Everyone get your pop and get out of here," she said. "And you-all leave this man alone. He ain't the one you're looking for." She walked the manager inside and again told everyone to go home.

I caught up with Price and asked him to explain what had happened.

"That Ay-rab slept with Coco," he said with a smirk. "But he didn't give her no disease. That little girl got that herself—she's a whore. Sixteen and she's been around already."

"So what was all that about, then?" I asked. "Why the screaming, and what's up with the beer and soda?"

"Like I said, the man was sleeping with Coco, but he was giving her diapers and shit for Coco's baby." I had heard rumors that some store owners gave women free food and household items in exchange for sex. Some residents were very upset at the practice. In fact, I heard Ms. Mae regularly plead with J.T. to put a stop to this behavior. J.T.'s answer to his mother was nearly identical to what Price now told me: "You can't stop that shit. It's been happening like that for the longest time. It's just how people do things around here."

I asked Price what his role had been today. "I told Boo-Boo that I would go over to the store with her and let her yell at that man," he said. "She said she was going to cut off his dick, take a picture of it, and put it up everywhere. He freaked out. That's why he ran. Then I told his brother, the one who owns the store, that he had to do something, 'cause people would burn the store down if he didn't. He said he'd put all the soda and beer he had on the sidewalk if people would leave the store alone. I told him, 'Cool.' But I told him that I needed to speak with him tomorrow, because I don't want Boo-Boo killing his little brother, which she *will* do. So tomorrow we'll figure all this shit out so no one gets hurt."

I was just about to ask Price why he was responsible for mediating a dispute like this. But he preempted me. "That's what BKs are about," he said. "We just help keep the peace. We take care of our community."

This explanation didn't satisfy me, and I wanted to talk to J.T.

about it. But he was so busy these days that I barely saw him—and when I did, he was usually with other gang leaders, working on the political initiatives that the BKs were putting together.

And then, just before Labor Day, J.T.'s efforts to impress his superiors started to bear fruit. He told me that he was heading south for a few days. The highest-ranking BK leaders met downstate every few months, and J.T. had been invited to his first big meeting.

The Black Kings were a large regional gang, with factions as far north as Milwaukee, southward to St. Louis, east to Cleveland, and west to Iowa. I was surprised when J.T. first mentioned that the gang operated in Iowa. He told me that most Chicago gangs tried to recruit local dealers there, usually by hanging out at a high-school basketball or football game. But Iowa wasn't very profitable. Chicago gang leaders got frustrated at how "country" their Iowa counterparts were, even in places like Des Moines. They were undisciplined, they gave away too much product for free, they drank too much, and sometimes they plain forgot to go to work. But the Iowa market was large enough that most Chicago gangs, including the Black Kings, kept trying.

J.T. had made clear to me his ambition to move up in the gang's hierarchy, and this regional meeting was clearly a step in that direction.

In his absence, he told me, I could hang out as much as I wanted around his building. He said he'd let his foot soldiers know they should be expecting me, and he left me with his usual caution: "Don't walk too far from the building. I won't be able to help you."

After J.T. told me about his plans, I was both excited and nervous. I had hung around Robert Taylor without him, but usually only for a few hours at a stretch. Now I would have more time to walk around, and I hoped to meet more people who could tell me about the gang from their perspective. I knew I had to be careful with the line of questioning, but at last I'd been granted an opportunity to get out from under J.T.'s thumb and gain a wider view of the Black Kings.

I immediately ran into a problem. Because I'd been spending so much time with the Black Kings, a lot of the tenants wouldn't speak to me except for a quick hello or a bland comment about the weather. They plainly saw me as affiliated with the BKs, and just as plainly they didn't want to get involved with me.

Ms. Bailey, the building president, was one of the few tenants willing to talk. Her small, two-room office was located in J.T.'s building, where she lived as well. This was in the northern end of the Robert Taylor Homes, sometimes called "Robert Taylor A." A few miles away, at the southern end of the complex, was "Taylor B," where a different group of gangs and tenant leaders held the power. On most dimensions daily life was the same in Taylor A and Taylor B: they had similar rates of poverty and drug abuse, for instance, and similar levels of gang activity and crime.

But there was at least one big difference, Ms. Bailey told me, which was that Taylor B had a large Boys & Girls Club where hundreds of young people could shoot pool, play basketball, use the library, and participate in youth programs. Ms. Bailey was jealous that Taylor A had no such facility. Even though Taylor B was walking distance from Taylor A, gang boundaries made it hard to move freely even if you had nothing to do with a gang. It was usually teenagers who got hassled when they crossed over, but even adults could have trouble. They might get searched by a gang sentry when they tried to enter a high-rise that wasn't their own; they might also get robbed.

The best Ms. Bailey could offer the children in Taylor A were three run-down apartments that had been converted into playrooms.

These spaces were pathetic: water dripped from the ceilings, rats and roaches ran free, the bathrooms were rancid; all these playrooms had were a few well-worn board games, some stubby crayons, and an old TV set. Even so, whenever I visited, I saw that the children played with as much enthusiasm as if they were at Disney World.

One afternoon Ms. Bailey suggested that I visit the Boys & Girls Club in Taylor B. "Maybe with your connections you could help us raise money for a club like that in our area," she said.

I told her I'd be happy to help if I could. That Ms. Bailey saw me, a middle-class graduate student, as having "connections" said a lot about how alienated her community was from the powerful people in philanthropy and government who could actually make a difference.

Since Taylor B was controlled by the Disciples, a rival to J.T.'s Black Kings, Ms. Bailey personally walked me over to the Boys & Girls Club and introduced me to Autry Harrison, one of the club's directors.

Autry was about thirty years old, six foot two, and thin as a rail. He wore large, round glasses too big for his face and greeted me with a big smile and a handshake. "You got any skills, young man?" he asked brightly.

"I can read and write, but that's about it," I said.

Autry led me into the poolroom and yelled at a dozen little kids to come over. "This young man is going to read a book to you," he said, "and then I'd like you to talk about it with him." He whispered to me, "Many of their parents just can't read."

From that day forward, Autry was happy to have me at the club. I quickly got to know him well. He had grown up in Robert Taylor, served in the army, and, like a few caring souls of his generation, returned to his neighborhood to work with young people. Recently he'd gone back to school to study criminal justice at Chicago State

University and was working part-time there as a research assistant to a professor who was studying gangs. Autry was married, with a three-year-old daughter. Because of his obligations at the club and at home, he told me, he sometimes had to drop classes and even take a leave of absence from school.

In his youth Autry had made his fair share of bad choices: he'd been a pimp and a gang member, for instance, and he had engaged in criminal activity. He'd also suffered the effects of project living—he'd been beaten up, had his money stolen, watched friends get shot and die in a gang war.

Autry sometimes sat for hours, leaning back in a chair with his skinny arms propped behind his head, telling me the lessons he'd learned from his days as a pimp. These included "Never sleep with your ladies," "Always let them borrow money, because you got the power when they owe you shit," and "If you *do* sleep with them, always, always, always wear a condom, even when you're shaking their hand, because you just never know where they've been."

We got along well, and Autry became a great source of information for me on how project residents viewed the gang. The club, it turned out, wasn't a refuge only for children. Senior citizens played cards there, religious folks gathered for fellowship, and social workers and doctors provided free counseling and medical care. Just like many of the hustlers I'd been speaking to, Autry felt that the gang did help the community—giving away food, mediating conflicts, et cetera—but he also stressed that the community spent a lot of time "mopping up the gang's mistakes."

"What do you mean?" I asked.

"They kill, sometimes for the most stupid reasons," he said. "'You spoke to my girlfriend. . . .' 'You walked down the sidewalk in my territory. . . .' 'You looked at me funny— That's it, I'll kill you!'"

"So it's not always fights about drugs?"

"Are you kidding me?" He laughed. "See, the gang always says it's a business, and it is. But a fifteen-year-old around here is just like any fifteen-year-old. They want to be noticed. They don't get any attention at home, so they rebel. And at the club we're always mopping up their mistakes."

"How does that work?"

"Well, we settle shit when it gets out of hand. Like the other day—Barry knifed somebody from a different gang because the other boy was hanging out near his building. Just for hanging out! So I called my friend Officer Reggie, and we let the two fight it out."

"Fight it out? I thought you said you *settled* it."

"We did. That's how you settle shit sometimes. Let boys fight each other—no guns, no knives. Then you tell them, 'Okay, you-all see that you can fight without killing each other?' "

Autry told me that the club played a broad peacekeeping role in the community. He and other staff members worked with school authorities, social workers, and police officers to informally mediate all kinds of problems, rather than ushering young men and women into the criminal-justice system. The police regularly brought shoplifters, vandals, and car thieves to the club, where Autry and the others would negotiate the return of stolen property as well as, perhaps, some kind of restitution.

I never saw any of these mediations in person. Autry just told me about them after the fact. It didn't seem as if he were lying, but perhaps bragging a little. He told me that he even invited rival gang leaders to the club late at night to resolve their conflicts. My conversations with Autry were a bit like some of my conversations with J.T.: it was not always easy to independently verify their claims.

One busy morning Autry surprised me by asking if I wanted to come to a private meeting at the club later that day. He explained that a few neighborhood organizations were planning a midnight basketball league.

It would be open to all teenagers, but the real goal was to attract gang members. Local community leaders liked the idea of getting unruly teens to play basketball at the club instead of spending their nights on the street. For the young men, the price of admission was to sit through a motivational speech by a pastor or some other speaker before each game. In exchange, the teenagers would get free sneakers, T-shirts, and the chance to win a trophy.

Autry's work would soon command wide attention, when the Clinton administration used the Chicago midnight basketball league as a model for a nationwide movement. In reality there was only anecdotal evidence that the leagues reduced teenage violence, but in a climate where few programs were successful on any level, policy makers were eager to showcase an uplifting idea like midnight basketball.

When I showed up at the club that afternoon, Autry was sitting at a table bearing coffee and doughnuts, a handmade sign behind him on the wall: MIDNIGHT BASKETBALL MEETING IN CONFERENCE ROOM.

"Welcome, Sudhir," Autry said, beaming. "Everyone is inside." He mentioned the names of several tenant leaders, pastors, a Nation of Islam official, an ex–police officer. The basketball league was turning into a big deal for Autry. It represented his entrée into the elite group of community leaders, whom Autry very much wanted to join.

"You sure they won't mind if I sit in?" I asked.

"Not at all," Autry said, shuffling some papers. "And the niggers won't mind either."

"Who?" I asked.

"Man, we got them all!" He rubbed his hands together excitedly.

"We got *all* the leaders—Disciples, Black Kings, MCs, Stones. Everyone is coming!"

"You didn't tell me they'd be there," I said meekly.

Autry could tell I was concerned. "Don't worry. Just sit in the back and keep your mouth shut. I'll say you're with me. But help me with these first." He handed me three sets of flyers that needed to be passed out to everyone. One of them was titled "Rules for Buy-In," which specified the mandatory donation of each sponsoring "organization." Each gang was expected to contribute five thousand dollars and field four teams of ten players. The money would be used to pay for the referees, uniforms, and the cost of keeping the gym open at night.

"You're getting the gangs to pay for this?" I asked. "That doesn't bother you?"

"What would you rather that they do with their money?"

"Good point," I said. "But something doesn't feel right about it."

"I see." Autry put down the flyers and pulled a cigarette from his shirt pocket. "Two thousand niggers in this project making money by selling that poison, killing each other, killing everyone who buys it. We can't do *nothing* about it. And now we tell them that if they want to be selling that shit, they have to give back. They have to step up. And you look at *us* funny? It's them you should be asking these questions to."

"I would if I knew them," I said.

"Don't lie to me, nigger."

Autry knew I was on good terms with J.T., although I'd been cagey about the extent of our relationship. Many times he'd told me I needed to have the courage to ask J.T. more difficult questions about the gang, even if it would upset him. "At least you can ask *one* of these niggers the question," he said. "And he'll be here tonight." Autry let out a loud laugh and went outside to smoke his cigarette.

Shit. It would be the first time I'd seen J.T. in several weeks. I was usually careful to ask his permission before attending any event involving gangs, both to show respect and because I needed a patron. Otherwise, as he always told me, my personal safety couldn't be guaranteed.

I decided to wait outside the club to talk to J.T. when he arrived. Autry offered to wait with me. We stood on the sidewalk and watched the busy, noisy traffic along Federal Street. The club sat in the shadow of a project high-rise. You could hear people yelling from the sidewalk up to the open windows—there was no intercom system—and you could smell the smoke of marijuana and menthol cigarettes.

Before long, J.T. and the leaders of the other gangs began pulling up with their respective security entourages. The scene was straight out of a gangsta-rap video. Each vehicle—there were sports cars, fancy trucks, and one long, purple Lincoln Continental—was immaculate, rims sparkling from a fresh wash. They drove up in a line, as if in a funeral procession, parking across the street from the club. The first man out of each car was a bodyguard, even if the gang leader was the one who drove.

Autry crossed the street, as nonchalantly as his excitement allowed, to ensure them that the club was safe, neutral territory. They were all dressed similarly: new tracksuits, white sneakers, and plenty of gold on their wrists and around their necks. As they approached, each leader was trailed by one or two bodyguards, with another one or two staying behind with the cars. All the bodyguards wore sunglasses and baseball caps.

J.T. noticed me standing there and pushed his bodyguards aside. "You-all go in!" he shouted to the other gang leaders, "I'll see you in a bit." Then he turned to me. He shrugged his shoulders and glared, the universal signal for "What the fuck?"

Autry intervened before I could answer. "Hey, man," he said, "no worries, he's with me."

"He's with *you*?!" J.T. wasn't smiling. "You *know* him?"

"Yeah, big boss man, today he's with me." Autry smiled, his front teeth glistening as he leaned over and hugged J.T.

"Oh, so he's with you now," J.T. repeated, shaking his head. He pulled out a cigarette, and Autry lit it for him.

"Sorry," I said, "I haven't seen you in a while. Autry and I just met, and he said I could come to this meeting. I should've told you."

"Yeah, the brother didn't mean nothing," Autry said. "Not a big deal. No taping today, right, my brother?" Autry loved to walk into a room with me at the club and yell, "Sudhir is from the university, and he'll be taping everything you say today!"

"Not a big deal?" J.T. said, turning to Autry. "You're more ignorant than I thought you were. You pulled all these people together, and you're going to fuck it up like this."

"Whoa, my brother. Like I said, he's with me."

"And what if he comes by *my* building? Is he with you then? Huh? Is he with you then, nigger?"

"Fuck, no!" Autry laughed. "Then he's with *you*! 'Cause I ain't stepping *foot* in that motherfucker. Hell no!"

Autry ducked inside, grinning broadly. He seemed to be having great fun.

"That's what I thought," J.T. said, turning to me. "If you walk in there, the first time all these other niggers see you, then you're with Autry, not me. You didn't think about that, did you? You're a motherfucking impatient nigger. And an ignorant one, from where I stand. You walk in there and I can't do nothing for you. No more. So it's up to you."

"I didn't think about any of this," I apologized. "I didn't know how—"

"Yeah, nigger, you didn't *think*." J.T. started walking inside. "Like I said, you're with me or you're with someone else. You decide."

Inside, I could see Autry, giggling at me. "Come in, boy!" he yelled. "Come in, little baby! You scared?"

I decided I wasn't willing to jeopardize my relationship with J.T., even if it meant missing an opportunity to learn more about the community and the gangs. So I turned and walked away. I started toward the university, and then I stopped. The last time I'd had an uncomfortable episode with J.T.—his beat-down of C-Note—I'd made a mistake. I'd waited too long before speaking to him about it. That made it harder to get a satisfying explanation. So this time I headed straight for J.T.'s building, figuring he'd go there when the meeting was over.

He did. He still seemed upset and started yelling at his mother. "No one understands what I deal with!" he said. "No one listens and does what I say." He sent his bodyguards out to buy some beer. He sat on the recliner and grabbed the remote control. He barely glanced at me.

"You pissed at me?" I asked.

"What the fuck have you been doing around here?" he asked.

I explained that Ms. Bailey had introduced me to Autry and that I was interested in what went on at the club. He seemed surprised that he no longer knew all the specifics about the people I was meeting. "I guess you were going to make some friends while I was gone," he said, and then he asked a question I'd been hoping he'd never ask: "What exactly are you doing around here? I mean, what are you writing about?"

He started changing channels on the TV. It was the first time I'd ever been with him when he didn't look me in the eye.

"Well, honestly, I'm . . . I'm fascinated by how you do what you do," I stammered. "Like I said before, I'm trying to understand how

your mind works, why you decided to come back to the neighborhood and run this organization, what you have to do to make it. But
if I don't get out and see how others look at you, how you have this
incredible effect on other people, then I'll never really understand
what you do. So while you were gone, I thought I'd branch out."

"You mean you're asking people what they think about *me*?"
Now he had turned to look at me again.

"Well, not really, because you know they would probably not feel
comfortable telling me. I'm at stage one. I'm trying to understand
what the organization does and how people have to deal with it. If
you piss people off, how do they respond? Do they call the police?
Do they call you?"

"Okay. So it's how others work *with me*."

He seemed appeased, so I was quick to affirm. "Yes! How others work with you. That's a great way of putting it." I hoped he
wouldn't ask what "stage two" was, for I had no idea. I felt a little
uneasy letting him think that I was actually writing his biography,
but at the moment I just wanted to buy myself some time.

He checked his watch. "All right, I need to get some sleep." He
got up and walked toward his bedroom without saying good-bye. In
the kitchen Ms. Mae kissed me good night, and I walked to the
bus stop.

J.T. was a little cool toward me the next few times I saw him.
So to warm things up, I stopped going to the club and
spent nearly all my time in and around J.T.'s building. I was unhappy
to be missing the opportunity to see how Autry worked with other
people behind the scenes on important community issues, but I
didn't want to further anger J.T. I just told Autry that I'd be busy for

a few weeks but I'd be back once I got settled in with my course work in the coming fall semester.

Soon after the school year began, a young boy and girl in Robert Taylor were shot, accidental victims of a drive-by gang shooting. The boy was eight, the girl nine. They both spent time in the hospital, and then the girl died. The shooting occurred at the border of Taylor A and Taylor B. J.T.'s gang had been on the receiving end of the shooting, with several members injured. The shooters were from the Disciples, who operated out of the projects near the Boys & Girls Club.

This single shooting had a widespread effect. Worried that a full-scale gang war would break out, parents began keeping their children inside, which meant taking time off from work or otherwise adjusting their schedules. Senior citizens worried about finding a safe way to get medical treatment. Local churches mobilized to deliver food to families too scared to walk to the store.

Ms. Bailey told me about a meeting at the Boys & Girls Club where the police would address concerned parents and tenant leaders. If I really wanted to see how the gang's actions affected the broader community, Ms. Bailey said, I should be there.

I asked J.T., and he thought it was a good idea, even though he never bothered with such things. "The police don't do nothing for us," he said. "You should understand that by now." Then he muttered something about how the community "takes care of its problems," mentioning the incident I'd seen with Boo-Boo, Price, and the Middle Eastern store manager.

The meeting was held late one weekday morning. The streets outside the club were quiet, populated by a smattering of unemployed people, gang members, and drug addicts. The leaves had already changed, but the day was unseasonably warm.

Autry was busy as usual, running to and fro making sure everything was ready. Although I hadn't seen him in some time, he shot me a friendly glance. The meeting was held in a large, windowless concrete room with a linoleum floor. There were perhaps forty tenants in attendance—all fanning themselves, since the heat was turned up too high. "If we turn it off, we can't get it back on right away," Autry told me. "And then it's May by the time you get it back on."

At the front of the room, several uniformed police officers and police officials sat behind a long table. Ms. Bailey nodded me toward a seat beside her, up front and off to one side.

The meeting was an exercise in chaos. Residents shouted past one another while the police officials begged for calm. A mother holding her infant yelled that she was "sick and tired of living like this." The younger and middle-aged parents were the most vocal. The senior citizens sat quietly, many of them with Bibles in their hands, looking as if they were ready for church. Nor did the police have much to say, other than platitudes about their continued efforts to disrupt the gangs and requests for tenants to start cooperating with them by reporting gang crimes.

After about forty-five minutes, the police looked very ready to leave. So did the tenants. As the meeting broke up, some of them waved their hands dismissively at the cops.

"Are these meetings always so crazy?" I asked Ms. Bailey.

"This is how it goes," she said. "We yell at them, they say nothing. Everyone goes back to doing what they were doing."

"I don't see what you get out of this. It seems like a waste of time."

Ms. Bailey just patted my knee and said, "Mm-hmm."

"I mean it," I said. "This is ridiculous. Where I grew up, you'd have an army of cops all over the place. But nothing is going on here. Doesn't that upset you?"

By now the room had cleared out except for Ms. Bailey and a few other tenant leaders, Autry, and one policeman, Officer Johnson, a tall black man who worked out of a nearby precinct. He was well groomed, with a short mustache and graying hair. They were all checking their watches and speaking quietly to one another.

I was about to leave when Ms. Bailey walked over. "In two hours come back here," she said. "But now you have to go."

Autry smiled and winked as he passed. What was he up to? I knew that Autry was still trying to groom himself as a local power broker, but I didn't know how much power, if any, he had actually accrued.

As instructed, I left for a while and took a walk around the neighborhood. When I returned to the club, Autry silently pointed me toward the room where the earlier meeting had been held. Inside, I saw Ms. Bailey and some other building presidents; Officer Johnson and Autry's friend Officer Reggie, a well-liked cop who had grown up in Robert Taylor; and Pastor Wilkins, who was said to be a long-standing expert in forging gang truces. Autry, I knew, saw himself as Pastor Wilkins's eventual successor.

They were all milling about, shaking hands and chatting softly before settling into the folding metal chairs Autry had arranged. A few of them looked at me with a bit of surprise as I sat down, but no one said anything.

And then, to *my* great surprise, I saw J.T., sitting with a few of his senior officers along one wall. Although our eyes didn't meet, I could tell that he noticed me.

Even more surprising was the group on the other side of the room: a gang leader named Mayne, who ran the Disciples, accompanied by *his* officers, leaning quietly against the wall.

I took a good look at Mayne. He was a heavyset man with a crumpled face, like a bulldog's. He appeared bored and irritated, and he kept issuing instructions to his men: "Nigger, get me a cigarette." "Boy, get me a chair."

Autry walked into the room. "Okay!" he shouted. "The club is closed, let's get going. Kids are going to come back at five."

Officer Reggie stood up. "Let's get moving," he said. "Ms. Bailey, you wanted to start. Go ahead." He walked toward the back of the room.

"First, J.T., get the other men out of the room," she said. "You, too, Mayne."

Mayne and J.T. both motioned for their senior officers to leave, and they did, walking out slowly with stoic faces. Ms. Bailey stood silently until they were gone. Then she took a deep breath. "Pastor, you said you had an idea, something you wanted to ask these young men?"

"Yes, Ms. Bailey," Pastor Wilkins said. He stood up. "Now, I know how this began. Shorties probably fighting over some girl, right? And it got all the way to shooting each other. That's crazy! I mean, I can understand if you were fighting over business, but you're killing people around here because of a spat in school!"

"We're defending our honor," Mayne said. "Ain't nothing more important than that."

"Yeah," said J.T. "And it *is* about business. Those guys come shooting down on our end, scaring people away."

Pastor Wilkins asked Mayne and J.T. to describe how the fight had escalated. Pastor Wilkins's original guess was mostly right: two teenage boys at DuSable High School got into a fight over a girl. One boy was in J.T.'s gang, the other in Mayne's. Over the course of a few weeks, the conflict escalated from unarmed to armed—first a knife fight and then the drive-by shooting. The shooting occurred during the afternoon, while kids were playing outside after school.

J.T. said that because his customers had b

shooting, and because tenants in his buildings

lives being interrupted, he wanted Mayne to

Mayne argued that the shooting took plac

two gangs' territory, near a park that neither g

fore, he argued, J.T. was ineligible for compensa

My mind raced as they spoke. I couldn't believe that a religious leader and a police officer were not only watching this mediation but were actually *facilitating* it. What incentive did they have to do so— and what would happen if people from the community found out they were helping gang leaders settle their disputes? I was also struck by how levelheaded everyone seemed, even J.T. and Mayne, as if they'd been through this before. These were the same two gang leaders, after all, who had been trying to kill each other, quite literally, with drive-by shootings. I wondered if one of them might even pull a gun here at any moment. Perhaps the very strangest thing was how sanguine the community leaders were about the fact that these men sold crack cocaine for a living. But at this moment it seemed that pragmatism was more important than moralism.

After a while the conversation got bogged down, with J.T. and Mayne merely restating their positions. Autry jumped in to try to re-focus things. "How much you think you lost?" he asked J.T. "I mean, you don't need to tell me the amount, but how many days did you lose business?"

"Probably a few days, maybe a week," J.T. said.

"Okay, well, we're going to bank this," Autry said. "Put it in the bank."

"What the fuck does that mean?" Mayne asked.

"Nigger, that means you messed up," Autry told him. "J.T. didn't retaliate, did he? I mean, he didn't shoot over at you. It was just you down at his end, right? So J.T. gets to sell his shit in the park week. The next time this happens, and J.T. fucks up, you get to sell *your* shit in the park for a week."

Ms. Bailey spoke up. "You-all do not get to sell nothing when the kids are there, okay? Just late at night."

"Sounds fine to me," J.T. said. Mayne nodded in agreement.

"Then we have a truce," Pastor Wilkins said. He walked over to J.T. and Mayne. "Shake on it."

J.T. and Mayne shook hands, not warmly and not willing to look at each other. The pastor and Ms. Bailey each let out a sigh.

As J.T., Mayne, and Pastor Wilkins sat down to work out the details of the deal, I walked out front. There was Autry, smoking a cigarette on the sidewalk. He shook his head; he looked fatigued.

"This stuff is hard, isn't it?" I asked.

"Yeah, I try to block out the fact that they could get pissed at me and kill me if I say something they don't like. You never know if they'll go home and think you're working for the other side."

"You ever get hurt before?"

"I got my ass kicked a few times—one time real bad—'cause they thought I wasn't being fair. I'm not sure I want to have that happen again."

"You don't get paid enough," I said.

J.T. came out of the club and stopped beside me. His head was lowered. Autry moved away.

"You wanted this, right?" he asked.

"Yes," I said, "this is what I'm looking for." He knew I'd been eager to see how the community and the gang worked out their differences. But he'd also made it clear that I could do so only if I had a patron, and I had to choose between J.T. and Autry. I chose J.T.

"Just remember, *you* wanted this," he said. "I didn't make you come here today. I didn't tell you about this. *You* wanted this." He pressed his finger into my chest every time he said "you." I sensed that despite our last conversation J.T. felt I was slipping from his grasp.

"I know," I said. "Don't worry."

"*I'm* not worried." He let out a sinister laugh. "But you should really think about this. Just remember, I didn't bring you here. I can't protect you. Not all the time anyway. You did this on your own."

"I get it, I'm on my own."

J.T. smiled, pressed his finger into my chest one last time, with force, and walked away.

FOUR

Gang Leader for a Day

After nearly three years of hanging out with J.T., I began talking to several of my professors about my dissertation topic. As it happened, they weren't as enthusiastic as I was about an in-depth study of the Black Kings crack gang and its compelling leader. They were more interested in the standard sociological issues in the community: entrenched poverty, domestic violence, the prevalence of guns, residents' charged relations with the government—and, to a lesser extent, how the community dealt with the gang.

If I explored these subjects well, my professors said, I could explain how the Robert Taylor tenants really behaved, rather than simply arguing that they didn't act like middle-class people.

Bill Wilson in particular was adamant that I adopt a wider lens on the gang and its role in Robert Taylor. Because sociology had such a strong tradition of "community studies," he wanted me to write the definitive report on everyday life in high-rise housing projects.

He also said he'd started worrying about my safety in the projects. By this point I had taken up golf as a way to spend more time with Wilson, an avid golfer. "I'm having nightmares, Sudhir," he said once in the middle of the fairway, staring out blankly. "You're worrying me, and I really want you to think about spending some time with others." He drifted off, never instructing me about which "others" I should be observing, but I knew this was code for *anyone* besides the gang.

I knew he had my best interests in mind, but it still came as a shock to me that I would have to widen my focus if I still planned to base my dissertation on this community. It meant that J.T. wouldn't be the sole target of my attention, and perhaps not even the primary target. A few of my professors were seasoned ethnographers, experts in the methodology of firsthand observation. They were insistent that I avoid getting so close to any one source that I would be beholden to him.

Easier said than done. I hadn't forgotten how agitated J.T. became when he saw me branching out into the community. I really didn't feel I could tell him that my project was moving away from a focus on his leadership. By now J.T. wasn't my only access to the community, but he was certainly my best access. He was the one who had brought me in, and he was the one who could open—or shut—any door. But beyond all that lay one simple fact: J.T. was a charismatic man who led a fascinating life that I wanted to keep learning about.

J.T. seemed to appreciate having the ear of an outsider who would listen for hours to his tales of bravado and managerial prowess. He often expressed how hard it was to oversee the gang, to keep the drug economy running smoothly, and to deal with the law-abiding tenants who saw him as an adversary. Sometimes he spoke of his job with dispassion, as if he were the CEO of

some widget manufacturer—an attitude that I found not only jar-
ring but, given the violence and destruction his enterprise caused, ir-
responsible.

He fancied himself a philanthropist as much as a leader. He spoke
proudly of quitting his mainstream sales job in downtown Chicago
to return to the projects and use his drug profits "to help others."
How did he help? He mandated that all his gang members get a
high-school diploma and stay off drugs. He gave money to some
local youth centers for sports equipment and computers. He willingly
loaned out his gang members to Robert Taylor tenant leaders, who
deployed them on such tasks as escorting the elderly on errands or
beating up a domestic abuser. J.T. could even put a positive spin
on the fact that he made money by selling drugs. A drug economy,
he told me, was "useful for the community," since it redistributed
the drug addicts' money back into the community via the gang's
philanthropy.

I have to admit that J.T.'s rhetoric could be persuasive, even when
I tried to play the skeptic. The fact was, I didn't yet have a good grip
on how his gang really affected the broader community. On an even
more basic level, I wondered if I really had a complete sense of what
J.T. did on a daily level. What kind of gang activities *wasn't* he showing me?

One cold February morning, I stood with him on a street corner as he met with one of his drug-selling crews. I was shivering, still
unaccustomed to the chilling lake winds, and trying hard to focus
on what J.T. was saying. He spoke to his men about the need to take
pride in their work. He was also trying to motivate the younger
members to brave the cold and sell as much crack as they could. In
weather like this, the youngest members had to stand outside and sell
while the ones with more seniority hung out in a building lobby.

After addressing his troops, J.T. said he was going off to play basketball. He climbed into his Malibu and I climbed in with him. We were parked near a busy intersection at State Street, within view of a Robert Taylor high-rise, some low-rise stores, and the Boys & Girls Club. Before he even turned the key, I mentioned, half joking, that I thought he was seriously overpaid.

"I don't see what's so difficult about your job," I said. "I mean, you *say* how hard it is to do what you do, but I just can't see it being that difficult." All I ever saw him do, I said, was walk around and shake hands with people, spend money, drive nice cars—he owned at least three that I knew of—and party with his friends. J.T. just sat for a moment, making no move to drive off. "Okay, well, you want to give it a try? If you think it's so easy, you try it."

"I don't think that would be possible. I don't think graduate school is really training me to lead a gang."

"Yeah, but you don't think I need any skills at all to do this. So you should have no problem doing it, right?"

It was true that *sometimes* his job looked hard. When his gang was warring with another gang, for instance, J.T. had to coordinate his troops and motivate fifteen-year-old kids to stand out in the open and sell drugs despite the heightened risk of being shot, beaten up, or arrested. And it wasn't as though these kids were getting rich for their trouble. The BKs, like most other street gangs, had a small leadership class. J.T. kept only a few officers on his payroll: a treasurer, a couple of "enforcers," a security coordinator, and then a set of lesser-paid "directors" who managed the six-person teams that did the actual street-level selling of crack.

But for the most part, it seemed that J.T.'s gang members spent their time hanging around on street corners, selling drugs, shooting dice, playing sports, and talking about women. Did it really take a self-styled CEO to manage *that*?

I expressed this sentiment to J.T. "I could do it," I said. "Probably. I mean, I don't think I could handle a war and I've never shot a gun, so it depends what you mean when you say 'try it.' "

"Just that—try it. There's no war on right now, no fighting. So you don't even have to touch a gun. But I can't promise that you won't have to do something you may not like."

"Such as?"

"I'm not telling you. You said you think it's easy, so you do it, and you'll see what I mean."

"Is this an offer?"

"Nigger, this is the offer of a lifetime. Guaranteed that if you do this, you'll have a story for all your college friends."

He suggested that I try it for a day. This made me laugh: how could I possibly learn anything worthwhile in a single day?

From inside the car, I watched as parents gingerly stepped out of the high-rise lobby, kids in tow, trying to get to school and out of the unforgiving lake wind. A crossing guard motioned them to hurry up and cross the street, for there were a couple of eighteen-wheelers idling impatiently at a green light. As they passed his car, J.T. waved. Our breath was fogging up the windshield. He turned on the defroster, jacked the music a bit louder. "One day," he said. "Take it or leave it. That's all I'm saying. One day."

I met J.T. at seven-thirty the next morning at Kevin's Hamburger Heaven in Bridgeport, a predominantly Irish-American neighborhood across the expressway from the projects. This was his regular morning spot. "None of these white folks here know me," he said, "so I don't get any funny looks."

His steak and eggs arrived just as I sat down. He always ate alone, he said. Soon enough he'd be joined by two of his officers, Price and T-Bone. Even though J.T.'s gang was nearly twice as large as most others on the South Side, he kept his officer class small, because he trusted very few people. All of his officers were friends he'd known since high school.

"All right," he began, "let's talk a little about—"

"Listen," I blurted out, "I can't kill anybody, I can't sell shit to any-body." I had been awake much of the night worrying. "Or even *plan* any of that stuff! Not me!"

"Okay, nigger, first of all you need to stop shouting." He looked about the room. "And stop worrying. But let me tell you what *I'm* worried about, chief."

He twirled a piece of steak on his fork as he dabbed his mouth with a napkin.

"I can't let you do *everything,* right, because I'll get into trouble, you dig? So there's just going to be some stuff you *can't* do. And you already told me some of the other stuff you don't *want* to be doing. But all that doesn't matter, because I got plenty of stuff to keep you busy for the day. And only the cats coming for breakfast know what you'll be doing. So don't be acting like you run the place in front of everybody. Don't embarrass me."

It was his own bosses, J.T. explained, that he was worried about, the Black Kings' board of directors. The board, roughly two dozen men who controlled all the neighborhood BK gangs in Chicago, kept a close eye on drug revenues, since their generous skim came off the top. They were always concerned that local leaders like J.T. keep their troops in line. Young gang members who made trouble drew unwanted police attention, which made it harder to sell drugs; the fewer drugs that were sold, the less money the board collected. So the board was constantly reminding J.T. to minimize the friction of his operation.

As J.T. was explaining all this, he repeated that only his senior of-ficers knew that I was gang leader for a day. It wouldn't do, he said, for the gang's rank and file to learn of our experiment, nor the community at large. I was excited at the thought of spending the day with J.T. I felt he might not be able to censor what I saw if I was with him for a full day. It was also an obvious sign that he trusted me. And I think he was flattered that I was interested in knowing what actually went into his work.

Impatient, I asked him what my first assignment was.

"You'll find out in a minute, as soon as I do. Eat up, you're going to need it."

I was nervous, to be sure, but not because I was implicating myself in an illegal enterprise. In fact, I hadn't even really thought about that angle. I probably should have. At most universities, faculty members solicit approval for their research from institutional review boards, which act as the main insurance against exploitative or unethical research. But the work of graduate students is largely overlooked. Only later, when I began sharing my experiences with my advisers and showing them my field notes, did I begin to understand—and adhere to—the reporting requirements for researchers who are privy to criminal conduct. But at the time, with little understanding of these protocols, I simply relied on my own moral compass.

This compass wasn't necessarily reliable. To be honest, I was a bit overwhelmed by the thrill of further entering J.T.'s world. I hoped he would someday introduce me to the powerful Black Kings leadership, the reputedly ruthless inner-city gang lords who had since transplanted themselves to the Chicago suburbs. I wondered if they were some kind of revolutionary vanguard, debating the theories of Karl Marx and W. E. B. Du Bois, Frantz Fanon and Kwame Nkrumah. (Probably not.) I also hoped that J.T. would bring me to some dark downtown tavern where large Italian men in large Italian suits met with black hustlers like J.T. to dream up a multiethnic, multigenerational, multimillion-dollar criminal plan. My mind, it was safe to say, was racing out of control.

Price and T-Bone soon arrived and sat down at our table. By now I knew these two pretty well—T-Bone, the gang's bookish and chatty treasurer (which meant he handled most of the gang's fiscal and organizational issues), and Price, the thuggish and hard-living security chief (a job that included the allocation of particular street corners to particular BK dealers). They were the two men most responsible for helping J.T. with day-to-day affairs. They both nodded in my direction as they sat down, then looked toward J.T.

"Okay, T-Bone," J.T. said, "you're up, nigger. Talk to me. What's happening today?"

"Whoa, whoa!" I said. "I'm in charge here, no? I should call this meeting to order, no?"

"Okay, nigger," J.T. said, again glancing around. He still seemed concerned that I was talking too loud. "Just be cool."

I tried to calm down. "T-Bone, you're up. Talk to me, nigger."

J.T. collapsed on the table, laughing hard. T-Bone and Price laughed along with him.

"If he calls me 'nigger' again, I'm giving him an ass whupping," T-Bone said. "I don't *care* if he's my leader."

J.T. told T-Bone to go ahead and start listing the day's tasks.

"Ms. Bailey needs about a dozen guys to clean up the building today," T-Bone said. "Last night Josie and them partied all night long, and there's shit everywhere. We need to send guys to her by eleven or she *will* be pissed. And I do not want to be dealing with her when she's pissed. Not me."

"Okay, Sudhir," J.T. said, "what do we do?" He folded his arms and sat back, as if he'd just set up a checkmate.

"What? Are you kidding me? Is this a joke?"

"Ain't no joke," said T-Bone flatly. "What do I do?" He looked at J.T., who pointed his finger at me. "C'mon, chief," T-Bone said to me. "I got about ten things I need to go over. Let's do this."

J.T. explained that he had to keep Ms. Bailey happy, since the gang sold crack in the lobby of her building and as building president she had the power to make things difficult. To appease her, J.T. regularly assigned his members to clean up her building and do other menial jobs. The young drug dealers hated these assignments not only because they were humiliating but because every hour of community service was one less hour earning money. Josie was a teenage member of J.T.'s gang who'd apparently thrown a party with some prostitutes and left the stairwells and gallery strewn with broken glass, trash, and used condoms.

"All right, who hasn't done cleanup in a while?" I asked.

"Well, you have Moochie's group and Kalia's group," T-Bone said. "Both of them ain't cleaned up for about three months." Moochie and Kalia were each in charge of a six-member sales force.

"Okay, how do we make a decision between the two?" I asked.

"Well, it depends on what you think is important," J.T. said. "Moochie's been making tall money, so you may not want to pull him off the streets. Kalia ain't been doing so hot lately, so maybe you want him to clean up, 'cause he isn't bringing in money anyway."

T-Bone countered by saying that maybe I should give the cleanup job to Moochie *because* he was making so much money lately. A little community service, T-Bone said, might ensure that "Moochie's head doesn't get too big." One of a leader's constant struggles was to keep younger members from feeling too powerful or independent.

Then Price threw in the fact that Moochie, who was in his early twenties, had been sleeping with Ms. Bailey, who was about fifty-five. This news shocked me: Was Moochie really attracted to a heavyset woman in her fifties? Price explained that younger guys often slept with older women, especially in winter, because otherwise they might not have a warm, safe place to spend the night. Also, a lease-holding woman might let her younger boyfriend stash drugs and cash in her apartment and maybe even use it as a freelance sales spot.

"Maybe Ms. Bailey gets to liking Moochie and she tells every-one not to buy shit from anyone but his boys," Price said. "You can't have that, because Moochie feels like he owns the building, and he doesn't."

"What if I flip a coin?" I asked, frustrated that I was spending so much time delegating janitorial duties. "I mean, you can't win one way or the other."

"Giving up already?" J.T. asked.

"Okay, let's send Moochie over there," I said. "It's better that his head doesn't get too big. Short run, you lose a little money."

"You got it," T-Bone said, and stepped away to make a phone call.

Price brought up the next item. The BKs had been trying to find a large space—a church or school or youth center—where they could hold meetings. There were several occasions, J.T. explained, when the gang needed to gather all its members. If a member vio-lated a major gang rule, J.T. liked to mete out punishment in front of the entire membership in order to encourage solidarity and, just as important, provide deterrence. If a member was caught stealing drugs, for instance, he might be brutally beaten in front of the whole gang.

J.T. might also call a large meeting to go over practical matters like sales strategies or suspicions about who might be snitching to the police. A big meeting also gave J.T. a captive audience for his ora-tory. I had already been to a few meetings in which the only con-tent was a two-hour speech by J.T. on the virtues of loyalty and bravery.

He often called the gang together on a street corner or in a park.

But this was far from ideal. There were about 250 young men in J.T.'s gang; summoning even 50 of them to the same street corner was sure to bring out the police, especially if a beating was on the agenda.

I was curious about the gang's relationship with the police, but it was very hard to fathom. Gang members brazenly sold drugs in public; why, I wondered, didn't the cops just shut down these open-air markets? But I couldn't get any solid answers to this question. J.T. was always evasive on the issue, and most people in the neighborhood were scared to talk about the cops at all—even more scared, it seemed to me, than to talk about the gang. As someone who grew up in a suburb where the police were a welcome presence, I found this bizarre. But there was plainly a lot that I didn't yet understand.

The Black Kings also needed to meet en masse if they were preparing for war with another gang. Once in a while, a war began when teenage members of different gangs got into a fight that then escalated. But leaders like J.T. had a strong incentive to thwart this sort of conflict, since it jeopardized moneymaking for no good reason. More typically, a war broke out when one gang tried to take over a sales location that belonged to another gang. Or one gang might do a drive-by shooting in another gang's territory, hoping to scare off its customers—perhaps right into the territory of the gang that did the shooting.

When this kind of spark occurred, J.T. might pick up the phone and call his counterpart in the other gang to arrange a compromise. But, more often, gang leaders ordered a retaliation in order to save face. One drive-by shooting begat a retaliatory drive-by; if a Black Kings dealer got robbed of his drugs or cash by someone from another gang, then the Black Kings would do at least the same.

The retaliation was what signaled the start of a war. In J.T.'s gang it was the security officer, Price, who oversaw the details of the war:

posting sentries, hiring mercenary gunmen if need be, planning the drive-bys. Price enjoyed this work, and was often happiest during gang wars.

I had never seen a war last beyond a few weeks; the higher-ups in each gang understood that public violence was, at the very least, bad for business. Usually, after a week or ten days of fighting, the leaders would find a mediator, someone like Autry, to help forge a truce.

"Pastor Wilkins says we can meet once a week at the church, at night," Price said. "I spoke to him yesterday. He says he would like a donation."

Price started to chuckle. So did T-Bone, who had returned from his phone call, and J.T.

"What's so funny?" I asked.

"Pastor Wilkins is a faggot, man," J.T. said. "That nigger sucks dick all night long!"

I had no idea whether Pastor Wilkins really did have sex with men, but I didn't think it much mattered. Price and the others enjoyed making fun of him, and that was that.

"I still don't see what's so funny," I said.

"Nigger, *you* have to meet with him," T-Bone said. "Alone!"

"Oh, I get it. Very funny. Well, how about this? Since I'm leader, then that meeting is now scheduled for tomorrow. Ha!"

"No, the pastor wants to meet today," J.T. said, suddenly stern. "And I need to find out today if we have a place to meet on Friday. So you're up, brown man. Get ready."

"All right, then. I'm delegating T-Bone to visit Pastor Wilkins. Now, you can't tell me that I can't delegate!"

"Actually, I can," J.T. said. "It says in the gang's rules that only the leader can make these kinds of meetings."

"Now you guys are making shit up. But fine, I'll do it. I say we give him fifty bucks for the use of the church."

"What!" Price said. "Are you crazy?"

"Fifty will just make sure the cops arrive on time," T-Bone said. "You better think a little higher."

"Well, what did we pay last time?" I asked.

"It depends," J.T. said, explaining that it was not uncommon for the less well-established clergy to rent out their storefront spaces to the gangs for business meetings. "Five hundred gets you the back room or the basement, but that's just one time. And the pastor stays in the building. Seven hundred fifty gets you the place to yourself. And sometimes you want to *be* by yourself, depending on what you're going to discuss."

"Yeah," Price chimed in. "If you have to beat somebody's ass, you might want to be alone."

I asked for a little time to think things over.

The four of us left the restaurant and got into J.T.'s Malibu for our next task: a meeting with Johnny, a man who owned a convenience store and no longer allowed members of the Black Kings inside. I already knew Johnny. He was a local historian of sorts who liked to regale me with stories of the 1960s and 1970s, when he was a gang leader himself. But he stressed how the gangs of that period were totally different. They were political organizations, he said, fighting police harassment and standing up for the community's right to a fair share of city services. In his view, today's gangs were mostly moneymaking outfits with little understanding of, or commitment to, the needs of Chicago's poor black population.

Johnny's store was on Forty-seventh Street, a busy commercial strip that bisected Robert Taylor. The strip was lined with liquor stores, check-cashing shops, party-supply and hardware stores, a few burned-out buildings and empty lots, a public-assistance center, two beauty salons, and a barbershop.

I wasn't very worried about meeting with Johnny until Price spoke up. "We've also got a problem with this nigger," he said, "because he's been charging us more than he charges other niggers."

"You mean he rips off only people in the Black Kings?" I asked.

"That's right," said J.T. "And this one is hard, because Johnny is T-Bone's uncle. He's also a dangerous motherfucker. He'll use a gun just like that. So you got to be careful."

"No, *you* have to be careful," I said. "I told you I won't use a gun."

"No one said *you* have to," Price offered, laughing from the back-seat. "But *he* might!"

"What exactly is it that I'm supposed to do?" I asked. "You want me to make him charge you fair prices?"

"Well, this is a tough one," J.T. said, "because we can't have people taking advantage of us, you dig? But the thing is, we provide this nigger protection."

"Protection?"

"Yeah, say somebody steals something. Then we find out who did it and we deal with it."

"So he can't tell us that we can't come in his store," Price said. "Not if we're providing him a service."

"Right," said J.T. "We have to try and remind him that he's paying us to help him, and it doesn't look good if he doesn't let us come in his store. See, what he's doing is trying to make back the money that he's paying us for protection."

Johnny was out front when we pulled up, smoking a cigarette. "What's up, Sudhir?" he said. "I see you wasting your time again, hanging around these niggers."

Johnny looked like a caricature of a disco-era hustler: bright orange pants, a polyester shirt that appeared to be highly flammable, cowboy boots with fake diamond trim, and lots of ghetto glitter—fake rubies and other stones—on his fingers. A tattoo on his arm read BLACK BITCH, and another on his chest said PENTHOUSE KINGS, which was the name of his long-ago street gang.

J.T., Price, and I followed Johnny into the back of the store while T-Bone peeled off to attend to some other business. The back room was musty and unswept. The walls were plastered with pictures of naked black women and a big poster of Walter Payton, the beloved Chicago Bears running back. The sturdy shelves and even the floor were crammed with used TV sets, stereo components, and microwaves that Johnny fixed and sold. A big wooden table held the remnants of last night's poker game: cards and chips, cigar butts, some brandy, and a ledger tallying debts. Through the open back door, a small homeless encampment was visible. J.T. had told me that Johnny paid a homeless couple fifty dollars a week to sleep outside and watch over the store.

We all sat down around the table. Johnny seemed impatient. "All right," he said, "what are we going to do?"

"Well, we were thinking more like what *you* were going to do, nigger," Price said.

"Listen, big black," Johnny said, cigarette dancing in his lips, "you can take that mouth outside if you can't say something useful."

J.T. told Price to go back to the car, leaving just me, J.T., and Johnny.

"You're paying us, Johnny," J.T. said, "and now you're *charging* us. You trying to make your money back? Is that it?"

Johnny replied in a calm monotone. "You niggers charge me two hundred and fifty dollars a month, and that shit has to stop," he said. "A man can't run a business if he has to pay that kind of money.

And your boys keep coming in here demanding free shit. I told Moochie and the rest of them that if they come in here anymore, this .22 is going to find their back." He gestured to a rifle hanging behind him on the wall.

"See now, that's the kind of talk we don't need," J.T. said. "I mean, we need to cooperate."

"Cooperate, my ass!" said Johnny. "You can cooperate with my fist."

"Whoa, whoa!" I yelled, trying to be useful. "Let's calm down now, boys. What I think we need is a little—"

"Is this Arab going to sit here all day with us?" Johnny said.

"Leave that boy alone," J.T. said. "I'll explain later." He shot me a glance, a *Shut the fuck up* glance. "Listen, you pay me two hundred dollars a month and you'll get the same shit from us." He was talking about the protection the gang afforded. "And I'll talk to Moochie and everyone else, tell them they can't steal shit. Okay?"

"Bitch, you better tell him not to bring his girlfriends up in here."

"What?"

"You heard me. He brings them bitches in here when I'm not around, showing off and taking shit off the shelves, eating candy and drinking soda like he owns the place. When my man tried to do something about it, he pulled a gun on him. Let him bring that shit on me. Try it once, I'll kill the little bitch."

"All right," J.T. said, putting his hand in front of Johnny's face to shut him up. "I told you *I'll* deal with the nigger."

"I pay you two hundred dollars and your boys get to come in here, but they have to promise to spend at least two hundred dollars a month on shit," Johnny said.

"And you're not going to jack up prices, right?" I said.

"Goddamn, Arab, you still here?" Johnny said. "Yeah, that's right, they pay what everyone else pays."

"Okay, then," I said, "we got ourselves a deal, boys!" I stood up to go.

"Boy, sit your ass down," J.T. said. "Johnny, we'll get back with you."

"Yeah, we'll get back with you," I said. "We need to deliberate." Johnny and J.T. started laughing.

"Goddamn!" Johnny shouted. "You bring this Arab with you wherever you go?"

"One day," J.T. muttered, clearly frustrated that I was taking my role a little too seriously. "One day, that's it."

We got back in the Malibu. Price drove, J.T. rode shotgun, and I sat in the back. My next duty, J.T. explained, was to settle a dispute between two gang members, Billy and Otis. Billy was the director of a six-man drug-selling crew. Otis, one of his six dealers, was claiming that Billy had underpaid him for a day's work. Billy, meanwhile, said that Otis lied about how much crack he sold and kept the extra money. My dilemma would be compounded by the fact that I already knew both Billy and Otis.

As we drove, Price explained my goal: to adjudicate the case and determine a fair punishment. "If Billy didn't pay Otis, then you have to punish Billy," he said. "The punishment for not paying one of your members would be two mouthshots, and Billy can't work for a week. And if you want, you get to make Otis the director for that week. But if Otis *stole* something, then we have a bigger problem. You have to beat the shit out of that nigger, not just hit him twice. *And* he has to work free for a month."

The thought of hitting someone in the face—delivering a "mouthshot"—made me nauseous. Growing up, I used to get picked on all the time. I was tall and athletic, but I was also a nerd, complete with pocket protector, bad haircut, and an armful of math and science books. I was a perfect target for the average football player or any other jock, especially since I played the less "manly" sports of tennis and soccer. I never even learned to throw a punch. In school most of the fights culminated with someone—most often a girl I was with—pleading for the bully to reconsider, or with me rolling up in a fetal ball, which I actually found to be quite a good strategy, since most bullies didn't want to fight someone who wouldn't fight back.

"Now, I don't mean to be picky," I said, "but isn't this why we have you here, Price? I mean, you're the security guy, no? *You* beat their ass—I mean, isn't that what you get paid for? And if I'm the leader, I can delegate, no?"

"Sudhir," J.T. said, "you have to realize that if you do that, then you lose respect. They need to see that you are the boss, which means that you hand out the beating."

"What if I make them do twenty pushups or fifty squat thrusts? Or maybe they have to clean my car."

"You don't own a car," J.T. said.

"That's right—so they have to clean *your* car for a month!"

"Listen, these guys already clean my car, wipe my ass, whatever I want, so that ain't happening," J.T. said calmly, as if wanting to make sure I understood the breadth of his power. "And if they can steal money or not pay somebody for working and they only have to clean a car, then think how much these guys will steal. You have to make sure they understand that they can't be stealing! Nigger, they need to *fear* you."

"So that's your leadership style? Fear?" I was trying to give the impression that I had my own style. Mostly, I was stalling out of worry that I'd have to throw a punch. "Fear, huh? Very interesting, very interesting."

We pulled up to the street corner where Billy and Otis had been told to meet us. It was cold, not quite noon, but the sun had broken through a bit. Aside from a nearby gas station, the corner was surrounded mostly by empty lots and abandoned buildings.

I watched Billy and Otis saunter over. Billy was about six foot six. He had been a star basketball player at Dunbar High School and won a scholarship to Southern Illinois at Carbondale, a small downstate school. He began using his connections with the Black Kings to deal marijuana and cocaine to students in his dorm. He eventually decided to quit the basketball team to sell drugs full-time. He once told me that the lure of cash "made my mouth water, and I couldn't get enough of it. Dumbest move I ever made." Now he was working in the gang to save money in hopes of returning to college.

I always liked Billy. He was one of thousands of people in this neighborhood who, by the time they turned eighteen, had made all sorts of important decisions by themselves. Fewer than 40 percent of the adults in the neighborhood had even graduated from high school, much less college, so Billy didn't have a lot of places to go for counsel. Even so, he was the first one to accept responsibility for the bad decisions he'd made. I'll never forget what he said when he moved back to the projects after dropping out of college: "I just needed someone to talk to. My mind was racing out of control, and I had no one to talk to."

I didn't want to think about hitting Billy today, because I really liked him—and because, at that height, his jaw was nearly out of reach.

Otis was a different story. He always wore dark sunglasses—even indoors, even in winter—and he kept a large knife underneath a long black jacket that he always wore, even in hot weather. He loved to cut people up and give them a scar. And he didn't like me at all.

This acrimony stemmed from a basketball game several months

earlier. I regularly attended the gang's midnight games at the Boys & Girls Club. If Autry came up one referee short, he sometimes pressed me into service. I had played basketball growing up, but not how it was played in the ghetto. In my neighborhood we set picks, passed the ball—and, perhaps most important, called fouls, even in pickup games. In the gang games, if you called even half the fouls that were actually committed, you'd run out of players by halftime. But during one game I refereed when Otis was playing, I called five quick fouls on him because . . . well, because he fouled somebody five times. He had to leave the game.

From the bench, with a cheap bottle of liquor in his hand, Otis shouted at me, "I'm going to kill you, motherfucker! I'm going to cut your balls off!" It was pretty hard to concentrate for the rest of the game.

I left the gym immediately afterward, but Otis chased me down in the parking lot. He was still in his uniform, so he didn't have his machete with him. He picked up a bottle from the asphalt, smashed it, and pressed the jagged edge to my neck. Just then Autry hustled into the parking lot, pulled Otis back, and told me to run. I stood there in shock while Autry kept yelling, "Run, nigger, run!" After about thirty seconds, he and Otis both started laughing, because my feet simply wouldn't move. They laughed so hard that they crumpled to the ground. I nearly threw up.

I was thinking of this incident now, as Otis walked toward us, and I wondered if he was, too. I got out of the car along with J.T. and Price.

"Okay, let's hear what happened," J.T. said. "I need to know who fucked up last week. Billy, you first."

J.T. seemed preoccupied, maybe a little upset. I didn't know why, and it wasn't the time to ask. It certainly didn't seem as if I had much chance of leading the conversation.

"Like I already said," Billy began, "ain't nothing to say. Otis got a hundred-pack and was a hundred dollars short. I want my money." He was stubborn and defiant.

"Nigger, please," Otis said. "You ain't paid me for a week. You *owed* me that money." Otis's eyes were bloodshot, and he looked as if he might reach out and hit Billy at any moment.

"Didn't pay?" said Billy. "You're wrong on that. I paid you, and you went out that night partying. I remember."

The director of a sales team—in this case, Billy—usually gave his street dealers an allotment of prepackaged crack. A "100-pack" was the standard. A single bag sold for ten dollars, so once the dealer exhausted his inventory, he was supposed to give his director one thousand dollars. Billy was saying that Otis had turned over just nine hundred dollars. Otis's only defense seemed to be that Billy owed him money from an earlier transaction—a charge that Billy denied. Otis and Billy kept arguing with each other, but they were looking at J.T., Price, and me, pleading their cases.

"Okay, okay!" J.T. said. "This ain't going nowhere. Get the fuck out of here. I'll be back with you later."

Billy and Otis walked away, joining the rest of their crew near some Dumpsters where they stored their drugs and money. Once they were out of earshot, J.T. turned to me: "Well, what do you think? You heard enough?"

"Yes, I did!" I said proudly. "Here's my decision: Otis clearly took the money and pocketed it. You notice that he never actually denied taking something. He just said that he was owed the money by Billy. Now, I can't tell whether Billy never paid Otis for the day's work, but the fact that Otis didn't deny stealing the money makes me feel that Billy forgot to pay Otis—or maybe he didn't want to. But all that doesn't matter, because Otis *did* steal some money. And, I bet, Billy *didn't* pay."

There was silence for about thirty seconds. Finally Price spoke up. "Hey, I like it. Not bad. That was the smartest thing you said all day!"

"Yeah," said J.T. "Now, what's the penalty?"

"Well, in this case we borrow from the NFL and invoke the offsetting-penalty rule," I said. "Both guys screwed up, so the two penalties cancel each other out. I know that Otis's crime is more serious because he stole, but both of them messed up. So no one gets hurt or pays a fine. How about that?"

More silence. Price watched J.T. for his reaction. I did the same. "Tell Otis to come over here," J.T. finally said. Price went to fetch him.

"What are you going to do?" I asked J.T. He said nothing. "C'mon, tell me." He ignored me.

Price returned with Otis.

"Wait for me over there," J.T. told me quietly, nodding toward the car.

I did as he said. I climbed into the backseat, which faced away from J.T. and the others. Still, I was close enough to hear J.T. tell Otis to put his hands behind his back. Then I heard a punch, fist hitting cheekbone, and after about ten seconds another one. Then, slowly, two more punches. I looked behind me through the back window and saw Otis, bent over, holding his face. J.T. was slowly walking back toward the car, shaking his fist. He got in, and then Price did, too.

"You can't let them steal," J.T. told me. "I liked your take on what happened. You're right, they both fucked up. Since we don't really know if Billy didn't pay, I can't beat him. But like you said, we *do* know that Otis stole something, because he didn't deny it. So I had to punish him. I let him off easy, though. I told him he only had to work free for a week."

I could hear Otis moaning in pain, like a sick cow. I asked quietly if he was okay. Neither J.T. nor Price answered. As we drove past Billy and Otis, I was the only one who looked over. Otis still had his head down, and he turned away as we passed. Billy just watched us drive by, completely expressionless.

We spent the next several hours driving around the South Side, covering the great swath of territory controlled not just by J.T.'s faction of the Black Kings but by other gangs within the BK nation.

As J.T. rose within the BKs' citywide hierarchy, part of his broader duty was to monitor several BK factions besides his own to make sure that sales proceeded smoothly and that neighboring gangs cooperated with one another. This meant that he now oversaw, directly or indirectly, several hundred members of the Black Kings.

There was a constant reshuffling and realignment of gang factions. This typically had less to do with dramatic events like a gang war and more to do with basic economics. When one local gang withered, it was usually because it was unable to supply enough crack to meet the demand or because the gang leader set his street dealers' wages too low to attract motivated workers. In such cases a gang's leadership might transfer its distribution rights to a rival gang, a sort of merger in which the original gang got a small cut of the profits and a lower rank in the merged hierarchy. If running a drug gang wasn't quite business as usual, it was nevertheless very much a business.

Today was the day that J.T. needed to visit all the four- and six-man sales teams occupying the street corners, parks, alleyways, and abandoned buildings where the Black Kings sold crack. He did this once a week. Because these visits were perhaps J.T.'s most important work, it was pretty obvious that I wasn't going to have much input.

But as J.T. drove to his first stop, he told me that I could at least tag along.

By now a second car had joined us, occupied by four junior gang members. They were J.T.'s security detail, driving ahead to each location and paging him to say it was safe from rival gangs.

As I watched J.T. question his sales teams, one after the next, I began to realize that he truly was an accomplished manager. All his members knew the drill. As soon as J.T. reached a site, the sales team's director would approach him alone and instruct his troops to stop all sales activity. One member, taking all the cash and drugs, left the area entirely so that the police couldn't link J.T. directly to the drug sales. It was unclear to me whether this was J.T.'s idea or standard practice in gangland, but when it came to avoiding the police, J.T. was meticulous.

In order to keep himself clear, he never carried a gun, drugs, or large amounts of cash. Even though he occasionally alluded to cops he knew personally, men who'd grown up with him in the neighborhood, he was always sketchy as to whether he held any real influence among the police. Whatever the case, he didn't seem all that concerned about getting arrested. In his view the police could come after him whenever they wanted, but it was in their best interest to let familiar faces run the drug businesses. "They just want to control shit," he told me, "and that's why they really only come after us maybe once in a while."

His street dealers, however, were constantly getting arrested. From a legal standpoint this was mostly a nuisance; from a business standpoint, however, it posed a disastrous disruption of J.T.'s revenue flow. If a dealer went to prison, J.T. sometimes sent money to his family, but he was also worried that the dealer might decide to give testimony to the police in exchange for a reduced sentence. J.T. was more generous when it came to dealers killed in the line of duty. He nearly always paid their families a generous cash settlement.

As he met now with each sales director, J.T. would begin by grilling him with a standard set of questions: *You losing any of your regulars?* (In other words, customers.) *Anybody complaining?* (About the quality of the crack.) *You heard of people leaving you for others?* (Customers buying crack from other dealers.) *Anybody watching you?* (The police or tenant leaders.) *Any new hustlers been hanging around?* (Homeless people or street vendors.) *You seen any niggers come around?* (Enemy gangs.)

After answering these questions, the director had to report on the sales activity over the past week: a summary of the week's receipts, any drugs that had been lost or stolen, the names of any gang members who'd been causing trouble. J.T. was most concerned with the weekly drug revenues—not just because his own salary derived from these revenues but because of the tribute tax he had to send each month to his superiors. J.T. had told me earlier that his bosses occasionally changed their tax rate, even doubling it, for no good reason (at least no good reason that J.T. was ever told about). When this happened, J.T. had to dip into his own pocket. A few months before, he'd had to contribute five thousand dollars to help build up the gang's arsenal of weapons, and he wasn't at all happy about it.

These pressures, combined with his constant fear that his junior members were planning a coup d'état, made J.T. paranoid about being ripped off. He had told me of several such coups in other neighborhoods. So he practically interrogated his sales directors, asking the same question in a variety of ways or otherwise trying to trip them up.

"So you sold fifty bags, okay, that's fine," J.T. might start.

"No, I said we sold twenty-five," the director would answer.

"No, you said fifty, I could have sworn you said fifty. Everyone else heard fifty, right?"

"No, no, no. I said twenty-five."

Invariably J.T. and the young man directing his sales team—these directors were usually in their late teens or early twenties—would go back and forth like this for several minutes, often over a trivial detail, until J.T. felt confident that he was getting the truth. On this day, as the cold afternoon stretched into night, I watched several of these young men sweat under J.T.'s questioning. Surely they all knew by now what to expect of him. But even a hint of suspicion could earn them a "violation": J.T. was quick to physically punish them or suspend their privileges—the right to carry a gun, for instance, or the right to earn money.

J.T. also asked his directors about any behavior in the past week that might have attracted the attention of the police—a dispute between a customer and a dealer, perhaps, or any gunfire. If one of his members had been suspended from high school or had drawn complaints from a tenant leader, he would have to submit to even tougher questioning from J.T.

For the directors, the worst part of this interrogation was that J.T. maintained his own independent sources. He kept a roster of informants in every neighborhood where the Black Kings operated. He had begun this practice when he first became responsible for monitoring neighborhoods that he didn't know as well as his own. While he may have been familiar with the streets and stores in these neighborhoods, he didn't know every pastor, tenant leader, police officer, and hustler as he did in his own.

Most of his informants were homeless people, squatters, or other hard-up adults. They came cheap—J.T. paid most of them just ten or fifteen dollars a day—and these ghetto nomads could easily hang out in drug areas and spy on J.T.'s gang members without raising suspicion. J.T. generally dispatched his senior officers to debrief these informants, but sometimes he met with them personally. Although they couldn't tell him if his own members were stealing from him, they were valuable for reporting problems like street fights or customer complaints.

As we drove through the neighborhood, past the blighted storefronts on Forty-seventh Street, J.T. told me that one of his sales groups was selling diluted product. The BKs' crack-selling chain began with J.T.'s senior officers buying large quantities of powder cocaine from a distributor in the outlying suburbs or a neighborhood at the city's edge. The officers usually cooked up the cocaine into crack themselves, using a vacant apartment or paying a tenant perhaps a hundred dollars a month to use her kitchen. Then the officers would deliver the prepackaged allocations to the sales directors.

Sometimes, however, the street crews were allowed to cook up the crack themselves. In such a case, J.T. explained, they might surreptitiously use an additive to stretch their cocaine allotment into more crack. They could turn each 100-pack of $10 bags into a 125-pack, which meant earning an extra $250. This money obviously wouldn't be susceptible to collection by J.T., since he could account only for 100-packs.

I was surprised that J.T. would give anyone a chance to rip him off like this. But he now had so many crews under management, with such overwhelming volume, that he occasionally farmed out the production. It was a relatively simple process: you mixed together powder cocaine with baking soda and water, then boiled off the water until all that remained were the crystallized nuggets of crack. Subcontracting the production also provided J.T. a hedge of sorts: even if the police raided one of the apartments where the crack was being processed, he wouldn't lose his entire supply of cocaine.

The sale of diluted crack troubled J.T. for reasons beyond the ob-

vious fact that his members were stealing from him. Such entrepreneurial energy could be infectious. If other factions of the gang
thought up schemes to increase their revenues, not only would J.T.
lose taxable receipts but his sales directors might feel empowered to
try to knock him off his throne. He was also concerned about the
physical dangers of diluted crack cocaine. Not long ago a teenager
in Robert Taylor had nearly died of an overdose, and rumor had it
that one of J.T.'s dealers had sold him crack that had been processed
with a dangerous additive. As a result the building president got the
police to post a twenty-four-hour patrol for two weeks, which shut
down drug sales. J.T.'s superiors nearly demoted him because of this
incident, out of concern that he couldn't control his members.

J.T.'s other worry about altered crack was a simple matter of
competitive practice: if word got out that the Black Kings were selling an inferior product, they would lose customers to other gangs.
This was what troubled him most, J.T. told me now as we drove to
meet with Michael, a twenty-year-old gang member who had recently been promoted to run a six-man sales team.

One of J.T.'s informants had told him that Michael's crew was
selling diluted product. The informant was in fact a crack addict; J.T.
had him buy the crack and turn it over to J.T., who could tell from
its color and brittle texture that the crack had indeed been stretched.

J.T. asked me what I would do if I were the gang boss and had
to deal with Michael.

"Kick him out!" I said.

J.T. explained that this decision couldn't be so straightforward.
"Most guys wouldn't even think of these ways to make money," he
said. "Here's a guy who is looking to make an extra buck. I have hundreds of people working for me, but only a few who think like that.
You don't want to lose people like that." What he needed to do, J.T.

told me, was quash Michael's tactic but not the spirit that lay at its root.

When we reached Michael, J.T. told his officers and security detail to leave him alone with Michael. He asked me to stay. We went into the alleyway behind a fast-food restaurant.

"See this?" J.T. said, holding up a tiny Ziploc bag to Michael's face. "What is it?"

"It's mine," Michael said. I had no idea how he could tell that the crack was his, and I wondered if he said so simply as a reflex.

Michael had a stoic look about him, as if he were expecting to be punished. The rest of his crew watched from perhaps ten yards away.

"Yeah, that's right, and it's half what it should be," J.T. said.

"You want us to fill it up with more than that?"

"Don't play with me, nigger. I know you been putting some shit in the product. I have the shit with me right here. How are you going to deny it?"

Michael was silent.

"I'm going to tell you what we're going to do," J.T. said. "I'm not going to put you on the spot. You're going to finish selling this, and next week you're not earning shit. Your take goes to all the other guys. And you know what? You're going to tell them, too. You're going to tell them why it's no good to make this weaker. You know why, right?"

Michael, his head down, nodded.

"Okay, then, you're going to tell them it's not right because we lose customers and then we don't have no work. And you're going to tell them that it was your idea, that you fucked up, and that as a way of dealing with it, you want them to have the money you would have made."

Michael was by now visibly upset, his face set in a sort of angry mope. Finally he looked up, groaned, shook his head, glanced away, kicked a few stones on the ground. It seemed as if he wanted to challenge J.T., but he had obviously been caught. So he said nothing. After a while J.T. called over the other members of Michael's group and finished obtaining his weekly report.

It had been dark for a few hours now. My stint as gang leader for a day—albeit in a very limited capacity—was finally over. It was both more banal and more dramatic than I could have envisioned. I was exhausted. My head was spinning with details, settled and unsettled. I never did manage to decide how much the Black Kings should pay Pastor Wilkins for the use of his church.

I had accompanied J.T. on site visits to roughly twenty Black Kings sales teams. Two sales directors had been taken off to a secluded area and given mouthshots for their transgressions. Another one, who had failed to make his weekly payment to J.T., was levied a 10 percent fine and a 50 percent deduction of his next week's pay. But J.T. used the carrot as well as the stick. The workers in one group who had done particularly well were allowed to carry guns over the weekend. (J.T. usually didn't let his members walk around armed unless there was a war going on; he also required that members buy guns directly from the gang.) And he gave a $250 bonus to the members of another group that had several weeks of above-average sales.

There seemed to be no end to the problems that J.T. encountered during this weekly reconnaissance, problems he'd have to fix before they spun out of control. There were several incidents of customers fighting in public with a BK member who sold them drugs; in each case the customer complained that the bag of crack was too small or that the product was not of suitable quality. A store owner reported to J.T. that several gang members demanded he give *them* his monthly "protection" payment; this couldn't have been a legitimate request, since J.T. allowed only his senior officers to pick up extortion receipts. A pastor called the police on one of J.T.'s members who used the church parking lot to receive oral sex (in lieu of cash payment) from a local drug user. And two gang members had been suspended from school for fighting, one of them for having a gun in his locker.

The next day I would wake up free of the hundreds of obligations and judgments I'd been witness to. But J.T. wouldn't. He'd still bear all the burdens of running a successful underground economy: enforcing contracts, motivating his members to risk their lives for low wages, dealing with capricious bosses. I was no less critical of what he did for a living. I also wanted to know more about his professed benevolence and how his gang acted on behalf of Robert Taylor's tenants. And I still knew very little about J.T.'s bosses.

But all that would take some time. My next set of answers about life in Robert Taylor came from the *second*-most-powerful force in my orbit, the woman known to one and all as Ms. Bailey.

FIVE

Ms. Bailey's Neighborhood

I ran into Ms. Bailey pretty regularly. Sometimes she accompanied J.T. as he made his rounds of the building; sometimes I'd see her with a police officer or a CHA official. She always said hello and politely introduced me to whomever she was with. But I didn't really know what she did or how she did it. Although she was present at the backroom gang negotiation I witnessed at the Boys & Girls Club, she hadn't gotten very involved. So I was curious to learn more about her.

Specifically, I wanted to know why residents spoke of her with a mixture of reverence and fear, much as they spoke of J.T. "Oh, you don't want to mess with Ms. Bailey," they'd say. Or, "Yeah, Ms. Bailey can tell you a lot about what's happening, but make sure you have five dollars with you." Even J.T., who agreed that I should spend some time with Ms. Bailey, vaguely hinted that I ought to be careful around her.

Part of my motivation to observe Ms. Bailey came from my advisers at the University of Chicago. Jean Comaroff, an accomplished ethnographer, said that I was spending too much time with men. Since two-thirds of the community were women raising children, she suggested that I try to better understand how women managed households, secured services from the CHA, and otherwise helped families get by. Bill Wilson told me that poverty scholars knew little about the role women played in community affairs, and he encouraged me to spend time with household leaders like Ms. Mae but also tenant leaders like Ms. Bailey. Wilson and Comaroff both advised me to exercise the same sort of caution with Ms. Bailey as I would with other powerful people, never taking what they told me at face value.

Ms. Bailey was of average height and stout. Because of arthritis in her knees, she walked slowly, but always looking straight ahead with great focus, like Washington crossing the Delaware. She had a tattoo on her right arm that read MO-JO—the nickname, Ms. Mae told me, of a son who'd passed away. Ms. Bailey had pudgy fingers and, when she shook your hand, the tightest grip I've ever felt.

Her title was building president of the Local Advisory Council (LAC). This was an elected position that paid a part-time wage of a few hundred dollars a month. The official duties of a building president included lobbying the CHA for better building maintenance, obtaining funds for tenant activities, and so on. Elections were held every four years, and incumbents were rarely deposed. Some LAC presidents were much more powerful than others, and from what I'd heard, Ms. Bailey was on the upper end of the power scale. She had actually fought for the creation of the LAC many years ago, and she kept her fighting spirit. I'd heard stories about Ms. Bailey getting medical clinics to give free checkups to the children in her building and local stores to donate food.

I witnessed this fighting spirit firsthand when I visited her small, decrepit office one day. I wanted to explain why I'd been hanging around her building and also explain my research. I began by discussing the prevailing academic wisdom about urban poverty and the factors that contributed to it.

"You planning on talking with white people in your study?" she snapped, waving her hand at me as if she'd heard my spiel a hundred times already.

I was confused. "This is a study of the Robert Taylor Homes, and I suppose that most of the people I'll be talking to are black. Unless there are whites who live here that I'm not aware of."

"If I gave you only *one* piece of bread to eat each day and asked why you're starving, what would you say?"

I was thrown off by this seeming non sequitur. I thought for a minute. "I guess I would say I'm starving because I'm not eating enough," I answered.

"You got a lot to learn, Mr. Professor," she said. "Again, *if I gave you* one piece of bread to eat each day and asked why you're starving, what would you say?"

I was getting even more confused. I took a chance. "Because you're not feeding me?"

"Yes! Very good!"

I felt relieved. I hoped no more tests were coming my way, but Ms. Bailey kept going. "Let's say I took away your house key and you had to sleep outside," she said. "A man from the city comes over and counts you as 'homeless.' What would you say?"

"Umm." This one seemed even harder. "I'd say you're wrong. I *have* a place to stay, so . . . no! I'm not homeless!" I thought I had nailed this one.

But she looked exasperated at my answer. "Wow, have you ever had to do *anything* for yourself?" she said.

I was at least smart enough to know that she wasn't literally asking me to reply.

"*If I took your house key away,*" she barked, "what does that make you?" She leaned across the desk, and I could feel her breath on my face.

"Well, I guess you robbed me. So I'm not homeless, I'm a victim."

"Okay, we're getting somewhere. Now let's say I tell the police to stop coming to *your* block and to go only where *I* live. And then I write that you live in a crime-infested neighborhood, that there's more crime on your block than mine. What would you say?"

"Well, I guess I'd say that it's not really fair because you have all the police, so—"

"Mr. Professor, we're really getting moving now!" Ms. Bailey threw up her hands in mock celebration. "Okay, so let's go back to the original question. You want to understand how black folks live in the projects. Why we are poor. Why we have so much crime. Why we can't feed our families. Why our kids can't get work when they grow up. So will you be studying white people?"

"Yes," I said. I understood, finally, that she also wanted me to focus on the people outside Robert Taylor who determined how the tenants lived day to day.

"But don't make us the victim," she said. "We'll take responsibility for what we can control. It's just that not everything is in our hands."

Our subsequent meetings were much the same. I would walk in to discuss an issue—the 60 percent dropout rate, for instance, among the project's high-school kids. "Research today says that if kids can get through high school, they have a twenty-five percent greater likelihood of escaping poverty," I said, as if giving a lecture. "So *early* education—keeping them in school—is the key. Also—"

Ms. Bailey interrupted. "If your family is starving and I tell you that I'll give you a chance to make some money, what are you going to do?"

"Make the money. I have to help my family."

"But what about school?" she said.

"I guess it will have to wait."

"Until what?"

"Until my family gets enough to eat."

"But you should stay in school, right?" she said, sarcasm rising in her voice. "That's what will help you leave poverty." She paused. Then she smiled triumphantly and made no effort to hide her patronizing tone. "So . . . you said you wanted to talk with me about high-school dropouts?"

It took a while, but I eventually realized there was no point in trying to act even remotely authoritative around Ms. Bailey. There was part of me that felt like the expert researcher, but only a very small part. Once I learned that there was no way around Ms. Bailey's Socratic browbeating, I decided to give in and just let her teach me.

I usually dropped by her office during the hours she reserved for open visitation from tenants; otherwise it could be hard to track her down. When a tenant came by, Ms. Bailey would ask me to step out. Our longest conversations, therefore, rarely lasted beyond fifteen minutes. Ms. Bailey remained formal with me, as if she were keeping her guard up. She never shared details about specific tenants; instead she spoke in generalities about "families who live around here."

After a few months of this, I told J.T. that I was frustrated by my interactions with Ms. Bailey. I couldn't tell if she trusted me.

J.T. enjoyed seeing me struggle. He had warned me that getting to know her wouldn't be easy and perhaps wasn't even worth trying. "It took a while before I let you talk with my boys," he said.

"What makes you think she'll just walk you around and show you everybody? Things don't go so fast around here."

He had a point. If Ms. Bailey needed time to feel comfortable with me, then I would just have to wait.

As the Chicago winter began to settle in, Ms. Bailey asked me to help her with a clothing drive. Tenants and squatters in her building needed winter coats, she said, as well as blankets and portable heaters. She wanted me to collect donations with her from several stores that had agreed to contribute.

A friend of mine let me borrow his car, a battered yellow and brown station wagon. When I went to collect Ms. Bailey at her building, she was carrying a large plastic bag. She grunted as she bent over to pick it up and again as she set it down on the floor of the car. With labored breaths, she directed me to our first stop: a liquor store a few blocks from her building.

She instructed me to drive around the back. She told me she didn't want the manager to see me, but she didn't explain why.

I parked in the alley as Ms. Bailey went inside. Five minutes later a few employees came out the back door and began loading the station wagon with cases of beer and bottles of liquor. Nothing expressly for winter, I noted, although a stiff bourbon could certainly help take the sting off the Chicago cold. Ms. Bailey climbed into the car. This donation, she told me, was made with the understanding that she would direct her tenants to visit this liquor store exclusively when they needed booze.

We drove a few miles to a grocery store on Stony Island Avenue. We went in the back way and met with a man who appeared to be the manager.

"Hey, sweetheart," Ms. Bailey said. She introduced me to Mr.

Baldwin, a large, pear-shaped black man with a round face and a wide grin. He had a clipboard in his hand, marking off the sides of beef hanging from a ceiling rack.

Mr. Baldwin gave Ms. Bailey a hug. "I got what you want, babe," he said. "All in the back. I got them ready for you yesterday."

He pointed us toward a younger man, who led us over to a few big garbage bags filled with puffy black jackets. At first glance they looked exactly like the jacket the young man was wearing, which had the name of the grocery store prominently displayed on the sleeves and chest. *Were* they the same jackets? I wondered if Ms. Bailey's tenants would wear clothing with a grocery store's name on it.

As I hauled the bags to the car, Ms. Bailey shouted at me. "And bring three cases of beer in here, Sudhir!"

I did as I was told. Even I, middle-class naïf that I was, could sense a horse trade.

Back in the car, Ms. Bailey anticipated my question. "I know you're wondering what we were doing at the food store," she said. "Take a look at the jackets." I reached into the backseat and grabbed one. It smelled distinctly of bleach, as if it had been disinfected. The store's patch had been either removed or covered up with another, even larger patch. It read ROBERT TAYLOR PRIDE.

Ms. Bailey smiled. "Those jackets are warmer than what most families can buy in the stores. These workers are sitting in a meat locker all day, so you know they have to stay warm. The manager donates about twenty to me each Christmas."

"And the patches?" I asked.

"The guy who makes the jackets for him does it for free—for us."

"And the beer?"

Ms. Bailey just smiled and told me where to drive next.

We hit several more stores that day. At Sears, Ms. Bailey exchanged pleasantries with the manager, and they asked about each other's families. Then he handed over a few boxes of children's coats; Ms. Bailey directed me to put the rest of the beer in his car. At a dollar store, Ms. Bailey traded some of the liquor for a bundle of blankets. At a hardware store, Ms. Bailey gave the manager the heavy plastic bag she'd brought along, and he gave her three portable heaters.

"Don't ask what's in the bag," she told me as I carried the heaters back to the car. "When I know you better, I'll tell you."

Only once did Ms. Bailey receive a donation that was actually a donation—that is, something for free. At one grocery store, she got some canned food without having to exchange any beer or liquor.

By the time we finished, we were on the far southern edge of the city. We hit traffic on the drive back to Robert Taylor, which gave me the opportunity to pepper Ms. Bailey with questions.

"When did you start doing this?" I asked.

Ms. Bailey told me that she had grown up in public housing herself. Back then, charities, churches, city agencies, and individual volunteers all helped out in the projects. "But the volunteers don't come around anymore," she said wistfully. "Have you seen any of those nice white people since you've been around? I didn't think so. Nobody gives us money, nobody runs programs. Not a lot of people are doing the free-food thing anymore. Even the churches really don't do what they did in the past."

"But I don't understand why the people we saw today want to give you things. I mean, how did you get to know them?"

"Well, first of all, most of them grew up in Robert Taylor or they have family in the projects. Lots of middle-class people don't like to talk about it, but they came from the projects. It's easy to forget where you came from. But I try and remind these people that they were once like us. And a few times a year, they do the right thing."

"So why give them beer and liquor?" I asked. "If it's a donation, it should be for free, no?"

"Well, things ain't always that simple," Ms. Bailey said. She brought up the incident I'd seen some months back, when the woman named Boo-Boo wanted to kill the Middle Eastern shopkeeper who'd slept with her teenage daughter. "That's what a *lot* of women have to do around here to get some free food," she said. "I don't want to see it come to that. So if I have to give away a few bottles of gin, that's fine with me."

Back at her office, Ms. Bailey organized the winter gear and prepared large baskets filled with canned food and meat. Word spread quickly, and families from her building soon began to drop by. Some were shy, others excited. But everyone seemed happy, and I watched as children smiled when they tried on a new coat or a warm sweater.

I noticed that some people received food but no clothing. Others got a jacket but no food. And some people just stood around until Ms. Bailey told them, "We don't have anything for you today." She said this even though the food baskets and clothing were in plain view, so I didn't know why she was withholding the gifts from them. Did she play favorites with some families?

One day Clarisse, the prostitute, walked into Ms. Bailey's office. There were several women already in front of her. Ms. Bailey's assistant, Catrina, was writing their names and noting exactly what each of them received.

"You got something for me today?" Clarisse asked, a lilt in her voice. Then her eyes landed on me briefly, but I didn't seem to register. She smelled like liquor; her blouse was undone so that one of her breasts was nearly popping out. Despite the cold weather, Clarisse was wearing a black miniskirt and sliding around perilously on high heels. Her face looked vacant, and her mouth was frothy. I had never seen her in this condition before. She had told me herself that she didn't do drugs.

"You're messed up," Catrina said, peering over her thick glasses. "You need to shower."

Ms. Bailey was in the next room, speaking with a tenant. "Ms. Bailey, look who's here!" Catrina called out. "Ms. Bailey, you need to tell her to get out of the office!" Catrina turned back to Clarisse and shot her a disapproving look.

Ms. Bailey came out and told Catrina to calm down. Then she motioned for Clarisse to come inside. As she closed the door, she rolled her eyes at me and sighed. I couldn't make out the whole conversation—it was unclear, in fact, if Clarisse was talking at all—but some of Ms. Bailey's proclamations were plainly audible.

"Get yourself clean or you ain't getting nothing! . . . Don't embarrass yourself, coming in here high on that shit! . . . You call yourself a mother? You ain't no mother. You *could* be one, if you stopped smoking that junk!"

The door opened, and Clarisse stumbled out, tears in her eyes. She dropped her purse and then, as she stopped to pick it up, tripped and fell, ramming into the pile of donation baskets. As she tried getting up, Clarisse vomited, some of it landing on the baskets.

Catrina and I jumped over to help her. Both of us slipped on the vomit. A strong wind blew in from outside, and the smell filled the room. Clarisse resisted our help, but she couldn't manage to get up by herself. Her pretty face had turned pale and pasty.

"Grab her and get her out of here!" Catrina yelled. She had to say this two more times before I realized that she was talking to me. "Sudhir! Grab her and take her home. Now!"

I tried being delicate with Clarisse. She was falling out of her clothes, and I didn't quite know how to touch her. She began throwing up again, and this time it landed on my arm.

"Sudhir!" Catrina yelled.

Clarisse was on all fours by now. She was drooling and heaving, but nothing came out. This time I wrapped my arms around her stomach and yanked her up. I figured I'd better get her out of the office even if I had to drag her.

"That bitch don't want me to feed my babies," Clarisse moaned. "I need food to feed my babies!" She started looking around frantically—for her purse, I realized.

"Clarisse, just a few more feet," I said. "I'll get your bag, don't worry. But let's get you out of the office."

"My bag!" she wailed. "My bag, I need my bag!"

She started kicking and flailing, trying to make her way back inside the office. With one last effort, I heaved her upright, causing us both to stumble and slam against the gallery's chain-link fencing. She sank back to the floor. I hoped I hadn't hurt her, but I couldn't tell.

As I turned to retrieve her purse, I saw Ms. Bailey, standing in the doorway. She held the purse in her hands.

"Is this what she wants?" Ms. Bailey asked. "Is it?!" I nodded. "Look inside. You want to help this lady, then look and see why she wants her bag."

I shook my head, staring at the floor.

"Look!" Ms. Bailey snapped at me. She strode over and held the bag up to my face. I saw a few condoms, some lipsticks, pictures of her daughters, and a few bags of either heroin or cocaine.

"Have to have that fix, don't you, baby?" Ms. Bailey asked Clarisse, sneering. We all stood there for what felt like an hour but was probably only a few seconds. Catrina tried to interrupt, but Ms. Bailey waved her off.

"Go ahead, Sudhir, take her home," Ms. Bailey said. She bent over to stare down at Clarisse. "If I see your babies coming over and telling me that they ain't eaten no food in three days, I'm taking them away. You hear?"

Ms. Bailey turned and left. Catrina, with a disinterested look, handed me some paper towels. I bent down to wipe the vomit and tears from Clarisse's face. She didn't resist this time when I helped her up.

I walked Clarisse upstairs to her apartment and led her to the couch. The apartment was dark, and I figured it would be best to let her sleep. In a back room, her two daughters were sitting on a queen-size bed. They looked to be about two and four years old and were watching the TV intently. I closed the door to their room and put a glass of water on the table next to Clarisse. The scene was a study in contrasts. The apartment was neat and cozy, with wall hangings and framed pictures throughout, some of Jesus Christ and some of family members. It smelled as if it had just been cleaned. And then there was Clarisse on the couch, breathing heavily, eyelids drooping, a total mess.

When I had first met her, on the gallery outside J.T.'s apartment, Clarisse had set herself apart from other prostitutes—the "hypes and rock stars"—who sold sex for drugs. Plainly, she had lied to me about not using drugs; I guess she'd wanted to make a decent impression. At this moment I wasn't too concerned about her lies. She needed help, after all. But it was pretty clear that I had to be careful about blindly accepting what people told me.

I sat on a recliner next to the couch. "I'm afraid to leave you here alone," I said. In the dim light, I couldn't really make out her facial expression. But she was breathing heavily, as if she'd just gone through battle. "Let me call an ambulance."

"I'm okay. I just need it to wear off."

"What about the kids? Have they eaten?"

"Ms. Bailey wouldn't give us nothing," she whimpered, a stage past crying. "Why she treat me like that? Why she treat me like that?"

I felt a sudden urge to make sure her kids were fed. I went into the bedroom, asked them to grab their jackets, and walked them over to a local sandwich shop. I bought them cheeseburgers, chips, and soda, and on the way home we stopped at a small grocery store. I had only fifteen dollars with me, but I told the owner, a Middle Eastern man, that the family hadn't eaten in a while. He shook his head—as if he'd heard this story a million times—and instructed me to get what I needed and just take it with me. When I told Clarisse's girls that we were going to fill up a shopping cart, they looked like I'd just given them free passes to Disney World. While they grabbed candy, I tried to sneak in a few cans of spaghetti—alas, one of the most nutritious items on the shelves—and some milk, cereal, and frozen dinners. When we got back, Clarisse was asleep. I put the food away, broke out a few Ring Dings for the kids, and put them in front of the TV again. They fixed on the cartoon images as if they'd never been gone. Since Clarisse was still sleeping, I left.

Two days later I returned to the building. Walking through the crowded lobby, nodding at the people I knew, I felt someone grab my arm and pull me into a corner. It was Ms. Bailey.

"You're sweet, you're young, you're good-looking, and these women will take advantage of you," she said. "Be careful when you help them."

"Her kids hadn't eaten," I said. "What could I do?"

"Her kids ate at my place *that morning*!" Ms. Bailey said. She tightened her grip on my arm and moved in even closer. "*I* make sure they eat. *No* children go hungry in my building. No, sir." She tightened her grip even further, and it hurt. "These women need to do the right thing if they have a baby. You remember that if you have a child someday."

"I will."

"Mm-hmm, we'll see about that. For now, be careful when you help the women. They'll take advantage of you, and you won't know what hit you. And I can't be there to protect you." I wasn't sure exactly what Ms. Bailey meant.

I nodded anyway, mostly so Ms. Bailey would loosen her grip. When she finally let go, I walked up to J.T.'s apartment to wait for him. It was the second time I'd been warned that I couldn't be "protected." First J.T. and now Ms. Bailey. I decided not to tell anyone, including J.T., about the conversation I'd just had with Ms. Bailey. In fact, the conversation had put me so out of sorts that by the time I got upstairs, I told Ms. Mae I had some schoolwork to do and had to get going. She fixed me a plate of food for the bus ride home.

A few weeks later, Ms. Bailey invited me to the building's monthly meeting. It was open to all tenants and posed one of the few opportunities for people to publicly voice their problems.

There were about 150 tenant families in Ms. Bailey's building. That included perhaps six hundred people living there legally and another four hundred living off the books. These were either boarders who paid rent to the leaseholders or husbands and boyfriends who kept their names off the leases so the women qualified for welfare. There were likely another few hundred squatters or people living temporarily with friends, but they were unlikely to attend a tenant meeting.

Ms. Bailey didn't seem all that enthusiastic about these meetings, but she let me know that she well understood their symbolic value. "They need to see that something is going on," she said, "even if nothing is going on."

The meeting was held in Ms. Bailey's office on a Saturday afternoon in December. Although it wasn't very cold outside, the radiator was at full blast and the windows were closed. Ms. Bailey entered the steaming room and calmly walked past the few dozen people assembled on folding chairs, parking herself up front. She always sat down in the same awkward way. Because she was so heavyset, and because she had arthritis in her legs, she usually had to grab someone or something to help ease herself into a chair.

I was surprised at the small turnout. The attendees were mostly women and mostly in their mid-fifties like Ms. Bailey. There were, however, a few younger women with children and a few men as well.

Ms. Bailey deliberately arranged a sheaf of papers in front of her. She motioned for a young woman to open up the window, but it wouldn't budge.

"Okay, this meeting is in session," Ms. Bailey said.

A well-dressed man toward the back of the room immediately jumped up. "I thought you said you'd talk with those boys!" he said. "They're still hanging out there, making all that damn noise. I can't get no sleep."

I assumed he was talking about the parties the Black Kings threw inside and outside the building.

"Did you make a note of that, Millie?" Ms. Bailey asked an old woman to her left. She was the official LAC recording secretary. Millie nodded while scribbling away.

"Okay," Ms. Bailey said, "go on, young man."

"Go on? I've *been* going on. I'm *tired* of going on. Each time I *come* here, I go on. I'm tired of it. Can you do something?"

"You got that, Millie?" Ms. Bailey asked, looking over the rims of her glasses.

"Mm-hmm," Millie answered. "He's tired of it, he's been going on, and he wants you to do something."

"You can probably leave out the tired part," Ms. Bailey said in a serious tone.

"Yes, okay," Millie said, scratching away in her notes.

"Will there be anything else, young man?" Ms. Bailey asked. He didn't say anything. "Okay, then, I'm figuring you don't want to talk about the fact that you're living here illegally. Is that right? Now, who's next? Nobody? Okay, then, we have some *serious* business to discuss. Before I take questions, let me tell you that Pride will be here on Tuesday registering all of you to vote. Please make sure to show up. It's very important we have a good turnout for them."

Pride was the organization I'd come across earlier, made up of ex–gang members and devoted to gang truces and voter registration. Ms. Bailey had already told me that she worked closely with them.

"What are we voting for?" asked a young woman in the front row.

"We're not actually voting, sweetheart. You need to register first. If you're already registered, you don't need to come. But I want every apartment in this building registered."

"Ain't you even a little bit concerned that we're just helping J.T. and the rest of them?" an older woman asked. "I mean, they're the only ones who seem to be getting something out of this."

"You want these boys to turn themselves around?" Ms. Bailey answered. "Then you got to take them seriously when they try to do right. It's better than them shooting each other."

"The voting hasn't done a damn thing for us!" someone cried out. "So why are you so accepting of what they're doing?" A chorus of "oohs" followed the question.

Ms. Bailey shushed the crowd. "Excuse me, Ms. Cartwright," she said. "If you're suggesting that I may be benefiting in any way by the voting stuff going on, you can just come out and say it."

"I'm not saying you *may* be benefiting," Ms. Cartwright said. "I'm saying you *are* benefiting. You get that new TV on your own, Ms. Bailey?"

This produced some more "oohs" and a round of outright giggling.

"Let me remind you," Ms. Bailey yelled, trying to reestablish order, "that we ain't had no harassment, no shooting, no killing for six months. And that's because these young men are getting right. So you can help them or you can just sit and moan. And about my TV. Who was the one that give you fifty bucks for your new fridge? And you, Ms. Elder, how exactly did you get that new mattress?"

No one answered.

"That's what I thought. You-all can keep up the bitchin' or you can realize that every one of us is benefiting from me helping these young men."

The rest of the meeting was similarly animated and followed this same pattern. Tenants accused Ms. Bailey of going easy on J.T.'s gang and personally benefiting from her alliance with them. She replied that her job was to help the tenants, period, and if that meant finding creative solutions to a multitude of problems, then she needed to be allowed such flexibility. To nearly every resident who complained, Ms. Bailey could cite an instance of giving money to that person for rent, for a utility bill, or to buy food or furniture. She plainly knew how to play the influence game. I'd been to her apartment a few times and, although she never let me stay for long, it was a testament to her skills: There were photos of her with political officials, several new refrigerators from the CHA, and cases of donated food and liquor. One bedroom was practically overrun with stacks of small appliances that she would give to tenants in her favor.

At one point during the meeting, Ms. Bailey mentioned the "donations" that she regularly procured from the gang, to be applied to various tenants' causes. J.T. had repeatedly told me that he had to keep Ms. Bailey happy—having his junior members carry out her orders, for instance, and paying her each month for the right to sell drugs in the lobby. But this was the first time I ever heard Ms. Bailey admit to this largesse. In fact, she discussed it with a measure of pride, highlighting her ability to put the gang's ill-gotten gains to good use. Although none of the tenants said so, I also knew from J.T. that some of *them* received payoffs from the gang—in exchange for their silence or for allowing the gang to stash drugs, cash, or weapons in their apartments. For a poor family, it was hard to turn down the gang's money.

"Why are we even talking about J.T.?" asked an older man. "Why don't we just go to the police? Can you tell me what you get from taking their help—or their money?"

"You-all want this place clean," Ms. Bailey said. "You want this place safe. You want this and that. And you want it right away. Well, the CHA ain't doing nothing. So I have to find ways to take care of it."

"But we can't walk around safely," the man said. "My car got the windows shot out last year."

"Right," Ms. Bailey countered. "That was *last* year, and sometimes that happens. But you see this place getting cleaned up. You see people getting rides to the store. Who do you think is doing that? Before you go yelling at J.T. and the rest of them, you better understand that they're family, too. And they're *helping*—which is more than I can say for you."

That a tenant leader—one who was respected by politicians,

shop owners, the police, and others—would praise a crack gang and work so closely with *its* leader made me realize just how desperate people could become in the projects. But I was learning that Ms. Bailey's compromising position also arose out of her own personal ambitions: in order to retain her authority, she had to collaborate with the other power groups, in this case the gangs, who helped shape the status quo. This resulted in the bizarre spectacle of Ms. Bailey's publicly defending the very people who were shooting and causing trouble for her tenant families. Even though it was obvious that tenant leaders had few good choices, I still wasn't convinced that they needed to operate in such murky ethical waters. Nevertheless I found myself wondering how much Ms. Bailey's actions were actually a response to hardships that limited her options and how much arose from her own desire to have power.

As the meeting broke up, people approached Ms. Bailey for one-on-one conversations. They all had their grievances: no hot water or a broken sink, a child getting in trouble, prostitutes taking clients into the stairwell, crack addicts partying the whole night.

Afterward Ms. Bailey motioned me into her office. Catrina was looking over some notes she'd taken at the meeting. Ms. Bailey asked her to get together with Millie, the LAC secretary, to prepare a list of tenant concerns to pass along to the CHA.

Ms. Bailey opened a small refrigerator and took out sodas for all of us. Grabbing a small blue rag, she wiped her sweaty forehead. "Did that live up to your expectations?" she asked me with a wink.

"Well, I thought you were just going to make a few announcements!" I said, laughing. "What do you do with everything you heard? I mean, a lot of it was directed at you. They were saying some pretty harsh things."

"We tell the CHA that things ain't working in the building, and we try to get them to fix it. That's it."

"And do you tell them about residents accusing you of taking gang money?"

"We tell the CHA that things ain't working in the building, and we try to get them to fix it."

She smiled cunningly and looked over to Catrina, who returned the dutiful glance of an ever-loyal junior officer.

"Sudhir, you have to remember something," Ms. Bailey continued. "In the projects it's more important that you take care of the problem first. Then you worry about *how* you took care of the problem." I opened my mouth to object, but she stopped me. "If no one dies, then all the complaining don't mean nothing, because I'm doing my job. If all I got to worry about is a few people wondering where the money's coming from, then around here that's a good day! No one dies, no one gets hurt, I'm doing my job."

"That's an awful way to live," I blurted out.

"Now you're starting to understand," she said in a tone somewhere between pedantic and patronizing. "Maybe you're even starting to learn."

Someone knocked on the door, and Ms. Bailey got up to answer it. Catrina leaned in toward me. "Watch how she helps people," she whispered. "She says it don't matter, but she's amazing. Have you seen how she gets apartments fixed around here?"

I told her that I hadn't.

"Have you seen how she helps women around here?" Catrina pushed her glasses up the bridge of her nose and kept her voice low. I felt as if we were in high school and I was sneaking a conversation with the teacher's pet.

"Well, Ms. Bailey gives away food to the mothers, right?" I whispered back.

Catrina shook her head and inhaled deeply, looking disappointed in me. "That's not what I'm talking about. You watch what she does when she helps women. Pay attention to *that*." Her voice was insistent, but she offered no more details. "She is *the* most amazing person I know."

As I spent more time with Ms. Bailey over the coming months, I found that most tenants were less suspicious of me than they'd been in the past. Sometimes, when a tenant came into Ms. Bailey's office to talk about a problem, the tenant would say, "It's okay, I don't mind if Sudhir listens."

Like J.T., Ms. Bailey seemed to enjoy the fact that I was interested in her. Perhaps she, too, thought I was going to be her personal biographer. I could see why she might make this assumption. I took every opportunity to express my fascination for her life, which seemed more fascinating the more I hung around.

One cold winter morning, I sat in Ms. Bailey's office with Catrina. It was a slow day, and only a few tenants visited. Ms. Bailey asked if I would go out and get her some coffee, and Catrina came with me. We bundled up and trudged through eight inches of fresh snow. The wind was nearly strong enough to blow you over; it was too cold for even a conversation. Catrina and I just concentrated on stepping in the footprints of people who'd made a first pass in the snow. Catrina wondered aloud what kind of God would make the earth so cold.

As we slogged our way back to the building, coffee and doughnuts in hand, a young woman hurried over to us as best as she could. "Catrina, you got to come quick," she said. "Ms. Bailey ran upstairs to Taneesha's apartment. She said you have to call Officer Reggie."

Catrina shoved the coffee at me and ran off as fast as possible under the circumstances. Since tenants had a tough time getting the police to respond, Ms. Bailey summoned Officer Reggie, the cop who'd grown up in Robert Taylor, when the situation warranted.

"Where's Taneesha live?" I yelled.

The young woman who'd summoned Catrina shouted back over her shoulder, "Twelve-oh-four!"

Approaching the building, I encountered a couple of J.T.'s gang members. They wore brown work boots and thick down jackets with the Oakland Raiders' distinctive silver-and-black insignia. To me it seemed too cold for business, but I could see a steady stream of cars coming down the alley to buy drugs. White and black addicts jumped out of their cars and ran into the lobby to buy crack. As I walked inside, one of J.T.'s men shouted to me, "They're up on the twelfth. Elevator's broken."

The stairwells were brutally cold. I had to stop a few times to catch my breath. I came across quite a few other people, all of them upset by the broken elevators. "Merry fucking Christmas," one said to me bitterly as he passed by with a heavy laundry bag.

As I stepped into the gallery on the twelfth floor, I saw a group of men standing outside Apartment 1204. I recognized C-Note and a few other squatters among them. They were all moving about, trying to keep warm, some of them jumping up and down. The gallery floor was concrete, so even if you were wearing thick-soled shoes, the cold still shot up your legs.

The door of 1204 was partially open. Ms. Bailey stood over the sofa and, when she caught sight of me, beckoned me inside. I had met Taneesha a few times, most recently at her twenty-first birthday party, which J.T. had thrown. She was tall and very pretty, with long, straight black hair, and she was trying to make a career as a model. She currently modeled clothes at various nightclubs—so-called lingerie parties—and also went to college at night. She had a baby boy,

Justin, named for her favorite high-school teacher, who had encouraged her to pursue modeling.

Everyone suspected that J.T. was the baby's father. He had told me never to ask him about the baby.

The light in her apartment was dim, but bright enough to show that her face was beaten badly and her white T-shirt was stained with blood. Her breathing was labored, her eyes closed; you could hear the blood gurgling in her mouth. Another young woman held her hand and comforted her. "They're coming," she said, "the ambulance is coming. Just relax, 'Neesha."

Ms. Bailey pulled me aside and asked if I would drive Taneesha to the hospital.

"I don't have a car, Ms. Bailey," I said. "Didn't you call the ambulance?"

"Okay, then, do me a favor," she said. "Ask C-Note to tell the boys in the lobby to take her."

"What about the ambulance?"

"Oh, no, baby," Ms. Bailey said softly. "They never come."

I wasn't sure whether to believe her, but at least fifteen minutes had passed since I'd arrived and there was no ambulance. Provident Hospital was only two miles away.

I walked out to the gallery and told C-Note, who simply leaned over and yelled down to the street twelve floors below. "Cheetah! Yo, Cheetah! Ms. Bailey says bring the car 'round! You got to take her to the hospital!"

"C-Note!" Ms. Bailey shouted out. "Don't yell! He's still in the building. Damn, we can't have him leaving the building."

I was confused. *Whom didn't she want to leave the building?* Before I could ask, she rounded up the men and addressed them as if she were a general and they, however ragged, were her troops. "She got hurt pretty bad. She'll make it, but she don't look so good. I need you-all to find him. He goes by 'Bee-Bee.' He may be in 407, inside that vacant apartment, or at his cousin's. I want to see him before you do anything to him."

I figured out that the man who had beat up Taneesha was hiding in the building.

"What if he starts to run or gets crazy?" one of the men asked. "Can we get him then?"

"Yeah, I suppose, but don't hurt him too bad before I talk to the fool. And *don't* let him get away. Sudhir, could you call J.T.?"

I nodded and followed C-Note and the others as they made for the stairwell. I recognized most of them as squatters who helped C-Note fix cars in the warmer months.

As soon as we were out of Ms. Bailey's earshot, I told C-Note I wanted to come with him.

"Call J.T.," he said, shaking his head. "Don't mess around with this. Do what Ms. Bailey says, *boy.*"

C-Note had called me "boy" only a few times, the last one when a friend of his was caught in a knife fight and C-Note instructed me to watch from inside a car, where I couldn't get hurt.

"I will, I will," I insisted. "But I want to go."

C-Note realized I wouldn't take no for an answer. "Just stay near me," he said. "But if shit gets crazy and I tell you to leave, you go, right? You hear me?"

Eight of us made our way down the stairwell, our breath leaving trails of hot steam in the frigid air. There were a lot of questions I wanted to ask. Who was Bee-Bee and what was his relationship with Taneesha? Did C-Note and the other men know him? But we were moving too fast, and C-Note was preoccupied, his eyes ablaze.

We stopped just above the fourth-floor stairwell, since it was thought that Bee-Bee had taken refuge in Number 407. "Charlie, you and Blue go ahead," C-Note said. "Shorty, you and them go to the other stairwell in case he runs past. Sudhir and me will stay in the back. Charlie, I'm right behind you, so if he got a knife, just let him go. I'll get him."

It struck me that I might not be as far out of the way as I'd planned.

All the men hurried to their positions. I could see the door to Number 407 from where I stood in the stairwell with C-Note. Charlie and Blue approached it. Like C-Note, they wore secondhand clothes and ill-fitting shoes. Charlie had a crowbar in his hand. Blue's fist was clenched, but I couldn't tell what he was holding.

Charlie knocked. The thin wooden door gave a hollow sound. All the other apartments on the floor had thick steel doors, but the CHA used wooden doors to designate which apartments were vacant. "Yo, nigger!" Charlie called out. "Hey, Bee-Bee! Taneesha says she wants to talk with you. Come on out. She says she's cool with everything." He looked back at us. C-Note waved his hands, signaling him to shout again. "Yo, Bee-Bee! Taneesha says she just wants to talk, nigger! I'll take you up there." *Why would Bee-Bee need an escort to go back upstairs?* I thought. *And why on earth would he believe any of this?*

Just then a voice rang out from the stairwell above us. "He's on eleven, and he's coming down the stairs! Get him, he's coming down!"

C-Note instinctively pinned me against the gallery, letting Charlie and Blue go past. They stopped just inside the stairwell. C-Note and I crouched down a few feet behind them. The intense cold made me shiver. Charlie pressed his hand toward the floor a few times, motioning us to stand still. I had never heard the building so quiet. Apart from the wind and some cars in the distance, the only sound I could make out was a mouse or rat scratching around in the incinerator room.

Then, from above, I heard some distant footsteps turning into a rumble. Someone was running down the stairs, breathing heavily. I found myself grabbing onto the back of C-Note's jacket. Charlie and Blue were crouched just in front of us. I made out what was in Blue's hand: brass knuckles.

Just as the footsteps reached the fourth floor, Charlie jumped up and swung the crowbar, waist high. He struck Bee-Bee full-on, bowling him over.

"Yeah, nigger!" Blue shouted, then jumped over and started pounding Bee-Bee in the side. His head hit the wall of the stairwell and snapped back. "Leave that bitch alone, you hear me?" Blue shouted, punching him repeatedly in the gut. "You better leave her alone, nigger!"

Bee-Bee was tall and strong, and he threw Charlie off him. He stood up and began shouting, but Blue tackled him, smashing Bee-Bee into the wall. The two of them started tumbling down the stairs. Charlie grabbed Bee-Bee's leg, so he, too, fell down the stairwell.

"Grab his other leg!" Charlie yelled in our direction. C-Note jumped down the stairs and made a grab. Blue, meanwhile, was struggling to get out from under Bee-Bee, who had Blue's head in a choke hold. I could see that Blue was struggling to breathe; he looked like he might pass out, or worse. I felt as if I had to do something. Running over to them, I kicked Bee-Bee in the stomach, which made him relax his grip on Blue. The other men smothered him, and I could hear his muffled words: "Okay, okay. All right, enough."

Blue, the strongest of them, bent Bee-Bee's arms behind his back, bringing him to his knees. I don't know whether it was the cold air, the adrenaline, or the swift kick I'd delivered, but I was badly out of breath. I leaned against the wall near the incinerator room. "Charlie, run back up the stairs and make sure he didn't drop nothing," C-Note said. "We'll meet you at the office."

The rest of us walked Bee-Bee downstairs to Ms. Bailey's office. She wasn't in, so C-Note sent another squatter to fetch her. We all stood outside the office, silent. No one seemed to worry that Bee-Bee would run away.

He sat down on the floor with his head pitched back, resting against the wall. This was my first opportunity to get a good look at him. He was young, his face light-skinned and boyish but with a menacing air. And he appeared to be aging fast. His nostrils were black, his eyes hollow and glazed, telltale signs of crack use. He wore a brown sweatshirt over a stained white tank top, with loose jeans and unlaced sneakers dirtied by the winter slush. I saw a gang tattoo on his neck, the crescent-and-star pattern of the Black P. Stone Nation. The Stones had been largely dismantled in the 1980s by the feds, with some remaining factions now aligned with the Black Kings. Why, I wondered, was Taneesha hanging around with *this* guy?

C-Note had caught his breath by now. "You really fucked up this time, Bee-Bee."

Bee-Bee said nothing. He wiped the sweat from his face.

I heard Ms. Bailey coming. I'd never seen her move so fast before—she was practically galloping, trailed by Catrina and a few older women in blue Tenant Patrol jackets.

Ms. Bailey hurried past without looking at me. Catrina, however, gave me one of her signature looks that I now recognized as meaning this: *Ms. Bailey's got the situation under control, and all will soon be right with the world.* Ms. Bailey unlocked her office door and went inside. Blue and Charlie, who'd returned from upstairs, picked up Bee-Bee and brought him into the office. Bee-Bee seemed cooperative. The three of them entered the back room in Ms. Bailey's office, and then someone shut the front door. I stayed outside, along with the other squatters and the Tenant Patrol women. C-Note, his work done, took off.

Then Catrina poked her head out the door and waved me inside. *Get in here!* she mouthed silently. I did, and she pointed me to a chair.

It was hard to make out the full conversation behind Ms. Bailey's closed door, but once in a while her voice was loud enough for me to hear: "You got some nerve, young man! . . . Beat her like that. . . . Where do you live, huh, where do you live?! . . . She's a good girl. She owe you money? She wouldn't fuck you? Why did you do that? . . . Say something!"

Then came the beating. Charlie or Blue, or maybe both of them, started hitting Bee-Bee. I also heard Ms. Bailey cry out in a muffled tone. *Maybe Ms. Bailey is hitting him as well,* I thought. I heard chairs scuffing the floor. Then, for the first time, I heard Bee-Bee's voice: "Oh, shit! . . . Get off me. . . . Fuck that! She deserved it."

Ms. Bailey started to yell louder. "Deserved it? . . . You'll get worse if you come around here. . . . Don't ever, don't *ever* touch her again, you hear me? *You hear me?* Don't ever come in this building again."

Ms. Bailey threw open the door. Blue dragged Bee-Bee out. His face was badly worked over; he was drooling and mumbling something unintelligible. Blue hustled him past Catrina and me and threw him to the floor on the gallery. Two other men grabbed him and led him toward the stairwell. Ms. Bailey followed them, with the members of the Tenant Patrol right behind.

I started to get up, but Catrina stopped me. "Sudhir! No, let them go! They're just taking him in the car, and they'll leave him on State Street. Come up with me and see how Taneesha's doing."

Taneesha's aunt answered our knock. She and Taneesha's mother told us that Taneesha was at the hospital; she had some bad bruises, but it seemed as if she'd be okay. "I don't know what she's going to *look* like, though," said the aunt. "He beat her pretty good." Tanee-sha's mother promised to call Ms. Bailey later that night.

We went back downstairs to Ms. Bailey's office. She hadn't re-turned yet—she was apparently visiting Taneesha at the hospital—so Catrina told me what she knew. Bee-Bee had been managing Taneesha's modeling career, booking her at lingerie shows and dances. For this, he received a 25 percent cut—and, according to Cat-rina, he made Taneesha sleep with him. When Bee-Bee heard that Taneesha was going to sign up with a legitimate modeling agency, he got mad and started beating her. Today wasn't the first time this had happened. In fact, Ms. Bailey had repeatedly warned Bee-Bee to stop. But he kept harassing Taneesha, even stealing money from her apartment. It was only because Ms. Bailey felt there was no other recourse, Catrina explained, that today she had rounded up C-Note and the others to form a sort of militia. In the projects this was a long-standing practice. Militias were regularly put together to track down stolen property, mete out punishment, or simply obtain an apology for a victim.

In a neighborhood like this one, with poor police response and no shelter for abused women, the militias sometimes represented the best defense. "It's hard when you can't get nobody to come around," Catrina said solemnly. She was sitting in Ms. Bailey's chair, a soda in hand and her voice assured, seeming for all the world like the heiress to Ms. Bailey's throne. "No police, nobody from the hospital. We can't live like this! That's why Ms. Bailey is so important. And espe-cially for women. She makes sure we're safe."

"I suppose," I said. "But it's a horrible way to live. And wouldn't you rather have the police come around?"

"I'd rather not live in the projects," Catrina shot back. "But women are always getting beat on, getting sent to the hospital. I mean, you have to take care of yourself. Ms. Bailey makes these men take care of us. I don't see what's wrong with that. Unless you live here, you can't judge us, Sudhir."

For some reason I couldn't restrain the judgmental voice of my middle-class self. "You all didn't call the police, did you?" I blurted out.

For the first time since I knew Catrina, she couldn't look me in the eye. "No, we didn't."

"Why?"

She took a deep breath and raised her head. "Because we're scared of them."

"*You* are scared? *Women* are scared? *Everyone* is scared?" I asked. "Who *exactly* is scared? I hear this all the time."

"Everybody. But for women it's different. You wouldn't understand." She paused. "At least we have C-Note and the rest of them when things go crazy." It was clear that Catrina didn't want to talk further. I decided to ask Ms. Bailey about this when things calmed down.

I'd seen some police around the neighborhood, and I'd seen them work with Autry at the Boys & Girls Club. But since most tenants were so distrustful of the cops, I kept my interactions with them to a minimum, since I didn't want to be thought of as being "with" the cops.

Still, I had a hard time accepting the idea that tenants wouldn't call the police for something as serious as an assault. I also found it tough to believe that the police wouldn't show up—or, for that matter, that an ambulance wouldn't respond either. But as Catrina sat now in total silence, staring at me expressionlessly, I realized I might well be wrong.

I told her that I'd better get back to my apartment. She didn't acknowledge me. I wanted to do something to help her.

"Would you like to get something to eat?" I
She shook her head.

"Do you want to write me another essay?" I
to write about what just happened?"

Catrina liked to write essays, which I read so that we could discuss them. This was a good way for her to talk through her aspirations as well as the shadows of her past: intense poverty and a bad
family situation that I was just starting to learn about.

She shrugged. I couldn't tell if that meant yes or no.

"Well, I'm happy to read it if you do write something. Whenever."

"Thanks," she said. The barest hint of a smile came to her face,
and she pushed her thick, black-framed glasses up on her nose. She
started sniffling and reaching for a tissue. She looked no more than
twelve years old. "I'll see you around," she said. "I'm sure things will
be okay."

With Catrina having gone quiet and Ms. Bailey at the hospital
and C-Note and the other squatters nowhere to be seen, there wasn't
anyone left for me to talk with. I thought about visiting J.T., but
every time I asked him anything about Ms. Bailey, he'd shut me
down. "You want to know what she's like, *you* hang out with her,"
he said. "I ain't telling you shit." J.T. didn't care much for Ms. Bailey's authority, as it occasionally challenged his own. It was well
within her power, for instance, to close off the lobby to his sales crew.
J.T. wanted me to experience Ms. Bailey for myself to see what he
had to deal with.

I took the bus back to my apartment but decided to stop first at
Jimmy's, a local bar where a lot of U of C professors and students
hung out. No one knew me there, and I could sit quietly and process

had just happened in my fieldwork. Sometimes I would go
ere to write up my notes, but more often I just sat and stared
blankly into my glass. With increasing frequency, Jimmy's was a ritual stop on my way home. At Jimmy's, as at the best bars, no one
cared what troubles I brought to the table. Most of the people were
sitting alone, like me, and I figured they were dealing with their
own problems.

Jimmy's gave me a place to take off one hat (the fieldworker) and
put on the other (the student). I needed this break, because I was
starting to feel schizophrenic, as if I were one person in the
projects—sometimes I caught myself even talking in a different
way—and another back in Hyde Park.

Increasingly I found that I was angry at the entire field of social science—which meant, to some degree, that I was angry at
myself. I resented the fact that the standard tools of sociologists
seemed powerless to prevent the hardships I was seeing. The abstract
social policies that my colleagues were developing to house, educate, and employ the poor seemed woefully out of touch. On the
other hand, life in the projects was starting to seem too wild, too
hard, and too chaotic for the staid prescriptions that social scientists
could muster. It struck me as only partially helpful to convince
youth to stay in school: what was the value in giving kids low-
paying, menial jobs when they could probably be making more
money on the streets?

In the poverty seminars that Bill Wilson sponsored, where some
of the best academic minds congregated to discuss the latest research,
I acted as if I had a unique insight into poverty by virtue of my prox-
imity to families. I prefaced my questions by blurting out a self-
serving objection: "No one here seems to have spent much time with
the poor, but if you did, you would see that . . ." or, "If you actually

watched poor people instead of just reading census tables, you would understand that . . ." I felt as though the other scholars were living in a bubble, but my arrogant tone did little to help anyone hear what I was trying to say. I worried that my behavior might embarrass Wilson, but I was too bitter to take a moderate stance.

I wouldn't say that I was disillusioned with the academic life per se. I still attended classes, worked with professors and met my deadlines, earned pretty good grades, and even received a few prestigious fellowships. I still saw myself on the road to being a professor like Wilson. But day by day, it was getting harder to reconcile my life at the U of C with my life in the projects.

Rather than sharing my frustration with my girlfriend, my roommates, and my friends—most of whom were actually quite supportive and curious about my research—I just kept my experiences to myself. How could I explain the vigilante justice that C-Note and the others had just delivered? How could I explain my own role in the beating? I didn't understand it myself, and I feared that I'd open myself up to my friends' advice: *You need to call the police if they don't. . . . You're getting too involved. . . . You've gone too far. . . .*

When I did try talking about my fieldwork, I felt awkward. In fact, I sometimes came off as defending the gangs and their violent practices or as romanticizing the conditions in the projects. So, to stay sane, I'd usually just tell people about Autry's work at the Boys & Girls Club or, if pushed, a few stories about life in the gang.

I was growing quieter and more solitary. My fellow graduate students and even some faculty members thought of me as unapproachable. Rumors circulated that I was too ambitious, too aloof, but I figured I'd just have to live with them. A small part of me hoped that life would get back to normal once my fieldwork was over. But the end didn't seem very near, so I just kept to myself.

I was eager to know more about the incident with Bee-Bee. Why had Ms. Bailey sicced the squatters on him instead of leaving it to the police? *Had* the police been called—Catrina said they hadn't, but I wanted to be sure—and if so, why didn't they respond? What were the consequences for Ms. Bailey of taking such matters into her own hands?

I waited until "check day" to go see Ms. Bailey. That's when welfare checks were distributed, which meant that most tenants were out buying food and clothing and household items—and not, therefore, coming to Ms. Bailey with demands.

On the way up to her office, I stopped in to see J.T. He was lying on the sofa, watching TV. Ms. Mae gave me a big hug and told me to sit down for lunch. She had cooked some of my favorites—okra, greens, mac and cheese—and so I gladly obliged. J.T. quipped that I was eating his share of food. "You're becoming the little brother I never wanted," he said.

I told him about Ms. Bailey and the Bee-Bee incident. "Oh, man!" he said with a laugh. "That's why she's so upset. She keeps asking if I've seen you."

"Why's she upset at *me*?"

"Because you beat the shit out of that man, the one who beat Taneesha. I told you to be careful with Ms. Bailey, not to do things for her."

"First of all, I didn't do anything. Blue was choking, so I kicked the guy to help him."

"That's not *really* why she's upset." J.T. sat up. "She thinks that you were spying for us. Remember when I said that she doesn't use us as much anymore? We could've taken care of the man who did that, but she didn't ask us. She asked those fools, C-Note and those crackheads."

I knew that J.T. had tried to persuade Ms. Bailey to call him when a woman in the building got beat up. But I also knew, from Catrina, that Ms. Bailey wouldn't call J.T. because his gang members were known to physically and sexually abuse women.

By now J.T. was in lecture mode. "*That's* why I told you not to do things with her. Because I can't be there to protect you. She already knows that you're with me, so she doesn't trust you." According to this theory, Ms. Bailey must have thought I was spying for the gang, keeping track of how often she used non-gang affiliates for enforcing justice in the building.

I was taken aback when J.T. said that I was "with" him. I hadn't thought my relationship with J.T. would affect my work with Ms. Bailey—and I certainly wouldn't have predicted she would see me as a spy. His casual aside left me unsure of how to talk with different people in the projects. Once again I was being asked to pick sides. Was it possible, I wondered, to be in the projects for any length of time and remain neutral, an outsider, an objective observer?

J.T. urged me to go see Ms. Bailey immediately. "You might as well deal with this shit," he said. "It's not going away." He changed the channel.

As I headed for Ms. Bailey's office, I thought that I should probably just confess the truth: I hadn't asked her permission to join C-Note, and I had participated—however minimally—in the beating of Bee-Bee.

Catrina was leaving as I entered. She said nothing, just shook her head as if in disapproval. I stepped into Ms. Bailey's office. "Ms. Bailey, I have to apologize." I told her about my involvement with Bee-Bee.

She stared at me for a while. I fidgeted.

"That's not really what bothers me, Sudhir," she finally said. "What bothers me is that you are seeing things and you may not be ready for it."

"I'm not sure I understand."

"See, if you were in a war and you were a reporter, you could just say what's going on. No one would be mad at you. But this ain't a war. I try to tell you that all the time. It's *every day.* Every day something happens like what happened to 'Neesha. And you're getting yourself in the middle. People are saying, 'Sudhir's tough, he beat up that man almost by himself. He'll do things for us.' You understand why that's a problem?"

"I'm not sure. You think they'll hire me to beat up people?"

"They might, they might not. But they *will* start talking about you. Sometimes they'll give you credit, and sometimes they'll blame you. Understand?"

I didn't answer.

"And when you say, 'No, I can't help you with that,' they'll say, 'But you helped 'Neesha, so why won't you help me?' Then they'll say, 'Sudhir don't care about *us,*' or 'Sudhir is 'Neesha's manager.' Then they'll say, 'Sudhir is working for Ms. Bailey, and he don't do nothing unless he gets paid.' Get it?"

"I think I get it." I sat silently and stared into my hands. "When do you think I *should* see these things?"

"Well, *why* do you want to see what we do? I mean, why don't you hang around the police? You should figure out why they don't come."

"Ms. Bailey, I wanted to ask you about that. Did you really call the police? Or the ambulance?"

"Sudhir, the hardest thing for middle-class white folk to understand is why those people don't come when we call."

Ms. Bailey didn't think I was actually white, but she always tried to show me how my middle-class background got in the way of understanding life in the projects.

"They just don't come around all the time. And so we have to find ways to deal with it. I'm not sure how much better I can explain it to you. Why don't you watch out for the next few months? See how much they come around."

"What about Officer Reggie?"

"Yes, he's a friend. But can I tell you how he can be helpful? Not by coming and putting Bee-Bee in jail. Because he'll be out in the morning. But Officer Reggie *can* visit Bee-Bee after we're through with him. Maybe put the fear in him."

"Put the fear in him? I don't understand."

"He could visit Bee-Bee and tell him that we won't be so nice the next time he does that to 'Neesha. If Bee-Bee knows that the cop don't care if we kick his ass, that may make him think twice. *That* is what we need Officer Reggie for."

"Ms. Bailey, I have to tell you that I just don't get it. I've been watching you for a while, and it just seems to me that you shouldn't have to be doing everything you're doing. If you got the help you needed, you wouldn't have to act like this."

"Sudhir, what's the first thing I told you when you asked about my job?"

I smiled as I thought of something she'd told me months earlier: "As long as I'm helping people, something ain't right about this community. When they don't need me no more, that's when I know they're okay."

But she'd been helping for three decades and didn't see any end in sight.

One day in the middle of February, the Wilson family lost their front door. The Wilsons lived on the twelfth floor, just down the hall from Ms. Bailey. Their door simply fell off its hinges, leaving the family exposed to the brutal cold of a Chicago winter.

Even *with* a front door, the Robert Taylor Homes weren't very comfortable in the winter. Because the galleries are outdoors, you can practically get blown over by the lake wind as you walk from the elevator to your apartment. Inside, the winter wind inevitably finds its way through the seams in the doorframe.

Chris Wilson worked for the city and moved in and out of Robert Taylor, living off-the-lease with his wife, Mari, and her six children. Chris and Mari were, unsurprisingly, pretty anxious when they lost their door. It wasn't just the cold; they were worried about being robbed. It was common knowledge that drug addicts would pounce on any opportunity to steal a TV or anything else of value.

The Wilsons tried calling the CHA but got no response. They put up a makeshift door of wooden planks and plastic sheeting, but it didn't keep out the cold. Neighbors who said they'd keep an eye on the apartment didn't show up reliably. So after a few days, the Wilsons called Ms. Bailey.

Ms. Bailey leaped into action. She asked J.T. to station a few of his gang members in the twelfth-floor stairwells to keep out potential burglars. As a preventive measure, J.T. also shut down a nearby vacant apartment that was being used as a crack den. Then Ms. Bailey contacted two people she knew at the CHA. The first was a man who obtained a voucher so the Wilsons could stay at an inexpensive motel until their door was fixed. The second person was able to speed up the requisition process for obtaining a new door. It arrived two days after Ms. Bailey placed her first call.

The door didn't come cheap for the Wilsons. They had to pay Ms. Bailey several hundred dollars, which covered the fees that she paid to her CHA friends, as well as an electrician's bill, since some of the wiring in the Wilsons' apartment went bad because of the cold. Ms. Bailey presumably pocketed the rest of the money. Mari Wilson was, on balance, unperturbed. "Last summer we didn't have

running water for a month," she told me, "so one week without a
door was nothing."

Having watched Ms. Bailey help women like Taneesha and families like the Wilsons, I was left with deeply mixed feelings about her
methodology—often ingenious and just as often morally questionable. With such scarce resources available, I understood why she believed that the ends justified the means. But collaborating with gangs,
bribing officials for services, and redistributing drug money did little to help the typical family in her building. Ms. Bailey had told me
that she would much rather play by the rules if only the rules
worked. But in the end I concluded that what really drove Ms. Bailey
was a thirst for power. She liked the fact she could get things done
(and get paid for it), and she wasn't about to give that up, even if it
meant that sometimes her families might get short shrift. Many families, meanwhile, were too scared to challenge her and invite the
consequences of her wrath.

I was left discouraged by the sort of power bestowed upon building presidents like Ms. Bailey. People in this community shouldn't
have to wait more than a week to get a new front door. People in
this community shouldn't have to wonder if the ambulance or police would bother responding. People in this community shouldn't
have to pay a go-between like Ms. Bailey to get the services that most
Americans barely bother to think about. No one in the suburb where
I grew up would tolerate such inconvenience and neglect.

But life in the projects wasn't like my life in the suburbs. Not only
was it harder, but it was utterly unpredictable, which necessitated a
different set of rules for getting by. And living in a building with a
powerful tenant leader, as hard as that life could be, was slightly less
hard. It may have cost a little more to get what you needed, but at
least you had a chance.

SIX

The Hustler and the Hustled

Four years deep into my research, it came to my attention that I might get into a lot of trouble if I kept doing what I'd been doing.

During a casual conversation with a couple of my professors, in which I apprised them of how J.T.'s gang went about planning a drive-by shooting—they often sent a young woman to surreptitiously cozy up to the rival gang and learn enough information to prepare a surprise attack—my professors duly apprised *me* that I needed to consult a lawyer. Apparently the research I was doing lay a bit out of bounds of the typical academic research.

Bill Wilson told me to stop visiting the projects until I got some legal advice. I tried to convince Wilson to let me at least hang out around the Boys & Girls Club, but he shot me a look indicating that his position was not negotiable.

I did see a lawyer, and I learned a few important things.

First, if I became aware of a plan to physically harm somebody,

I was obliged to tell the police. Meaning I could no longer watch the gang plan a drive-by shooting, although I could speak with them about drive-bys in the abstract.

Second, there was no such thing as "researcher-client confidentiality," akin to the privilege conferred upon lawyers, doctors, or priests. This meant that if I were ever subpoenaed to testify against the gang, I would be legally obligated to participate. If I withheld information, I could be cited for contempt. While some states offer so-called shield laws that allow journalists to protect their confidential sources, no such protection exists for academic researchers.

It wasn't as if I had any intention of joining the gang in an actual drive-by shooting (nor would they ever invite me). But since I could get in trouble just for driving around with them while they *talked* about shooting somebody, I had to rethink my approach. I would especially have to be clearer with J.T. We had spoken several times about my involvement; when I was gang leader for a day, for instance, he knew my limits and I understood his. But now I would need to tell him, and perhaps a few others, about the fact that I was legally obligated to share my notes if I was ever subpoenaed.

This legal advice was ultimately helpful in that it led me to seriously take stock of my research. It was getting to be time for me to start thinking about the next stage: writing up my notes into a dissertation. I had become so involved in the daily drama of tagging along with Ms. Bailey and J.T. that I'd nearly abandoned my study of the broader underground economy my professors wanted to be the backbone of my research.

So I returned to Robert Taylor armed with two objectives: let people know about my legal issues and glean more details of the tenants' illegal economic activities.

I figured that most people would balk at revealing the economics of hustling, but when I presented the idea to J.T., Ms. Bailey, and several others, nearly everyone agreed to cooperate. Most of the hustlers liked being taken seriously as businesspeople—and, it should be said, they were eager to know if they earned more than their competitors. I emphasized that I wouldn't be able to share the details of anyone else's business, but most people just shrugged off my caveat as a technicality that could be gotten around.

So with the blessing of J.T. and Ms. Bailey, I began devoting my time to interviewing the local hustlers: candy sellers, pimps and prostitutes, tailors, psychics, squeegee men.

I also told J.T. and Ms. Bailey about my second problem, my legal obligation to share notes with the police.

"You mean you didn't know this all along?" Ms. Bailey said. "Even *I* knew that you have to tell police what you're doing—unless you give them information on the sly."

"Oh, no!" I protested. "I'm not going to be an informant."

"Sweetheart, we're all informants around here. Nothing to be ashamed of. Just make sure that you get what you need, I always say. And don't let them beat you up."

"I'm not sharing my data with them—that's what I mean."

"You mean you'll go to prison?"

"Well, not exactly. I just mean I won't share my data with them."

"Do you know what being in contempt means?"

When I didn't reply, Ms. Bailey shook her head in disgust. I had seen this look before: she was wondering how I had qualified for higher education given my lack of street smarts.

"Any nigger around here can tell you that you got two choices," she said. "Tell them what they want or sit in Cook County Jail."

I was silent, trying to think of a third option.

"I'll ask you again," she said. "Will you give up your information, or will you agree to go to jail?"

"You need to know that? That's important to you?"

"Sudhir, let me explain something to you. You think we were born yesterday around here. Haven't we had this conversation a hundred times? You think we don't know what you do? You think we don't know that you keep all your notebooks in Ms. Mae's apartment?"

I shuddered. Ms. Mae had made me feel so comfortable in her apartment that I'd never even entertained the possibility that someone like Ms. Bailey would think about—and perhaps even page through—my notebooks.

"So why let me hang out?" I asked.

"Why do you *want* to hang out?"

"I suppose I'm learning. That's what I do, study the poor."

"Okay, well, you want to act like a saint, then you go ahead," Ms. Bailey said, laughing. "Of course you're learning! But you are also *hustling*. And we're all hustlers. So when we see another one of us, we gravitate toward them. Because we need other hustlers to survive."

"You mean that people think I can do something for them if they talk to me?"

"They *know* you can do something for them!" she yelped, leaning across the table and practically spitting out her words. "And they know you *will*, because you need to get your information. You're a hustler, I can see it. You'll do anything to get what you want. Just don't be ashamed of it."

I tried to turn the conversation back to the narrow legal issue, but Ms. Bailey kept on lecturing me.

"I'll be honest with you," she said, sitting back in her chair. "If you *do* tell the police, everyone here will find you and beat the shit out of you. So that's why we know you won't tell nobody." She smiled as if she'd won the battle.

So who should I be worried about? I wondered. *The police or Ms. Bailey and the tenants?*

When I told J.T. about my legal concerns, he looked at me with some surprise. "I could've told you all that!" he said. "Listen, I'm never going to tell you anything that's going to land me in jail—or get me killed. So it don't bother me what you write down, because I can take care of myself. But that's really not what you should be worried about."

I waited.

"What you should be asking yourself is this: 'Am I going to be on the side of black folks or the cops?' Once you decide, you'll do whatever it takes. You understand?"

I didn't.

"Let me try again. Either you're with us—you feel like you're in this with us and you respect that—or you're just here to look around. So far these niggers can tell that you've been with us. You come back every day. Just don't change, and nothing will go wrong, at least not around here."

J.T.'s advice seemed vague and a bit too philosophical. Ms. Bailey's warning—that I would get beat up if I betrayed confidences—made more sense. But maybe J.T. was saying the same thing, in his own way.

I decided to focus my study of the underground economy on the three high-rise buildings that formed the core of J.T.'s territory. I already knew quite a bit—that squatters fixed cars in the alleys, people sold meals out of their homes, and prostitutes took clients to vacant apartments—but I had never asked people how much money they made, what kind of expenses they incurred, and so on.

J.T. was far more enthusiastic about my project than I'd imagined he would be, although I couldn't figure out why.

"I have a great idea," he told me one day. "I think you should talk to all the pimps. Then you can go to all the whores. Then I'll let you talk to all the people stealing cars. Oh, yeah! And you also have folks selling stolen stuff. I mean, there's a whole bunch of people you can talk to about selling shoes or shirts! And I'll make sure they cooperate with you. Don't worry, they won't say no."

"Well, we don't want to force anyone to talk to me," I said, even though I was excited about meeting all these people. "I can't *make* anyone talk to me."

"I know," J.T. said, breaking into a smile. "But *I* can."

I laughed. "No, you can't do that. That's what I'm saying. That wouldn't be good for my research."

"Fine, fine," he said. "I'll do it, but I won't tell you."

J.T. arranged for me to start interviewing the pimps. He explained that he taxed all the pimps working in or around his buildings: some paid a flat fee, others paid a percentage of their take, and all paid in kind by providing women to J.T.'s members at no cost. The pimps had to pay extra, of course, if they used a vacant apartment as a brothel; they even paid a fee to use the stairwells or a parking lot.

As I began interviewing the pimps, I also befriended some of the freelance prostitutes like Clarisse who lived and worked in the building. "Oh, my ladies will love the attention," Clarisse said when I asked for help in talking to these women. Within two weeks I had interviewed more than twenty of them.

Between these conversations and my interviews with the pimps, some distinctions began to emerge. The prostitutes who were managed by pimps (these women were known as "affiliates") had some clear advantages over the "independents" who worked for themselves. The typical affiliate was beaten up far less frequently—about once a year, as against roughly four times a year for the independents. The affiliates also earned about twenty dollars per week more than the independents, even though their pimps took a 33 percent cut. (Twenty dollars wasn't a small sum, considering that the average Robert Taylor prostitute earned only about one hundred dollars per week.) And I never heard of an affiliate being killed in the line of work, whereas in one recent two-year stretch three independents were killed.

But the two types of prostitutes had much in common. Both groups had high rates of heroin and crack use, and they were bound to the projects, where the demand for sex came mostly from low-income customers. At the truck stops on the other side of the Dan Ryan Expressway—barely a mile away from Robert Taylor but a different ecosystem entirely—a different set of pimps catered to a clientele of white truckers who paid more than the typical black customer in a housing project. Around Robert Taylor a prostitute usually earned ten to twenty dollars for oral sex, sometimes as little as twenty-five dollars for intercourse, and at least fifty dollars for anal sex. But if she was in need of drugs, she would drop her price significantly or accept a few bags of drugs in lieu of any cash.

Once my prostitute research was under way, I asked Ms. Bailey if she would help me meet female hustlers who sold something other than sex. I had casual knowledge of any number of off-the-books businesses: women who sold food out of their apartments or catered parties; women who made clothing, offered marital counseling or baby-sitting; women who read horoscopes, styled hair, prepared taxes, drove gypsy cabs, and sold anything from candy to used appliances to stolen goods. But since most of these activities were conducted out of public view, I needed Ms. Bailey to open some doors.

She was cautious. For the first week, she selectively introduced me to a few women but refused to let me meet others. I'd suggest a name, and she'd mull it over. "Well," she'd say, "let me think about whether I want you to meet with her." Or, just as often, "No, she's not good. But I got someone else for you." Once, after Ms. Bailey introduced me to a psychic, I asked if many other psychics worked in the building. "Maybe, maybe," she said, then changed the subject and left the room.

I eventually figured out why she was reluctant to let me explore the underground economy. As it turned out, tenant leaders like Ms. Bailey always got their cut from such activities. If you sold food out of your kitchen or took in other people's children to baby-sit, you'd better give Ms. Bailey a few dollars, or you might find a CHA manager knocking on your door. If you occasionally cut hair in your apartment, it was probably a good idea to give Ms. Bailey a free styling once in a while. In these parts Ms. Bailey was like the local IRS—and probably a whole lot more successful at collecting her due.

So the people she let me talk to were the ones she probably trusted most not to speak out of line. But I didn't have much choice: Without Ms. Bailey's say-so, *no one* was going to speak with me about any illegal activities.

Truth be told, nearly everyone Ms. Bailey introduced me to had a fascinating story to tell. One of the most fascinating women I met was Cordella Levy, a close friend of Ms. Bailey. She was sixty-three years old and had lived in public housing her entire life, the past thirty years in Robert Taylor. (She had a Jewish surname, she said, because her grandmother had married a Jewish man; someone else in her family, however, told me that they were descended from black Hebrew Israelites.) Cordella had raised seven children, all but one of whom had moved out of Robert Taylor. Although she used a walk-

ing crutch to get around, Cordella had the fight of a bulldog inside her.

She now ran a small candy store inside her apartment. All day
long she sat on a stool by the door and waited for children to stop
by. Her living room was barren except for the candy: boxes and
boxes of lollipops, gum, and candy bars stacked invitingly on a few
tables. If you peeked around the corner, you could see into the back
bedroom, where Cordella had a TV, couches, and so on. But she liked
to keep her candy room sparse, she told me, because if customers saw
her furniture, they might decide to come back and rob her.

"You know," she told me, "I didn't always sell candy."

"You mean you didn't go to school for this?" I joked.

"Sweetheart, I never made it past the fourth grade. Black folks
weren't really allowed to go to school in the South. What I meant
was that I used to be somebody different. Ms. Bailey didn't tell you?"
I shook my head. "She told me you wanted to know how I used
to hustle."

"I'd love to hear," I said. Cordella seemed itching to tell her story.

"Sweetheart, I've made money around here every which way you
can. You know, I started out working for Ms. Bailey's mother, Ella
Bailey. Ella was a madam, used to have parties in the building. Oh,
Lord! She could throw a party!"

"Ms. Bailey's mother was a madam?" I laughed. "That explains
a lot!"

"Yes, sir, and when she passed, I took over from her. Three apartments on the fourteenth floor. Cordella's Place, they used to call it.
Come in for a drink, play some cards, make a friend, have a nice time."

"Make a friend? Is that what they used to call it?"

"Ain't nothing wrong with friendship. And then I started making clothes, and then I sold some food, drove people around for a

while to the store. My mother taught me how to sew wedding dresses, so I was doing a lot of—"

"Wait!" I said. "Slow down, please. Let's get back to helping people make friends. I'm curious why you stopped running the parties. What happened? I ask because all the people doing that today are men: J.T. and the pimps. I haven't heard about any women."

"That's because they took over. The men ruined everything for us. The first one was J.T.'s mama's cousin, Miss Mae's cousin. He just decided to start harassing all the women who were making money. I think it was around 1981. He would beat us up if we didn't pay him money to work out of the building. I had to pay him a few dollars each week to manage my women and throw my parties. He nearly killed my friend because she wouldn't give him money for doing hairstyling in her apartment. He was real awful. On heroin, used to carry around a big gun, like he was in the movies. And he was a very violent man."

"So what happened, he took over your parties?"

"Well, all of a sudden, he told me I had to give him fifty percent of what I was making, and he'd protect me—keep the cops away. But I knew he couldn't keep any cops away. The man was a thug and wasn't even no good at that. I figured I had been doing it for a while, and so I just gave up and let him have the whole thing. But what I'm saying is that the women ran things around here, before the gangs and the rest of them took over. It was different, because we also helped people."

"How?"

"See, people like me had a little power. I could get your apartment fixed or get you out of jail, because the cops were my best customers. These folks today, like J.T., they can't do that."

"What about Ms. Bailey?"

"Yeah, she can, but she's just one person. Imagine if you had about fifty people like her doing their thing! Now, that was a sight. Fifty women, all powerful women with no shame. It was a different time. It was a time for women, a place for women."

For several days after I interviewed Cordella, I kept thinking of what she said: "It was a time for women, a place for women." Her nostalgia reminded me of how Catrina, Ms. Bailey's assistant, spoke so reverently of women helping each other in the building.

I spent the next three months focused on meeting the matriarchs of the high-rises. There were plenty to choose from: more than 90 percent of the four thousand households in Robert Taylor were headed by a female. Whenever Ms. Bailey introduced me to an elderly dressmaker or a grandmother who offered day care to working parents, I tried to solicit stories about the past as well as details of her current enterprise.

Many of these women had protested for civil rights in the 1960s and campaigned for black political candidates in the 1970s; they took the need to fight for their community very seriously. But during the 1980s and 1990s, as their plight was worsened by gangs, drugs, and even deeper poverty, they struggled just to keep their families together. By then the housing authority had grown corrupt and unsupportive, the police were largely unresponsive, and the tribe of strong women had been severely marginalized.

While the official statistics said that 96 percent of Robert Taylor's adult population was unemployed, many tenants did have part-time legitimate jobs—as restaurant workers, cabdrivers, cleaning ladies in downtown corporate offices, and nannies to middle-class families. But nearly all of them tried to hide any legitimate income from the CHA, lest they lose their lease or other welfare benefits.

There were also working men living in Robert Taylor, perhaps a few dozen in each building. But they stayed largely out of sight, again because of the CHA limits on how much money a tenant family could earn. Sometimes a man would leave home for a few weeks just to keep the CHA inspectors off guard. So when I or someone else they didn't recognize came into an apartment, the men might head for the back room. They didn't attend many tenant meetings, and for the most part they let the women handle the battle for better living conditions. The absence of men in Robert Taylor had made it that much easier for the gang members and pimps to essentially have the run of the place.

As I began compiling statistics on the illicit earnings generated by women throughout Robert Taylor, it became obvious that all their illicit earnings combined hardly constituted a lucrative economy. Selling food or candy out of your apartment might net you about twenty dollars per week. (Cordella Levy managed to do better than that, having persuaded a local grocery store to sell her candy wholesale in return for steering her customers to that store for their groceries.) Day care brought in five or ten dollars per day per child, but business wasn't steady. A woman could earn more selling sex, but that was risky in a few ways. One of the favored moneymaking options, therefore, was to take in a boarder, which could generate a hundred dollars a month. There was never any shortage of people who needed a place to stay.

But I also discovered something more interesting, and probably more important, than the money that changed hands in these various transactions. Many households participated in a vast web of exchange in which women borrowed, bartered, and pooled their resources to survive. One woman might offer day care for a large group of women, another might have a car and contribute by driving folks to buy groceries, and other women might take turns cooking for various families. In some cases the members of a network maintained a fixed formula of exchange: If you cook my family five dinners, I'll take care of your kids for two days.

Often a network of women would share their apartments as well. Let's say there were five women on one floor whose apartments had maintenance problems (which, given the condition of the buildings, wasn't uncommon). There was little chance that the CHA would respond to all their repair requests, and the women couldn't afford to pay five different bribes to Ms. Bailey or the CHA building manager. These women would pool their money to make sure they *could* pay the necessary bribes so that at least one apartment in their network had hot water and at least two had working refrigerators and stoves; perhaps one of them would also pay for pirated cable TV. Everyone would shower in one apartment, cook in another apartment, keep their food elsewhere, sit in the one air-conditioned room to watch the one TV with cable, and so on. To have your own apartment with all utilities functioning was a luxury that few people expected in Robert Taylor.

I met most of the neighborhood's male hustlers by hanging out in the local parking lot with C-Note. He let people know that it was safe to speak with me. There were always a lot of men milling around, talking and drinking, who represented the diversity of the neighborhood hustlers: carpenters who did inexpensive home repairs, freelance preachers, truck drivers who worked off the books for local factories, car thieves, rappers and musicians, cooks and cleaners. All of them made their money under the table.

Most of them had once held legitimate jobs that they lost out of either misfortune or misbehavior. Until a few years earlier, they could have gotten a few hundred dollars a month in welfare money, but by

1990, Illinois and many other states eliminated such aid for adult men. The conservative revolution launched by President Ronald Reagan would lead eventually to a complete welfare overhaul, culminating in the 1996 directive by President Bill Clinton that made welfare a temporary program by setting time limits on just about every form of public aid—for men, women, and children.

For men like the ones in Robert Taylor, the welfare changes only exacerbated their poverty. They all learned to keep track of which restaurants and churches offered free food and which abandoned buildings were available for sleeping. Like the women, the men also had a network: One would cook while another looked for work while yet another tried to find a place for all of them to sleep. If they heard of a vacant apartment, they'd pool their resources to bribe the CHA building manager, gang leader, tenant leader, or whoever else happened to have the key. These men also passed along information to cops in exchange for "get out of jail free" promises, and they could always make a few dollars from CHA janitors—who regularly paid off hustlers to clean the buildings when they felt like taking a day off.

C-Note introduced me to Porter Harris, a bone-thin man, sixty-five years old, who spent much of his time scouring the South Side for recyclable junk. When I met him, he was pushing a shopping cart filled with wire, cans, and metal scrap, trolling the tall grass between the high-rises and the railroad tracks. Years ago, Porter told me, *he* was the one who dictated where various hustlers in Robert Taylor could work, sell, and trade, much as C-Note did now. But he'd had to leave because of a battle with a gang leader.

"Booty Caldwell, real name was Carter," he told me in a southern drawl. "That was the one who kicked me out of here for good." Porter picked at his few remaining teeth with a blade of grass. He wore a floppy straw hat that made him look as if he'd stepped out of a faded photograph from the Old South. "There were about ten of us. I controlled Forty-seventh Street to Fifty-first. I had this whole area—you couldn't sell your *soul* without letting me know about it, yessir."

"Sounds like a good living," I said, smiling. "You were the king of hustlers?"

"Lord, king, and chief. Call it what you want, I ran that area. And then one day it all was taken away. By Booty Caldwell. He was part of the El Rukn gang." By the late 1960s, El Rukn had become the most powerful gang in Chicago. They were widely credited with uniting many independent gangs, making peace treaties and cooperative arrangements that resulted in a few El Rukn "supergangs." But a federal indictment in the mid-1980s weakened El Rukn, allowing other gangs, including the Black Kings, to take over the burgeoning crack trade.

From Porter, C-Note, and others, I learned that the most profitable hustling jobs for men were in manual labor: you could earn five hundred dollars a month fixing cars in a parking lot or roughly three hundred dollars a month cleaning up at the local schools. The worst-paying jobs, meanwhile, often required the longest hours: gathering up scrap metal or aluminum (a hundred dollars a month) or selling stolen clothes or cigarettes (about seventy-five dollars a month). While just about every hustler I interviewed told me that he was hoping for a legit job and a better life, I rarely saw anyone get out of the hustling racket unless he died or went to jail.

One day, after I'd spent hours interviewing Porter and some of the other male hustlers, I was summoned to Ms. Bailey's office. I'd been so busy that I hadn't seen her in a while. It was probably a good idea, I thought, to have a catch-up session.

I said hello to Catrina on my way in, and she gave me a smile. She was assuming more and more duties and seemed to be acting nearly as a junior officer to Ms. Bailey. Inside, J.T. and Ms. Bailey were laughing together and greeted me heartily.

"Mr. Professor!" J.T. said. "My mother says you haven't been by in a month! What, you don't like us anymore? You found somebody who cooks better?"

"You better not piss off Ms. Mae," Ms. Bailey said. "You'll never be able to come back in the building again."

"Sorry, all this interviewing has kept me really busy," I said, exasperated. "I just haven't had time to do much of anything else."

"Well, then, sit down, baby," Ms. Bailey said. "We won't keep you long. We just wanted to know who you've been meeting. We're curious about what you've learned."

"Hey, you know what, I could actually use the chance to tell you what I've been finding," I said, taking out my notebooks. "I've been meeting so many people, and I can't be sure whether they're telling me the truth about how much they earn. I suppose I want to know whether I'm really understanding what it's like to hustle around here."

"Sure," J.T. said. "We were just talking about that. You used to ask us to find you people. Now you do it yourself. We feel like you don't need us no more." He started laughing, and so did Ms. Bailey.

"Yeah," Ms. Bailey said. "Don't leave us behind, Mr. Professor, when you start to be successful! Go ahead, tell me who you've been talking to. If you tell us who you met and what they're doing, maybe we can check for you and see if folks are being straight."

For the next three hours, I went through my notebooks and told them what I'd learned about dozens of hustlers, male and female. There was Bird, the guy who sold license plates, Social Security cards, and small appliances out of his van. Doritha the tax preparer.

Candy, one of the only female carpenters in the neighborhood. Prince, the man who could pirate gas and electricity for your apartment. J.T. and Ms. Bailey rarely seemed surprised, although every now and then one of them perked up when I mentioned a particularly enterprising hustler or a woman who had recently started taking in boarders.

I finally left, riding the bus home to my apartment. I was grateful for having had the opportunity to discuss my findings with two of the neighborhood's most formidable power brokers. As I looked out the bus windows, I realized just how much I owed Ms. Bailey and J.T. If it weren't for the two of them, and a few other people like C-Note and Autry, I wouldn't ever have made any progress in learning how things really worked around Robert Taylor.

I spent the next few weeks turning the information in my notebooks into statistical tables and graphs that showed how much different hustlers made. I figured that J.T. would appreciate this data at least as much as my professors would, since he was always talking about the importance of data analysis within his managerial technique. So I headed over to Robert Taylor to show him my research.

In the parking lot, I ran into C-Note, who was in his usual spot with a few other squatters, fixing flat tires and washing cars.

"Hey, what's up, guys?" I shouted out. "Long time—how you been?"

Nobody replied. They looked at me, then turned away. I walked closer and stood a few feet from them. "What's up?" I said. "Everything all right?"

One of the men, Pootie, picked up a tool and started to loosen a tire from the rim. "Man, sometimes you just learn the hard way," he said to no one in particular. "That's life, isn't it? Sometimes you realize you can't trust nobody. They could be a cop, a snitch—who knows?"

C-Note simply shrugged. "Mm-hmm," he said.

"Yup, you just learn you can't trust *nobody*," Pootie continued. "You tell them something, and then they turn on you. Just like *that*! You can't predict it. Especially if they're not from around here."

Once again C-Note shrugged. "Mm-hmm," he muttered. "You got that right."

They kept ignoring me, so I walked over to J.T.'s building. A young woman I knew named Keisha was standing on the grass with her kids. They looked like they were waiting for a ride.

"Hey, Keisha," I said. "How are you doing?"

"How am I *doing*?" she asked, shaking her head. "I was doing a lot better before I started talking to *you*." She picked up her things and walked her kids a few yards away.

In the lobby some of J.T.'s gang members were hanging out. We shook hands and said hello. I went upstairs to see Ms. Bailey and J.T., but neither of them was home.

Down in the lobby again, I could feel people staring at me, but I couldn't figure out why. I felt myself growing paranoid. Did people suddenly think I was a cop? What was up with Pootie, C-Note, and Keisha? I decided to go back home.

I spent a few days trying to track down J.T., but nobody knew where he was. I couldn't wait any longer, so I went back to Robert Taylor and found C-Note in the parking lot. He and two other men were working on a car.

"C-Note, please," I begged, "what did I do? Tell me."

C-Note stood up and wiped the oil off a wrench. He motioned for the two other men to leave us alone. One of them gave me a nasty look and muttered something that sounded equally nasty, but I couldn't quite make it out.

"You need to learn to shut your mouth," C-Note finally said.

"Shut my mouth? I don't know what you're talking about."

"Don't play with me. All that shit I told you. All them niggers I introduced you to. If you told me you were going to tell J.T. they were making that money, I wouldn't have told you nothing."

My heart sank. I thought of my long debriefing with J.T. and Ms. Bailey. I had given them breakdowns on each hustler's earnings: how much every one of them made, when and where they worked, what they planned for the future. I didn't hand over my written data, but I'd done the next-best thing.

"J.T. is all *over* these niggers," C-Note said. He looked disgusted and spit on the ground. I could tell he was angry but that he wasn't comfortable expressing it to me. Until now our relationship had been based on trust; I rarely, if ever, spoke to anyone about what I learned from C-Note.

"He's taxing every one of them now," he said. "And he beat the shit out of Parnell and his brother because he thought they were hiding what they were doing. They weren't, but you can't convince J.T. of nothing. When he gets his mind to something, that's it. And then he tells Jo-Jo and his guys that they can't come around no more because *they* were hiding things from him. Jo-Jo's daughter lives up in here. So now he can't see *her.*" C-Note kept talking, getting angrier and angrier as he listed all the people that J.T. was cracking down on. "There's no way he could've found out if you didn't say nothing."

There was an awkward silence. I thought about lying, and I began to drum up an excuse. But something came over me. During the years I'd been in this community, people were always telling me that I was different from all the journalists and other outsiders who came by, hunting up stories. They didn't eat dinner with families or hang around at night to share a beer; they typically asked a lot of questions and then left with their story, never to return. I prided myself on this difference.

But now it was time to accept my fate. "I was sitting in Ms. Bailey's office," I told C-Note. "She and J.T. always help me, just like you. And I fucked up. I told them things, and I had no idea that they would use that information. Man, I had no idea that it would even be useful to them."

"That has to be one of the stupidest things I *ever* heard you say." C-Note began putting away his tools.

"Honestly, C-Note, I had no idea when I was talking to them—"

"No!" C-Note's voice grew sharp. "You knew. Yes you did. But you were too busy thinking about your own self. That's what happened. You got some shit for your professors, and you were getting high on that. I know you ain't *that* naïve, man."

"I'm sorry, C-Note. I don't know what else to say. I fucked up."

"Yeah, you fucked up. You need to think about *why* you're doing your work. You always tell me you want to help us. Well, we ain't never asked for your help, and we sure don't need it now."

C-Note walked away toward the other men. They stood quietly drinking beer and watching me. I headed toward the building. I wanted to see if Ms. Bailey was in her office.

Then an obvious thought hit me: If J.T. had acted on my information to tax the male street hustlers, Ms. Bailey might have started taxing the women I told her about. Worse yet, she might have had some of them evicted for hiding their income. How could I find out what had happened because of my stupidity? As I stood in the grassy expanse, staring up at the high-rise, I tried to think of someone who might possibly help me. I needed a tenant who was relatively independent of Ms. Bailey, someone who might still trust me enough to talk. I thought of Clarisse.

I hustled over to the liquor store and bought a few bottles of Boone's Farm wine. Clarisse wasn't going to talk for free.

I walked quickly through the building lobby and took the stairs up. I didn't want to get trapped in the elevator with women who might be angry with me for selling them out to Ms. Bailey. Clarisse opened her door and greeted me with a loud burst of laughter.

"Oooh! Boy, you fucked up this time, you surely did."

"So it's all over the building? Everyone knows?"

"Sweetheart, ain't no secrets in this place. What did Clarisse tell you when we first met? *Shut the fuck up.* Don't tell them nothing about who you are and what you do. Clarisse should have been there with you. You were spying for Ms. Bailey?"

"Spying! No way. I wasn't spying, I was just doing my research, asking questions and—"

"Sweetheart, it don't matter what you call it. Ms. Bailey got pissed off and went running up in people's houses, claiming they owed her money. I mean, you probably doubled her income, just like that. And you're really not getting *any* kickbacks? Just a little something from her?"

"Wait a minute," I said. "How do they know I was the one who gave Ms. Bailey the information?"

"Because, you fool, she *told* everyone! Even if she didn't tell them, she was running around saying, 'You made twenty-five dollars last month,' 'You made fifty dollars last week,' 'You made ten dollars this week, and you owe me ten percent plus a penalty for not telling me.' I mean, the only folks we told all this information to was you!"

"But did she charge you, too?"

"No, no! She don't charge the hos, remember? J.T. already charges us."

I sat and listened with my head down as Clarisse listed all the women who'd been confronted by Ms. Bailey. I had a sinking feeling that I'd have a hard time coming back to this building to continue my research. I also had to face the small matter of managing to leave here today still in one piece.

Clarisse sensed my anxiety. As she talked—laughing heartily all the while, at my expense—she started massaging my shoulder. "Don't worry, little baby! You probably never had an ass whuppin', have you? Well, sometimes that helps clear the air. Just don't take the stairs when you leave, 'cause if you get caught there, they may never find your body."

I must have looked truly frightened, for Clarisse stopped laughing and took a sincere tone.

"Folks forgive around here," she said gently. "We're all religious people, sweetheart. We have to put up with a lot of shit from our own families, so nothing you did to us will make things much worse."

At that moment, sitting with Clarisse, I didn't think that even the Good Lord himself could, or would, help me. It was embarrassing to think that I had been so wrapped up in my desire to obtain good data that I couldn't anticipate the consequences of my actions. After several years in the projects, I had become attuned to each and every opportunity to get information from the tenants. This obsession was primarily fueled by a desire to make my dissertation stand out and increase my stature in the eyes of my advisers. After I'd talked with C-Note and Clarisse, it was clear to me that other people were paying a price for my success.

I began to feel deeply ambivalent about my own reasons for being in the projects. Would I really advance society with my research, as Bill Wilson had promised I could do if I worked hard?

Could I change our stereotypes of the poor by getting so deep inside the lives of the families? I suddenly felt deluged by these kinds of questions.

Looking back, I was probably being a little melodramatic. I had been so naïve up to this point about how others perceived my presence that any sort of shake-up at all was bound to send me reeling.

I couldn't think of a way to rectify the situation other than to stop coming to Robert Taylor entirely. But I was close to finishing my fieldwork, and I didn't want to quit prematurely. In the coming weeks, I spoke to Clarisse and Autry a few times for advice. Both suggested that the tenants I had angered would eventually stop being so angry, but they couldn't promise much more than that. When I asked Autry whether I'd be able to get back to collecting data, he just shrugged and walked off.

I eventually came back to the building to face the tenants. No one declined to speak with me outright, but I didn't exactly receive a hero's welcome either. Everyone knew I had J.T.'s support, so it was unlikely that anyone would confront me in a hostile manner. When I went to visit C-Note in the parking lot, he simply nodded at me and then went about his work, talking with customers and singing along with the radio. It felt like people in the building looked at me strangely when I passed by, but I wondered if I was just being paranoid. Perhaps the best indicator of my change in status was that I wasn't doing much of anything *casual*—hearing jokes, sharing a beer, loaning someone a dollar.

One sultry summer day not long after my fiasco with the hustlers, I attended the funeral of Catrina, Ms. Bailey's dutiful assistant. On the printed announcement, her full name was rendered as Catrina Eugenia Washington. But I knew this was not her real name.

Catrina had once told me that her father had sexually abused her when she was a teenager, so she ran away from home. She wound up living in Robert Taylor with a distant relative. She changed her name so her father wouldn't find her and enrolled in a GED program at DuSable High School. She took a few part-time jobs to help pay for rent and groceries. She was also saving money to go to community college; she was trying to start over. I never did find out her real name.

As a kid she had wanted to study math. But her father, she told me, said that higher education was inappropriate for a young black woman. He advised her instead just to get married and have children.

Catrina had a love of knowledge and would participate in a discussion about nearly anything. I enjoyed talking with her about science, African-American history, and Chicago politics. She always wore a studious look, intense and focused. Working as Ms. Bailey's assistant, she received just a few dollars a week. But, far more significant, she was receiving an apprenticeship in Chicago politics. "I will do something important one day," she liked to tell me, in her most serious voice. "Like Ms. Bailey, I *will* make a difference for black people. Especially black women."

By this time Catrina had been living in Robert Taylor for a few years. But over the July Fourth holiday, she decided to visit her siblings in Chicago's south suburbs, an area increasingly populated with African-American families who'd made it out of the ghetto. From what I was told, her father heard that she was visiting and tracked her down. A skirmish followed. Catrina got caught between her brother, who was protecting her, and her angry father. A gun went off, and the bullet hit Catrina, killing her instantly. No one around Robert Taylor knew if either the brother or the father had been arrested.

The funeral was held in the back room of a large African Methodist Episcopal church on the grounds of Robert Taylor. The hot air was stifling, the sun streaming in shafts through dusty windows. There were perhaps fifty people in attendance, mostly women from Ms. Bailey's building. A few members of Catrina's family were also there, but they came surreptitiously because they didn't want her father to hear about the funeral. Ms. Bailey stationed herself at the room's entrance, welcoming the mourners. She looked as if she were presiding over a tenant meeting: upright, authoritarian, refusing to cry while consoling those who were. She had the air of someone who did this regularly, who mourned for someone every week.

Sitting in a corner up front was T-Bone, his head down, still as stone. He and Catrina had been seeing each other for a few months. Although T-Bone had a steady girlfriend—it wasn't uncommon for gang members, or practically any other young man in the projects, to have multiple girlfriends—he and Catrina had struck up a friendship and, over time, become lovers. I sometimes came upon the two of them studying together at a local diner. T-Bone was about to leave his girlfriend for Catrina when she was killed.

Any loss of life is mourned in the projects, but there are degrees. Young men and women who choose a life of drugs and street gangs may, understandably, not be long for this world. When one of them dies, he or she is certainly mourned, but without any great sense of shock; there is a general feeling that death was always a good possibility. But for someone like Catrina, who had refused to follow such a path, death came with a deep sense of shock and disbelief. She was one of thousands of young people who had escaped the attention of social workers, the police, and just about everyone else. Adults in the projects pile up their hopes on people like Catrina, young men and women who take a sincere interest in education, work, and self-betterment. And I guess I did, too. Her death left me with a sting that would never fade.

The essays that Catrina used to write covered the difficulties of family life in the projects, the need for women to be independent, the stereotypes about poor people. Writing seemed to provide Catrina a sense of relief, as though she were finally acknowledging the hurdles of her own past; it also helped her develop a strong, assertive voice, not unlike that of her hero, Ms. Bailey.

In tribute to Catrina, I thought I'd try to broaden this idea by starting a writing workshop for young women in the building who were interested in going back to school. I brought up the possibility with Ms. Bailey. "Good idea," she said, "but take it slow, especially when you're dealing with *these* young women."

I was nervous about teaching the workshop, but I was also eager. My relationship with tenants up to this point had largely been a one-way street; after all this time in Robert Taylor, I felt as though I should give something back. On a few occasions, I had managed to solicit donations from my professors, fifty or a hundred dollars, for some kind of program in the neighborhood. This money might do a great deal of good, but it seemed to me a fairly impersonal way of helping. I was hoping to do something more direct.

In the past I hadn't been drawn to standard charitable activities like coaching basketball or volunteering at a school, because I wanted to differentiate myself from the people who helped families and ran programs in the community. I had heard many tenants criticize the patronizing attitudes of such volunteers. The writing workshop, however, seemed like a good fit. Having hung out in the community for several years, I believed I could avoid the kind of fate—

exclusion, cold stares, condescending responses—that often greeted the people who rode into town to do good.

I was also still reeling from the fact that I had alienated so many people around J.T.'s territory. I was feeling guilty, and I needed to get people back on my side again.

Of all the people in the projects, I had the least experience spending time with young women, particularly single mothers. I was a bit nervous, particularly because Ms. Bailey, Ms. Mae, and other older women warned me not to get too close to the young women. They felt that the women would begin looking to me as a source of support.

In the beginning the group convened wherever we could—in someone's apartment, at a diner, outside under a tree. At first there were five women in the group, and then we grew to roughly a dozen as more people heard about it. The meetings were pretty casual, and attendance could be spotty, since the women had family and work obligations.

From the outset it was an emotional experience. The women wrote and spoke openly about their struggles. Each of them had at least a couple of children, which generally meant at least one "baby daddy" who wasn't in the picture. Each of them had a man in her life who'd been either jailed or killed. They spoke of in-laws who demanded that the women give up their children to the father's family, some of whom were willing to use physical force to claim the children.

Their material hardships were overwhelming. Most of them earned no more than ten thousand dollars a year, a combination of welfare payments and food stamps. Some worked part-time, and others took in boarders who paid cash or, nearly as valuable, provided day care so the young women could work, run errands, or just have a little time for themselves.

The most forceful stories were the tales of abuse. Every single woman had been beaten up by a boyfriend (who was usually drunk at the time), some almost fatally. Every one of them had lived in fear for days or weeks, waiting for the same man to return.

One cold autumn evening, we congregated at a local diner. We found a large table in the back, where it was quiet. The owner was by now accustomed to our presence, and he didn't mind that we stayed for hours. If business was particularly good, he'd feed us all night long and then waive the tab. He and I had struck up a friendship—I often came to the diner to write up my field notes—and he liked the fact that I was trying to help tenants.

The theme of this week's essay was "How I Survive." Tanya was the first to read from her journal. She was twenty years old, a high-school dropout with two children. She'd stayed with her mother after the first child was born but eventually got her own apartment in the same building, then had a second baby. She didn't know the whereabouts of the first father; the second had died in a gang shooting. In her essay she bragged about how she earned twice her welfare income by taking in boarders.

"But sometimes it doesn't go so well, Sudhir," said one of the other women, Sarina, who liked to be the voice of reason. She stared down Tanya as she spoke. Sarina had three children, the fathers of whom were, respectively, in jail, dead, and unwilling to pay child support. So she, too, had taken in boarders. "I remember when my brother came into the house, he started dealing dope and they caught him. Almost took my lease away."

"Yeah, but that's just because you didn't pay the building manager enough money," Tanya said. "Or I think that it was because you didn't sleep with him!"

"Well, I'm not doing either one of those things," Sarina said in a moralistic tone, shaking her head.

"You got some nerve," interrupted Keisha. "Sarina, you put your ass out there for any man who comes looking." At twenty-six, Keisha was one of the oldest women in the group. Even though she had grown angry with me for sharing information about hustlers with Ms. Bailey, she hadn't held the grudge for long. She had two daughters and was the best writer in the group, a high-school graduate now planning to apply to Roosevelt College. "Hell, there ain't no difference between some ho selling her shit and you taking some man in your house for money."

"Hey, *that's* survival!" Tanya said. "I mean, that's what we're here to talk about, right?"

"Okay," I jumped in, trying to establish some order. "What's the best way for you to take care of whatever you need to? Give me the top ten ways you survive."

Sarina began. "Always make sure you know someone at the CHA you can turn to when you can't make rent. It helps, because you could get evicted."

"Yeah, and if you have to sleep with a nigger downtown, then you got to do it," said Keisha. "Because if you don't, they *will* put your kids on the street."

Sarina went on, ignoring Keisha. "You got to make sure you can get clothes and food and diapers for your kids," she said. "Even if you don't have money. So you need to have good relations with stores."

"Make sure Ms. Bailey's always getting some dick!" Keisha shouted, laughing hard.

"You know, one time I had to let her sleep with *my* man so I wouldn't get kicked out of the building," Chantelle said.

"That's awful," I said.

"Yeah," Chantelle said. "And he almost left me, too, when he found out that Ms. Bailey could get him a job and would let him stay up there and eat all her food." Chantelle was twenty-one. Her son had learning disabilities, so she was struggling to find a school that could help him. She worked part-time at a fast-food restaurant and depended on her mother and grandmother for day care and cash.

Chantelle's hardships weren't uncommon in the projects. Unfortunately, neither was her need to appease Ms. Bailey. The thought that a tenant had to let the building president sleep with her partner was alarming to me. But among these women such indignities weren't rare. To keep your own household intact, they said, you had to keep Ms. Bailey happy and well paid. As I heard more stories similar to Chantelle's, I found myself growing angry at Ms. Bailey and the other LAC officials. I asked Chantelle and the other women why they didn't challenge Ms. Bailey. Their answer made perfect sense: When it became obvious that the housing authority supported a management system based on extortion and corruption, the women decided their best option was to shrug their shoulders and accept their fate.

I found it unconscionable that such a regime existed, but I wasn't going to confront Ms. Bailey either. She was too powerful. And so while the women's anger turned into despair, my disgust began to morph into bitterness.

The women's list of survival techniques went well beyond ten. Keep cigarettes in your apartment so you can pay off a squatter to fix things when they break. Let your child pee in the stairwell to keep prostitutes from congregating there at night. Let the gangs pay you to store drugs and cash in your apartment. (The risk of apprehension, the women concurred, was slim.)

Then there were all the resources to be procured in exchange for sex: groceries from the bodega owner, rent forgiveness from the CHA, assistance from a welfare bureaucrat, preferential treatment from a police officer for a jailed relative. The women's explanation for using sex as currency was consistent and pragmatic: If your child was in danger of going hungry, then you did whatever it took to fix the problem. The women looked pained when they discussed using their bodies to obtain these necessities; it was clear that this wasn't their first—or even their hundredth—preference.

"Always know somebody at the hospital," Tanya blurted out. "Always have somebody you can call, because that ambulance never comes. And when you get there, you need to pay somebody, or else you'll be waiting in line forever!"

"Yes, that's true, and the people at the hospital can give you free baby food," Sarina said. "Usually you need to meet them in the back alley. And I'd say you should keep a gun or a knife hidden, in case your man starts beating you. Because sometimes you have to do something to get him to stop."

"You've had to use a knife before?" I asked. No one had spoken or written about this yet. "How often?"

"Many times!" Sarina looked at me as if I'd grown up on Mars. "When these men start drinking, you can't talk to them. You just need to protect yourself—and don't forget, they'll beat up the kids, too."

Keisha started to cry. She dropped her head into her lap and covered up so no one could see. Sarina leaned over and hugged her.

"The easiest time is when they're asleep," Tanya said. "They're lying there, mostly because they've passed out drunk. That's when it runs through your mind. You start thinking, 'I could end it right here. I could kill the motherfucker, right now. Then he can't beat me no more.' I think about it a lot."

Keisha wiped her eyes. "I stabbed that nigger because I couldn't take it no more. Wasn't anybody helping me. Ms. Bailey said she couldn't do nothing, the police said they couldn't do nothing. And this man was coming around beating me and beating my baby for no reason. I couldn't think of any other way, couldn't think of nothing else to do. . . ."

She began to sob again. Sarina escorted her to the bathroom.

"She sent her man to the hospital," Tanya quietly explained. "Almost killed him. One night he was asleep on the couch—he had already sent *her* to the hospital a few times, broke her ribs, she got stitches and bruises all over her body. She grabbed that knife and kept putting it in his stomach. He got up and ran out the apartment. I think one of J.T.'s boys took him to the hospital. He's a BK."

Because the boyfriend was a senior gang member, Tanya said, J.T. refused to pressure him to stop beating Keisha. She still lived in fear that the man would return.

One day Ms. Bailey called and asked that I come to a building-wide meeting with her tenants. She hadn't invited me to such a meeting in more than a year, so I figured something important was afoot.

I hadn't been keeping up with Ms. Bailey's tenant meetings in part because I'd already amassed sufficient information on these gatherings and also because, in all honesty, I'd grown uncomfortable watching the horse-trading schemes that she and other tenant leaders used to manage the community.

My own life was also starting to evolve. I had moved in with my girlfriend, Katchen, and we were thinking about getting married. Visiting our relatives—mine in California and hers in Montana—took time away from my fieldwork, including much of our summers and vacations. My parents were thrilled, and they pushed me to think seriously about starting a family along with a career. Katchen was applying to law school; neither of us was ready for children just yet.

And then there was the matter of my dissertation, which I still had to write. I began to meet more regularly with Bill Wilson and other advisers to see whether I could plausibly move toward wrapping up my graduate study.

Ms. Bailey's office was packed for the meeting when I arrived, with a few dozen people in attendance, all talking excitedly. As usual, most of them were older women, but there were also several men standing in the back. I recognized a couple of them as the partners of women in the building; it was unusual to see these men at a public meeting. Ms. Bailey waved me up front, pointing me to the chair next to hers.

"Okay," she said, "Sudhir has agreed to come here today so we can clear this up."

I was taken aback. Clear *what* up? Everyone was suddenly staring at me, and they didn't look happy.

"Why are you sleeping with my daughter?" shouted a woman I didn't recognize. "Tell me, goddamn it! Why are you fucking my baby?"

"Answer the woman!" someone else hollered. I couldn't tell who was talking, but it didn't matter: I was in a state of shock.

One man, addressing me as "Arab," told me I should get out of the neighborhood for good and especially leave alone their young women. Other people joined in:

"Nigger, get out of here!"

"Arab, go home!"

"Get the fuck out, Julio!"

Ms. Bailey tried to restore order. Amid the shouting she yelled out that I would explain myself.

I was still confused. "Let Sudhir tell you why he's meeting them!"

Ms. Bailey said, and then I understood: It was the writing workshop. People had seen me picking up the young women and driving away with them. Apparently they thought I was sleeping with them, or maybe pimping them out.

As I tried to explain the writing workshop, I kept getting drowned out. I began to feel scared. I had seen how a mob of tenants nearly tore apart the Middle Eastern shopkeeper who'd slept with Boo-Boo's daughter.

Ms. Bailey finally made herself heard above the riot. "He's trying to tell you that he's just helping them with homework!"

That quieted everyone down a little bit. But still, I was stung: Why weren't any of the women from the workshop in attendance? Why hadn't anyone come to defend me, to tell the truth?

After a few more minutes, things having calmed down a bit, Ms. Bailey told me to leave. There was other business to take care of, she said, laughing—at me—and clearly enjoying herself at my expense.

Leaving the building that night, I wondered how much more time I could afford to spend in J.T.'s territory. It was hard to think of any tenants who *weren't* angry with me.

SEVEN

Black and Blue

O f all the relationships I'd developed during my time at Robert Taylor, it turned out that the strongest one by far was my bond with J.T. As unusual and as morally murky as this relationship may have been, it was also undeniably powerful. Our years together had produced a close relationship. This bond would become even more intimate, to the point that J.T. felt personally indebted to me, when I had the opportunity to help save the life of one of his closest friends.

It was a classic Chicago summer afternoon: a cloudless sky, the muggy air broken occasionally by a soft lake breeze. I was hanging around at Robert Taylor, outside J.T.'s building, along with perhaps a hundred other people. Tenants were barbecuing, playing softball, and taking comfort in the cool shadow of the building. Few apartments had a working air conditioner, so on a day like this the lawn got more and more crowded as the day wore on.

I was sitting on the lawn next to Darryl Young, one of J.T.'s uncles, who relaxed on a lawn chair with a six-pack of beer. Since the beer was warm, Darryl sent a niece or nephew inside every now and then to fetch some ice for his cup. Darryl was in his late forties and had long ago lost most of his teeth. He had unkempt salt-and-pepper hair, walked with a stiff limp, and always wore his State of Illinois ID on a chain around his neck. He left the project grounds so rarely that his friends called him "a lifer." He knew every inch of Robert Taylor, and he loved to tell stories about the most dramatic police busts and the most memorable baseball games between competing buildings. He told me about the project's famous pimps and infamous murderers as well as about one tenant who tried to raise a tiger in his apartment and another who kept a hundred snakes in her apartment—until the day she let them loose in the building.

Suddenly Darryl sat up, staring at an old beater of a Ford sedan cruising slowly past the building. The driver was a young white man, looking up at the building as if he expected someone to come down.

"Get the fuck out of here, boy!" Darryl shouted. "We don't need you around here. Go and sleep with your own women!" Darryl turned and hollered to a teenage boy playing basketball nearby. "Cheetah! Go and get Price, tell him to come here."

"Why do you want Price?" I asked.

"Price is the only one who can take care of this," Darryl said. His face was tight, and he kept his eyes on the Ford. By now the car had come to a stop.

"Take care of what?" I asked.

"Damn white boys come around here for our women," Darryl said. "It's disgusting. This ain't no goddamn brothel."

"You think he's a john?"

"I *know* he's a john," Darryl said, scowling, and then went back to shouting at the Ford. "Boy! Hey, boy, get on home, we don't want your money!"

Price sauntered out of the building, trailed by a few other members of the BK security squad. Darryl stood up and hobbled over to Price.

"Get that boy out of here, Price!" he said. "I'm tired of them coming around here. This ain't no goddamn whorehouse!"

"All right, old man," Price said, irritated by Darryl's enthusiasm but clearly a bit concerned. "Don't worry. We'll take care of him."

Price and his entourage approached the car. I could hear Price speaking gruffly to the driver while the other BKs surrounded the car so that it couldn't drive off. Then Price opened the door and gestured for the white guy to get out.

Just then I heard the loud squeal of a car rounding the corner of Twenty-fifth and Federal. Some kids shouted at people to get out of its path. It was a gray sedan, and I could see it roaring toward us, but unsteadily, as if one of the wheels were loose.

The first shots sounded like machine-gun fire. Everyone seemed to duck instinctively, except for me. I was frozen upright; my legs were stuck in place and everything turned to slow motion. The car came closer. Price and the other BK security men ran toward the building as more shots were fired. The car flew past, and I could see four people inside, all black. It looked as if two of them were shooting, one from either side.

Price got hit and dropped to the ground. The rest of his entourage reached the lobby safely. Price wasn't moving. I saw Darryl lying flat on the grass, while other tenants were crawling toward shelter—a car, a tree, the building itself—and grabbing children as they went. I was still standing, in shock, though I had managed to at least hunch over. The gray car had vanished.

Then I heard a second car screeching down the back alleyway. I was puzzled. In most drive-by shootings, a gang wouldn't risk a second pass, since the element of surprise had been used up. Indeed, looking around now at the expanse in front of the building, I saw perhaps a dozen young men with guns in their hands, crouching behind cars or along the sides of the building. I had never seen so many guns in Robert Taylor.

Price still hadn't gotten up. I could see that he was gripping his leg. Somehow the sight of him lying motionless moved me to action. I headed toward him and saw that one of the BKs had come back outside to do the same. We grabbed Price and started to drag him toward the building.

"Get Serena! Get Serena!" someone shouted down from an upper floor. "She's out there with her baby!"

The BK helping me with Price ran over to help Serena and her children to a safe spot. I dragged Price the rest of the way by myself and made it to the lobby just as the second car emerged from the alley. I heard some shouts and some more gunshots. I saw that the BK who'd gone to help Serena had draped his body atop her and her kids.

In the dim light of the lobby, I could see that Price's leg was bleeding badly, just above the knee. J.T.'s men pushed me out of the way. They carried Price farther inside the building, toward one of the ground-floor apartments. I wondered where J.T. was.

"Sudhir, get inside, go upstairs to Ms. Mae's—now!" It was Ms. Bailey. I gestured toward Price, to show that I wanted to help. She just yelled at me again to get upstairs.

About five flights up the stairs, I ran into a group of J.T.'s men on the gallery, looking out. "I don't see no more!" one of them shouted to some BKs on the ground outside. "It don't look like there's any more! Just get everyone inside and put four in the lobby."

I heard a stream of footsteps in the stairwell. Parents yelled at their children to hurry up, and a few mothers asked for help carrying their strollers. I heard someone say that J.T. was in the lobby, so I hustled back downstairs.

He stood at the center of a small mob, taking reports from his men. There was a lot of commotion, all of them talking past one another:

"Niggers will do it again, I know they will!"

"We need to get Price to the hospital, he's still bleeding."

"No, we need to secure the building."

"I say we drive by and shoot back, now!"

As instructed, four young men now stood armed guard in the lobby, two at each entrance. Under normal circumstances young gang members like these bragged about their toughness, their willingness to kill for the family. But now, with the danger real, they looked shaky, eyes wide and fearful.

J.T. stood calmly, wearing dark sunglasses, picking his teeth. When his eyes fell upon me, he fixed me with a glare. I didn't know what he was trying to communicate. Then he pointed toward the ceiling. He wanted me upstairs, at his mother's place, out of the way.

Instead I walked even farther into the lobby, out of his view. I asked a rank-and-file BK where Price was. He pointed down the hall. J.T. approached, patted me on the back, and pulled me in close. "Price isn't doing so hot," he whispered. "He's bleeding real bad, and I need to get him to the hospital."

"Call the ambulance," I said instinctively.

"They won't come. Listen, we need your car. If they see one of our cars come up to Provident, they may call the police. We need to borrow your car."

"Sure, of course," I said, reaching for my keys. I had recently bought a junker, a 1982 Cutlass Ciera. "Let me get it."

"No," J.T. said, grabbing my hand. "You can't leave the building for a while. Go upstairs, but let me have the keys. Cherise will take him."

I gave J.T. my keys and watched him walk toward the apartment where Price was being looked after. It was common practice to have a woman drive a BK to the hospital so that he wouldn't immediately be tagged as a gangster. Cherise lived in the building and let the Black Kings use her apartment to make crack cocaine. J.T. sometimes joked that the young women in the projects would never turn on their stoves if it weren't for his gang cooking up crack.

J.T. commandeered a vacant apartment on the fourteenth floor to use as a temporary headquarters. The scene was surreal, like watching an army prepare for war. I sat in a corner and watched as J.T. issued commands. Small groups of men would come inside, receive their orders, and hurry off. J.T. assigned several men to take up rifles and sit in the windows of the third, fifth, and seventh floors. He instructed other groups of men to go door-to-door and warn tenants to stay away from the west-facing windows.

He told one young BK that there probably wouldn't be another shooting for at least a few hours. "Get some of the older people out of here," he ordered. "Take them to 2325." A BK foot soldier told me that Price had made it to the emergency room but was said to be still bleeding badly.

J.T. came over and told me what he knew. The first car, the beat-up Ford, was a decoy to lure some Black Kings out of the building. The attack appeared to be a collaboration between the MCs and the Stones. They were deeply envious, J.T. told me, that the BKs had been able to attract so many customers to their territory. The MCs and the Stones were a constant source of worry for J.T., since they were led by "crazy niggers," his term for the kind of bad business-men who thought that a drive-by shooting was the best way to compete in a drug market. J.T. much preferred the more established rival gangs, since a shared interest in maintaining the status quo decreased their appetite for violence.

Every so often J.T. sent out an entourage to buy food for people in the building. A few tenants carried on as usual, paying little attention to the Black Kings' dramatic show of security in the lobby. But except for a couple of stereos and some shouting in the stairwells, the building was eerily quiet. We all baked in the still, hot air.

Occasionally one of J.T.'s more senior members would throw out a plan for retaliation. J.T. listened to every proposal but was noncommittal. "We got time for all that," he kept saying. "Let's just see what happens tonight."

Every half hour Cherise called from the hospital to report on Price's condition. J.T. looked tense as he took these reports. Price was a friend since high school, one of the few people J.T. allowed in his inner circle.

I was just nodding off to sleep on the floor when J.T. walked over.

"Thanks, man," he said quietly.

"For what?"

"You didn't have to get mixed up in this shit."

He must have heard that I'd helped drag Price into the lobby. I didn't say anything. J.T. slapped my leg, asked if I wanted a Coke, and walked off to the fridge.

There were no more shootings that night, but the tension didn't let up. I never went home.

Within a few days, once he figured out exactly who was responsible for the attack, J.T. rounded up T-Bone and several other officers and went after the shooters. J.T. personally helped beat them up; the BKs also took their guns and money. Because these young rivals had "no business sense," as J.T. told me later, there was no hope of a compromise. Physical retaliation was the only measure to consider.

Price stayed in the hospital for a few days, but the bullet caused no irreparable damage, and he was soon back in action.

T-Bone called me one day with big news: J.T. was on the verge of receiving another important promotion within the citywide Black Kings organization. If all went according to plan, J.T., T-Bone, and Price would be responsible for taking on even more BK factions, which meant managing a considerably larger drug-trafficking operation. I could hear the excitement in T-Bone's voice. For him, too, the promotion meant more money as well as a boost in status. "Two years, that's it," he told me. "Two more years of this shit, and I'm getting out of the game." Ever practical, T-Bone was saving for his future—a house, full-time college, and a legal job.

J.T. wouldn't be around Robert Taylor much for the next several weeks, T-Bone told me, since his new assignment required a lot of preparation and legwork. But he had asked T-Bone to give me a message: "J.T. wants you to go with him to the next regional BK meeting. You up for it?"

I had been waiting for this phone call for a few years. I desperately wanted to learn about the gang's senior leadership, and now that J.T. was one of them, it looked like I'd finally have my chance.

By this point in my research, I still felt guilty sometimes for being as much of a hustler, in my own way, as the other hustlers in the neighborhood. C-Note had called me on it, and C-Note was right. I constantly hustled people for information—stories, data, in-

terviews, facts—anything that might make my research more interesting.

So I was happy whenever I had the chance to give a little bit
back. The writing workshop hadn't worked out as well as I'd wanted,
and I was searching for another way to act charitably. An opportunity fell into my lap when the Chicago public-school teachers went
on strike. Since BK rules stipulated that each member graduate from
high school, J.T. asked Autry to set up a program during the strike
so that J.T.'s members could stay off the streets and do some homework. Autry had set up a similar program at the Boys & Girls Club,
but gang boundaries forbade J.T.'s members to go there.

Autry agreed, and he asked me to run a classroom in J.T.'s building. I obliged, pretty sure that lecturing high-schoolers on history,
politics, and math shouldn't be too hard.

We met in a dingy, darkened apartment with a bathroom that
didn't work. On a given day, there were anywhere from twenty to
fifty teenage gang members on my watch. The air was so foul that I
let them smoke to cover the odor. There weren't enough seats, so the
kids forcibly claimed some chairs from neighboring apartments, with
no promise of returning them.

On the first day, as the students talked loudly through my lecture
on history and politics, J.T. walked in unannounced and shouted at
them to pay attention. He ordered Price to take one particularly
noisy foot soldier into the hallway and beat him.

Later I asked J.T. not to interrupt again. The kids would never
learn anything, I insisted, if they knew that he was going to be monitoring them. J.T. and Autry both thought I was crazy. They didn't
think I had any chance of controlling the unruly teens without the
threat of an occasional visit by J.T.

They were right. Within a day the "classroom" had descended

into anarchy. In one corner a few guys were admiring a gun that one of them had just bought. (He was thoughtful enough to remove the bullets during class.) In another corner several teenagers had organized a dice game. The winner would get not only the cash but also the right to rob the homeless people sleeping in a nearby vacant apartment. One kid brought in a radio and improvised a rap song about their "Injun teacher," replete with references to Custer, Geronimo, and "the smelly Ay-Rab." (It never seemed to occur to anyone that "Arab" and "Indian" were not in fact interchangeable; in my case they were equally valuable put-downs.) The most harmless kids in the room were the ones who patiently waited for their friends to return from the store with some beer.

Things got worse from there. Some of my students started selling marijuana in the classroom; others would casually leave the building to find a prostitute. When I conveyed all this to J.T., he said that as long as the guys showed up, they weren't hanging out on the street and getting into any real trouble.

Given that they were using my "classroom" to deal drugs, gamble, and play with guns, I wondered exactly what J.T. meant by "real" trouble.

My role was quickly downgraded from teacher to baby-sitter. The sessions lasted about two weeks, until news came that the teachers' strike was being settled. By this time my admiration for Autry's skill with the neighborhood kids had increased exponentially.

D espite my utter failure as a teacher, Autry called me again for help. The stakes were a little higher this time—and, for me, so was the reward.

Autry and the other staffers at the Boys & Girls Club wanted me to help write a grant proposal for the U.S. Department of Justice, which had advertised special funds being allocated for youth programs. The proposal needed to include in-depth crime statistics for the projects and the surrounding neighborhood, data that was typically hard to get, since the police didn't like to make such information public. But if I took on the project, I'd get direct access to Officer Reggie Marcus—"Officer Reggie" to tenants—the local cop who had grown up in Robert Taylor himself and was devoted to making life there better. I jumped at the chance.

I had met Reggie on several occasions, but now I had an opportunity to work closely with him and cultivate a genuine friendship. He was about six feet tall, as muscular and fit as a football player; he always dressed well and carried himself with a quiet determination. I knew that Reggie often dealt directly with gang leaders in the hopes of keeping violence to a minimum and that he was a diplomatic force among the project's street hustlers. Now I would be able to ask as many questions as I wanted about the particulars of his work.

Why, for instance, did he try to reduce gun violence by making sure that the *gangs* were the only ones who had guns?

"They don't like gun violence any more than the tenants, because it scares away customers," he explained. "So they try to keep things quiet."

One wintry afternoon I met Reggie at the police station in the Grand Boulevard neighborhood, a few blocks from J.T.'s territory. When I arrived, he told me he still had some phone calls to make, so I went to find a water fountain. The police station was drab, row after row of bland gray cubicles; the air was cold and damp, the tile floor slippery from the tracked-in snow.

Near the water fountain, I came upon a wall covered with Polaroid pictures. They were all of black men in their teens and twenties, most of them looking dazed or defiant. Beneath each photo was a caption with the person's name and gang affiliation.

Taped next to the photos was a party flyer headlined "MC South-side Fest." J.T.'s gang hung similar flyers all around the buildings when they were sponsoring a party or a basketball tournament. On the MC flyer, there were several names handwritten along the right margin, as if it were a sign-up sheet: "Watson," "O'Neill," "Brown."

Reggie came by as I was inspecting the flyer.

"Let's not hang out here," he said, looking concerned. "And let's not talk about that. I'll explain later."

We were heading over to the Boys & Girls Club to talk to Autry about the Department of Justice grant. As we walked to Reggie's SUV, parked behind the police station, I was still thinking about the MC flyer.

I recalled a party the Black Kings had thrown a few years back, having rented out the second floor of an Elks Lodge. The women were dressed up, and the men wore spiffy tracksuits or pressed jeans. They drank beer and wine coolers, danced, and passed marijuana joints around the room.

As J.T. and I stood talking in a corner, a group of five men suddenly busted into the room, all dressed in black. One of them held up a gun for everyone to see. The other four ran to the corners of the room, one of them shouting for everyone to get up against the wall. Four of the men were black, one white. J.T. whispered to me, "Cops." He and I took our places against the wall.

One of the partying gangsters, a huge man, at least six foot two and 250 pounds, started to resist. "Fuck you, nigger!" he shouted. Two of the men in black promptly yanked him into the bathroom— where, from the sound of it, they beat him brutally. We all stood silently against the wall, listening to his grunts and groans.

"Who's next?" shouted one of the men in black. "Who wants some of this?"

Two of them pulled out black trash bags. "Cash and jewels, I want everything in the bag!" one shouted. "Now!"

When the bag reached us, J.T. calmly deposited his necklace and his money clip, fat with twenties. I put the cash from my pocket, about fifteen dollars, into the bag. As I did so, the man holding the bag looked up and stared at me. He didn't say anything, but he kept glancing over at me as he continued his collection rounds. He seemed puzzled as to what I, plainly an outsider, was doing there.

When they were done, the five men dropped the bags out the window and calmly filed out. After a time J.T. motioned for me to follow him outside. We walked to his car, parked in the adjoining lot. Some other BK leaders joined him, commiserating over the robbery.

"Fucking cops do this all the time," J.T. told me. "As soon as they find out we're having a party, they raid it."

"Why? And why don't they arrest you?" I asked. "And how do you know they were cops?"

"It's a game!" shouted one of the other BK leaders. "*We* make all this fucking money, and they want some."

"They're jealous," J.T. said calmly. "We make more than them, and they can't stand it. So this is how they get back at us."

I had a hard time believing that the police would so brazenly rob a street gang. But it didn't seem like the kind of thing that J.T. would lie about; most of his exaggerations served the purpose of making him look *more* powerful, not less so.

I had forgotten the incident entirely until I saw the MC flyer at the police station. I wondered if the names written in the margin were the cops who had signed up to raid the party. So I told Reggie about the BK party and J.T.'s claim that the robbers were cops.

He took a deep breath and looked straight ahead as he drove. "You know, Sudhir, you have to be careful about what you hear," he said. Reggie drove fast, barreling over the unplowed snow as if he were off-roading. Our breath was fogging up the windshield. "I'm not going to say that all the people I work with are always doing the right thing. Hell, *I* don't do the right thing all the time. But—"

"You don't have to tell me anything if you don't want to."

"I know that, I know that. But you *should* know what's going on. Yes, some of the people I work with raid the parties. And you know, sometimes I feel like I should do it, too! I mean, guys like J.T. are making a killing off people. And for what? *Peddling* stuff that kills. But it's not for me. I don't participate—I just don't see the point."

"I've ridden along with J.T. and a few of his friends in their sports cars," I said. "Sometimes a cop will pull us over for no reason. And then—"

"He asks to see a paycheck stub, right?"

"Yeah! How did you know I was going to say that?"

"Think about how frustrating it is to do policing," Reggie said. "You've been hanging out with these guys. You know that they never hold the cash that they make. They have all these investments in other people's names. So what can we do? We can't arrest their mothers for living in a nice house. But when we stop them in their fancy cars, we can legitimately ask whether they stole the car or not. Now, again, I don't do that stuff. But some other people do."

"But *I* don't have to carry around a paycheck stub. Why should they?" I knew this was a naïve-sounding question, and I was fully aware that there was a big difference between me and the gang members. But because naïveté had worked in the past, I'd stuck with this strategy.

"*You* are not peddling that shit," Reggie said, stating the obvious. I wasn't sure if his explanation was meant to be sarcastic, whether he was humoring me, or whether he just wanted to make sure I understood precisely the police officers' rationale. "*You* aren't making millions by killing people. Sometimes we'll take their car away."

"What do you do with it?" I asked. I knew Reggie didn't believe that the drug dealers were each "making millions," but some of their earnings were still sufficiently greater than the cops' to make Reggie upset.

"A lot of times, we'll sell it at the police auction, and the money goes to charity. I figure it's a way of getting back at those fools."

On a few occasions, I'd been riding in a car with some gang members when a cop stopped the car, made everyone get out, and summarily called for a tow truck. On a few other occasions, the cop let the driver keep the car but took everyone's jewelry and cash. To me the strangest thing was that the gang members barely protested. It was as if they were playing a life-size board game, the rules of which were well established and immutable, and on this occasion they'd simply gotten a bad roll of the dice.

A few weeks later, Reggie invited me to a South Side bar frequented by black cops. "I think you're getting a real one-sided view of our work," he said.

His offer surprised me. Reggie was a reserved man, and he rarely introduced me to other police officers even if they were standing nearby. He preferred to speak with me behind closed doors—in Ms. Bailey's office, inside the Boys & Girls Club, or in his car.

We met at the bar on a Saturday afternoon. It was located a few blocks from the precinct and Robert Taylor. It was nondescript on the outside, marked only by some neon beer signs. On either side of it lay fast-food restaurants, liquor stores, and check-cashing shops. Even Reggie didn't know the bar's actual name. "I've been coming

here for fifteen years," he said, "and I never even bothered to ask."
He and the other cops just called it "the Lounge." The place was
just as nondescript inside: a long wooden bar, several tables, dim
lighting, some Bears and Bulls posters. It had the feel of a well-worn
den in a working-class home. All the patrons were black and at least
in their mid-thirties, with a few old-timers nursing an afternoon beer.

Reggie sat us down at a table and introduced me to three of his
off-duty colleagues. From the outset they seemed wary of speaking
about their work. And since I never liked to question people too
much until I got to know them, the conversation was stiff to say the
least. In a short time, we covered my ethnic background, the Chicago
Bears, and the strange beliefs of the university crowd in Hyde Park.
The cops, like most working-class Chicagoans, thought that Hyde
Park liberals—myself included, presumably—held quaint, unrealistic views of reality, especially in terms of racial integration. To these
men Hyde Park was known as the "why can't everyone just get
along?" part of town.

One of the cops, a man named Jerry, sat staring at me the entire
time. I felt sure I'd seen him before. He was quietly drinking whiskey
shots with beer chasers. Once in a while, he'd spit out a question:
"So you think you know a lot about gangs, huh?" or "What are you
going to write about, Mr. Professor?" I got a little nervous when he
started calling me "Mr. Professor," since that's how I was known in
J.T.'s building. Was this just a coincidence?

The more Officer Jerry drank, the more belligerent he became.
"You university types like to talk about how much you know, don't
you?" he said. "You like to talk about how you're going to solve all
these problems, don't you?"

Reggie shot me a glance as if to say that I'd better defend myself.

"Well, if you think I don't know something, why don't you teach me?" I said. I'd had a few beers myself by now, and I probably sounded more aggressive than I'd intended.

"Motherfucker!" Jerry leaned in hard toward me. "You think I don't know who you fucking are? You think we *all* don't know what you're doing? If you want to play with us, you better be real careful. If you like watching, you may get caught."

A shiver ran over me when he said "watching." Now I knew exactly where I'd seen him. In J.T.'s buildings Officer Jerry was well known, and by my estimation he was a rogue cop. Some months earlier, I'd been sitting in a stairwell interviewing a few prostitutes and pimps. I heard a commotion in the gallery. The stairwell door was partially open; looking out, I could see three police officers busting open an apartment door. Two of them, one black and one white, ran inside. The third, who was black, stayed outside guarding the door. He didn't seem to notice us.

A minute later the cops hauled out a man and a teenage boy. Neither of them resisted, and neither seemed very surprised. The teenager was handcuffed, and they forced him to the floor. The mother was screaming, as was the baby in her arms.

Then a fourth cop showed up, swaggering down the hall. It was Officer Jerry. He wore black pants, a black and blue fleece jacket, and a bulletproof vest. He started to beat and kick the father violently. "Where's the money, nigger?" he shouted. "Where's the cash?"

I was shocked. I glanced at the folks I'd been talking to in the stairwell. They looked as if they'd seen this before, but they also looked anxious, sitting in silence in the apparent hope that the cops wouldn't come for them next.

Finally the man relented. He, too, lay on the floor, bloodied. "In the oven," he said, "in the oven."

Officer Jerry went inside and returned with a large brown bag. "Don't fuck with us," he told the father. "You hear me?"

The father just sat there, dazed. The other cops took the handcuffs off the teenager and let him back into the apartment.

Just as Officer Jerry was leaving, one of the pimps sitting next to me accidentally dropped a beer bottle. Officer Jerry turned and looked down the gallery, straight at us. I jumped back, but he stomped into the stairwell. He cast his eye over the lot of us. "Get the fuck out of here!" he said. Then, noticing me, he smirked, as if I were no more significant than a flea.

Once he left, I asked one of the pimps, Timothy, about Officer Jerry. "He gets to come in the building whenever he wants and get a piece of the action," he said. Timothy told me that Sonny, the man that Officer Jerry had just beaten, stole cars for a living but had apparently neglected to pay his regular protection fee to Officer Jerry. "We always joke that whenever Officer Jerry runs out of money, he comes in here and beats up a nigger," Timothy said. "He got me once last year. Took two hundred bucks and then my girl had to suck his dick. Asshole."

In the coming months, I learned that Officer Jerry was a notorious presence in the building. I heard dozens of stories from tenants who said they'd suffered all forms of harassment, abuse, and shakedowns at the hands of Officer Jerry. It was hard to corroborate these stories, but based on what I'd seen with my own eyes, they weren't hard to believe. And to some degree, it probably didn't much matter whether all the reports of his abusive behavior were true. In the projects, the "bad cop" story was a myth that residents spread at will out of sheer frustration that they lived in a high-crime area where the police presence was minimal at best, unchecked at worst.

Now, sitting across the table from him at the Lounge, I started to feel extremely nervous. What if he somehow knew that I had recorded all these incidents in my notebooks?

He sat there sputtering with rage, shaking the table. I looked over at Reggie, hoping for some help.

"Jerry, leave him alone," Reggie said quietly, fiddling with his beer. "He's okay."

"Okay? Are you kidding me? You trust that motherfucking Ay-rab?!" Jerry tossed back his shot and grabbed the beer. I thought he might throw the bottle at me. He let out a nasty laugh. "Just tell him to stay out of my way."

"Listen, I'm only trying to get a better understanding of what you do," I said. "Maybe I could tell you a little bit about my research."

"Fuck you," Jerry said, staring me down. "You write any of that shit down, and I'll come after your ass. You got me? I don't want to talk to you, I don't want you talking to nobody else, and I don't want to see you around these motherfucking projects. I know who you are, motherfucker. Don't think I don't know what you're doing."

Reggie grabbed my arm and threw a twenty-dollar bill on the table. "Let's go," he said.

When we got to the car, Reggie started the ignition but didn't drive away. He began to speak gently but firmly, his tone almost parental. "Sudhir, I brought you here today because these guys wanted to know who you are and what you're up to. I didn't want to tell you that, because I knew you'd be nervous. They know you're watching, they know you've seen them in the building, they know you're going to be writing something. I told them that you were a good person. Jerry was too drunk—I'm sorry about that."

Reggie held his silence for a few minutes, looking out at the busy street.

"I think you have to make a decision, Sudhir," he said. "And I can't make it for you. I never really asked you what you'll be writing about. I thought you were just helping the club, but then Autry told me last week that you're writing about life in the projects. You and I have talked about a lot of things. But we never talked about whether you would write what I say. I hope not. I mean, if you are, I'd like you to tell me right now. But that's not really the problem, because I'm not afraid of what I do or what I am."

Up to this point, Reggie knew that I was interviewing families and others for my graduate research. A few months later, we wound up talking further about my dissertation, and he said it would be okay to include anything he'd told me, but we agreed to change his name so he couldn't be identified.

At this moment, however, what really concerned me was the reaction of his colleagues. "Reggie, are you telling me I need to worry if I write about cops?"

"Police don't talk a lot to people like you," he said. "Like Jerry. He doesn't want people watching what he does. I know you've seen him do some stupid shit. I know you've seen a *lot* of people do some stupid shit. But you need to decide: What good does it do to write about what he does? If you want to work around here, maybe you keep some of this out."

I left Reggie that evening not knowing what I should do. If I wanted to write about effective policing—like the good, creative work that Reggie did—I would feel compelled to write about abusive policing as well.

A week later I was talking to Autry about my dilemma. We were having a beer in the South Shore apartment where he lived with his wife and children. South Shore was a stately neighborhood with pockets of low-income apartments that someone like Autry could afford. He had moved there to keep his children away from street gangs.

Autry insisted that I not write about the police. His explanation was revealing. "You need to understand that there are two gangs in the projects," he said. "The police are also a gang, but they *really* have the power. I mean, these niggers run around with money and cars, but at any moment the cops can get them off the street. They know about you. They've been talking with me, and I've been telling them you're okay, but they want to know what you're looking for."

"Why didn't you tell me this before?" I asked.

"I didn't want to worry you, and you haven't done nothing wrong," he said. "But you need to do what I do. Never, never, *never* piss off the police."

When I pressed Autry on the subject, he wouldn't say anything more, other than flatly repeating his advice: "Don't write about them."

Two weeks later my car was broken into. It was parked across the street from the Boys & Girls Club. Curiously, however, neither the lock nor the window was broken; instead the lock had been expertly picked. My backpack and the glove compartment had both been thoroughly rummaged, with some pens, paper, a couple of candy bars, and my gym clothes strewn about. But nothing seemed to be missing. Although I sometimes kept a few notebooks in my backpack, on this occasion I hadn't.

I went inside to tell Autry. "Let's call Reggie," he said. "Don't touch anything."

We waited for Reggie inside the club, where a children's Christmas party was in progress. The mood was happy, especially since some local stores had donated crates of food for tenant families.

Reggie arrived wearing a Santa hat. He'd been at another Christmas party, passing out toys donated by police officers. When he saw my car, he dropped his head and then peered at Autry.

"Did you talk with him?" he asked Autry.

"I did, but he's pigheaded. He don't listen."

I was confused.

"Sudhir, is there any way you could let me know when you're going to come around here?" Reggie asked. "I mean, maybe you could page me and leave a message."

"What are you talking about? I come over here nearly every day! Can you guys please tell me what's going on?"

"Let's go for a walk," Reggie said, grabbing my arm.

It was freezing, and the wind was howling. We walked around the project buildings. The fresh snow made the high-rises look like gravestones sticking up from the ground.

"Sudhir, you're getting into something you shouldn't be messing with," Reggie said. "You've been reading about the gang busts, right?"

Yes, I told him. The newspapers had been reporting the recent arrests of some of the highest-level drug dealers in Chicago. These arrests were apparently intended to interrupt the trade between the Mexican-American gangs who imported cocaine and the black gangsters who sold crack.

Word on the street was that the FBI and other federal agencies were behind the arrests. Although I hadn't been in touch with J.T. lately—he was still busy settling into his expanded Black Kings duties—he had told me in the past that federal involvement frightened the gangs. "Once you see the feds, that's when you worry," he said. "If it's local, we never worry. As long as you don't do something stupid, you'll be okay." Although the recent arrests involved gang leaders more senior than J.T., and not even in his neighborhood, he was habitually concerned that federal officials would work their way down the ladder to him. He also reasoned that the feds would specifically target the Black Kings if possible, considering that the gang ran what was probably the city's smoothest drug operation.

Reggie now told me that the feds were indeed working Chicago—and hard. They were hoping to indict the drug gangs under the powerful Racketeer Influenced and Corrupt Organizations (RICO) Act, which was instituted in 1970 to combat the Mafia and other crime groups that dealt in money laundering, gambling, and union shakedowns. RICO had been so successful in disrupting Italian, Irish, and Jewish crime gangs that the feds were now using it to go after street gangs, claiming that they, too, were organized criminal enterprises.

Reggie explained that he, like most street cops, hated it when federal agents came to town. They were so eager for high-profile indictments, he said, that they'd use allegations of police improprieties to leverage local cops into turning over their gang intelligence. This in turn would disrupt the relationships that cops like Reggie had carefully built up in the community.

"What does all this mean for you?" I asked. "And for me?"

"For me it means I got to do everything by the book. For you it means you have to be very, very careful. I heard from Ms. Bailey that you're asking a lot of people about us. Now, that doesn't bother me, like I said before. But there are a lot of folks where I work who think you're trying to bust them, do you understand?"

"Bust them?"

"They think you're looking for dirt. Looking to find something to hold against them. I wouldn't worry about your car. Just trust me, it won't happen again."

After this talk with Reggie, I began to fear the police much more than I had ever feared J.T. and the gangs. As Autry had told me, it was the cops who had the real power. They controlled where and how openly the gang could operate, and, if so inclined, they could put just about anyone in jail. Still, as both Autry and J.T. had told me, the cops rarely arrested gang leaders, since they preferred to know who was in control rather than having to deal with an unpredictable leader or, even worse, a power vacuum. When I asked Reggie if this was really true, his response—he dropped his head and asked me not to press him on the issue—seemed to indicate that it was.

Not every cop in the projects was corrupt or abusive, but I had become nervous about getting on the cops' bad side. I had no desire to get beaten up or be regularly harassed. I'd grown up thinking of cops as people you trusted to help when things went bad, but that wasn't the way things worked here, even for me. Not that I'd endeared myself to the cops: I came into the projects by befriending a gang leader, after all, and I hung out with a lot of tenants who did illegal things for a living.

Looking back, I think it would have been better to learn more about the neighborhood from the cops' perspective. But this wouldn't have been easy. Most tenants probably would have stopped speaking with me if they thought I was even remotely tied to the police. One reason journalists often publish thin stories about the projects is that they typically rely on the police for information, and this reliance makes the tenants turn their backs.

As it was, the best I could do was try to learn a little bit from cops like Reggie. He could be just as creative in his approach to police work as some of the tenants were in their approach to survival. If this meant sharing information with gang members to ensure that their wars didn't kill innocents, so be it. Rather than arresting young gang members, Reggie and other cops used "scared straight" tactics to try to get them to stop dealing. I also watched many times as the police mediated disputes between hustlers; and even though they weren't always responsive to domestic-abuse calls, many cops did help Ms. Bailey scare perpetrators so they wouldn't come into the high-rise again.

It wasn't until months after my car was broken into that Reggie

confirmed it had been the police who did it. Officer Jerry and a few
of his friends were apparently concerned about the contents of my
notebooks and wanted to find them. Bad Buck, a young man from
Robert Taylor whom I'd befriended, had told the police that I kept
my notes in my car. Reggie said that Buck had been caught holding a thousand dollars' worth of cocaine and had surrendered the information about my notes in exchange for not going to jail.

I n early 1995 the newspapers began to report another story of
major import for the residents of Robert Taylor, this one with even
greater consequences than the federal drug busts. Members of Congress and the Clinton administration had begun serious discussions
with mayors across the country to propose knocking down housing
projects. Henry Cisneros, the secretary of housing and urban development, claimed that "high-rises just don't work." He and his staff
spoke of demolishing these "islands of poverty," with the goal of
pushing their inhabitants to live where "residents of different in-
comes interact with one another." Cisneros singled out Chicago's
projects as "without question, the worst public housing in America
today." The Robert Taylor Homes were said to be at the very top of
the demolition list. They were to be replaced by an upscale town-
house development called Legends South, which would include just
a few hundred units of public housing.

Most of the tenants I spoke with greeted this news with disbelief. Did the politicians really have the will or the power to relocate
tens of thousands of poor black people? "The projects will be here
forever," was the phrase I heard from one tenant after another. Only
the most elderly tenants seemed to believe that demolition could be
a reality. They had already seen the government use urban renewal—
or, in their words, "Negro removal"—to move hundreds of thou-

sands of black Chicagoans, replacing their homes and businesses with highways, sports stadiums, universities—and, of course, huge tracts of public housing.

From the outset urban renewal held the seeds of its own failure. White political leaders blocked the construction of housing for blacks in the more desirable white neighborhoods. And even though blighted low-rise buildings in the ghetto were replaced with high-rises like the Robert Taylor Homes, the quality of the housing stock wasn't much better. Things might have been different if housing authorities around the country were given the necessary funds to keep up maintenance on these new buildings. But the buildings that had once been the hope of urban renewal were already, a short forty years later, ready for demolition again.

Amid all this uncertainty, I finally heard from J.T. He called with the news that his promotion was official. He asked if I still wanted to join him in meetings with some citywide BK leaders.

"They're actually interested in talking with you," he said, surprise in his voice. "They want someone to hear their stories, about jail, about their lives. I thought they might not want to talk because of what's going on"—he meant the recent gang arrests—"but they were up for it."

I told J.T. that I'd been talking to my professors about winding down my field research and finishing the dissertation. I had completed all my classes and passed all my exams, and I was now focused on writing my study about the intricate ways in which the members of a poor community eked out a living. Bill Wilson had arranged for me to present my research at various academic conferences, in hopes of attracting a teaching position for me. My academic career probably started the day I met J.T., but the attention of established sociologists made me feel as though I had just now reached the starting gate. Katchen had completed her applications to law school, and both of us were expecting to leave Chicago soon.

There were other factors, too: Many of the tenants in Robert Taylor felt betrayed by me, cops were warning me not to hang out, and now the projects themselves were about to come down. All this combined to make it pretty clear that I wouldn't be spending time in the projects much longer.

J.T. reacted dismissively, saying I shouldn't even think about leaving now. "We've been together for the longest," he said. "If you really want to know what my organization is about, you got to watch what happens. We're on the move, we're only getting bigger, and you need to see this."

J.T. wouldn't take no for an answer. There was something childlike about his insistence, as if pleading with someone not to abandon him. He laughed and chatted on spiritedly about the future of the BKs, about his own ascension, about the "great book" I would someday write about his life.

I tried to take it all in, but the sentences started to bleed into one another. I simply sat there, phone to my ear, mumbling "Uh-huh" whenever J.T. took a breath. It was time to acknowledge, if only to myself, exactly what I'd been doing these past several years: I came, I saw, I hustled. Even if J.T. wouldn't allow me to move on just yet, that's what I was ready to do.

Not that this acknowledgment of my inner hustler gave me any peace. I was full of unease about my conduct in the projects. I had actively misled J.T. into thinking that I was writing his biography, mostly by never denying it. This might have been cute in the early days of our time together, but by now it was purely selfish not to tell him what my study was really about. I tended to retreat from conflict, however. This was a useful trait in obtaining information. But as my tenure in the projects was ending, I was noticing the darker side of avoidance.

With other tenants I played the role of objective social scientist, however inaccurate (and perhaps impossible) this academic conceit may be. I didn't necessarily feel that I was misrepresenting my intentions. I always told people, for instance, that I was writing up my findings into a dissertation. But it was obvious that there was a clear power dynamic and that they held the short end of the stick. I had the choice of ending my time in the projects; they did not. Long after I was finished studying poverty, they would most likely continue living as poor Americans.

EIGHT

The Stay-Together Gang

One July day in 1995, I drove to Calumet Heights, a neighborhood that lay just across the expressway from Chicago's South Side. In an otherwise run-down working-class area, Calumet Heights stood out for its many middle- and upper-class black families who took great pride in the appearance of their houses. The neighborhood was also home to several of the most powerful gang leaders in the Midwest, including Jerry Tillman and Brian Jackson of the Black Kings. In a practice common among gang leaders, Jerry and Brian had each bought a big suburban home for their moms, and they both spent considerable time there themselves.

Today they were throwing a BK pool party at Brian's house; Jerry was supplying the food and beer. Brian lived in a long, white, Prairie-style home built in the style of Frank Lloyd Wright. Parked on the lawn were a dozen expensive sports cars, which belonged to the BK senior leadership, and a lot of lesser sports cars parked along the curb, which belonged to the junior leadership. A bunch of young men stood around idly on the lawn, caps shading their eyes from the sun. These were BK foot soldiers, in charge of guarding their bosses' cars.

I parked my own rusting Cutlass at the curb and approached the house. I spotted Barry, one of J.T.'s foot soldiers, standing next to J.T.'s purple Malibu. He nodded me toward the house's rear entrance.

J.T. had been meeting regularly with Chicago's highest-ranking BK leaders for some time before he invited me to this party. I was excited. I had envisioned half-naked women sitting poolside and rubbing the bosses with sunscreen while everyone passed around marijuana joints and cold beer.

What I saw for real was far less glamorous. True to stereotype, there was an expensive stereo blasting rap music through a dozen speakers and some big crystal statues of wild animals, and a few people were indeed rolling joints. But overall the place looked as worn as an old fraternity house. The leather couches were badly stained, and so were the carpets. I found out later that the gangsters' mothers felt lonely in the suburbs and told their sons they preferred living in the ghetto, with their friends. Nor were there any half-naked women to be seen, or any women at all. It was a members-only party, and seemingly a pretty tight-knit affair. J.T. had told me that these gatherings were held every few weeks, more often if there were pressing matters to discuss. Although the events were mostly social, he said, the gang leaders inevitably wound up talking business as the evening wore on: Which wholesaler was offering the best and cheapest cocaine? Which neighborhood gangs were acting up and needed discipline?

I bumped into J.T. as he came out of the kitchen. We shook hands and hugged; he seemed to be in a good mood. Small groups of men were congregating in the kitchen, the dining room, and the living room; I could hear the roar of computer games in a back room. Everyone seemed relaxed and at ease.

J.T. brought me over to a group of men and introduced me as "the Professor," which prompted laughs all around. Most of the men were large, their potbellies perhaps the best evidence of a capacity for self-indulgence. They were all tattooed and wore showy gold and silver jewelry. As I would find out later, every one of them had been jailed on a felony at least once.

J.T. hadn't told me exactly how he'd explained my presence to his colleagues and superiors. I just had to trust him. No one seemed even remotely threatened—but then again I wasn't walking around with a tape recorder or asking intrusive questions. In fact, I didn't need to. The men would randomly come up to me and start talking about themselves and, especially, the history of the Black Kings. "In the 1960s, gangs were leading a black revolution," one of them said. "We're trying to do the same." Another took a similar tack, echoing what J.T. had told me many times: "You need to understand that the Black Kings are not a *gang;* we are a *community organization,* responding to people's needs."

One of the men put his arm around me warmly and escorted me into the dining room, where a poker game was being played. There must have been thirty thousand or forty thousand dollars in bills on the table. My guide introduced himself as Cliff. He was a senior BK, in his late forties, who acted as a sort of consigliere for the gang, providing advice to the up-and-coming leaders. "All right, folks, listen up!" he said, trying to gain the poker players' attention. They glanced up briefly. "This is our new director of communications," Cliff said. "The Professor is going to help us get our word out. Make sure you all talk with him before you leave."

I shuddered. J.T. was sitting on the couch with a beer in his hand. He just smiled and shrugged. Two thoughts ran through my mind. On the one hand, I was impressed that J.T. had the confidence to invite me and nominate me for such an exalted position (although part of me felt like I was on the receiving end of a surreal practical joke; perhaps they were just testing my mettle?). On the other hand, knowing that these men managed an organized criminal enterprise, I was scared that I was falling into a hole I could never dig myself out of. I had repeatedly tried to distance myself from the gang, or at least stake out my neutrality. But J.T.'s warning from years earlier rang just as true today: "Either you're with me or you're with someone else." In this world there was no such thing as neutral, as much as the precepts of my academic field might state otherwise.

I attended several of these high-level BK gatherings. Although I didn't conduct any formal interviews, in just a few months I was able to learn a good bit about the gang leaders and their business by just hanging around. Over time they seemed to forget that I was even there, or maybe they just didn't care. They rarely spoke openly about drugs, other than to note the death of a supplier or a change in the price of powder cocaine. Most of their talk concerned the burdens of management: how to keep the shorties in line, how to best bribe tenant leaders and police officers, which local businesses were willing to launder their cash.

I did harbor a low-grade fear that I would someday be asked to represent the BKs in a press release or a media interview. But that fear wasn't enough to prevent me from attending as many parties and poker games as J.T. invited me to. I would joke on occasion with J.T.'s superiors that I really had no skills or services to offer them. They never formally appointed me as their director of communications—

or even made such an explicit offer, so I just assumed that no such role really existed.

As a member of the younger set of leaders who had only recently been promoted to these ranks, J.T. was generally a quiet presence. He didn't speak much with me either. But my presence seemed to provide him with some value. It signaled to the others that J.T. had leadership capacities and unique resources: namely, that he was using his link with a student from a prestigious university to help remake the gang's image in the wider world. To that end, the gang leaders continued to approach me to discuss the gang's history and its "community-building" efforts. I took most of this with a grain of salt, as I'd come to consider such claims not only blatantly self-serving but greatly exaggerated.

Watching J.T. operate in this rarefied club, I couldn't help but feel a sense of pride in him. By now I had spent about six years hanging out with J.T., and at some level I was pleased that he was winning recognition for his achievements. Such thoughts were usually accompanied by an equally powerful disquietude at the fact that I took so much pleasure in the rise of a drug-dealing gangster.

Now that he'd graduated into the gang's leadership, J.T. became even more worried about the basic insecurities of gang life—the constant threat of arrest and imprisonment, injury and death. This anxiety had begun to grow in the weeks after Price was wounded in the drive-by shooting. J.T. began asking me to review his life year by year so that I wouldn't be missing any details for his biography. By this point my dissertation had little to do with J.T., and I believe he knew that, even though I'd been hesitant to say so outright. Still, the arrests were making him nervous, and he wanted to be sure that I was faithfully recording the events of his life. He also became obsessed with saving money for his mother and his children in case something happened to him. He even began selling off some of his cars and expensive jewelry.

At the same time, he started to make more money because of his promotion. Not only were there additional BK sales crews whose earnings J.T. could tax, but, as if in an investment bank or law-firm partnership, he also began receiving a share of the overall BK revenues produced by drug sales, extortion, and taxation. By now he was probably earning at least two hundred thousand dollars a year in cash.

His promotion also carried additional risk. At the suburban meetings I attended, the leaders spoke anxiously about which gang leaders had been named in federal indictments and who was most likely to cooperate with the authorities. I also heard about a young gang member who'd been severely beaten because his bosses thought he had turned snitch.

Amid the beer drinking, gambling, and carousing at these parties, there was a strong undercurrent of paranoia. For me it was a bizarre experience, since the leaders began voicing their fears to me privately, as if I were a confessor of some sort, knowledgeable about their trade but powerless to harm them. Cold Man, a forty-five-year-old leader who ran the BKs' operation on the city's West Side, asked me to step outside for a cigarette so we could talk. He tended to take the long view. "We need to be careful in these times of war," he told me, alluding to the arrests and their potential to create turncoats within the gang. "Don't trust nobody, especially your friends. I love these niggers, they're my family, but now is not the time to go soft."

Pootchie, a smart thirty-year-old leader who'd recently been promoted along with J.T., one night asked me to sit with him in his car to talk. "I'm not going to do this forever," he said. "I'm here to make my money and get the fuck out."

"What will you do next?" I asked.

"I'm a dancer—tap, jazz, all of it. I'd like to get my own place and teach."

I couldn't help laughing. Pootchie looked sheepish. "Sorry!" I said. "I don't mean to laugh, but it's just surprising."

"Yeah, my father used to dance, and my mother was a singer. I dropped out of school—stupidest thing I ever did—but I got a business sense about me. I probably saved a few hundred grand. And I *ain't* getting arrested. No way. I got bigger things I'm into. Not like some of these jailhouse niggers. I ain't one of them. I'm an operator."

I learned that Pootchie's distinction between "jailhouse niggers" and "operators" was an essential one. These were the two kinds of leaders within the Black Kings. The first was devoted to building solidarity and staying together during difficult times, like the present threat of widespread arrests. These leaders were known as "jailhouse niggers," since they had learned from prison that you didn't survive unless you formed alliances and loyalties. These men tended to be the older leaders, in their late thirties or forties, and they tended to speak more of the BK "family" as opposed to the BK "business." The "operators," meanwhile, were a more entrepreneurial breed, like Pootchie and J.T. They were usually younger—J.T. was about thirty by now—and saw the gang primarily as a commercial enterprise. J.T. wanted to be a respected "community man," to be sure, but that was more of a practical gambit than an ideological one.

Riding back to the South Side one night with J.T. from a suburban poker game, I sat quietly in the dark. J.T. was in a somber mood. As we pulled up to my apartment building, he admitted that the federal indictments were driving everyone a bit mad. "No one trusts nobody," he said. "They'll shoot you for looking funny." J.T.

shook his head. "I never realized how easy life was when it was *just* the projects. If they think I'm talking with the cops, I'll be killed right away. Sometimes I think I should get my money and get out."

As he said this, I immediately thought, *I'd better get my data and get out!* But I didn't. I kept going back to the BK meetings. With the gang's most senior officers talking to me, I figured I'd better be careful about how I chose to exit the group. As paranoid as everyone was these days, now was not the time for sudden movements.

J.T.'s life had also become complicated by the possible demolition of the Robert Taylor Homes. He was smart enough to know that his success was due in considerable part to geography: The concentration of people around Robert Taylor and its great location, near traffic corridors and expressways, guaranteed a huge customer base. J.T. might have been a good businessman, but every drug dealer in Chicago knew that Robert Taylor was among the best sales locations in the city.

So if the projects were torn down, J.T. would lose his customer base as well as much of his gang membership, since most of his young members lived in Robert Taylor.

Accordingly, J.T. was far less sanguine about the demolition than some tenants were. He thought it was folly to think that poor families could alter the buildings' fate. Sometimes he'd just sit detachedly when we were together, muttering to himself, "Man, I need a plan. I need a plan. I *have* to think what I'm going to do. . . ."

He also had to worry about retaining his senior leaders, Price and T-Bone. They, too, were getting anxious, since their best shot at success—and their biggest incentive to stay in the gang—was the opportunity to become a leader. If Robert Taylor was torn down, then J.T.'s stock would probably fall, and so would theirs.

When I asked T-Bone how he felt about the future, he soberly described his vulnerability as a lieutenant to J.T. "I'm not protected, that's my main problem," he said. "I got nothing, so I have to be real careful. I mean, I save my money and give it to my mom. Like I told you, I want to get my degree and do something else with my life, start a business maybe. But with all the police coming around, I got to be careful. It's people like me who go to prison. The ones up on the mountain always strike a deal."

But if he left the gang suddenly, I asked him, wouldn't his bosses suspect he was collaborating with the police?

"Yeah," he said with a laugh. "If I leave the gang, these niggers will come after me and kill me. If I stay in the gang, the police will throw me in jail for thirty years. But that's the life. . . ."

As his voice trailed off, I wanted to cry. I liked T-Bone, so much so that sometimes I almost forgot he was a gang member. At the moment he seemed like a bookish kid, working hard and worrying about passing his classes.

Not long afterward T-Bone's girlfriend left a message instructing me to meet him at dusk in a parking lot near the expressway. I did as I was told. "You were always interested in how we do things," T-Bone said, "so here you go." He handed me a set of spiral-bound ledgers that detailed the gang's finances. He seemed remorseful—and anxious. He wondered aloud what his life would have been like if he'd "stayed legit." I could tell he was expecting a bad ending.

The pages of the ledgers were frayed, and some of the hand-writing was hard to decipher, but the raw information was fascinating. For the past four years, T-Bone had been dutifully recording the gang's revenues (from drug sales, extortion, and other sources) and expenses (the cost of wholesale cocaine and weapons, police bribes, funeral expenses, and all the gang members' salaries).

It was dangerous for T-Bone to give me this information, a blatant violation of the gang's codes, for which he would be severely punished if caught. T-Bone knew of my interest in the gang's economic structure. He saw how delighted I was now, fondling the ledgers as if they were first editions of famous books.

I never shared the notebooks with anyone in law enforcement. I put them away for a few years until I met the economist Steven Levitt. We published several articles based on this rich data source, and our analysis of the gang's finances easily received the most notoriety of all the articles and books I have written. T-Bone probably had no idea that I would receive any critical acclaim, but he certainly knew that he was handing me something that few others—in the academy or in the world at large—had ever seen. Looking back, I think he probably wanted to help me, but I also believe he wanted to do something good before meeting whatever bad ending might have been coming his way. Given his love of books and education, it is not altogether inconceivable that T-Bone wanted this to be a charitable act of sorts, helping the world better understand the structure of gangland.

Perhaps the most surprising fact in T-Bone's ledgers was the incredibly low wage paid to the young members who did the dirtiest and most dangerous work: selling drugs on the street. According to T-Bone's records, they barely earned minimum wage. For all their braggadocio, to say nothing of the peer pressure to spend money on sharp clothes and cars, these young members stood little chance of ever making a solid payday unless they beat the odds and were promoted into the senior ranks. But even Price and T-Bone, it turned out, made only about thirty thousand dollars a year. Now I knew why some of the younger BK members supplemented their income by working legit jobs at McDonald's or a car wash.

So a gang leader like J.T. had a tough job: motivating young men to accept the risks of selling drugs despite the low wages and slim chance of promotion. It was one thing to motivate his troops in the Robert Taylor Homes, where BK lore ran deep and the size of the drug trade made the enterprise seem appealingly robust. It would be much harder to start up operations from scratch in a different neighborhood.

I got to witness this challenge firsthand one evening when I accompanied J.T., Price, and T-Bone to West Pullman, a predominantly black neighborhood on the far South Side. Although there were poor sections of West Pullman, it also had a solid working-class base, with little gang activity. That was where the three Black Kings were trying to set up a new BK franchise. J.T. had arranged a meeting with about two dozen young men, a ragtag group of high-school dropouts and some older teenagers, most of whom spent the majority of their time just hanging out. J.T. wanted to help them become "black businessmen," he told them.

They sat on wooden benches in the corner of a small neighborhood park. Most of them had boyish faces. Some looked innocent, some bored, and some eager, as if attending the first meeting of their Little League team. J.T. stood in front of them like their coach, extolling the benefits of "belonging to the Black Kings family, a nationwide family." He pointed to his latest car, a Mitsubishi 3000GT, as a sign of what you could get if you worked hard in the drug economy. He sounded a bit like a salesman.

A few of them asked about the particulars of the drug trade. Were they supposed to cook the crack themselves, or were they provided with the finished product? Could they extend credit to good customers, or was it strictly a cash business?

"My auntie said I should ask you if she could join also," one teenager said. "She says she has a lot of experience—"

J.T. cut him off. "Your auntie?! Nigger, are you kidding me? Ain't no women allowed in this thing."

"Well, she said that back in the day she was into selling dope," the teenager continued. "She said that you should call her, because she could help you understand how to run a business."

"All right, we'll talk about this later, my man," J.T. said, then turned to address the rest of the young men. "Listen, you all need to understand, we're taking you to a whole 'nother level. We're not talking about hanging out and getting girls. You'll get all the pussy you want, but this is about taking pride in who you are, about doing something for yourself and your people. Now, we figure you got nobody serving around here. So there's a real need—"

"Serving what?" the same teenager interrupted.

J.T. ignored him. "Like I said, you got no one responding to the demand, and we want to work with you-all. We're going to set up shop."

"Is there some kind of training?" asked a soft, sweet voice from the back. "And do we get paid to go? I got to be at White Castle on Mondays and Thursdays, and my mama says if I lose that job, she'll kick me out of the house."

"White Castle?!" J.T. looked over in disbelief at T-Bone, Price, and me. "Nigger, I'm talking about taking control of your *life*. What is White Castle doing for you? I don't get it—how far can that take you?"

"I'm trying to save up for a bike," the boy replied.

Hearing that, J.T. headed for his car, motioning for Price to finish up with the group.

"We'll be in touch with you-all," Price said assertively. "Right now, you need to understand that we got this place, you dig? If anyone else comes over and says they want you to work with them, you tell them you are Black Kings. Got it?"

As Price continued speaking to the teenagers, I walked over to J.T. and asked if this meeting was typical.

"This shit is frustrating," he said, grabbing a soda from the car. "There's a lot of places where the kids ain't really done nothing. They have no idea what it means to be a part of something."

"So why do you want to do this?"

"Don't have a choice," he said. "We don't have any other places left to take over." Most city neighborhoods, he explained, were already claimed by a gang leader. It was nearly impossible to annex a territory with an entrenched gang structure unless the leader died or went to jail. Even in those cases, there were usually local figures with enough charisma and leverage to step in. This meant that J.T. had to expand into working- and middle-class neighborhoods where the local "gang" was nothing more than a bunch of teenagers who hung out and got into trouble. If today's meeting was any indication, these gangs weren't the ideal candidates for Black Kings membership.

"I can't believe I'm doing this shit," J.T. said, walking around his car, kicking stones in the dirt. Between the dual threats of arrest and demolition, he seemed to be coming to grips with the possibility that his star might have peaked.

The Black Kings weren't the only ones anxious about the threat of demolition. All the tenants of Robert Taylor were trying to cope with the news. Although demolition wouldn't begin for at least two years, everyone was scrambling to learn which building might come down first and where on earth they were supposed to live.

Politicians, including President Clinton and Mayor Richard J. Daley of Chicago, promised that tenants would be relocated to middle-class neighborhoods with good schools, safe streets, and job opportunities. But reliable information was hard to come by. Nor would it be so easy to secure housing outside the black ghetto. The projects had been built forty years earlier in large part because white

Chicagoans didn't want black neighbors. Most Robert Taylor tenants thought the situation hadn't changed all that much.

The CHA began to hold public meetings where tenants could air their questions and concerns. The CHA officials begged for patience, promising that every family would have help when the time came for relocation. But there was legitimate reason for skepticism. One of the most inept and corrupt housing agencies in the country was now being asked to relocate 150,000 people living in roughly two hundred buildings slated for demolition throughout Chicago. And Robert Taylor was the largest housing project of all, the size of a small city. The CHA's challenge was being made even harder by Chicago's tightening real-estate market. As the city gentrified, there were fewer and fewer communities where low-income families could find decent, affordable housing.

Information, much of it contradictory, came in dribs and drabs. At one meeting the CHA stated that all Robert Taylor residents would be resettled in other housing projects—a frightening prospect for many, since that would mean crossing gang boundaries. At another meeting the agency said that some families would receive a housing voucher to help cover their rent in the private market. At yet another meeting it was declared that large families would be split up: aunts and uncles and grandparents who weren't on the lease would have to fend for themselves.

With so much confusion in the air, tenants came to rely on rumors. There was talk of a political conspiracy whereby powerful white politicians wanted to tear down Robert Taylor in order to spread its citizens around the city and dilute the black vote. There was even a rumor about me: word was going around that I worked for the CIA, gathering secret information to help expedite the demolition. I assumed that this theory arose out of my attempt to procure a Department of Justice grant for the Boys & Girls Club, but I couldn't say for sure.

Many tenants still clung to the idea that the demolition wouldn't happen at all, or at least not for a long time. But I couldn't find a single tenant who, regardless of his or her belief about the timing of the demolition, believed that the CHA would do a good job of relocation. Some people told me they were willing to bribe their building presidents for preferential treatment. Others were angry at the government for taking away their homes and wanted to stage protests to halt the demolition.

There was also a deep skepticism among tenants that their own elected leaders would work hard on their behalf. Ms. Bailey and other building presidents were being besieged by constituents desperate for advice.

One day I sat in Ms. Bailey's office as she waited for a senior CHA official to show up for a briefing. Several other tenant leaders were also waiting, in the outer room. Ms. Bailey made no effort to hide the fact that she, along with most of the other tenant leaders, had already agreed to support the demolition rather than try to save the buildings. "The CHA made things perfectly clear to us," she explained. "These buildings *are* coming down." She spoke to me as if I were a five-year-old, with no understanding whatsoever of city politics. "Of course, you got a few people who think they can stop this, but I keep telling them, 'Look out for your own family, and get out while you can.' I'm looking out for *myself*."

"What does that mean?" I asked.

"That means I got one shot to get what I can from the CHA for me and for my people. The CHA don't have no money, Sudhir! They made that clear to us. And you know they just want to get us out of here, so I'm going to get *something* out of this."

"Like what?"

"Well, I already told them I need a five-bedroom house in South Shore," she said with a rich laugh. Then she told me the building presidents' personal requests. "Ms. Daniels wants the CHA to give her son's construction company a contract to help tear down the buildings. Ms. Wilson made a list of appliances she wants in her new apartment. Ms. Denny will be starting a new business, and the CHA needs to hire her to help relocate families."

"And you think the CHA will actually agree to these demands?"

Ms. Bailey just sat and stared at me. Apparently my naïveté was showing once more.

I tried again. "You already got them to agree, didn't you?"

Again she was silent.

"Is that what this meeting is about?" I motioned toward the outer room where the other building presidents were waiting. "Is that why this guy from the CHA is coming?"

"Well, no," she said. "We already had *that* conversation. Today is about the families. Let me tell you how this process is going to go. I know it's early, but they're already tearing down the projects on the West Side, so there ain't no mystery anymore." The Henry Horner projects on the West Side were being razed to make way for a new sports arena, the United Center, which would host the Chicago Bulls, the Chicago Blackhawks, and, eventually, the 1996 Democratic National Convention. "We'll make our list, and they'll take care of our people."

"Your list?"

"I already told you the CHA has no money, Sudhir! What part of this don't you understand?" She grew very animated and then suddenly quieted down. "They can't help everyone. And you know what? They'll mess up like they messed up in the past. Not everyone is going to be taken care of."

Ms. Bailey said that she would likely be able to help only about one-fourth of the families move out safely. Her bigger job, she said, was to make sure that the remaining three-fourths grasped this reality. The CHA, she said, "plans to use most of their money to demolish the buildings, not help people move out."

So Ms. Bailey and the other building presidents made lists of the families who they felt should have priority in obtaining rent vouchers, assistance in finding a new apartment, or free furniture and appliances. This list, it turned out, didn't necessarily comprise the neediest families—but, rather, the building presidents' personal friends or tenants who had paid them small bribes.

I asked Ms. Bailey how much she was getting.

"Sudhir, I'll be honest with you," she said, smiling. "We'll be taken care of. But don't forget to put in your little book that the CHA also gets their share. We're all washing each other's hands around here."

It wasn't very pleasant to watch this entire scenario play out in two parallel worlds. In the media all you heard were politicians' promises to help CHA tenants forge a better life. On the ground, meanwhile, the lowest-ranking members of society got pushed even lower, thanks to a stingy and neglectful city agency and the constant hustling of the few people in a position to help. In the coming months, the place began to take on the feel of a refugee camp, with every person desperate to secure her own welfare, quite possibly at the expense of a neighbor.

Not everyone, however, was so selfish or fatalistic. For some tenants demolition represented a chance to start fresh with a better apartment in a safer neighborhood. It was particularly inspiring to watch such tenants work together toward this goal while their elected leaders mainly looked out for themselves.

One such optimist was Dorothy Battie, a forty-five-year-old

mother of six who had spent nearly her entire life in the projects. Dorothy lived in a building a few blocks away from J.T. She was a heavyset woman, deeply religious, who always had a positive demeanor despite having suffered through everything the projects had to offer. Her father and several nieces and nephews had been killed in various gang shootings. Dorothy had fought through her own drug addiction, then helped other addicts enter rehab. Some of her children were now in college, and one was a leader in a Black Kings gang.

Dorothy had never been an elected tenant leader, but she was a self-appointed godmother to countless families. She helped squatters find shelter, fed tenants who couldn't afford to eat, and provided day care for many children, some related by blood and others not. Spurred on now by the demolition, she began to act as a sort of relocation counselor for several families who were determined to live near one another in a new neighborhood. They thought that sticking together was their best, and maybe only, chance for survival. These families became informally known as "the Stay-Together Gang," and their undisputed ringleader was Dorothy.

I caught up with her one day in her living room as she was looking over a list of the families she most wanted to help.

"Let's see," she said, "I got Cherry, three kids. Candy, two kids. Marna, a son and a daughter. Princess, three kids. Carrie, two young girls. And there's probably a few more." All these young women were friends who shared baby-sitting, cars, and cooking. Now their mission, with Dorothy's help, was to find a place to live where they could keep their network intact.

"See, here's the problem," Dorothy explained. "I know what it's like out there in the private market. You end up in some apartment, with no one around, no one to help you. And you're scared. At least if a few people can move with each other, stay together, they can help each other. Lot of people out there don't like us because we come from the projects. They may not answer the door if we knock for help. So I want to make sure people don't get stuck in the cold."

It was important, she said, to start with the most stable family in the network. That was Cherry, who worked thirty hours a week as a fast-food cashier and also went to night school. Dorothy's plan called for Cherry to find an apartment in a good neighborhood and then bring the other families over.

While this plan seemed pretty straightforward, Dorothy told me that success was hardly guaranteed. "Things never go as planned," she said bluntly, "because we're dealing with poor people."

Dorothy's first obstacle was Ms. Reemes, a powerful tenant in her building, who was not elected to any office but had great influence with the CHA and police. Like Ms. Bailey, Ms. Reemes expected families to pay her a fee, anywhere from fifty to two hundred dollars, for smoothing the relocation process. Every family that Dorothy helped meant one less potential bribe for Ms. Reemes. Although the building hadn't even been singled out yet for demolition, Ms. Reemes was already accepting "deposits" from families who wanted a rent voucher or relocation services.

"She wanted *me* to give her a cut," Dorothy said, "and I told her I'm not even getting paid to help these people! So I told her to go to hell. That lady is so selfish."

As Dorothy told it, Ms. Reemes was so miffed by Dorothy's refusal to play the payoff game that she went on a harassment campaign. First, Dorothy said, Ms. Reemes put in a bad word about Dorothy with the CHA. Within a week Dorothy's two grown daughters, both of whom lived in the same building, received eviction notices for late payment of rent. This was particularly surprising, since one of her daughters had no income and was therefore excused from paying any rent at all. Dorothy successfully got the

eviction notices rescinded. Then a CHA janitor cut off the electricity in Dorothy's apartment, but Dorothy paid a squatter to restore it.
Ms. Reemes then tried to get the gangs to harass Dorothy, not real-
izing that Dorothy's own son was a senior gang leader. He paid Ms.
Reemes a personal visit, and she backed down.

Through a classified ad in the *Chicago Sun-Times,* Dorothy found
a two-bedroom apartment for Cherry's family in Woodlawn, a poor
but stable neighborhood about two miles away, near Hyde Park and
the university. Because Dorothy had a CHA connection who helped
Cherry get a $500-a-month housing voucher, she had to pay only
$150 a month out of pocket.

Soon after Cherry moved in with her children and an aunt who
would provide day care, Dorothy found a large apartment nearby for
Princess and her three children. The only problem was that Princess's
brother and uncle heard about this and decided that they also wanted
to move in. If they were found to be living there, Princess would lose
her rent voucher on the grounds of illegal tenancy. Worse yet, her
brother and uncle were drug dealers who wanted to use Princess's
apartment as a new base of operations. "Princess has put up with
those two fools for too long, and it's hurting her kids," Dorothy told
me. "I wanted her to start over, and now her brother and uncle are
going to mess everything up."

So Dorothy, with Princess in tow, went to confront the two men
at a local bar where they hung out. Princess was worried, since both
of them smoked crack and were prone to violence, but Dorothy
feared no one. As Princess later described it, Dorothy stormed into
the bar and loudly told the two men they'd have *her* to deal with if
they moved in with Princess. The men threatened to beat up
Dorothy and then stomped away. They retaliated by calling Princess's
new landlord and, posing as CHA officials, warned the landlord that
Princess was a gang member. The landlord promptly called Dorothy.

He didn't necessarily believe that Princess was in a gang, he said, but he wasn't willing to take the chance. So Princess lost her lease. Dorothy eventually found Princess another apartment, but it was smaller, more expensive, and a few miles away from Cherry.

And then Marna was thrown in jail for six months for stabbing her boyfriend. Dorothy moved Marna's children around from one apartment to another so that the social workers couldn't find them and send them to foster care. Soon after, Dorothy heard that Candy had promised J.T. that the Black Kings could stash guns and drugs in the new apartment that Dorothy was helping her rent. Since J.T. was paying Candy for this service, Dorothy had little leverage to persuade her to do otherwise. Within a year Candy would lose her lease (and her rent subsidy) when the landlord called the police, having seen so many people tromping in and out of her apartment.

The most astounding story concerning Dorothy—one that I could never independently verify—also had to do with the police. She told me that Ms. Reemes called in Officer Jerry, the rogue cop, who caught her in the lobby, dragged her into a vacant apartment, planted drugs on her, and threatened to arrest her for possession if she didn't stop competing with Ms. Reemes. When Dorothy refused, Officer Jerry arrested her, but she managed to enlist some other police officers, including Officer Reggie, to set her free. According to Dorothy, Officer Jerry returned two weeks later and told Dorothy that if she just paid Ms. Reemes a share of "her cut"— which, Dorothy insisted, didn't exist—then he would leave her alone.

In the end Dorothy's list included twelve families chosen for the Stay-Together Gang. Despite her perseverance, she was able to help only four of them move out together, to neighboring apartments in Woodlawn and South Shore. I would spend much of the next decade keeping track of the Robert Taylor Homes' former tenants to see how they adapted to life beyond the projects. As it turned out,

Dorothy's success rate was easily as good as that of the various social-services agencies contracted by the CHA, each of which was awarded hundreds of thousands of dollars to carry out the job. Dorothy herself would stay in Robert Taylor until it was demolished, and then she joined her daughter, Lee-Lee, in Englewood, a high-crime, predominantly black neighborhood a few miles away.

Dorothy's move to Lee-Lee's house was, unfortunately, a typical outcome for many tenants who left Robert Taylor and other CHA projects. While the goal of the demolition was to move families to safer, integrated communities, the CHA was so inept that nearly 90 percent of the relocated tenants wound up living in poor black areas that left them as badly off as being in the projects, or worse.

In place of the projects, the city began to build market-rate condominiums and town houses, three-story structures tucked cozily together instead of the sixteen-story high-rises separated by vast expanses. Robert Taylor tenants had been promised the right to return to the community once construction was done, but fewer than 10 percent of the units were set aside for public-housing families. It is little wonder that the prevailing wisdom in Chicago is that the Daley administration and the powerful real-estate interests, rather than creating new and improved low-income housing, in fact knocked down the projects to initiate a land grab. As of this writing, the new apartments are set to house mostly middle- and upper-class families.

A few months after T-Bone gave me the Black Kings' financial ledgers, Ms. Bailey invited me to a back-to-school party for the children in her building. J.T. had given her a thousand dollars to throw the party and to buy the kids some sneakers, clothes, and school supplies.

I hadn't been spending much time around J.T.'s building in the months leading up to the party. I was generally holed up in the library, working on my dissertation. My advisers and I had agreed that it should explore how families cope with poverty—specifically, how CHA tenants solved problems and kept the community together without much help from the government or charities.

When I arrived for the party, it felt like my first visits from years earlier. There were cars parked all around the basketball court, rap music blasting away, kids running everywhere, and squatters grilling burgers and hot dogs to earn a little money. J.T. and his senior officers were drinking beer and casting an eye over the entire scene. J.T., Ms. Mae, Ms. Bailey, and some of the other tenants greeted me with the same carefree attitude they had showed me when I first began coming around. As I watched Ms. Bailey and some of the other older women tend to the children, I couldn't help but feel kind of nostalgic. Everyone looked a bit older and more fatigued—just like me, I suppose.

I saw something out of the corner of my eye that stopped me cold: a small garden bursting with bright orange, red, and purple geraniums. In this vast stretch of concrete and patchy lawn, littered with broken bottles, used condoms, and empty crack vials, here was an oasis. I laughed to myself. Why hadn't I ever noticed it before?

I'd been so caught up with gangs, political chicanery, and the life of poverty that I had missed something so beautiful right there in front of me. What else had I missed because of my incessant drive to hustle?

I thought back to the last time I'd noticed any flowers in Robert Taylor. It had been well over a year earlier. The tenants were preparing for a visit from President Bill Clinton. They were incredibly excited, but also unnerved. His visit was meant to highlight the unprecedented levels of gang violence in Chicago public housing.

Clinton supported the use of police "sweeps," the warrantless searches that the Chicago Police Department was using to combat the gang and drug problems. While the ACLU and other groups decried the sweeps as a violation of constitutional rights, Clinton argued that the right to "freedom from fear" was more important. He wanted inner-city residents to believe, as he believed, that the scourge of street gangs required extraordinary measures, and his trip to Robert Taylor provided a firsthand opportunity to persuade them.

In the weeks before his visit, the project was turned upside down. The police conducted even more sweeps than usual, sometimes ransacking apartments indiscriminately. They also conducted random spot checks in the building lobbies, arresting a great many suspected drug dealers, including many young men who had nothing whatsoever to do with dealing drugs.

J.T. didn't go so far as to halt drug sales, but he was a bit more cautious, sometimes having his dealers take customers inside to an apartment to obtain the drugs rather than getting them on the street. He also stopped extorting from local stores, fearing that that might lead to arrest. And he stopped laundering money, stowing his cash in garbage bags until the neighborhood quieted down.

On the streets, city tow trucks hauled away abandoned vehicles—as well as a lot of vehicles that might have looked abandoned but were in fact just old and beat up. On top of all this disorder, the weather was unrelentingly hot and humid.

Still, there was hope in the air. Because of Bill Clinton's overwhelming popularity among African Americans, even the most cynical tenants—including the people whose cars had been towed—were excited about his visit. Tenant leaders led campaigns to spruce up their buildings' lobbies, hallways, and playgrounds. Tenant patrols went door-to-door asking people to tidy up their living rooms and clean their toilets; in one building, snakes and other strange pets were confiscated from certain households. And throughout the project, aged flower beds sprang to life.

In the early days of Robert Taylor, the buildings had competed against one another with flower gardens and other beautification projects. This dormant practice was now reborn in anticipation of the president's visit. He obviously couldn't visit all twenty-eight Robert Taylor buildings, and he might have time for just one. But this only heightened the intensity of the competition. A few tenant leaders called in favors with city officials to try to make sure their building was on the president's list. Some of them curried additional favor by turning in drug dealers to the police.

The 5011 building, located on the far south side of Robert Taylor, showed particular enthusiasm. This was fueled by the belief that a new construction project next door to 5011 was in fact the construction of a presidential podium. The tenant leader taxed the local gang twenty-five hundred dollars to fund a wide-scale restoration effort. The building's children were given new clothes and shoes; a mural of historic African-American figures was painted along the building's ground floor; a few particularly civic-minded tenants even wrote speeches, just in case the president called them up to the podium. And families planted rows and rows of flowers in a garden that had seen nothing but trash for years.

By the morning of June 17, 1994, the day of President Clinton's visit, the residents of 5011 were fully ready. But his entourage sped past quickly, without so much as a wave. He gave his speech in another part of Robert Taylor. A few of the tenants in 5011 moaned and groaned, but generally they were satisfied that the president had showed up at all. Parents broke out soda and beer, and their kids caught the spirit and launched a party. After the initial disappointment, no one seemed willing to utter a spiteful word. For a time at least, the community shared a deep spirit of satisfaction, of having pulled together. Over and over again, you could hear tenants remark that they hadn't seen such solidarity in decades.

Now, a year later, the flower bed outside J.T.'s building stood as a similar sign of hope—and, in light of the imminent demolition of the projects, a sign of proud obstinacy.

The back-to-school party was in full swing. Kids and grown-ups alike loaded their plates with food. A softball game started up, and a crowd of people gathered to watch. I milled about, saying hello to a lot of people I hadn't seen in a while.

Suddenly the sound of gunshots pierced the air, and everyone ran for cover. There were four or five shots, rapid fire, from what sounded like a pistol. Parents grabbed their kids and ducked behind cars or ran for the lobby. Above the blaring music, you could hear women screaming for their children. J.T. hollered for everyone to get down.

I found myself crouching behind a car parked near the building. Beside me were a few of J.T.'s foot soldiers, young men I barely knew. I asked where the shooting was coming from. They immediately pointed up toward the upper floors of the building.

"Niggers are probably high on dope," one of them whispered. "Or else you got an MC who snuck up in the building. It used to be an MC building before we took it over."

Some distance away I could see a thin, dark-skinned woman staggering toward us across the grassy expanse in front of the building. Her clothes were sloppy, and she was practically falling down, probably either drunk or high. As she came closer, you could hear her talking to herself, most of it gibberish. People started yelling at her to take cover. A few of J.T.'s men shouted nasty names and threw beer bottles at her. It was pretty common for drug dealers to treat drug users with disdain; they often justified their line of work by pointing out that they took money from the most useless members of the community.

Some more shots rang out from above, the bullets kicking up clouds of dirt a few feet from the woman.

"That ain't the MCs firing at us," said the foot soldier beside me. "That's just some nigger who is fucked up and looking to cause trouble."

Finally an older gentleman ran out, grabbed the staggering woman, and hustled her into the lobby. After about ten minutes with no more gunfire, most people felt comfortable enough to come out from their hiding places. Parents and children ran into the building, abandoning the party. The squatters and the hustlers, meanwhile, got back to their food and listened to the music. My heart kept racing for several minutes, but even I wasn't surprised by now that nobody even bothered to call the police.

In the spring of 1996, I learned that I had received a junior fellowship at Harvard's Society of Fellows. I was ecstatic; it was a much-sought-after position, a three-year salaried research post. I went to tell J.T. the good news, and that I would soon be leaving town, although I still planned to maintain my ties to Chicago.

The smells of Ms. Mae's cooking—collard greens, cornbread, and smothered chicken—hit me as I walked in the door. "You still manage to get here right when the food is ready, don't you?" J.T. said with a laugh.

I apologized for missing the last few suburban Black Kings meetings.

"They still think you're the director of communications," he said, laughing again but looking at the TV instead of at me. "There's another meeting next Sunday if you want to come with me."

"Sure," I said, trying to sound enthusiastic. "That would be great." I explained why I'd been so busy lately. Until I learned of the Harvard fellowship, I had been applying for teaching jobs at universities all over the country, including Columbia University in New York.

J.T. interrupted my explanation. "You remember Curtis, that tall, dark boy you met?" He suddenly sat up and began to speak with great enthusiasm. "Curtis is from New Jersey, or at least he has work out there. Hey, what do you think about heading out there with me? I've been wanting to go and see how they do things. He and I have this bet. He says the women are hotter in *his* projects. Says I should come out and see."

I did remember Curtis, a nerdy-looking drug dealer who worked out of the housing projects in Newark. We had exchanged a few words at most when he came to visit J.T. about a year earlier.

"Somehow," I said to J.T., trying to sound appreciative, "I don't think that would be such a good—"

"Yeah, you're probably right. Probably not the best time for us to leave right now, especially with everything that's going on. You need to watch me do my thing, I know." He grew pensive. "I got a couple of big meetings next week, and you probably want to be around for that."

Before I could ask him about these meetings, he had another idea: "You know something? You remember how we talked about how gangs are different across the country?"

I had once told J.T. that gangs in New York and Boston were said to be much smaller than Chicago's gangs, rooted in local neighborhoods as opposed to being part of a citywide wheel. But no one, I told him, had managed to write an in-depth, multi-city study of street gangs.

"I could help you meet people all over the place!" he continued. He stood up to get a beer from the fridge. "We got people we know in L.A., in Las Vegas, St. Louis. Black Kings are nationwide! I mean, you and I could figure out how the whole thing works."

"So you'll be my research assistant!" I said with a laugh, not quite sure what he was proposing.

"No, no! You'll still be writing about *me*. The book will still be about *me*, but this will add a new dimension to it."

"Yes, it would add a lot, but I'd really have to check with my professors. I mean, I'm not sure what's going to happen once I move. . . ."

J.T.'s voice immediately took on a guarded tone. "No, I understand," he said. "I know you got a lot to think about. I'm just saying that I could help you. But yeah, you talk to your professors first. No big thing. . . ."

We sat there, not speaking, eyes on the TV. I kept hoping we'd be interrupted by Ms. Mae calling us for dinner, but we weren't. I didn't even have the energy to muster up a question about J.T.'s business or his life, as I'd always done previously whenever he sensed that my interests were shifting. Finally a college basketball game came on, and the blare of the crowd and the cheerleaders drowned out the silence between us.

With the demolition of Robert Taylor now formally scheduled to begin within a year, the drug economy in J.T.'s buildings was already faltering. Some of his best customers were tenants, and they were starting to move out. So were a lot of the BK foot soldiers who still lived at home with their moms. (J.T. offered to rent Ms. Mae a home in one of several neighborhoods, and she tried out a few, but she wound up coming back to a cousin's house a few hundred yards from Robert Taylor.) The whole place had also grown thick with police, called in to protect the streams of contractors, engineers, city planners, and other bureaucrats who were plotting the massive demolition.

With less demand for drugs, there was less work for J.T.'s rank-

and-file members. It was in his interest to place these young men in a new gang, since he never knew when he might need their help in the future. Given his standing in the BKs, it was certainly within J.T.'s power to reassign his foot soldiers to other BK factions throughout the city. But he was able to place only a handful at a time, and no more than a few dozen overall. Worse yet, this strategy tended to fail in the long term, since in most cases the host gang wouldn't fully accept the new member.

J.T.'s gang also had a lot of older members, in their thirties and even forties, who were unwilling to accept a transfer, since that typically meant a drop in seniority and, accordingly, income. Some of these men began to leave J.T.'s command altogether, trying to secure positions within other gangs around the city—occasionally, to J.T.'s deep displeasure, within a rival gang.

A few of J.T.'s men traveled as far as Iowa to try to set up shop. I never went along on any of these out-of-state recruiting trips, but judging from the frustration of the BK missionaries who returned to Chicago, this plan wasn't going to work out very well.

J.T. tried to hold things together, but the new economics of his situation conspired against him. He grew lonely, feeling as if he were being abandoned by his own BK family. His sense of paranoia grew even more acute. Whenever I saw him, he immediately began to speculate that the more senior BK defectors were revealing the gang's secrets to rival outfits: where the BKs stored guns and drugs, which cops were open to bribery, which local merchants were willing to launder money.

And then there were the arrests. The federal indictments that had begun to tear apart other gangs were now striking the Black Kings as well. Barry and Otis, two of J.T.'s younger members, had recently been arrested. I wondered how long J.T. would be able to stay free himself. One night, driving back from one of the suburban gang meetings, he mused that jail might actually be the best of his options, since anyone who escaped arrest for too long was suspected of being a snitch and placed himself in real danger on the streets.

Soon after this conversation, I heard that T-Bone had been arrested. He was eventually convicted of trafficking narcotics and sentenced to more than ten years in prison. His prompt transfer to an out-of-state prison fueled speculation that he was testifying against his peers to get a reduced sentence. I tried every avenue I could think of, but I had no luck reaching T-Bone. I eventually heard that he had died in prison, and he became celebrated in death for never having cooperated with the police to sell out other gang members.

For a time I thought that J.T. and I might remain close even as our worlds were growing apart. "Don't worry," I told him, "I'll be coming back all the time." But the deeper I got into my Harvard fellowship, the more time passed between my visits to Chicago, and the more time passed between visits, the more awkward J.T. and I found it to carry on our conversations. He seemed to have grown nostalgic for our early days together, even a bit clingy. I realized that he had come to rely on my presence; he liked the attention and the validation.

I, meanwhile, grew evasive and withdrawn—in large part out of guilt. Within just a few months at Harvard, I began making a name for myself in academia by talking about the inner workings of street gangs. While I hoped to contribute to the national discussion on poverty, I was not so foolish as to believe that my research would specifically benefit J.T. or the tenant families from whom I'd learned so much.

As demolition became a reality, and as J.T.'s gang continued to fall apart, so did our relationship. When I told him that I'd been offered a job teaching sociology at Columbia University upon completing my Harvard fellowship, he asked me what was wrong with teaching in Chicago. "What about high school?" he said. "Those people need education, too, don't they?"

The breakdown of the gang affected Ms. Bailey as well. When the gang didn't make money, Ms. Bailey didn't make much money either. And with demolition so near, she needed all the money she could get to help the tenants she wanted to help. She paid for day care so single mothers could go look for new apartments. She hired a car service to take tenants on their housing searches. She helped others settle their outstanding electricity bills so they'd be able to get service once they entered the private market.

But as the money ran out, some tenants began to turn on her. Even though the CHA was supposed to provide relocation services, it was Ms. Bailey who had stepped into the breach, for a fee, and so she was the one who now caught the blame. She was widely accused of pocketing the gang's money instead of using it for the tenants.

I had never seen Ms. Bailey cry until the moment she told me about these accusations. "I have lived here for almost my whole life, Sudhir," she said mournfully.

We were sitting in her office on a hot spring day. The old bustle was long gone. It used to be that we couldn't sit and talk for ten minutes before Ms. Bailey was interrupted by a needy tenant; now we had the room to ourselves for well over an hour.

"You've been told before that you work too closely with the gangs," I said. "Why does it bother you now?"

"Out there they don't have anybody," she said. "Out there they think they can make it on their own, but . . ." She tried and tried, but she wasn't able to finish her sentence.

I wanted to say something worthwhile but couldn't think of anything. "They'll . . . they'll be okay," I sputtered. "Hell, they lived through the projects."

"But you see, Sudhir, I know that and you know that, but *they* sometimes forget. It's like I told you many times: What scares *you* ain't what scares *them*. When they go to a new store or they have to stand at a bus stop in a place they never been to before, *that's* what scares them. I wanted to help them feel okay. And just when they need me, I can't be there for them."

"You can still do things—" I started to say. But I stopped. The pain on her face was evident, and nothing I could say would console her. I just sat quietly with her until we'd finished our coffee.

I saw Ms. Bailey a few more times, but she was never again the same. For health reasons she moved into her nephew's home in the middle of West Englewood, a poor black community about two miles from the projects. I visited her there. She had several ailments, she told me, but it was hard to sort out one from the other. "I stopped going to the doctor's," she said. "One more test, one more drug, one more thing I got to pay for. And for *what*? To live *here*?"

She waved her hands out at the miles and miles of poor tracts surrounding her nephew's house, tracts that held far too few of the people from her old high-rise home, the people who'd once given her life meaning.

Winter in Chicago comes fast, and it comes hard. The cold delivers a wallop, making you shudder longer than you'd expect. The first blasts of chilling wind off the lake feel like an enemy.

It was a late Sunday morning in November 1998, and I was waiting outside J.T.'s building one last time. About a half dozen Robert Taylor buildings had already been torn down, and his was due for demolition within a year. Nearby businesses had started to close, too. The whole place was starting to feel like a ghost town. I had changed as well. Gone were the tie-dyed shirts and the ponytail, replaced by the kind of clothes befitting an edgy young Ivy League professor. And also a leather briefcase.

I leaned against my car, stamping my feet to keep warm while waiting for J.T. I was just about to get back into the car and turn on the heater when I saw his Malibu charge down Federal Street.

J.T. had called the night before to request a meeting. In his characteristically ambiguous way, he wouldn't divulge any details. But he sounded excited. He did tell me that the federal indictments were probably over and that he wouldn't be arrested. I wanted to know how and why he had escaped arrest, but I didn't have the guts to ask. He'd always been secretive about his contacts in law enforcement. He also asked a few questions about what kind of research I'd be doing in New York. I mentioned some possible ideas, but they were vague at best.

We greeted each other with a handshake and a smile. I told him he looked like he'd put on a little weight. He agreed; between his work and the needs of his growing children, he said, there wasn't as much time to exercise. He pulled a small piece of paper from his pocket and handed it to me. There were several names and phone numbers printed in J.T.'s scratchy handwriting. Among the names was that of Curtis, the gang leader in Newark we'd talked about before.

"You should call these people," J.T. said. "I told Curtis that you wanted to see how things worked out there. He'll take care of you. But Billy Jo, that's the one who really knows what's happening in New York. Here, give him this."

J.T. had often talked about his friends who ran drug-dealing operations in New York. But what with the federal indictments, the demolition of Robert Taylor, and my own career moves, I had pretty much forgotten about them. Also, given how things had turned out with me and J.T.—it was pretty obvious by now that I wasn't going to write his biography—I was surprised that he'd go out of his way to put me in touch with his contacts back east.

He took out another sheet of paper, tightly folded over in fours, the creases a bit worn, as if he'd been carrying it in his pocket for a while. His hands were so cold that they shook as he unfolded it. He gave the paper to me and blew on his hands to warm them up.

"Go ahead, nigger, read it," he said. "Hurry up, it's cold!"

I began to read. It was addressed to Billy Jo: *Billy, Sudhir is coming out your way. Take care of the nigger. . . .* My eyes scanned down and caught a phrase in the middle of the page: *He's with me.*

I could feel myself breaking into a wide smile. J.T. reached into his car and pulled out two beers.

"I'm not sure I'm ready for another big research project just yet," I said.

"Oh, yeah?" he said, handing me one of the beers. "What else are you going to do? You can't fix nothing, you never worked a day in your life. The only thing you know how to do is hang out with niggers like us."

I nearly choked on my beer when he summarized my capacities so succinctly—and, for the most part, accurately.

J.T. leaned back on the car, looking up at the high-rises in front of us. "You think niggers will survive out there?" he asked. "You think they'll be all right when they leave here?"

"Not sure. Probably. I mean, everything changes. You just have to be ready, I guess."

"You hungry?" he asked.

"Starving."

"Let's go down to Seventy-ninth. There's a new soul-food place."

"Sounds good," I said, chugging the beer quickly. "Why don't you drive?"

"Oh, yeah," he said, jumping into the car, "and I got one for you! What would you do if you were me? I got this new bunch of guys that think they know everything. . . ."

He began telling me about his latest management dilemma with a gang he was running in Roseland, a neighborhood where a lot of the Robert Taylor families were relocating. As he spoke, I became lost in his voice. His steady and assured monologue comforted me; for a few moments anyway, I could feel as though little had changed, even though everything had. He turned on some rap music, opened up another beer, and kept on talking. The car screeched out of the parking lot, J.T. waved to a few women pushing strollers in the cold, and we sped down Federal Street.

Within a few years, J.T. grew tired of running a gang. He managed his cousin's dry-cleaning business, and he started up a barbershop, which failed. He had put away enough savings, in property and cash, to supplement his lower income. Once in a while, he did consulting work for Black Kings higher-ups who tried to revive their citywide hold on the drug economy. But this effort never came to fruition, and with the crack market severely depleted, Chicago's gangland remains fragmented, with some neighborhoods having little if any gang activity.

I still see J.T. now and then when I'm in Chicago. Although we've never discussed it explicitly, I don't sense that he begrudges my success as an academic, nor does he seem bitter about his own life. "Man, as long as I'm not behind bars and breathing," he told me, "every day is a good day." It would be hard to call us friends. And I sometimes wonder if we ever were.

But he was obviously a huge part of my life. For all the ways in which I had become a rogue sociologist, breaking conventions and flouting the rules, perhaps the most unconventional thing I ever did was embrace the idea that I could learn so much, absorb so many lessons, and gain so many experiences at the side of a man who was so far removed from my academic world. I can still hear J.T.'s voice when I'm on the streets far away from Chicago, somewhere in the unruly Paris suburbs or the ghettos of New York, hanging around and listening to people's stories.

AUTHOR'S NOTE

Many of the names and some of the identities in this book have been changed. I also disguised some locations and altered the titles of certain organizations. But all the people, places, and institutions are real; they are not composites, and they are not fictional.

Whenever possible, I based the material on written field notes. Some of the stories, however, have been reconstructed from memory. While memory isn't a perfect substitute for notes, I have tried my best to reproduce conversations and events as faithfully as possible.

ACKNOWLEDGMENTS

There is one basic truth in the South Asian immigrant experience: Do as your parents tell you. This notion was put to the test during my junior year of college, when I informed my father and mother that I wanted to study sociology. My mother seemed agnostic, but such decisions were made by my father, who said he preferred that I stay on the path toward a degree in bioengineering. I was not interested in science, and after several conversations we reached a compromise: I would study theoretical mathematics.

I knew that my father supported me, and I even understood his rationale. We were immigrants with no connections, no wealth, and all we had lay between our ears; a math degree would at least guarantee me a job.

A year later, when I told my father I wanted to apply to graduate programs in sociology, he continued to support me, giving advice that I now share with my own students. His counsel often took the form of parables and was laden with examples of people he had seen succeed (and fail). What he told me might take a full evening to relay, over wine and my mother's cooking, but the essence was always clear: write every day, visit your professors with well-formed questions, and always read everything that is recommended, not just what the professor requires.

He also taught me to shut up and listen to my advisers. In contemporary American institutions of higher learning, most people would find this instruction quaint; during a time in which the "student" has become the "customer," this sort of thinking is considered anathema. But my father was no fan of the American educational system, so he insisted that I spend my time listening. I owe my father more than he will ever know. In life, love, and work, his wisdom would prove exceedingly valuable.

Within a few weeks of my arrival at the University of Chicago, I was lucky enough to meet William Julius Wilson, the eminent scholar of urban poverty. He made an unforgettable impression on me: he was thoughtful, choosing his words carefully, and it was obvious that I'd learn a lot if I simply paid attention. My father's counsel echoed in my head: Listen to Bill, follow his advice, always work harder than you need to.

Throughout the course of my graduate studies, I ran into many obstacles, and Bill was always there to guide me. I brought him many typical grad-student dilemmas (*How should I prepare for my exams?*) and some that were less typical (*If I find out that the gang plans to carry out a murder, should I tell somebody?*). More than once I tested his patience; more than once he told me to stop going to my field site until things cooled off. I am one in a long line of students who have benefited from Bill Wilson's tutelage. For his patient direction, I remain grateful.

None of this is meant to discount the role that my mother has played in my life and career. She is the most caring and thoughtful person I have ever known; her voice always rang in my head when I needed to get around a roadblock. Thanks, Mom.

I can recall the initial conversations with my sister, Urmila, when I signed up to write this book. I was nervous, while she was over-joyed. She has always productively channeled her enthusiasm by keeping me honest and mindful of those who are less fortunate and who may never benefit from my writings.

At the University of Chicago and at Columbia, Professors Peter Bearman, Jean Comaroff, John Comaroff, Herbert J. Gans, Edward Laumann, Nicole Marwell, and Moishe Postone guided me through difficult waters. Katchen Locke, Sunil Garg, Larry Kamerman, Ethan Michaeli, Amanda Millner-Fairbanks, David Sussman, Benjamin Mintz, Matthew McGuire, and Baron Pineda were ever supportive, whether with humor, advice, or a glass of wine. Farah Griffin's writings inspired me to push on, Doug Guthrie encouraged me to pursue the venerable path of public sociology, and Eva Rosen read drafts diligently and is on her way to becoming an outstanding sociologist.

I never would have written this book if I hadn't met Steven Levitt, an economist who took an interest in my fieldwork. Over dinner one night at the Harvard Society of Fellows, Steven and I spent hours trying to connect the worlds of economics and sociology. To this day Steven remains a close collaborator and friend. I couldn't have attempted this act of hubris without his encouragement. Steven kindly introduced me to Suzanne Gluck, who helped shepherd me through the byzantine world of trade publishing. Suzanne is one of the wisest souls I have ever met. At Penguin, Ann Godoff has been a pleasure to work with, and I hope this is the first of many journeys under her stewardship.

In writing this book, I drew on the intellectual gifts and emotional sustenance of my close friend Nathaniel Deutsch. I pulled Nathaniel away from his precious daughter, Simona, on many occasions to rant, cry, or just throw up my hands. Nathaniel, I may never be able to return the favor, but I will certainly make sure Simi knows how kind you have been.

To Stephen Dubner, I owe an inexpressible debt. Stephen had the unenviable task of helping me put my thoughts on paper. It was not always easy for me to visit my past, and Stephen listened to my meanderings patiently, offering the right amount of criticism and feedback. I doubt that Stephen thinks of himself as a teacher, but he is one of the best.

I remain especially grateful to the tenants of the Robert Taylor Homes for letting me into both their apartments and their lives. Dorothy Battie has been a close friend, and Beauty Turner and the staff at the *Residents' Journal* newspaper have given of their time generously.

I still feel guilty about all those years that I let J.T. think I would write his biography. I hope that he at least reads these pages someday. While a lot of it is my story, it plainly could never have happened without him. He let me into a new world with a level of trust I had no reason to expect; I can only hope that this book faithfully represents his life and his work.

TRANSACCION CON ARTS

BBVA Bancomer

IGLI CANCUN
APTO INTHAT CENTON L 30 Col. CENTRO
Cd. CANCUN CROO
E896688-00900001

HORA: 16:02
BMG121 A242

FECHA: 22/06/12
FILIAL: 0132193
************ K0037

BBVA Bancomer

VISA   VENTA USD
                        USD86.00

TOTAL
BANCOS DEI 000027 000278   9/8661
APROBACION:

*** COPIA CLIENTE ***

BBVA Bancomer

FIRMA   JOSHUA S CHAMPAIGN

PCM

prometo y me obligo
a pagar a la orden de la
e la Tarjeta relacionada al
ficinas, la cantidad que
l de este título el cual
del contrato que tengo
Institución para el uso de

to que el presente es
operación señalada al
e pleno valor probatorio y
de que firmé y/o digité mi
cual es de mi exclusiva
lo que manifiesto plena
o al cargo efectuado a la
e deriva esta Tarjeta. El
negociable únicamente
ncarias, a excepción que
por Tarjetahabientes de

GOCIABLE

PCM

prometo y me obligo
a pagar a la orden de la
e la Tarjeta relacionada al
ficinas, la cantidad que
l de este título el cual
del contrato que tengo
Institución para el uso de

to que el pr
opera

INDEX